The White Indian Boy
and
The Return of the White Indian

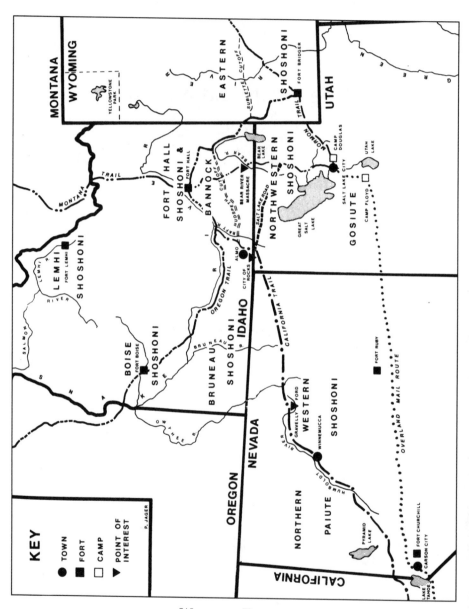

WESTERN TRAILS

The White Indian Boy
and its sequel
The Return of
the White Indian

by

Elijah Nicholas Wilson

and

Charles A. Wilson

THE UNIVERSITY OF UTAH PRESS

Salt Lake City

The Defiance House Man colophon is a registered trademark of the University of Utah Press. It is based upon a four-foot-tall, Ancient Puebloan pictograph (late PIII) near Glen Canyon, Utah.

18   17   16   15   14   5   6   7   8   9

LIBRARY OF CONGRESS CATALOGING-IN-PUBLICATION DATA

Wilson, Elijah Nicholas, 1842-1915.
  [Among the Shoshones]
  The white Indian boy ; and its sequel, The return of the white Indian / by Elijah Nicholas Wilson and Charles A. Wilson.—University of Utah Press ed.
  p. cm.
  The white Indian boy originally published in 1910 as Among the Shoshones; this manifestation originally published: Rapid City, S.D. : Fenske Print., c1985.
  ISBN-13: 978-0-87480-834-6 (pbk. : alk. paper)
  ISBN-10: 0-87480-834-0 (pbk. : alk. paper)
  1. Wilson, Elijah Nicholas, 1842-1915.   2. Pioneers—Wyoming—Biography.   3. Frontier and pioneer life—Wyoming.   4. Shoshoni Indians. 5. Wyoming—Biography.   I. Wilson, Charles Alma. Return of the white Indian. II. Title.   III. Title: Return of the white Indian.
  F761.W55.A3 2005
  978.7'092—dc22
  [B]

2005015069

Contents

Foreword by John J Stewart vii

Preface by Charles Alma Wilson xiii

Acknowledgments...xvii

A Note on the Family Tree of Elijah Nicholas Wilson xix

The White Indian Boy 1

The Return of the White Indian 151

Foreword

BY JOHN J STEWART

When I was a child a favorite book in our family was *The White Indian Boy* by Elijah Nicholas "Nick" Wilson. It was read over and over again. Our interest in it was enhanced by summer vacation visits to Jackson Hole, Wyoming, a land of enchantment nestled between the Tetons on the west and the Wind Rivers on the east.

Our parents, Robert and May Stewart, sometimes rented a cabin at Leeks' Lodge on the east shore of Jackson Lake, where we could go boating, swimming, and fishing. One day the elderly owner of the resort, Steve Leek, took us in his boat across the lake to see a cabin he had built on the west side of the lake at the base of the Tetons. What we did not know at that time was that Steve Leek was a son-in-law of Nick Wilson.

More often our parents rented a log cabin from Ida Lundy, an early pioneer in the village of Wilson, which was settled by and named in honor of Nick Wilson. The cabin was on the bank of Fish Creek, and upstream just a short distance from it was Nick Wilson's tiny cabin, long since abandoned. Near his cabin stood the rustic hotel that Nick and his son-in-law Abe Ward built, and where Nick entertained many travelers with his tales of life among the Shoshone Indians. Nearby were the former homes and farms of some of Nick's many children and grandchildren.

In his book, which was first published under the title *Uncle Nick Among the Shoshones*, Nick tells of catching trout from his cabin's front dooryard. To verify Nick's claim my father also caught trout from Nick's front dooryard. Fish Creek was indeed aptly named.

It was in Nick's cabin that two of his children were reared, including his son Charley, author of the sequel published here, *The Return of the White Indian*. On one of our summer trips to Jackson Hole I inquired around as to whether any of Nick Wilson's children were still alive, for if so I would like to get acquainted with them. A Wilson relative told me, "No, they're all dead".

Unwilling to let them all be dead I asked others the same question and one man told me he believed there was a son still alive, perhaps living on the Shoshone Indian Reservation east of the Wind River Mountains. He told me the relative who had misinformed me had lied because of a grudge he had against one branch of the Wilson family.

I drove through the mighty Wind Rivers to the Indian Reservation where I fortunately found Charley Wilson. I asked him whether he was dead or alive. Lying on his sick bed he confessed that he was nearly dead and believed the end was near. I told him of my keen interest in his famous father's book and remarked that I would like to shake the hand of Nick's son. Charley kindly reached up a trembling hand and I felt fully rewarded for my journey. Believing he was seriously ill I told him I would not burden him further by lingering. I bid him good-bye and wished him a speedy recovery.

Charley said, "Please don't go. I need you. I know you're a writer. I believe God sent you here. I've always wanted to write a book about my father. To tell about his later years. I need your help." I told Charley I would be glad to help him in whatever I could.

Thus began a warm friendship and collaboration. With the hope of getting his sequel done, Charley's health and spirits improved. With very little help from me he wrote a sequel that is as interesting as Nick's book. It is a book that I am confident you will thoroughly enjoy. Like Nick's it is truly a classic of the Old West.

Charley was especially proud of the fact that Nick as a young man had been a Pony Express rider. A friend of mine, Rowe Findley, an assistant editor at *National Geographic*, was doing a story on the Pony Express and I was happy to put him in touch with Charley. He included in his subsequent article prominent mention of Charley and a portrait photo of him, which greatly pleased Charley.

Once when Charley and his wife Dorotha were staying with us at our cabin in Teton Valley, Idaho, Charley asked me whether I was acquainted with an elderly man named Charley

Williams. I told him I was. He lived in a cabin three miles from mine. I had visited him several times, to learn more about Teton Valley's history.

Charley Wilson asked me to take him to see Charley Williams. As we neared the Williams' place Charley said, "Now when we get there don't tell him who I am. I haven't seen him in over fifty years. I want to see whether he recognizes me. If he doesn't then tell him to look at the back of my neck. He told me that no matter how many years passed he could always tell me by the back of my neck."

When we got to Charley Williams's house he was sitting in his rocking chair as usual. He immediately recognized me because of my recent visits. I asked him, "Do you know who this man is?" He looked carefully at Charley and shook his head no. I said, "Look at the back of his neck." He climbed out of his rocker and looked at the back of Charley's neck, puzzled by the request. "Now do you know him?" I asked. He did not.

Then Charley Wilson gave him a big bear hug and said, "I'm Charley Wilson!" Charley Williams came alive. "Charley Wilson? Charley Wilson!" Those two old codgers were ever so happy, and for the next three hours I heard the most wondrous tales as they shared their memories of when they were tough young cowboys and farmhands in Teton Valley.

The little town of Tetonia once had a movie theater; remains of it are still there. One summer evening after a long hot day at work the two Charleys stopped at the local beer hall for some refreshments and then decided to see the movie playing next door. Unfortunately, the ticket taker did not notice that they were each carrying a pistol. Midway through the movie, when the villain seemed to be getting the upper hand, the two Charleys whipped out their pistols and shot him dead. Others in the audience screamed and scurried out of the theater. The owner called the sheriff and had the two Charleys arrested.

Charley Williams's family lived in Teton Valley so he was allowed to stay, after making due restitution. Charley Wilson's family lived in Jackson Hole, across the high mountain. The sheriff ordered him to get out of Teton Valley and never return or he would be imprisoned for life. Thus it was that the two Charleys had never seen each other again until this day of re-union that I witnessed.

Years later, when Charley and his niece Trilba Nethercott Redding were staying overnight with us at our home in River Heights, Charley awoke in the middle of the night shouting hysterically. I rushed to his room, switched on the light, and found him standing up, fiercely fending off some attacker, be-having much like his bellicose grandfather Alfred Alexander Nethercott who he describes in his book. Between curses he told me that the devil was in the room threatening him. I had to wonder whether the angry ghost of the Teton Valley sheriff or the drunken ghost of old Grandpa Nethercott had seized him.

On only three points did Charley and I have any serious disagreement about the combined book: Nick had used pho-netic spelling in his book and that is the way the first edition was published. Charley was determined to have it that way in the combined edition. I finally persuaded him to use Howard Driggs's revised version.

I won that point, but lost the other two: I asked him to let me find an established publisher for it, and also have it in-dexed. But Charley was in his eighties and naturally anxious to get it published without delay. He had plenty of funds to do it on his own and wasn't concerned about an index, so he hired a commercial printing firm and included no index.

Charley decided to write and publish a second book, fo-cused on his dual careers as a private big-game hunting guide and a government hunter and trapper. I had nothing to do with that effort but was especially delighted with the colorful title he gave it: *Bloody Tracks on the Mountain Where the Wild Winds Blow.* That title alone should be worth the price of the book.

I don't know how well that second book fared but there was an immediate demand for the combined book of *The White In-dian Boy* and *The Return of The White Indian,* so much so that it and a second printing were soon out of print. Charley and I had kept in touch through the years and in his mid-nineties he asked me to try to get it republished, which I agreed to do.

Prior commitments on some of my own books, other chores, and my wife's tragic death, delayed my fulfilling my promise to Charley. But I never forgot it and eventually I did get to it. I was very pleased when the University of Utah Press recognized its worth.

Charley died December 4, 1999, at 98 years of age, and is buried near Nick in the South Park Cemetery close to Wilson.

We buried him where the wild winds blow.

Preface

BY CHARLES ALMA WILSON

Many of you have read the story of *The White Indian Boy* who lived with Chief Washakie of the Shoshone Indian Tribe along about 1856 when the Indians were wild and the mighty West was yet untamed. It is an intriguing story and never enough of it was told. The White Indian boy's name was Elijah Nicholas Wilson; he was my father.

This exciting and interesting story was written by him and he never went to school a day in his life! You ask, how is this possible? I will tell you that many people have asked me this question; I even received one letter from Switzerland asking, "What is lumpy Dick?" And, "Did Nick Wilson ever go back to live with the Indians?" "Was he ever married?" "What about his later life?" "Did he stay in the West?" And many, many more questions. Among some of the more pertinent inquiries were regarding his Mormon background, and how did that affect his life? I will try to answer all these questions and picture his life as I have known it as his son and as he has told it to me.

Nick Wilson was a bonafide rider for the Pony Express when he was eighteen years of age, and his name is found among the sixty-five Express riders on the records in the Archives of the Pony Express in Washington, DC. Large bronze plaques were made and issued by the American Trails Association, of which Howard R. Driggs was president at that time. These plaques were to be placed at the graves of these Pony Express riders or issued to the nearest relative of those whose graves could not be found. Such a Pony Express plaque is displayed at the grave of Elijah Nicholas Wilson in the South Park Cemetery located in Jackson Hole.

Nick also drove for the famous Overland Stage and was the leader in the settlement of Jackson Hole Valley in Wyoming. He spoke five Indian languages very fluently, and in Utah and Nevada, he was guide and interpreter for Albert Sidney Johnston, who achieved Civil War fame as a Confederate General and who was killed at Shiloh in one of the hardest-fought battles of the Civil War.

In his later life, after Indians were placed on reservations, Nick Wilson was an interpreter for the United States Government at both Fort Washakie on the Wind River Indian Reservation in Wyoming and at Fort Hall on the Blackfoot Indian Reservation in Idaho.

He was an avid story teller and it was his telling stories of Indian and frontier life that led to his writing the book *The White Indian Boy,* which was first published by the Skelton Book Company of Salt Lake City, Utah, and was know as *Uncle Nick Among the Shoshones* in 1910.

It was later edited by Howard R. Driggs for his Pioneer Series and was called *The White Indian Boy.* It was so well edited as to language and composition that it became a textbook in schools all over America. In later years, since the old copyright expired, this book has been published very successfully by several book companies. It has had at least three different titles, i.e., *Uncle Nick Among the Shoshones,* printed by Skelton Publishing Company; *The White Indian Boy,* edited by Driggs and published by the World Book Company in New York; and more recently by Book Craft Company of Salt Lake City, Utah, and called *Among the Shoshones* by Elijah Nicholas Wilson, and also by Pine Cone Publishers of Medford, Oregon, also called *Among the Shoshones,* but now here is the more complete story of the real Nick Wilson as he really was, written by himself, and by myself, Charles A. Wilson, son of the White Indian Boy!

I have listed above some of the many questions I have been asked regarding my father's life, questions which until now have not been fully answered or explained. I think I will start with the one regarding his Mormon background, and which really is the basis for all the rest.

My father, Elijah Nicholas Wilson, was born in Nauvoo, Illinois, April 8, 1842. The furor over the beginning of the Mormon Church by Joseph Smith (Apostle and Prophet) was at its height. The church, called Mormon, or Latter-Day Saints, was already established in 1830, and my father's family was among the first converts.

My Uncle James Wilson was one of Joseph Smith's body-guards at Nauvoo, just prior to the martyrdom at Carthage Jail on June 27, 1844. I am not going to stand on exact dates for this biography, as it would require too much research and I do not have the time, as I am 83 years old and already have let too much time go by, so will suffice on approximate dates.

Upon Joseph Smith's death came the first major division in the Mormon Church. His first wife, Emma Hale Smith, wanted the Church to continue under the Smith family's leadership, but most of the original Church members followed Brigham Young to the Salt Lake Valley in Utah. My father's family went with Brigham Young. There are now over one hundred divisions or branches of the Mormon Church, due to persecution from outsiders and among themselves.

The first pioneer immigrants reached the Salt Lake Valley in July, 1847. My father's family crossed the plains to Salt Lake in 1849 when he was seven years old. As a small lad I listened to his tales of adventures on this terrible, but exciting trip west with wagons and oxen and the awful hardships they endured, both on the trip and after arrival in the Salt Lake Valley.

He told of the great herds of buffalo encountered on this trip and the packs of grey wolves that followed the caravans day after day, feeding on any strayed or abandoned stock, and even digging up newly made graves to eat the dead. He said the wolves got so bad that the pioneers hauled the bodies of their dead along with them until they came to rocky ground where they could bury and cover the dead with rocks so the wolves could not dig them up.

After arriving in the Salt Lake Valley, my father's family settled at what today is Grantsville, and it was here he spent his childhood up to about twelve or fourteen years of age when he ran away with a wild band of Indians and lived with them for over two years.

I will now let you read my father's book, *The White Indian Boy*, just as he wrote it on an old French typewriter of 1906 vintage. Due to his lack of schooling, the writing of this story became very hard work for him, but he kept pounding along for over two years on this manuscript, finally finishing it in 1910. Then, after you read that, I will try to answer some of the other questions mentioned above, but first, his Mormon background will follow his manuscript.

He was only forty-seven years old when he settled in Jackson Hole Valley and seventy-three when he died there in 1915, and so there is a lot of his life that has not been told until now. I will also tell the true story of Jackson Hole and its people during his life there, and after my father passed away onto the happy hunting grounds where he hoped to find his old Indian friends had become "a white and beautiful people."

It is almost impossible to obtain a copy of any of the four books mentioned above, all of the same story, but published after the old copyright expired. They have all become collectors' items, and especially the original book called *Uncle Nick Among the Shoshones*, published by Skelton Publishing Company in 1910, is greatly sought after.

In republishing the story of *The White Indian Boy*, I have the full edited collection of all four of these books, plus the sequel, *The Return of the White Indian*, so that now the reader has the complete history of Elijah Nicholas Wilson from the age of seven years, when he crossed the American Plains in a Mormon caravan in 1849 to the Great Salt Lake Valley, Utah, to the settling of the Jackson Hole Valley in Wyoming in 1889 of which he was the leader and settled with the first pioneers that came to make this Valley their home, dying there on December 27, 1915.

Charles A. Wilson

CHARLES A. WILSON

Acknowledgments

With grateful appreciation, I want to thank some special people, for without their help, it would have been almost impossible to have compiled this manuscript.

First: To Trilba Nethercott Redding, I am eternally indebted for the hundreds of hours she spent in untangling and typing my handwritten pages of this manuscript. It was a herculean job because after my writing cools off I can hardly read it myself.

Second: To John Stewart, English Professor at the University of Utah at Logan, Utah, for the many days he spent in editing this manuscript for me in spite of my seemingly ingratitude, which was really shock! I humbly learned to eat crow and I want him to know that I do understand, and deeply thank him for his patience and love to the end of a job well done.

Third: To Rowe Findley, Assistant Editor for National Geographic Magazine, Washington, D.C., who encouraged me to provide a sequel to my father's book, telling of his later years and adding some details of my own very interesting life, I give thanks.

Fourth, but not least: My gratitude and thanks to all my friends, relatives and other acquaintances who contributed to the success and publishing of this volume. Without your trust, help and generosity, it would never have been possible. Hundreds of you responded to my brochures and sent me your checks and letters of encouragement even before the books came off the press! Your trust and faith made this all possible. Without your money, your encouragement and your faith in me, I would have had to give up on a dream that became almost an obsession!

I, also, dedicate this book to my brother George Washington Wilson for his support and encouragement, which means so much to me.

To all of you, I give my love! May the Great Spirit bless you all real good!

Charles A. Wilson

CHARLES A. WILSON

A Note on the Family Tree
of Elijah Nicholas Wilson

Elijah Nicholas Wilson, born April 8, 1842, in Nauvoo, Illinois, son of Elijah Wilson and Martha Kelley. Died December 26, 1915, in Wilson, Wyoming. Buried in South Park Cemetery in Jackson Hole.

Nick Wilson had three wives:

> First wife: Matilda Rebecca Patten, born February 27, 1848, in Big Pidgeon, Iowa, daughter of William Cornwell Patten and Jane Crouse. Died November 10, 1899, in Wilson, Wyoming. Buried in South Park Cemetery, Jackson Hole.

> Second wife, in plural marriage: Sena Logan

> Third wife (after the death of Matilda and departure of Sena): Charlotte Rachel Nethercott, born October 4, 1870, in Sacramento, California, daughter of Alfred Alexander Nethercott and Charlotte Pearce. Died May 3, 1950, in Evanston, Wyoming, and is buried there.

Nick and Matilda Wilson had fifteen children:

1. Matilda Wilson, born August 23, 1866, in Oxford, Idaho. Married Hyrum Tharnik. Death date unknown.

2. Edna Jane Wilson, born December 26, 1867, in Bloomington, Idaho. Married Abraham Ward. Died September 18, 1917.

3. Martha Melvina Wilson, born May 19, 1869, in Bloomington, Idaho. Died January 5, 1875.

4. Hannah Louise Wilson, born January 12, 1871, in Bloomington, Idaho. Married Ellington Smith. Died May 11, 1897.

5. Elijah Nicholas Wilson, Jr., born September 25, 1872, in Oxford, Idaho. Died June 17, 1891.

6. Catharine Ann "Kate" Wilson, born March 12, 1874, in Oxford, Idaho. Married George Goodrick. Died November 16, 1923.

7. Sarah Wilthy "Ett" Wilson, born October 20, 1875, in Oxford, Idaho. Married Steve Leek. Died May 20, 1931.

8. Polly Ann Wilson, born August 17, 1877, in Bloomington, Idaho. Died May 18, 1879.

9. William Patten Wilson, born April 4, 1879, in Bloomington, Idaho. Death date unknown.

10. Mary Olivia Wilson, born November 23, 1880, in Ovid, Idaho. Death date unknown.

11. Fannie Pricilla Wilson, born January 28, 1882, in Ovid, Idaho. Death date unknown.

12. Elias Henry Wilson, born November 22, 1884, in Bloomington, Idaho. Death date unknown.

13. Nellie Guena Wilson, born July 11, 1886, in Salem, Idaho. Married Enoch Burns Ferrin. Died January 16, 1950.

14. Ray Leon Wilson, born March 16, 1888, in Salem, Idaho. Died May 18, 1891.

15. Milton J. Wilson, born March 5, 1891, in Rexburg, Idaho. Died March 20, 1891.

Nick Wilson and Sena Logan had two sons:

1. Wallace Wilson. Died at approximate age of 10.

2. William "Bill" Wilson. Bill Wilson and his wife had two sons: Leo and William.

Nick and Charlotte Wilson had three children:

1. Charles Alma Wilson, born October 12, 1901, in Wilson, Wyoming. Married Dorotha F. Stark. Charles and Dorotha had four sons: Steve, Philip, Stark, and Paul. After Dorotha's death he married his niece, Trilba Nethercott Redding, whom he acknowledges helped with the preparation of the book. Died December 4, 1999. Buried in South Park Cemetery in Jackson Hole. His second wife, Trilba, died February 9, 1999.

2. Sarah Charlotte Wilson, born July 15, 1903, in Wilson, Wyoming. Died June 7, 1905.

3. George Washington Wilson, born February 22, 1905, in Wilson, Wyoming. Married Edna Harris. Died April 16, 1999.

The wolves got so bad that emigrants had to haul their dead until they could reach rocky ground, where they could cover the bodies with rocks to keep the wolves from digging them up. Picture taken about 1849 near Independence Rock on Sweetwater River in Wyoming.

The White Indian Boy

or

Uncle Nick Among the Shoshones

by
Elijah Nicholas Wilson

E. N. WILSON
"UNCLE NICK"

Contents

THE WHITE INDIAN BOY

1. Pioneer Days.. 1
2. My Little Indian Brother 4
3. Off With the Indians 8
4. The Great Encampment 13
5. Village Life 19
6. My Mother 24
7. The Crows 26
8. A Long Journey 39
9. The Fierce Battle 50
10. Lively Times 56
11. Old Morogonai... 61
12. The Big Council.. 65
13. Homeward Bound 69
14. Year of th eMove 75
15. The Pony Express.. 84
16. Johnston Punishes the Indians......................... 97
17. The Overland Stage 104
18. A Terrible Journey 112
19. My Old Shosone Friends 123
20. Trapping With an Indian 131
21. Working on the Indian Reservation 135
22. Frontier Troubles.. 139

Preface

Perhaps you have read, or heard old frontiersmen tell about the many terrible outrages and bloody massacres that have been committed by the red men upon the early settlers in the valleys of the Rocky Mountains. Many a large emigrant train has been overpowered and every one of the people killed and scalped, and their little childrens' brains dashed out against the hub of a wagon wheel. Houses have been burned and the inmates murdered; barns and hay-stacks destroyed by fire; and cattle and horses driven off.

Now, my dear friends, I know this to be too true, for I am one of the early settlers of the Rocky Mountains, and I have passed through some of the most heart-rending experiences that have ever been described.

I have had many narrow escapes from being killed. I have had my friends shot down by my side, and I have been very badly wounded twice.

I was one of the first Pony Express riders and stage drivers of the early days, and I have seen some terrible things committed by the low-down Gosiute Indians of Utah and Nevada.

Many a poor boy has been shot from his horse when carrying the express. The stations have been burned and the hostlers killed and scalped. This kind of thing happened very often during a period of about two years.

The Humboldt Indians were considered the most cruel and blood-thirsty Indians of those days. Pocatello was the name of their chief, and in later years I got very well acquainted with him. His small band of about five hundred warriors would attack small trains of emigrants, capture the people, tie them down, and burn their eyes out with red hot irons, cut their ears off, and thus torture them until they died. I have not the language to describe these terrible and bloody crimes, but what I do say shall be the truth, and any of the old timers will bear me out in what I say.

Elijah Nicholas Wilson

ELIJAH NICHOLAS WILSON

CHAPTER 1 — **Pioneer Days**

I came to Utah in 1850 with my parents when I was a very small boy. We moved to one of the outside settlements where the people were having serious trouble with the Indians. We had to group our houses close together and build a high wall all around them to protect ourselves from the savages. Some of the men would generally have to stand guard while the rest worked in the fields, and even then we lost many of our cattle, and very often some of the people would be killed. We had to keep close watch over our cows during the day, and corral them at night, and place a strong guard around the pen.

We built a log schoolhouse in the center of the town, or fort, and near it we erected a very high pole on which we could run a white flag as a signal if the Indians attempted to run off our cattle, or attack the town, or the men at work in the fields. In the log schoolhouse were two old men that would take turns in stopping there all the time to give the signals if necessary, by raising the flag in day time, or by beating a big drum at night, for we had in the house a large bass drum so that if the Indians should make a raid on the cowpen or the town in the night, one of the guard would notify the man with the drum and he would turn loose on the old thing and make it rattle to beat time.

When the people heard the drum, all the women and children were supposed to rush for the schoolhouse, and the men would hurry for the cow corral or take their places along the wall. Often in the dead hours of night when we would be quietly sleeping, we would be startled by the sound of this old drum. Then you would hear the kids coming and squalling from every direction. You bet, I was there, too. Many a time I have run for that old schoolhouse expecting to be filled with arrows before I could get there. Yes, sir, many is the time I have run for that schoolhouse while clinging to my mother's apron and squalling like sixty.

Those Gosiute Indians were the lowest and most degraded and treacherous tribe in the Rocky Mountains. They would go almost naked in the summer time, but when winter came, they would take rabbit skins and twist them into a long string like a rope, and then fold it back and forth and tie the folds together, and in that way make it into a kind of robe. This robe was generally all they had to wear in the day time and all they had to sleep in at night. They would eat almost anything they could get.

The Shoshones and the Bannocks were not so bad. They were cleaner and had many ponies to ride, and they were not so ugly as the mean Gosiutes that we had so much trouble with.

We could not go outside the wall without endangering our lives, and when we would lie down at night we would not know what would happen before morning. That is the way, my dear friends, we were fixed. We did not know at what time, what minute, we would all be massacred.

While we were fighting the Indians, the grasshoppers and crickets came down from the mountains, ate every green thing, and left the country as bare as though there had never been anything growing in the first place. Fine gardens, crops, meadows — everything was destroyed and the country left a barren desert. To make the situation worse, most of the people hadn't supplies enough even to last until harvest time, but now, alas! there would be no harvest. My kind readers, imagine yourselves a thousand miles from civilization among tribes of hostile Indians, with the sun darkened by grasshoppers, and the earth covered with crickets, and with nothing on hand to eat.

I cannot collect words to describe the misery and suffering of the poor people through those two years. The third year things commenced to look somewhat better. The Indians became friendly, the grasshoppers and crickets disappeared, and the people who could muster a little seed raised a small crop that year. Those of us who were left after the starvation period would gather together and sing. "Oh, hard times, come again no more." During those troublous two years many of our friends had been killed by the Indians and others had died for want of proper food, and clothing to protect them from the severe weather.

My little Indian brother.

CHAPTER 2 — **My Little Indian Brother**

A few Indians hung around the settlement begging their living. The people thought it best to put them to work, so my father made a bargain with one old Indian to work for him. His family consisted of his wife and one small son about my age.

At that time my father had a small bunch of sheep, and he wanted to move out on his farm, which was two miles from the settlement, so he could take better care of them. The old Indian thought it would be safe to do so, as most of the Indians in the neighborhood were becoming more friendly, and the wild Indians were so far away that it was thought they would not bother us. So we moved out to the farm and father put the Indian boy and myself to herding the sheep. I had no other boy to play with, so Pansuk the little Indian boy, and myself became greatly attached to each other.I soon learned to talk his language and Pansuk and I had great times together for four years, when the poor little fellow took sick. We did all we could for him, but he kept getting worse until he died. It was hard for me to part with my dear little friend. I loved him as much as if he had been my own brother.

After Pansuk died, I had to herd the sheep by myself. The summer wore along very lonely for me, until about the first of August, when there came a band of Shoshone Indians and camped near where I herded sheep. Some of them could talk the Gosiute language which, thanks to my little Indian brother, I could speak, too. They seemed to take quite a fancy to me and would be with me every chance they could get. They said they liked to hear me talk Indian, for they never heard a white boy talk as well as I did.

One day an Indian came to the place where I was herding sheep. He had with him a little pinto pony which I thought was the prettiest thing I ever saw. The Indian could talk Gosiute very well. He asked me if I did not want to ride the pony. I said that I would like to ride him, but was afraid to, for I had never been on a horse in my life. He said that the pony was very gentle. He helped me on to his back and led him around awhile. The next day he came again with the pinto pony and had me ride it again. Four or five of the

My little Indian brother, Pansuk and his mother. They came to us when he was about six years old. My father hired this Gosiute family to work on his farm near Grantsville, Utah, about 1849. I was one year older than Pansuk. I learned the Indian language from him very fast during the four years we herded my father's sheep together.

Herding sheep was lonely business. Nick's older brother had to take over after Nick ran away with a wild tribe of Indians in 1856.

Indians came this time and they would take turns leading the pony with me on his back. I soon got so I could ride him without their leading him for me. They kept this up for several days.

Finally the Indian came one day as he had been doing and let me ride quite a while, and when I got tired and gave him back the horse, he asked me if I did not want to keep him. I told him that I would sooner have the pony than anything I ever saw. He said I could have the horse, and I could ride him all the time, if I would go away with him. I said I was afraid to go. He said he would take good care of me and would give me bows and arrows, and all the good buckskin clothes I wanted if I would go. I asked him what they had to eat. He said they had all kinds of meat and berries and fish, sage chickens, ducks, geese, and rabbits. I thought this surely beat herding sheep and living on greens and lumpydick, so I told him I would think the matter over. When he came the next day I told him that I had decided to go with him.

In five days they were going to start up north to meet the rest of their tribe. This Indian was to hide for two days after the rest had gone and then meet me at a bunch of willows about a mile above my father's house after dark with the little pinto pony. Now, my dear friends, how many little boys of my age, lacking only a few months of being twelve years old, would run away from home and friends and go off with a tribe of wild Indians? You will see that I went with them and it was for two years that I never saw a white man. This was in the month of August, 1856.

CHAPTER 3 — Off With the Indians

The night came at last when we were to start. Just after dark I slipped away from the house and started for the bunch of willows where I was to meet the Indian. When I got there, I found two Indians waiting for me instead of one. The sight of two of them almost made me weaken and turn back, but as soon as I saw with them my little pinto pony it gave me new courage, so I went up to them. They had an old Indian saddle on the pony, with very rough rawhide thongs for stirrup straps. At a signal from them, I mounted my horse and away we went.

The Indians wanted to ride pretty fast. It was all right at first, but after a while, I got very tired. My legs began to hurt me and I wanted to stop, but they urged me along until the peep of day, when we stopped by some very salty springs. I was so stiff and sore that I could not get off my horse, so one of them lifted me off and stood me on the ground, but I could not stand up. The rawhide straps had rubbed all the skin off my legs so that they were as raw as fresh meat. The Indians told me if I would take off my pants and jump into the salt springs it would make my legs better, but I found that I could not get them off for they were stuck to my legs. After some very severe pain we succeeded in getting my pants off, but not a bit of skin was left for about a foot up my legs. They said: "Come on, now, and get into this water and you will be well in a little while." Well, I jumped into the spring up to my waist. O, gosh! O, blazes! I jumped out again. O, Lordy! O, Lordy! O, Lordy! Well, my dear friends, I cannot describe the sensations in my wounded parts. I jumped and I kicked. I bucked and tore up the ground and mashed down the grass until it looked as if a bunch of sheep had been bedded there. Well, after a half hour, I wore myself out, and fell to the ground, and oh, how I cried! The Indians put down a buffalo robe and rolled me on it and spread a blanket over me. I lay there and cried myself to sleep.

When I awoke, the Indians were sitting by a small fire. They had killed a duck and were broiling it for my breakfast. When they saw that I was awake, they said, "Come and eat some duck." I started

Chief Washakie
Advocate of Peace, if not — then war

In his left hand, Chief Washakie clasps the Peace Pipe showing he is an advocate of peace, first and last. But in his good right hand he holds his trusty rifle as a symbol and harbinger of war as a last resort.

to get up, and oh! how sore I was. I began to cry again. They kept coaxing me to come and have something to eat, until finally I got up and went to them, but I had to walk on the wide track. I ate some duck and dried meat and then I felt better. They had the horses all ready and said:"Come and get on your horse." I said I could not ride, that I would walk. They said that they were going a long ways and that I could not walk, but they would try to fix the saddle so it would not hurt me. They put a buffalo robe over the old saddle and put me in it. It was not so bad as I thought it would be. I had no pants on so the soft hair of the buffalo robe was all right. One of them tied my pants to my saddle. That day I lost them and I didn't have another pair on for over two years. I had a blanket over my legs to keep the sun from burning them.

We traveled all day over a country that was more like the bottom of an old lake than anything else, and camped that night by another spring. The Indians pulled me from my horse, piled me down on a robe, started a fire, then caught some fish and broiled them on the coals. Oh, what a fine supper we had that night; the next morning I felt pretty well used up, but I ate some fish and a large chunk of dried elk meat for my breakfast and felt better. Then we started again. Near mid-afternoon, we saw about six miles ahead of us the Indians we had been trying to catch up with. They had overtaken another large band of Indians so it looked as if there were an awful lot of them. By the time we caught up with them, they had just stopped and were unpacking, and some of them had their wickiups up. We rode through the camp until we came to a big wickiup where a large, good looking Indian was standing. They said this man was their chief, that I was to stop with him, and that he would be my brother. They said his name was Washakie.

An old squaw came up to my horse and stood looking at me. These two Indians told her that my legs were badly skinned and were very sore. One of the Indians that had brought me told me that this old woman was the Chief's mother and that she would be my mother, too, and would be very good to me, then Washakie helped me off my horse. The old squaw came up to me and put her hand on my head and began to say something very pitiful to me, and I began to cry. She cried, too, and taking me by the arm, led me into the wickiup, and pointed to a nice bed that the chief's wife had made for me. I lay down on the bed and sobbed myself to sleep. When I woke up, this new mother of mine brought me some soup and some fresh deer meat to eat, and oh, how good it tasted to me!

The next morning my new mother thought she would give me a good breakfast. They had brought some flour from the settlements so she thought she would make me some bread, such as I had been used to having at home, She had no soda, nothing but flour and water, so you may judge what kind of bread it was. She would have had to whip a hungry dog to make him eat it. Along with the bread she gave me some good, fried sage-chicken, some dried meat, and some fresh service berries. I think she did not like it very well when she found that I did not eat the bread.

That day my mother and the chief's wife started to make me something to wear, for after I had lost my breeches, I had nothing on but an old, thin shirt and a straw hat that had met with an accident and lost part of its brim. The elbows were out of my shirt and it did not have a very long tail, either. The two women worked for several hours and finally got the thing finished and gave it to me to put on. I did not know what to call it, for I had not seen anything like it before, but it may have been what the girls now call a mother-hubbard. It was all right, anyhow, when I got it on and my belt around me to keep the thing close to me, but I had to pull the back up a little above the belt to keep it from choking me to death when I stooped over. My dear old mother rubbed my legs with skunk oil and they got better fast. All of the Indians were very kind to me.

We stayed at this camp for five days to give me time to get well. It had got noised around by this time that my legs were very bad, and one day when I was out in front of the wickiup, a lot of kids wanted to see them. One stooped to raise my mother-hubbard to look at them, and the rest began to laugh, but they didn't laugh long, for I gave him a kick that sent him winding. Then his mother came out after me and I thought she was going to eat me up. She gave me quite a lecture, but I did not know what she said, so it made no difference to me. My old mother, hearing the noise, came and, taking me by the hand, led me into the wickiup and gave me some dried serviceberries. I thought that was pretty good and if that was the way they were going to treat me, I would kick another one if I got a chance.

It was not long until I got another chance, for the next day the kids gathered around me again and another one about my size went to raise my mother-hubbard. I fetched him a kick that sent him about a rod and he gave out a war whoop that you could have heard a mile. It brought about half of the tribe to see how many I had killed. That kid's mother turned loose on me, too, with her tongue and everlastingly ribbed me up. The chief happened to see the trouble and I think that is what kept me from being cremated. Anyhow, after that the kids left my mother-hubbard alone. My mother began to teach me the Shoshone language, and I got along pretty well. Being able to talk the Gosiute language helped me for the two languages were a good deal alike.

One night the hunters came in loaded with meat, and the next day we started to move. The horses were brought in and among them was my pinto pony. When I saw him it seemed as if I had met some one from home, and I ran up and hugged him as if he had been my sweetheart.

My dear old mother had fixed me up a pretty good saddle and had cushioned it off in fine style to keep it from hurting me. We traveled about fifteen miles that day and camped on a small stream which they called Kohits. Mother told me to wade out into the water and bathe my legs. I said, "Not by a d—n sight, I have had all the baths I want." She said the water would make my legs tough, and when she saw that I wouldn't go into the stream, she brought some cold water and told me to wash them. Then I wanted to know if it was salty. She said it was not a bit salty. So I bathed my legs, and when I found the water didn't hurt me, I waded out into the stream. My brother Washakie said it was "tibi tsi djant," which means, "very good."

CHAPTER 4 — **The Great Encampment**

It was the custom in those early days for all the Indians of this tribe to come together every three years, and this was the year for them to meet again. We started for the great camp ground, and after traveling for three days, we came to a large river, which they call Piupa (Snake River), where we joined another large band of Indians belonging to the same tribe.

In order to cross the river, the squaws built boats of bul-rushes tied in bundles and the bundles lashed together until there were enough to hold up six or eight hundred pounds. The Indians swam the horses, and some of the little boys rode their horses across. I wanted to swim my horse, but my mother would not let me. We spent about a week in getting across the river, and during this time I had more fun than I ever had before in my life.

My mother gave me a fish hook and a line that was made out of hair from a horse's tail. With these I caught my first fish, and some of them were very large ones, too. I had lots of fun with the other boys and we became friendly, but my mother kept pretty close around for fear I would kick some of their heads off. After that I learned to talk Shoshone faster by playing with the kids than I did from my mother.

Nothing of importance happened until we got to Big Hole Basin. There I saw the first buffalo I had seen since I crossed the Plains. One morning we saw seven head on the bench about a mile away. Ten Indians started after them. One having a wide spear with a long handle would ride up to a buffalo and cut the ham strings of both legs and the others would come along and kill it. About fifteen squaws went up to skin the buffaloes and get the meat. Mother and I went with them. The squaws would rip the animals down the back from the head to the tail and then rip them down the belly and take off the top half of the hide and cut all the meat on that side from the bones. They would then tie ropes to the feet of the buffaloes and turn them over with their ponies, and do the other side the same. After they got the meat home, they would slice it up in thin pieces and hang it up to dry. When it was about half dry they would take a piece at a time and pound it between two rocks until it was very soft, and then hang it up again until it was dry. The dried meat was put into a sack and the older it got the better it was. This is the way they did all of their buffalo meat. This meat was generally kept for use in the winter and during the general gatherings of the tribe. I know that we had about five hundred pounds of it when we got to the place where the tribe was to assemble. It was about the last of August when the tribe had all assembled in Deer Lodge Valley, now in Montana.

It was a great sight to see so many Indians together and to think I was all the white person within three hundred miles. I could not begin to count the wickiups that were strung up and down the small stream as far as I could see, and the whole country was covered with horses and dogs. As nearly as I could find out, there were about six thousand Indians in this great camp, but there might have been more. When I asked the chief how many there were, he said there were so many that he could not count them.

Mother kept very close watch over me for fear that I would get hurt or lost among so many Indians, and when I went around to see what was going on, she was nearly always with me to take care of me. She told me that Pocatello's Indians were very bad and that they would steal me and take me away off and sell me to Indians that would eat me up. She scared me so badly that I stuck pretty close to her most of the time. The Indians would run horses and bet so heavily on the races that I saw one Indian win fifty head of ponies on one race. Two Indians were killed while racing their horses, and a squaw and her papoose were run over and the papoose was killed.

Some of Pocatello's Indians had several white scalps they had taken from some poor emigrants they had killed. I saw six of these scalps. One was the scalp of a woman with red hair, one a girl's scalp with dark hair, and four were men's scalps, one with gray hair, the rest with dark hair. I cannot describe my feelings when I saw the red devils dancing around those scalps. It made me wish that I were home again herding sheep and living on greens and lumpy-dick.

Washakie's Indians had a few Crow scalps, for at this time the Crows and Shoshones were at war with each other. I am pretty sure they had no white scalps, or if they had, they did not let me see them.

The Indians had great times dancing around the scalps. They would stick a small pole in the ground and string the scalps on it and then dance around them and sing and yell at the top of their voices, and make the most horrible noises I ever heard. The leaders of the different bands would take the inside, then the warriors would circle around them, then came the squaws and the children on the outside, and the noise they made would shame a band of coyotes. I have seen five hundred Indians at a time in this kind of dance, and they would keep at it until I would get sick and tired of it, but they thought they were having a high time, and most of those who were not gambling or racing horses would keep up this dancing and singing at intervals for a week or more.

The time was drawing near when we were to separate and I was glad of it. Some of Pocatello's Indians started out a few days ahead of the rest of his band. A day or two before we were to start my horse got away and went off with some other horses, and I slipped away from my mother and went after him. I had not gone far until I met some Indians hunting horses, who said they had not seen my horse. I went on quite a ways further when an Indian came up to me and said that he had seen some horses go over a ridge about a mile away, and if I would get on his horse behind him he would take me over and see if my horse was there. I got on behind him and we started, but when we got to the top of the hill I could not see any horses in sight, and after we got over the hill he started to ride fast. Then I began to get scared, for I thought of the man-eating Indians my mother had told me about, and I asked him to stop and let me get off, but he whipped his horse the harder and went the faster. Watching my chance, I jumped off and about broke my neck, but I got up and started back for camp as fast as I could run. He turned and came up to me and threw his lasso over me. After dragging me about ten rods, he stopped and hit me with his quirt and told me to get back on the horse or he would put an arrow through me. I cried and begged him to let me alone, but he made me get on again and started off as fast as his horse could go, but I noticed that he kept looking back every little while. Pretty soon he stopped and told me to get off. I jumped off, and as I did so he hit me such a lick over the head with his quirt that it made me see stars for a few minutes. Then he started off on a run, but after going about fifty yards he stopped, pulled his bow and arrow out of the quiver and started towards me as if he intended to put an arrow through me. He only came a few steps, then suddenly whirled his horse and away he went over the prairie. I soon saw what caused his hurry, for a short distance away were some Indians coming towards me as fast as they could travel. When they got to me they stopped, and one of them told me to get on behind him and he would take me to my mother. I climbed up mighty quick, and before we got to the wickiup I met my mother. She had come out to meet me and was crying. She lifted me from the horse and hugged me in great fashion. She said one of Pocatello's Indians was trying to steal me, and she never expected to see me again.

Some Indians happened to see me get on the horse behind the Indian and told my mother, and Washakie sent those Indians after me before we had a chance to get very far away. Mother stuck pretty close to me after that while we stopped in this place, but I had such a scare that I didn't go very far from the wickiup unless mother was with me. The chief told me never to go alone after my horse if he got away again, but to let him know and he would have him caught for me; that the Pocatello Indians wanted me and they would get me if they could and sell me for a great many ponies, and then it would by "goodby, Yagaiki," Yagaiki was my Indian name. For a long time after that I had to go to bed as soon as it began to get dark for my mother would not allow me out after night-fall.

The camp finally began to break up in earnest, as small bands started off in different directions, and they were about all gone when we started. There were about sixty wickiups and two hundred and fifty Indians in our band. We had about four hundred head of horses, and more than five hundred dogs, it seemed to me, all of them half breed coyotes. Chief Washakie was at that time about twenty-seven years old, a very large Indian, and quite good looking. His wife did not appear to be over twenty years old, and had one little girl papoose about six months old.

We got started from the big camp at last, and I was very glad of it for I was tired of being looked at by so many Indians. There were hundreds of young Indians in the big camp, and some old ones, too, who had never seen a white person before. They would gather around me like I was some wild animal. If I moved suddenly towards them, they would jump back and scream like wild cats. My mother told them I would not bite, but if they bothered me very much I might kick some of their ribs loose, for I could kick worse than a wild horse.

We had not traveled more than two or three hours before one of the horses turned his pack under his belly and began to run and kick like mad. This started all of the other horses, and as they came running by us, mother tried to stop them and one of the horses ran against her and knocked her horse down and it rolled over with her. I thought she was killed. I jumped from my horse and raised her up and then I saw that she was not dead, but that one of her arms was broken. Washakie's wife was there and told me to go ahead and tell Washakie to hurry back. I think I never cried harder in my life than I did then, for I thought my poor old mother was going to die. She told me not to cry, that she knew she would be all right soon. We had to stop here for a week to let mother get better. There were lots of antelope in the valley and plenty of fish in the stream by the camp, so when mother would go to sleep, I would go fishing. I could tell every time she woke up, for when Hanabi, the chief's wife, came out and called, "Yagaiki, come," I knew that mother was awake and had missed me. Then I would get back to her in double quick time.

While we were waiting for my mother to get better, I went out with Washakie to see the Indians run antelope. About fifty of us circled around the antelope and would take turns in running them. It was not long until we had them run down. The poor little animals became so tired that they would stick their heads under a bush and lie there until we had shot them with our bows and arrows. I killed two myself, and it tickled me nearly to death. When I got to camp I told mother how it all happened and she bragged on me so much, that I thought I was a heap big Indian. Well, mother's arm was doing nicely, for the medicine man had fixed it up pretty well.

We started again and traveled for several days, and then stopped where there were a great number of buffaloes and antelope. We stayed there for about three weeks. During the time that mother was not able to watch me, she had Washakie take me with him on his hunting trips, which just suited me. I went out with him to kill buffaloes, and the first day we killed six—two large bulls and four cows. One Indian, with a broad spear, would run up behind them and cut their ham strings so that they could not run and then we would go up and shoot them in the neck with arrows until we killed them; then the squaws would come and take the hide and meat and leave the bones. I told Washakie that my bow was too small to kill buffaloes with. He laughed and said I should have a bigger one.

When we got back to camp he told some of the Indians what I had said, and one very old Indian by the name of Morogonai gave me a fine bow and another Indian gave me eight good arrows. You bet, I felt big then, and I told mother that the next time I went out I would kill a whole herd of buffaloes. She said she knew I would, but that she did not know what they would do with all the meat. Washakie said I was just like the white men, they would kill all the buffaloes they could see and let them lie on the prairie for the wolves. He said it was not that way with the Indians, for they save all of the meat and hides. That the Great Spirit would not like it if they did as the white men; for they would have bad luck and would go hungry if they wasted meat and killed buffaloes and deer when they did not need to.

Two or three days after this we went out again and killed two more buffaloes. When we got back that night, mother asked how many I killed. I told her that I shot twice at them and I believe I hit one once. She said I was all right, and that I would be the best hunter in the whole tribe after a while. I told her that I would get a gun and then I would kill buffaloes for the whole band. She said I was a bully boy, and that I would be a chief some day. It took mother's arm a long time to get well and she suffered with it very much, but I was having a fine time and was getting fat. The bucks would kill the meat, but the squaws would have to carry it to camp and cook or dry it. They had to carry all the wood and the water. The men would lie around until they ran out of meat and then they would go out and hunt again.

CHAPTER 5 — **Village Life**

Cold weather was coming, for already some snow had fallen in the mountains. Hanabi and some of her friends went to work and made me some fine clothes. They were made somewhat like the chaps of the cowboys, open in front, with no seat, but on the sides wedge-shaped strips that ran up to the belt. The leggings fit pretty tight, but the women left a seam about as wide as my hand on the outside so they could be let out if necessary. They gave me a pair of new moccasins that came up to my knees. They also made me another mother-hubbard out of nice, smoked buckskin, that fit me better than the first one did. The sleeves came down a little below my elbows, and had a long fringe on the outside from the shoulder down and all around the neck. The skirt part of the thing came down almost to my knees and had fringe all around the bottom of it, with beads in heart and diamond shapes all over the breast. The clothes were all very fine and when I got them on I couldn't tell whether I was a boy or a little squaw papoose. I didn't care much, either, for they fit me pretty well and were warm and comfortable. Mother made me a hat out of muskrat skin. It ran to a peak and had two rabbit tails sewed to the top for tassels. With my new clothes on, I was fixed up better than any other kid in the camp.

We now started for the elk country. When we got there the Indians killed about one hundred elk and a few bear, but by that time it was getting so cold that we set out again for our winter quarters. After traveling for several days we stopped on a large river which we called Paitapa, and which the whites call the Jefferson River, in Montana.

By this time, most of the buffaloes had left for their winter range, but we could see a few once in a while as they passed near our camp. The Indians did not bother them because we had plenty of dried meat and for fresh meat there were lots of white tail deer near the village that we could snare by hanging loops of rawhide over their trails. There were also a great many grouse and wild chickens. I have killed as high as six or seven a day with my bow and arrows.

Winter passed very slowly. Nothing very exciting happened until along towards spring when one day we had a terrible fracas. Washakie had gone up the river a few miles to visit another large Indian village to stay a day or two. While he was gone pretty nearly all the camp got into a fight. We had a fishing hole close to the camp where the squaws and kids would fish. Mother and I had been down there with a lot of others fishing through the ice, and had caught quite a nice lot of fish when mother took what we had to the wickiup. She told me not to stay long. As soon as she had gone, a girl, a little larger than I was, wanted to take my pole and fish in my hole. I let her take it, and she caught several fish. Then I heard mother call me and wanted her to give me back my pole, so I could go home, but she would not do it. I tried to take it away from her, but she jerked it away from me and hit me over the head with it and knocked me onto my knees. I jumped up and gave her a whack that knocked her down, and when she got up she gave a few of the awfulest yelps I ever heard. I did not know that one person could make so much noise as she did. Then she put for her home as fast as she could go, and knowing that something was likely to happen pretty quick, I gathered up what fish the kids hadn't run away with and went home, too. I was just inside our wickiup when the girl's mother came rushing up with a big knife in her hand. She said: "Give me that little white devil till I cut his heart out." She started for me, but mother stopped her, pushed her back and got her out of the wickiup.

They made such a racket that the whole camp gathered around to see the fun. The squaw hit mother over the head with the knife, and when I saw the blood fly, I grabbed a big stick and struck the squaw over the head and knocked her down. Then I saw another squaw take hold of mother and I sent her spinning. Then others mixed in and took sides and soon the whole bunch was yelling and fighting fit to kill. One boy grabbed the stick to take it away from me, but I gave him a kick that settled his hash. Hanabi took the stick away from me and then I ran into the wickiup and got my bow and arrows, but a big Indian took the bow away from me and broke the string. If he had only left me alone I would have made a few good squaws in quick time. I guess it was for the best anyway. More Indians came up and stopped the fracas, but not before a lot of them went off howling with sore heads. That night Washakie came home and they held a big council. I don't know what they did, but the next day two or three families left our camp and went to join another band.

Everything passed along very well for a while. I helped mother pack wood and water, and the other little boys called me a squaw for doing it because carrying wood and water was squaw's work. I told mother I would break some of their darn necks if they didn't stop it. She said, "Let them alone, they are bad boys." But one day we were packing wood, and having cut more than we could carry in one trip I went back for it, when a boy came up to me and said, "Oh! you are a squaw," and spit at me. I threw down my wood and started after him. He ran and was yelping at every jump, expecting me to kick the top of his head off. Washakie happened to see me before I caught him and called to me to stop. It was lucky for that kid that Washakie was there, you bet, for if I had caught him I would have fixed him so that his mother would not have known him. I went back and got my wood and took it to the wickiup. Washakie wanted to know what it was all about, so I told him what the boy had called me and how he spit at me. He said he did not want me to start another camp fight, but that he did want me to take my own part, even if it caused the whole tribe to go to fighting. He said he had been watching how things were going, and was glad to say that so far as he knew, I had never started a fuss and that he did not think I was quarrelsome if I was let alone. He said that if I was cowardly and afraid to stand up for myself, the little boys would give me no peace and so he was glad to see me take my own part.

One day I heard an Indian talking to Washakie and telling him that it was not right for him to let me do squaw's work, and that it was setting a bad example for the other little boys. Washakie said he thought it was setting a good example, and if some of the older ones would take it, it would be better for their wives. He said: "We burden our women to death with hard labor. I have never noticed it before so much as I have the last year since we have had Yagaiki. I see how much he helps mother and what lots of hard work she has to do while we sit around and do nothing. Yagaiki appears to be happier when helping mother than he is when playing with the other little boys, and he is so much comfort to her that I firmly believe mother would have gone crazy if it had not been for him. Her troubles were so great after my father and my two brothers were killed, nearly at the same time, that it was more than she could have stood. I do believe it was the Great Spirit that sent the little white boy to her."

I think if anything happened to me it would have killed my mother. She would say to Washakie: "You have no idea how smart

My dear old Indian Mother.

CHAPTER 6 — **My Mother**

My Indian mother was as good and kind to me as any one could be, but she did not seem to realize that there was another loving mother miles and miles away, whose heart was filled with sorrow on account of the absence of a child and to whose mind would come these words: "Oh! where is my boy tonight?" My Indian mother would often ask me a great many questions about my white mother. She asked me if I did not want to go home. I told her that I would like to see my folks very much, but if I went home they would keep me there and I did not want to herd sheep. I told her I would sooner play with the white boys than with the Indian boys; and that I liked my bow and arrows which I could not have at home for my father said I was all the time shooting at the cats and chickens and he would not let me have them on the place. "I like my horse and I could not have him at home; and I love you, too, my good mother, and I couldn't have you with me if I went away, so taking it all around, I would sooner stay with you." This always seemed to please her, for her face would light up and sometimes a tear would roll down the brown cheeks and then she would grab me and hug me until you could hear my ribs crack.

She would often tell me of her husband and of her two sons that were killed in a snow slide. She told me how her husband was shot in the knee with a poisoned flint arrow, while fighting with the Crow Indians. He lived a little over a year after the battle, but suffered greatly before he died. Soon after his death her two boys, named Piubi and Yaiabi, went out hunting mountain sheep, and while they were climbing a steep hill the snow gave away above them and came dashing down, sweeping them into a deep gorge in the bottom of the canyon, where they lay under many feet of snow until late in the following spring. The Indians took long sticks and pushed them down into the snow, but could not find the bodies. She told how she would go up there every day and dig in the snow with a stick in the hope of finding her boys, until she got so sick that Washakie and some other Indians brought her home and there she lay for two months very near to death from sorrow and exposure. As soon as she could walk she went up again to where the snow slide was.

The warmer weather of spring had by this time melted some of the snow away, and as she came near she found the body of one of her boys partly uncovered and one of his feet had been eaten off by the wolves. She quickly dug the body out of the snow, and nearby she found her other boy. She was too weak to carry them back to her wickiup and she couldn't leave them there all night alone for the wolves. The next morning, Washakie found her lying on the snow beside the bodies of her children. He took them up tenderly and carried them back to the village, but the poor, old mother was very sick for a long time after that. She was just getting well when the band of Indians she was with came to the settlement where I lived and first saw me.

She would tell me about things that happened when she was a little girl. She said her father was a Shoshone and her mother a Bannock. She said she was sixty-two years old when I came, and had had four children, three boys and a girl. The girl was seven years old when she was dragged to death by a horse. Her oldest and youngest sons were killed in the snow slide, and Washakie and I were the only ones she had left. She had passed through many hard and sorrowful events in her life, but was having better times now than she ever had before, and if I would stay with her she knew she would be happy once more. She said she had fifteen head of horses of her own and when she died she wanted Washakie and me to divide them between us. She said she wanted me, when she died, to bury her like the white folks bury their dead, for she thought that way was the best.

CHAPTER 7 — **The Crows**

The winter was breaking up and we commenced to get ready to move to the spring hunting grounds, but when we started to gather the horses we found that about fifty head were missing. After a while the Indians found the trail where they had been driven off by the Crow Indians. Our Indians followed them, but the Crows had so much the start that they could not overtake them, so we lost fifty head of our best horses. Mother lost six head, Washakie eleven head, and the rest belonged to the other Indians of the band. My little pinto was all right, for I had kept him near the camp with the horses that we used through the winter. Our Indians declared that they would make them all back before another winter. I found that was the way they would do. The Crows would steal every horse they could from the Shoshones, and our Indians would do the same with them, so I could not see that there was much harm done. It was as fair for one as it was for the other, and they would fight every time they met. The Crows were always on the watch and if they ran on to a small bunch of Shoshones they would make it hot for them, and the Shoshones would do the same to them, so there was excitement and war dances going on all the time.

We left our winter camp and started south. After two days' travel, we came to another large Indian camp and both camps kept together during the rest of the summer. We traveled south for three or four days and stopped where there was plenty of all kinds of game, such as buffalo, elk, deer, and antelope. We stayed here a few days, then went east three days' travel and came to a beautiful lake that was fairly alive with fish. Oh, how I did catch them! There was plenty of game everywhere. We could see buffaloes at any time and in any direction that we looked. I had great fun fishing and running antelope. Washakie said I was riding my horse too much, that he was getting poor, and that I had better turn him out and he would give me another. I was glad to do this for I knew my horse was getting thin, and I wanted to give him a rest and let him get fat. The horse that Washakie gave me was a pretty roan, three years old, and partly broke. When Wasakie saw how well I managed my new horse, he told me that I could break some young horses for him to pay for the one he gave me. That just suited me, for I did like to be around wild horses. The horses were very small, especially the two-year old colts which he wanted broke. I wanted to get right at it, but he said I must wait until they got fat so they could buck harder.

We were not far from the line that was in dispute between our Indians and the Crows. One day some of the hunters came in scared nearly to death, and said the Crows were coming right on to us. I never saw such excitement in my life. Everybody was running around and talking at the same time, and the bucks were getting their war fixings on as fast as they possible could. The horses were rounded up and driven into camp, and you never saw such a mixup in your life—horses, squaws, dogs, papooses and wickiups, all mixed together. The war chief told all the young warriors to get out and meet the Crows, and the old men to stay and guard the camp. I said if I was going to fight, I wanted my pinto; but mother said, "You are not, you little fool, you can't fight anything." I said, "That is what I came out here for." She said: "I will tell you when to fight. You come and sit down by me; I doubt if there is a Crow in five days' ride from here. I have had too many such scares." I said, "And aren't they coming?" She said, "Don't be afraid." I told her I was not afraid, that I would like to see the Crows and see if they had wings. I said the crows in our country all had wings. She said that the Crows were Indians like the Shoshones. By this time the squaws had everything packed up to put on their horses that were standing ready with their saddles on, and the old men had gathered in small bunches, all talking at the same time. It was not long until we saw the bucks coming back, and when they came up they said it was nothing but a herd of buffaloes running this way—no Crows at all. I began to think they were all cowards, the whole bunch of them. I was disappointed, for I hoped to see some fun.

Well, the next day about fifty of the young warriors left for some place, I could not find out where. Everything passed off in peace for a while. We fished and chased antelope, and one day I went with Washakie up in the mountains to kill elk. We had not gone far when we saw a large herd of elk lying down. We left our horses and crept up close to them. Washakie had a good gun, and his first shot hit a big cow elk. She ran abut a minute and fell. Washakie told me to slip up and shoot her in the neck with my arrows until

I killed her, then cut her throat so that she would bleed, and then stay there until he came back. Well, I crept up as close as I dared, and shot every arrow at her I had, and then climbed a tree. I guess she was dead before I shot her, but I did not know it, and I was too much afraid to go up to her. Washakie followed the herd that ran down the canyon.

I stayed up in the tree for about two hours, then came down softly and went up to the elk and threw sticks at her, but she didn't move. Then I thought she must be dead, so I went up to her and cut her throat; but she had been dead so long that she did not bleed a bit. I stayed around there a long time. After a while I began to get scared. I thought the bear would smell the elk and come and find me there and eat me up, so I started to where we left the horses, but I could not find them; then I started back to the elk, but I couldn't find it, either; then I did not know what to do. The timber was very thick and I was getting more scared all the time. I went back to where I thought the horses were and hunted all around, but I could not find them. By this time the sun had gone down and it was very dark and gloomy among the trees. I climbed another tree and waited a long time. I was afraid to call for fear of bringing the bear onto me.

Afterwards, I learned that I had not left the elk long until Washakie came and took the entrails out of it, and as he did not see my horse he thought I had gone on to camp. Before following the elk, he had tied my horse to a tree, but he had broken loose and gone off. When Washakie got to camp and found I was not there, and heard some of the Indians say they had seen my horse loose with the saddle on, he didn't know what to do, and mother almost went crazy. She started right out to hunt me, and about seventy-five Indians followed her. A little after dark, I heard the most awful noise. I thought sure the Crows were coming after me, but pretty soon I heard some one call my name, "Yagaiki! Ya-gai-ki!" Then I knew they were our Indians, so I answered him. Pretty soon I heard the brush cracking right under my tree and he hallooed again. I said, "Here I am." He said, "What are you doing up there?" I told him I was looking for my horse. "Your horse is not up there." I said, "I know it." He told me to come down which I did in a hurry. He said: "Get on behind me, the whole tribe is looking for you, and your poor mother is nearly crazy about you. It would be better for her if some one would kill you, and I have a notion to do it. It would save her lots of trouble." When we got out of the timber he began to halloo just as loud as he could to let the rest know that I was found, then I could hear the Indians yelling all through the timber. He started for camp and when we got there, mother had not yet come in, so I was going back to look for her, but Hanabi would not let me go. She told me that I might miss her and get lost again; that I had given her enough trouble for one night. It was not long until mother came. She grabbed hold of me and said: "Yagaiki! Yagaiki! where have you been? I was afraid a big bear had got you" She talked and cried for almost an hour. She blamed Washakie for going off and leaving me alone. She said that I should never go with him again, that I must stay with her.

The next morning, as a squaw and mother and I were starting out to get the elk, Washakie asked me if I was sure I could find it. I told him I knew I could, so we started and I took them right to it. Mother said, "Where was it you were lost?" I said I was not lost, that I knew where camp was all the time. She said, "Why did you not come home, then?" I replied that I was waiting for Washakie to come, because he had told me to stay there until he came. "Well," she said, "you had better stay with me until you get a little older." I told her I liked to hunt, but she said I had lots of time and could go hunting another year. As we were skinning the elk, mother remarked that I had spoiled the skin by shooting it so full of holes. We got back to camp with our meat, and found it very fat and nice.

Everything went along all right during the next few days, and nothing happened worth speaking of until the Indians that went off about ten days before got back. They had thirty-two head of the Crow's horses, but one of our Indians had been killed by the Crows. A young Indian that was with them told me about their raid. He said after they left camp they went over on the head of the Missouri river, which the Indians call Sogwobipa, where they found a small band of Crow Indians, but the Crows had seen them first and were ready for them. He said they saw a bunch of horses and watched them until after dark. Then they started to get the horses and just before getting to them, they were met by a shower of arrows and a few bullets which killed one of their party, and wounded five or six of their horses. One of the horses was so badly crippled that he could not travel so the rider jumped onto the dead Indian's horse, and they all broke back as fast as their horses could carry them with one hundred Crows after them. They were chased by the Crows all night, but they finally made their escape.

A few days after this, as they were going through a range of mountains, they came suddenly upon a small band of the Crows, killed two of them, and took all their horses. They thought the whole tribe of Crows was following them, so they cut a line for home. I thought it was pretty tough for about fifty to jump on a few like that, rob them, and leave them without horses. I think Washakie didn't like it, either. I told him it was not fair. He said it was too bad, but the Crows would treat us that way, but it was not right for either to do it. Well, the Indians were quite uneasy, for they thought the Crows would follow them up and be on us at any minute, so we kept a strong guard out all the time.

Washakie thought it best to get a little further from the line and in a more open country so they could watch their horses better. They did not appear to value their own lives so much as they did their horses. I asked Washakie why it wouldn't be better for the chiefs to get together, talk the matter over and fix things up and stop this stealing from one another. He laughed and said that when I got a little older I might fix things up to suit me, but as things were going now, he had to be rather careful; that Pocatello had poisoned the minds of many of his tribe and drew them off, and that he could not do just as he wanted to, but if he could, there would not be any more fighting.

The camp packed up and made a start for the open country, and there was a long string of us. We traveled south, down the river from this beautiful lake, for about seven days and came to another large stream that came from the east, and when the two came together it made a very large river, which the Indians called Piupa. We put our wickiups by a small stream that came out of the north fork of this big river. It was not very wide, but quite deep, and was full of fish. What fun I had catching them! After we had been here a few days, Washakie said that when I was ready I could start in to breaking the colts. That was just what suited me, so we caught one, tied it to a tree and let it stand there until it stopped pulling back, then it would lead. We let it stand there all day and at night he helped me to lead it to water. Then we staked it near camp and let it eat there all night.

The next morning I found I could lead it to water alone, so I thought I would try to ride him. I was putting my saddle on him, but mother said to ride him bareback. I told her I could not stick to him without my saddle. She said, "Well, do as you like;" so I went to work to saddle him, but he objected to that, and came nearly getting away from me. Mother said, "Tie this old blanket over his head so he can't see." I fastened him to a bush, and threw the blanket over his head, and mother came and helped me tie it on. By this time about fifty kids had gathered around to see the fun. Well, I got my saddle on him and mother said, "Now you get on and I will pull the blanket off." I got on and said, "Let him go." Off came the blanket and away went the horse. He whirled and sprang in the air, and came down with his head between his front legs. I went flying towards the creek and didn't stop until I got to the bottom of it. When I crawled out and wiped the water out of my eyes, I could see the colt going across the prairie, with the saddle under his belly, and kicking at every jump. Mother said, "Let him go." I said I would ride that horse if I never killed another Indian. She said, "How many did you ever kill?" I said that the number that I had killed was nothing to what I was going to kill, and I had a notion to start in on some of these black imps now if they did not look out and quit laughing.

When I got some dry clothes on a young Indian came up on a horse and I got him to go and catch the colt for me. When he brought him in, he helped me tie a strap around him as tight as we could get it, just so I could put my fingers under it, then he held the colt while I got on him. When I said, "Let him go," Mr. Colt started off on a run, and the young Indian followed after me and kept the colt out of the brush and away from the other horses that were staked around. The colt soon got tired and stopped running. I had a fine ride. The Indian boy stayed with me until the colt got tired, then we took him to camp, and I staked him out. It took mother and me two days to gather up my saddle, and when we got it all it was in such a bad fix that we could hardly tell what it had been in the first place. It took us about a week to fix it up again, but we made it a great deal stouter than it was. The next day I rode the colt again and I soon had him broke. The next colt was not so bad for me to ride, and I soon got so I could ride any of them without much trouble.

About this time we had another stampede. One night the Indians thought the Crows were on us sure, for one of the guard came running in and said he had seen a big band of Crows coming. It was in the middle of the night, but all the squaws and papooses were pulled out of bed and told to get into the brush and stay there until morning. I told mother that I would not go one step without my horse. She said that I could not find him in the dark, but I said I could for I knew right where he was. I started for the horse and mother started after me, but I outran her. I could hear her calling,

"Yagaiki! Yagaiki! kamy, Yagaiki! kamy!" I happened to find my pinto and jumped on to his back, and was at my mother's side in a few minutes. She said, "You little fool, the Crows might have got you." I said, "There are no Crows in a thousand miles of us." She said, "How do you know?" I said I would have to see them before I would believe they were coming. Well, the Indians gathered up all the horses and stayed around them all night. Mother and I and Hanabi went down the river about a mile where there were seven or eight hundred squaws and papooses scattered through the willows. They made such a noise that nobody could sleep, for they thought they would all be killed before morning.

Well, morning came and no Crows. The Indians were all as mad as hornets, or at least they all acted that way. Washakie sent out a few men to where the guard said he saw the Crows, and when they got back they said there were no signs of Indians, but that the guard saw a big dust, and thought it was the Crows coming. I told Washakie that guard ought to be killed, that if a white man had done such a thing he would have been put in prison for ten years. I told him I had got so that I could not believe any of them but him. He said it was a shame, but they would do that way and he could not help it. I asked him how he could tell when the Crows were really coming. He said he had a few good, trusty men, and when he thought there was much danger he would send out some of these, or would go himself. I asked him if he thought there was any danger of the Crows coming to attack us. He said he did not look for them to come to fight at this place, but that they might watch around to try to steal our horses, and if they could run on to a few of our men out a little way from camp, they might kill them.

Everything went on quietly again for a while. I kept on breaking colts and whipping kids every once in a while. One day I was out riding a wild colt and there was a lot of boys along with me. Among them was a boy that I had kicked in the head for trying to raise my mother-hubbard to see my sore legs, when I first came to live with the Indians. He had a long stick and would punch my colt with it every time he got a chance. At last I said, "See here, young man, what do you mean by jabbing my horse?" He said that he wanted to make him throw me off for kicking him that time. I said, "Now, look here, if I get another kick at you, I will break your darned, black neck." Pretty soon he jabbed my horse again. I had a long rawhide rope tied around my colt's neck. I took the other end and made a noose in it and when he punched my horse the next time, I threw the noose over his head and jerked him off his pony. That scared my colt and he broke and ran. Before I could stop him, I had nearly choked the life out of that kid. The blood was coming out of his nose and mouth, and I thought I had surely killed him. As soon as I loosened the noose though, I found he could squall in good shape, and when he got up he started for camp, lickety split, and at every step he groaned as bad as a dying calf.

I started for camp, too, for I knew that hell would be popping very soon. He went past our wickiup and mother asked him who hurt him. He said, "Yagaiki." Before I got home I met mother. She said, "Yagaiki, what have you been doing?" I said, "Trying to kill a blamed kid." "Well, you have come very nearly doing it this time. How did it happen?" I told her all about it. She said, "It will cause another camp fight." "I don't care," I said, but I really did care a great deal. I turned loose the colt I was riding and started after my pinto pony. She said, "Where are you going?" I said, "After my horse." "What for?" she asked. "Because I want him," I said. When I had caught and saddled him, I saw the boy and his father and mother and a few more coming, so I jumped on my horse and started off. Mother called for me to stop, but I didn't stop. I thought if they wanted to fight, they could fight; I did not want to fight, so I got out of it as fast as pinto could carry me. I went up the river and hid in the brush. About dark, I could hear Indians calling. "Yagaiki!" but I did not answer them.

After a while the mosquitoes got so bad in the brush that I could not stay there, so when everything was still I crept out, but then did not know where to go or what to do, so I sat down on a stump and tried to think what was best for me to do. I knew there would be a racket in camp over what I had done, and I hated it like everything on account of mother. I was not a bit sorry for the kid, and I felt then as if I wouldn't have cared much if I had killed him. I had some pretty tough feelings as I sat there on the stump. I was more homesick just then than I had ever been before. I was so far from home, and with a lot of Indians who were mad at me. I did not know but what they would burn me as soon as they got hold of me. I felt pretty bad, and these lines that I had heard my sister sing came to my mind:

> *"Oh! pity the fate of a poor young stranger*
> *That has wandered far from his home;*
> *He sighs for protection from Indians and danger,*
> *And knows not which way to roam."*

Well, after thinking the matter over, I decided it would be better for me to go back and face the music, let it be what it would. When I got near the camp I met a lot of Indians that mother had sent to hunt me. When I saw them I stopped and they came running up to me and said, "Yagaiki, we are hunting you." "What for?" I asked. They said that my mother had sent them, and they asked me if I had seen Washakie. They said that he was out hunting for me. When I asked them what the Indians would do to me, they said they would do nothing to me, that I had done just what any one else would have done. I said I was afraid it was going to start another fight, but they laughed and said it would not. This made me feel much better. When I got to camp and mother saw me, she said, "Yagaiki, where have you been?" When I told her, she said I was the most foolish boy she ever saw for running off like that. "Well," I said, "I thought if I went away it might keep down another fight in camp." It was not long until Washakie came in, and he gave me a long talk. He said for me never to run off that way any more, that when I got into trouble, to come to him and he would see that I was not hurt. I told him I had better go home, for I was always getting into trouble and making it hard for mother and him. He said he would not let me go home for that, but that I must be a little more careful, for I might have killed the boy if I had not stopped just when I did. He said a rope tied to a wild horse and around a boy's neck hasn't much fun in it for the boy. I told him I did not think about the rope being tied to the horse or I would not have done it, but the boy made me so mad I did not know what I was doing. I told him the boy was doing all he could to make the horse throw me off, and if he ever did it again I would wring his blasted neck off. He told me the boy's neck was much skinned, and his father and mother felt very badly about it, but he would talk to them and try to fix it up. The other little boys that were with us said I did just right. Washakie had a long talk with the boy's parents and I heard no more about it, but I saw the boy going around with a greasy rag around his neck, and when he came around where I was he would look very savagely at me.

The mosquitoes got so bad at this place that we had to move. We went east nearly to the Teton Peaks, where we found all kinds of game plentiful and the streams full of trout. We came to a beautiful valley with a river running north and south through the center of it. There was no timber growing on its banks, but there were great patches of willows from one to one and one-half miles wide extending for about twenty miles up and down the river. The white-tailed deer were plentiful among the willows. I killed five while we were there and mother tanned the skins and made a suit of clothes for me out of their hides. The clothes were quite nice and warm. There were also a number of moose killed among the willows.

Washakie told me that his tribe had a great fight with the Sioux Indians in this valley many years ago when he was a small boy, and that his people lost about two thousand of their best men. He took me all over the battle ground.

We stayed in this valley about 30 days and I started to breaking more colts. When I got up the first one after our racket, mother said, "Leave your rope here." I told her that I could not do without it. "Well, don't use it on any more kids," she said. Everything passed off here very quietly except for two or three scares the Indians had when they thought the Crows were after them. If they saw a dust made by the wind they would send out to see what caused it. They were like a band of sheep that had been run by wolves. Every little thing would scare them. It made me tired to see them so cowardly. I told Washakie that I did not think they would fight if they had a chance. I said, "When are you going to send more Indians out to steal the Crows' horses?" He said, "Why, do you want to go with them?" I said, "Not much, I have not lost any horses." "Well, we have," he said, "but I have nothing to do with that kind of business, the War Chief attends to all that. If the Crows do not come after us we will send out a party against them after awhile, but I do not know just when. We must, though, get back the horses we have lost, and do it before the snow comes." I asked him if he was going to winter here in this valley. "Oh, no, the snow falls too deep here. After the buffalo get fat and we get what meat we want for our winter use, we will go west, a long way off, to winter where no buffalo run, but where there are plenty of deer and antelope and fine fishing." He said that some of those fish were as long as I was.

The Indians killed a great many elk, deer, and moose, and the women had all they could do tanning the hides and drying the meat. Berries were getting ripe so we would go up in the mountains and gather them to dry. I had lots of fun going with mother to gather the berries. One day while we were up in a deep canyon we found plenty of berries and were busy gathering them, when all at once we heard some awful screaming. Pretty soon here came a lot of squaws and papooses. "Wudutsi nia baititsi ke kudjawaia. Wudutsi!" one said. That means, "A bear has killed my girl." I jumped onto my pinto, for I was riding him that day, and started up through the brush as fast as I could go. When I got a little way up the canyon, the brush was not quite so thick, and I could see a bear running up the hill. I went a little further and found the girl stretched out on the ground as if she were dead. Then I yelled as loud as I could for some of the Indians to come back, but they had all gone. I tried to lift her onto the horse, but she was too heavy for me, so I laid her down again. Then she asked for a drink. I took the cup she was picking berries in and gave her some water. I asked her if she felt better. She said, "Yes, where is my mother?" I said they all went down the canyon like a lot of scared sheep, and that they must be nearly home by this time. Seeing that she felt better, I took her by the arm and helped her up.

She was crying all the time and said her head and her side hurt her very much and that her arm hurt her, too. I asked her if she could ride. She said she would try, so I helped her on to the horse and led it about three miles until we got out of the canyon, then she said, "You get on behind, I think I can guide the horse." So I got on behind her, for we had to go about four miles yet to reach camp. When we got in sight of camp, we saw some Indians coming full tilt, and when we met them there was the greatest hubbub I ever heard. When we got to camp, her mother came running up and threw her arms around the girl and hugged and kissed her, and cried and went on like she was crazy. She would have hugged me, too, if I had been willing. She said I was a brave boy. Mother came up to me and said, "Yagaiki, I thought you had come down to camp ahead of me, or I never would have come without you." I said, "You were as scared as any of them." She said, "I know I was scared, but I never would have left you if I had known that you had not come out of the canyon."

That night the girl's mother and father came to our wickiup to see what I wanted for saving their daughter's life. I told them that I wanted nothing for doing what I ought to do. Her father said, "You are a good boy, and a brave boy, too." I asked her mother why she ran off, and left the girl behind in that way. "Well," she said, "I saw the bear knock her down and jump on her, and I thought she was dead, and that if I went up to her the bear would kill me, too; then there would be two of us dead." Her father said the way so many got killed by bears was because, if a bear caught one, others would run in and get killed. He said it was best if one got caught by a bear for the rest to run and get away while the bear was killing that one. I said that I did not like that way of doing, that I thought if a bear got hold of one, the rest should go after the bear and kill it, and that I would try to save anyone that got caught by a bear, even if I got killed myself. "I know you would, my brave boy. You have already shown what you would do," said my mother. Washakie said: "Don't brag on the boy too much or you will make him think he is a hero. Well, it was a brave act in the boy, and he will be more thought of by everybody in the tribe after this." Mother said that I would be one of the greatest war chiefs the tribe ever had when I got to be a man. She said she always knew there was something about me that was more than common. Washakie said, "Well, that is all right, let us go to sleep." The girl's mother told me that I could have her daughter for a wife when I got big enough, but I told her she could keep the girl for I did not want her. She said, "Maybe you will change your mind when you get older." The next day, I wanted mother and a lot more Indians to go up the same canyon to gather some more service berries. "No, sir," they said, "you don't get us up that place any more after berries." The thoughts of the bear scared them nearly to death. The Indians did not have much to do with bears, but if they came across one out of the brush in open ground, they would sometimes attack him.

One morning we saw two bears crossing the valley, and about fifty Indians on horses started after them. I ran and got Pinto, and when I came for my saddle mother said, "Where are you going?" "I am going to help kill those bears." "What bears?" "Those bears going yonder." "You are not." When Washakie told her to let me go, she consented, so I jumped on to the horse and started after the bears as fast as I could peg it. The Indians had headed them off from the timber and were popping arrows to them in good style. My horse was not a bit scared of them, so I ran up pretty close to one of the bears and put three arrows into his side. The Indians said, "Keep back, you little fool, that bear will tear you to pieces." But Mr. Bear was too full of arrows to tear much, for by this time you could hardly see him for arrows. He looked like a porcupine with the quills sticking out all over him. We soon killed the two bears, but the skins were so full of holes that they were not worth much, and the meat wasn't much good, either. That night they had a big dance around the two hides, and would have me join them and sing as loud as any of them, for they said I was the most daring one among them. One old Indian said, "The little fool don't know any better. If a bear ever got hold of him he would not be so brave." Anyhow, they gave me the best hide. Mother tanned it and sewed up most of the holes, and it made a very good robe for me to sleep on.

Another small band of Indians came to our camp and the girl that hit me with the fishing pole was with them. After she saw that the Indians were so kind to me, and liked me so much, she wanted to make up with me. She came around several times before she said anything to me, but finally, one day, she came to where I was helping mother stake down a moose hide so it would dry, and said, "Yagaiki, I am sorry that I hit you that day with your fish pole." I said, "I am not." She said, "Why?" I said, "Because we had lots of fun that day." Mother said, "Yagaiki, why don't you make up with her?" I said I did not want to; that I would rather give her a few more kicks. "Kiss her, you mean boy," said my mother. Well, I didn't kiss her but I told her it was all right, that we would be friends again. She said, "Good! Come to our wickiup some day and play with me." "Not much," I said, "your mother will cut my head off with that big knife she has, if I go near her." "No, she will not hurt you. She is coming over to make it all right with your mother. She is very sorry for what we did to your folks, and so is my father." Well, everything was fixed up and we became pretty good friends after that.

By this time we had gathered all the berries that grew along the foot hills, for the squaws were afraid to go up into the mountains after the bear excitement. They also went to work in dead earnest in tanning the elk and deer skins, and in drying meat for use during the coming winter. The Indians had quit hunting for elk and deer for they had all the skins that the women could get ready to take to some trading post where they could be swapped for red blankets and beads and other Indian goods. About every fall they would go to Salt Lake City to sell their buckskins and buffalo robes. Mother and Hanabi worked all day and away into the night to get their skins ready in time, and I helped them all I could. I took an old horse of mother's, went to the foothills and snaked down enough wood to last while we were there. I packed all the water for them, too, and no kid dared to call me a squaw, either.

Well, the time had come for us to start killing buffaloes for the winter supply of meat. We did not have to hunt them, either, for we could see them at any time, and in almost any direction. Many a time I would go with Washakie to see the Indians kill the buffaloes. Washakie only wanted five, and we soon got them; but it would take mother and Hanabi many days to tan their hides for market, and dry the meat for winter use.

CHAPTER 8 — **A Long Journey**

Nothing went wrong while we were getting ready for the long trip to market, and finally everything was in shape to pack up. Our camp was very large by this time for Indians had been coming in every few days, until they numbered over a thousand, and there must have been all of five thousand horses. When we got ready and started, I could not see half of the long string of pack horses. We had for our family twenty pack horses loaded with buffalo robes, and elk and deer skins, besides our camp outfit. Washakie had a fine, big wickiup of elk hides, made so it would shed rain. It could be divided into two parts, and sometimes we would put up only half of it, if we were going to stop one night, but if we were going to stay for some time, we would put it all up.

After we got started, I noticed that the Indians broke up into small bands. That night there were about twenty-five wickiups left in our camp, but I could see many other camps scattered up and down the river. Washakie said that it was better to travel in small parties, for we could get along faster, and the horses could get better pasture and would not be so much bother. In two or three days we got to the Big River where I had come near choking the boy to death with my rope. It was quite wide and the current was very swift where we forded it. When we got in the deepest place, mother's horse stumbled over a cobble stone and fell, and away went mother down the stream, for it was so swift that she could not withstand the current. I saw her going and started after her, but I could not catch her until she was carried down into deep water. My horse was a good swimmer, so I was soon at her side. I pulled her to the bank and helped her out of the water. By this time we were quite a distance down the stream where the willows were very thick, and we had a hard time getting out. We soon met Washakie coming to help us. When he came up he said "Mother, you came nearly going to the happy hunting grounds that time." "Yes," she said, "but I have someone with me to help me in time of need. I am not afraid of anything when Yagaiki is with me." Washakie thought we had better camp there so mother could put on dry clothes and get over her scare, for he was afraid it would make her sick.

That night we camped in a grove of cottonwoods near the river, and just before dark an Indian came running in and told Washakie that the Crows had overtaken a small bunch of the tribe, had killed them, and taken all their horses.

Washakie told the war chief to take every one of our Indians and follow them even to the Crow country if he had to. The war chief told his men to get ready for a long trip, and the women and children to hide in the willows until they heard from him. I never saw such excitement among the squaws and kids in my life as we had there. Mother said, "Come on, Yagaiki, let us get to the brush." "Not by a d—n sight," I said. "I am going with the warriors to kill Crows." Mother got me by one arm and Hanabi by the other, and mother began to cry and said to Washakie, "Make him come." Washakie laughed and said that I was just fooling, that I had not lost any Crows, and that I would go with them. He said he was going to guard the camp. "So am I," I said. Mother said, "I want you to guard me and Hanabi." Washakie said, "Go with them and see that nothing hurts them." I ran out, caught Pinto, put my saddle and a few buffalo robes on him, and mother and Hanabi and I started down the river.

When we got down to where the rest of the crowd was, and I could hear the kids howling like young coyotes, I said, "What is the use of hiding when there is such a noise as this going on? If the Crows have any ears they can hear this noise for five miles." Mother said that made no difference, for the Crows didn't dare to come into the brush after them. I asked her if the Crows were as big cowards as our crowd. She said they were. I said, "There is no danger, then, so we had better go to sleep." It was not long before we heard Washakie call for us to come to camp. "There," I said, "another scare is over with no Crows at all. I will never hide again." When we got to camp I learned that a few Crows had chased some of our Indians and had fired a few shots at them, but nobody had been killed, and not even a horse had been stolen. About fifty of our young warriors were following the Crows, but I knew they would never overtake them.

The next day we packed up early and hit the trail pretty hard, and for several days we headed south. We left the large river that the Indians called Piupa, crossed over the mountains, and came to a place they called Tosaibi, which I learned later to be Soda Springs, in the southeastern part of Idaho. We could not use the water of the springs, so we went a short distance and camped on a large river which the Indians called Titsapa. They said this river ran into a big salt lake that reached nearly to my old home. That started me to thinking of home and my dear mother, brothers, and sisters that I would like to see so well, and I could feel the hot tears running down my cheek. Mother saw them and came and sat down by my side and said, "Yagaiki, I fear you do not like to live with us." I said, "Why?" "What are you crying about?" she asked. I told her that I was thinking of my white mother. She said, "Am I not as good to you as your own mother?" I told her that she was.

We went down this river one day's travel, and there we stayed three days. From here part of our band was going to take the buffalo robes and buckskins and what furs we had to Salt Lake City to sell them. I wanted to go with this party, but mother would not let me. Hanabi and Washakie took twelve pack horses very heavily loaded and also two young horses to sell if he got a chance. They left mother and me with the camp outfit and sixty-four head of horses to look after. Those that were not going to Salt Lake City intended to go off northwest and strike the head of another river which was about four days' travel from where we were, and stay there until the others returned.

Well, Washakie and the rest of them started on their long journey to the big city of the white people. When mother and I went to pack up to go back we found we did not have pack saddles enough for all of our camp outfit. We had sixteen sacks of dried meat, two sacks of service berries, and all of our camp outfit and only eight pack saddles. Mother said we could get along if we had two more saddles. I told her that if my saddle would do for one to take it, for I could ride bareback. She said it would, but she did not like to take it. She did take it, however, and another boy let us have his saddle, so we packed up ten horses. You see we could not get off very early in the morning for, although it did not take long to pack one horse, it took quite a while to pack ten of them. There were fifteen squaws, about thirty-five children, and three old Indians in our camp. After traveling three days we came to the head of the river which they called Tobitapa, but which is called now by the white man, the Portneuf river.

Washakie thought it would take them fifteen days to go to Salt Lake City and get back to where we were. I asked mother if she was not afraid the Crows would come and kill the whole lot of us while the others were gone. She said, "No, the Crows never come this far south." I asked her why she did not want to go to Salt Lake

City with the others. She said we had too many horses, and that she was afraid the white men would take me away from her. I asked her if that was the reason that Washakie did not like to have me go with him. She told me that Washakie said if I ever got dissatisfied and wanted to go home he would give me my horse and fix me up in good shape, and send two Indians with me to see that I got home safe. "But," she said, "I hope you will never want to go away from me, for I believe it would kill me now if you should go away and leave me." I told her I thought I never would want to leave her. I could see that she always seemed happier when I would tell her that I would always stay with her. She would do anything to make me happy. If she ever saw me look unhappy, I could see that she would turn away and cry.

She was afraid that I would get sick by not having bread and milk to eat, for I had told her that I always had bread and milk for supper when I was at home, so she thought that eating all meat would not agree with me and would make me unhealthy. She would often have fried fish and fried chickens or ducks for supper, but she would not let me eat any of it if she could help it. When I first went to live with her she made a small sack and tied it to my saddle and would keep it full of the best dried fish, so that when we were traveling, I could eat if I got hungry, for she said I could not go all day without eating anything as the Indians did. Every morning she would empty my sack and fill it anew so that I could eat all the time if I wanted to. She soon found out what I liked best and she always had it for me, so you see I always had plenty to eat, even if I was with the Indians, and that is more than a great many white children had at home.

I was very healthy while I was with the Indians. I guess the reason was that I did not like the way they doctored. When any of them got a cold or was sick, they would dig a hole two or three feet deep by the side of a cold spring and put in a few cobblestones. Then they would build a fire in the hole, get the stones right hot, and then scrape the fire all out. The sick person had to get into the hole with a cup of water, and after the hole was covered with a buffalo robe, he would pour the water on the hot rocks and make a steam. This would soon make him sweat like sixty; and when he had sweat long enough, someone would jerk the robe off the hole, and he would jump into the cold water of the spring. As soon as he got out of the water they would throw a buffalo robe around him, put him to bed, and let him sweat a while, then they would cool him off gradually by taking the cover off a little at a time until he quit sweating. He was then thought to be well.

One cold, chilly day I was out hunting chickens and was quite a distance from camp when a heavy rainstorm came up and soaked me through and through before I could get home. That night I coughed all night so that nobody could sleep. The next day mother wanted to dig a hole for me. I told her not much, that I did not want a hole dug for me until I was dead. She begged me to take a sweat. I told her she would not get me to jump into any more springs like they did when I had sore legs. She said it would not hurt me. I told her that was played out, I would not do it. She said, "Well, you need not jump into the water, the heat of the ground, and the steam from the rocks will sweat you enough," and asked if I would do that. Washakie said, "Yes, do it and get well before you are down sick in bed." I said, "Go to digging." She soon had the hole dug and everything ready; then she said, "Come on now, pull off your clothes and get in here." I said, "Pull off nothing." She said,"You must." Washakie said, "Jerk them off, I will hold this buffalo robe over you so you will not be seen." They got me to pull off my clothes and get into the hole over the hot rocks, just like an old sitting hen does over her eggs, and mother gave me some water to pour on the rocks. She stood there to keep the robe over the hole, and would keep asking me if I was sweating. I told her that I was getting wetter than a fish, but for some cause she kept me there for quite a while, until I begged pretty hard to be let out, then she jerked off the robe and shewhack came three or four buckets of cold water all over me. Oh gosh! didn't I get out of that hole quick! Washakie stood there with the robe, threw it over me, carried me into the wickiup and put me to bed. He threw more robes over me and I lay there and sweat like a horse. This was after Washakie and his party had got back from Salt Lake, but they were gone twenty-two days instead of fifteen.

Snow had already fallen on the tops of the mountains when Washakie got back, so he was in a hurry to get the camp moved to the winter range, and mother and Hanabi began at once to arrange the packs for traveling. Washakie had disposed of his robes and skins at a good price, and he had sold the two horses, so he came back pretty well fixed. He had twenty-four red blankets, and a lot of calico, some red flannel for the tongues of moccasins and two pairs of drawers for me, and about a peck of beads of all colors and sizes. The beads were to swap for tanned buckskin and the blankets for buffalo robes. He brought me a butcher knife, a new bridle, two pounds of candy, and a lot of fish hooks.

We soon started for our winter quarters. We went down the Tobitapa (Portneuf) to the Piupa (Snake River), then up the Piupa, and then over the divide on to the headwaters of Angatipa (Rock Creek). At this place we stayed six days and killed sixteen buffaloes, two for each family. That was to be the last killing of buffaloes until the next year. Washakie bought four of the buffalo hides, which made him six in all. He said he wanted something for the women to do through the winter. When we started from here, we went west over a big mountain upon which we had to camp in about three feet of snow. We had to tie up all our horses to keep them from running away, for we had nothing for them to eat. We were off pretty early the next morning, and that night we got out of the snow, but it was still very cold. The next day we came to a beautiful stream. It was not very large, but it was fairly alive with mountain trout. We went down this stream two days' travel, and there we stayed for about a month, I think. When we stopped Washakie intended to stay there during the winter, but afterwards he changed his mind and we went down the stream until we came to another large stream. I do not remember what the Indians called this river, but they told me that fish as long as I was came up that river in the spring.

We had a very good camping ground that winter. It was sheltered from the wind, but we had a great deal more snow than we had the winter before. About six hundred yards above our camp was a large grove of dry quakingasp, which was pretty much all small poles. I told mother that if she would help me pile a lot, I would haul them down for her with the horses. She did not believe I could do it. But I got her to help me make a big pile of the poles. She said she knew we would have to pack it if we got it down to camp. Washakie had brought from Salt Lake City the inch auger I asked him to get for me, so I went to work to make a sled like I had seen my father make. I got two crooked sticks for runners, pinned on some cross pieces, and soon had the thing made. It did not look much like a sled, but it answered the purpose pretty well. I got up two lazy old horses of mother's, put on their pack saddles, and tied ropes from the sled to the pack saddles. I got on one of the horses and away we went for the grove. I put on quite a few sticks, tied them with a rope, and took the load to camp without any bother at all. All of the Indians and squaws and papooses were out watching me bring in my first load of wood. The old war chief said, "What cannot a white man do?" In a few days I had all of the wood down to camp. Hanabi said I was as good as two squaws.

After I got my wood down I loaned my sled to some of the Indians. They thought they could haul wood as well as I could, so they hooked up two horses like I had done and started for the grove. They went up a little higher than I did, where it was quite a bit steeper than where I got my wood. They put on a big load and started down; the sled ran into the horses' heels, scared them, and they started to run. The one the Indian was riding broke loose from the sled, but the other horse ran with the sled fastened to him, scattered the wood all over the side of the hill, and came bolting down through the camp. The sled jammed against the wickiups and jerked thee or four of them down. Then the frightened horse struck out through some cottonwoods, slammed the sled against the trees and broke it all to pieces. This discouraged the Indians and they said the squaws could pack the wood if they wanted any, that it was their work anyhow. That ended the wood hauling.

I got some of the Indian boys to help me fix up the sled again. We pulled it up on a hill with a horse and turned it towards camp. I wanted some of the boys to get on with me and slide down, but they were afraid to. They said that they wanted to see me do it first, so away I went down all right. They came down with the horse and we pulled the sled up again, and by hard begging, I got two of the boys on the sled with me. As soon as we started, one jumped off, but the other stayed on with me. When we reached the bottom, he said it was the finest ride he ever had. The next time several other boys said they would like to try it, and five got on. Away we went to the bottom. Oh, what fun we had! It was not long until they all wanted to get on, and the heavier it was loaded the faster it would go, and when the track was slick it would go nearly to the camp. We kept this up for days. When the track got well broke, we would pull the sled up ourselves without a horse. All the big boys and girls would join us in our coasting, and sometimes the older ones would ride, too. We kept the sled going all the time, until we wore the runners out, then we passed the rest of the winter in fishing and in hunting chickens and rabbits. Sometimes we would go for antelope, but when we went for them some of the older Indians would go along with us to keep us from killing too many.

Everything went off very peaceably this winter. There was no quarreling or fighting. One young papoose died and one old squaw did the same thing. We lost no horses. I had a real good time, and mother semed to enjoy the winter as well as I did. We were a long ways from the Crows, so we had no Crow scares. Along towards spring seven or eight of us little boys were in the cottonwoods shooting birds, when one boy's arrow hit the side of a tree, glanced, and struck me in the leg. He was scared, for he thought I was going to kick him to pieces. I told the boy to stop crying, that I knew it was an accident, and was not done on purpose. He quit crying, and the other boys thought I was getting to be a pretty good fellow after all, for before this they believed that if anybody hurt me, there would be a kicking scrape right away.

Spring came at last. We moved down the river about fifteen miles where we could get better grass for our horses. Here were plenty of white tailed deer and antelope, some elk, and a few mountain sheep; ducks and geese were plentiful. We stayed here until about the middle of May. The big fish that they told me about began to come up the river, and they were big, too. Two of them were all I could carry. They must have weighed at least thirty or thirty-five pounds each. Mother and Hanabi dried about two hundred pounds of these fish, which afterwards I learned were salmon. The first that came up were fat and very good, but they kept coming thicker and thicker until they were so poor they were not fit to eat.

We started to move camp again. We went down the river a little farther, and then up a very deep and rocky canyon where there had been many snow slides during the winter. We crossed over snow that had come down in these slides that was forty or fifty feet deep, and as hard as ice. There was not much timber in the canyon, and the cliffs were very high. Years afterwards very rich gold mines were found in this canyon, great quartz mills were built, and a big mining camp was started.

As we left this canyon, we climbed a very steep mountain for abut two miles, and then went down through thick timber, until we came out onto a beautiful prairie covered with the finest grass I ever saw. Off to the left was a deep canyon where one fork of the Big Hole River headed, and we camped here for a long time. Antelope and black tailed deer were plentiful, and we killed a great many of them and dried the meat. I think Washakie and I killed seventeen while we stayed here.

From this place we went down to the forks of the river, and I think we stayed there two or three weeks to give the women time to tan the deer skins. It was fine fishing in the Big Hole River. While we were staying here one of the war chief's boys was shot accidentally and killed. Oh! what crying we had to do. Every one in camp who could raise a yelp, had to cry for about five days. I had to mingle my gentle voice with the rest of the mourners. They killed three horses and buried them and his bow and arrows with him. The horses were for him to ride to the happy hunting grounds. When they got ready to bury him, every one in camp had to go up to him and put a hand on his head and say he was sorry to have him leave us. When it came my turn, I went into my wickiup and would not come out. Mother came after me. I told her I would not go, that I was not sorry to see him go, but was glad of it, for he was no good anyhow. Mother said, "Don't say that so they will hear it." Then she went back and told them I was afraid of dead folks and she could not get me to come, but that I was in the wickiup crying fit to break my heart.

They took him to a high cliff of rocks and put him in a crevice with his bedding, a frying pan, an ax, his bow and arrows, and some dried buffalo meat, and then covered him up with rocks. When they got back to camp they let out the most pitiful howls I ever heard. I got down to it, too, just as loud as I could scream. Could you have seen me, you would have thought I was the most broken hearted one in the whole camp. I got so hoarse I could hardly talk. When I was doing my best howling, I had to get behind a tree once in a while, or get in the brush where nobody could see me, for I would have to stop and laugh half of the time. Well, we kept this up for five days—a little every day. I did feel sorry for his poor mother. She cut her hair off close to her head. I asked mother why she did it. She said that all the mothers did it when their oldest boy died.

After our mourning came to an end, we moved down the Big Hole River to where the town of Melrose is now. Plenty of game was to be seen everywhere. The bitter weeping had ceased, except that of the poor mother, whose mourning could be heard for a mile. We stayed here about two weeks, then went down the Big Hole River until it emptied into the Beaver Head River, and formed the Jefferson River. We did not do anything here but fish, for the buffalo were not fat enough to kill, and besides, we had all the dried elk and deer meat we wanted. It was a beautiful place to camp, and we had the finest grass for our horses. I broke a few more colts—two for mother and four for Washakie. By this time our horses were getting fat and looking fine, but my little Pinto was the prettiest one of all. Hardly a day passed but what some Indian would try to trade me out of him. One Indian offered me two good horses for him, but I thought too much of him to swap him for a whole band of horses. He was just as pretty as a horse could be.

Our next journey took us a long ways northeast. Washakie said we would go to where the buffaloes were too many to count. We traveled for a week and came to the north fork of the Madison River, about on a line with the Yellowstone National Park, and oh! the Kwaditsi (antelope), and padahia (elk), and kotea (buffalo), were in great herds. Everywhere that we might look we could see

Indian tree burial in cottonwood tree somewhere along Wind River, before Indians were placed on reservations, 1865. This custom was altered and even abandoned after Indians were placed on reservations.

them. While we were at this camp, another boy was killed by a horse. When I heard of it, I told mother to get her voice ready and her throat fixed for another big time, and that I was going to do my best for him, but it would not be because I felt very sorry. Hanabi said, "Yagaiki, aren't you ashamed to talk that way?" and mother said she was afraid that I was a hard-hearted boy. Well, we all turned out and gathered up all the pieces of him we could find, for the horse had dragged him through down timber and over rocks, and when he stopped running there was not much left of the boy.

From there we went up the Madison River about ninety miles, where we stayed a month. The buffalo were getting fat, so we killed quite a few and dried the meat and made their hides into robes. Then we went on south and came to a beautiful lake where we had such a good time the summer before. This lake is now called Henry's Lake, and is the head of the north fork of the Snake River. We did nothing here but fish, for we had dried meat to last until we got to the usual hunting grounds.

CHAPTER 9 — **The Fierce Battle**

We were now traveling towards the Crow country, and I think our Indians were a little afraid that the Crows were going to try to stop them if they could; but Washakie said he was going through if half his tribe were killed, for he was not going to be bluffed off his best hunting ground any longer. I thought something was up, for small bunches of Indians were coming in all the time, and we had gathered a very large band of us, until we numbered about seven hundred warriors. We sent all of our surplus horses down the Snake River with Indians to guard them until we came back. Washakie and mother kept fifteen head for pack horses, and I kept my two horses to ride. After the extra horses and packs had gone, we started for the disputed hunting grounds.

The men all went out ahead, followed by the pack horses, with the women and children and the old men in the rear. Mother said I was to keep close to her, for Washakie said the Crows might tackle us that day. I said that kind of talk was too thin. But we hadn't been traveling very long before one of the three or four Indians that had been sent on ahead came tearing back and said that he had seen where a very large band of Crows had passed, and that he saw a smoke in the timber ahead. The men all stopped and bunched up. I heard Washakie tell them to go ahead and keep a good lookout, and if the Crows jumped onto them, to fight as long as there was a man left. I thought they must be getting brave. Well, we started again with the men on ahead of us as before, but riding very slowly. Six or eight Indians were riding back and forth to keep the squaws and pack horses from getting scattered. Pretty soon we stopped again, and the war chief said: "We will camp here for tonight. We know now that we must fight or go back, and we have done that so much that the Crows begin to think we are afraid of them; but I feel that we ought to give them a lesson this time that they will not forget soon." Washakie said, "That is the way I look at it. Now is the time to show them that we will fight for our rights." This seemed to be the way most of the warriors felt, for I heard them talking about it in the council that night.

"Yagaiki" leaving home to go with the Indians on his pinto pony.

Well, we camped right there all in a bunch, and hardly had room to make down our beds. A strong guard was sent out to look after the horses, but the night passed off without any trouble, and when morning came, ten men were sent to see if they could find any signs of the Crows. They were gone about an hour when back they came, and said that about a thousand Crows were camped over the ridge just ahead of us. The war chief said, "We shall go on the hunting grounds, if there are ten thousand of them."

The Indians painted up in grand style. They drew black streaks all over their faces to make themselves look fiercer, and then we got ready and started forward. We had not gone far, when the squaws were ordered to stop, but the warriors went on and passed over a small ridge out of our sight. Pretty soon we heard shooting, and an Indian came and told us to go back until we came to good water, and to stay there until we heard from the chief. He said, "They are fighting now." We had hardly reached the stream of water, before we saw the Indians come up on the hill and then disappear, and then come in sight again. We could see that they were fighting very hard, and we could hear them yelling to beat Old Billy. They had not been fighting over an hour before half or two-thirds of them were on top of the hill and slowly coming down the side towards us. The squaws began to cry and said the Crows were getting the best of our Indians and were driving them back. They kept coming closer and closer to us. When I looked around I saw that all the squaws were getting butcher knives and were ready to fight if they had to. Then I noticed that our men were not coming towards us any longer. I could see Washakie on his big buckskin horse riding around among his Indians and telling them what to do, and pretty soon they began to disappear over the ridge again and I could tell then that our Indians were getting the best of the Crows.

We could tell the Crow Indians from ours for they had something white over one shoulder and around under one arm, and they wore white feathers in their hair. There were about fifteen hundred Indians engaged in the fight on both sides, so you can know that the battle ground covered quite a piece of country. We could see lots of horses running around without riders. I believe that many of the squaws would have taken part in the battle if it had not been for the guard of about fifty old Indians that rode around us all the time to keep the squaws and the horses close together. I could see plainly now that our side was driving the Crows back. When they had driven the Crows back to the ridge, they seemed to stick there, but were still fighting and yelling and circling round and round. It looked as though they could not drive the enemy any further. I got so excited that I jumped on my horse and said to another little Indian boy, "Come, let us go up there and see what they are doing and try to help them." Mother grabbed my horse by the bridle and said, "You crazy little fool, haven't you got one bit of sense?" I said, "I might kill a whole flock of Crows for all you know." After they had been fighting about six hours, one Indian came back, very badly wounded, and told us to go back to the lake, but not to unpack until we got word from the war chief. We went back and when we got on top of the divide we could see the Indians fighting, although they were about two miles away, and we could see loose horses all over the prairie. We reached the lake when the sun was about an hour high. About dark half of our Indians came to us and the war chief said to unpack and put up the wickiups for very likely we would stay there for a while. He told us that about sundown the Crows broke and ran, and that Washakie with the other half of our Indians was following them to try to head them off and keep them from getting away. Washakie thought that he and his warriors could stop them until morning and then the whole of his band would attack them again. The war chief sent twenty Indians with one hundred fresh horses to overtake our Indians that were following the Crows, for their horses had been on the go all day and were about worn out. He said he saw twenty-five of our Indians were dead, and he did not know how many more had been killed. An Indian asked mother if she had any horses she could let them have to take back. She said she had two they could take, and I said they could take my roan pony. We had the horses staked close by and soon had them for him.

By this time three or four hundred squaws and papooses were wailing and moaning in such good shape that you could have heard them for two miles. I asked mother when our turn would come. Hanabi said, "Do hush and go to sleep." But there was not much sleep that night. When day came I never saw such a sight in my life. About two hundred Indians had been brought in during the night, all very badly wounded. I went around with mother to see them. One poor fellow had his nose shot off and one eye shot out, and he said that he did not feel very well himself. Many of them were so badly hurt that I knew they could not live until sundown, and I thought about half of them would die that day. A few old Indians were sent over to the battle field to keep the eagles and wolves from eating the Indians that had been killed. The war chief had been shot in the arm and in the leg, but was not very badly hurt. He had gone before I got up that morning, and had taken with him all the warriors that were able to go.

Well, that night a little after dark all of our Indians came back. Washakie said the Crows had gone into the thick timber so that he could not get them out, but that there were not many of them left anyhow. Our men brought in a very large band of the Crow's horses and saddles, and when they were unpacked, I never before saw such a pile of buffalo robes, blankets, bows and arrows, and guns.

The next morning we all started out for the battle ground to bury the dead, and, oh! what pitiful wails the squaws and papooses made when they saw the dead Indians lying around. Wives were hunting among the dead for their husbands, and mothers were looking for their sons. I went around picking up arrows. I had gathered quite a few when mother saw me with them. She said, "Throw them down, quick. The old Indians will come around to gather them. Don't touch anything." I said, "What do they want with them?" She said that they would keep them until another fight. The squaws scalped every Crow they could find. I saw mother scalping one and I said, "Aren't you going to scalp our Indians?" She said, "No!" I said, "You ought to scalp them and send the scalps to the Crows, for they killed them and ought to have the scalps." She said, "Go off. You don't know what you are talking about." Our Indians carried our dead to a deep washout in the side of the hill, put them in and covered them with dirt and rocks. The dead Crows were left to the wolves and buzzards. That night, when I got back to camp, I was very tired and hungry, and I had seen so many Indians scalped that I felt sick and wished from the bottom of my heart that I was home with my kindred.

About two hundred and fifty horses were captured from the Crows. We had thirty-one Indians killed, and three hundred wounded in the battle. Eighteen of the wounded died afterwards, which made forty-nine that we lost in this terrible fight. Washakie sent out a few of our men to count the Crows that had been killed, and when they got back they said they found one hundred and three dead Crows, and Washakie said that about that many more were badly wounded and would die. That would make over two hundred killed on the Crow side, and forty-nine on our side. I began to change my mind about our Indians being cowards after seeing that fight. I have seen many a hard fight between white men and Indians, and only in one of them did I see greater bravery than was shown by our Indians in that great battle. We had to stay here about three weeks on account of our wounded.

By the time the wounded could be moved, it was too late for us to go the rounds Washakie had planned, so we thought we had better get ready for winter. We moved camp over to the Angatimpa and started to kill buffaloes and dry the meat. We split up into small bands again. The Indians had quite a few widows to kill buffaloes for, and they had to go to market with the robes and skins, and it was getting late in the fall. The worst of it was that the man who was the best to cut the ham strings of the buffaloes had been killed in the battle, so we could not get along as fast with our hunting. However, we soon got all the buffaloes we wanted, and now the hides were to be made into robes. Poor old mother and Hanabi worked very hard to get them ready so they could be sent to Salt Lake with the crowd that was going.

Washakie had a good many buffalo robes. Besides what he got from hunting, he had bought quite a number, and a lot had been captured from the Crows, so he had sixteen horses packed with nothing but buffalo robes and buckskins. We had six packs of dried meat, and the camp outfit made three more. We were, therefore, so heavily loaded that we could not travel very fast. When we got over the divide, Washakie said that mother and I had better stop there with some of the others to take care of the extra horses. I did not like to do this, for I wanted to go to Salt Lake this time, but I would do anything Washakie said. He told us we could come on slowly after they got started.

When they started for Salt Lake they took with them about thirty head of the Crow's horses to swap for anything they could get for them. After they were gone, there were about one hundred of us left behind, mostly squaws and papooses and old and wounded Indians, to take care of, and six hundred head of horses.

CHAPTER 10—Lively Times

After the party had been gone two days, the balance of us moved down the creek to where it sank in the sand hills. Here three of the wounded Indians got so bad that we had to stop for some time, but we had the finest grass for the horses, and the sage-chickens were as thick as could be.

One day I was out shooting chickens and had killed four with arrows and was coming home, when, as I was passing a wickiup, a dog jumped out and got me by the leg and tore off quite a lot of flesh. I shot him through with an arrow, leaving the feathers on one side of him and the spike sticking out on the other. As I was trying to catch the dog to get my arrow back, the old squaw who owned him ran up with a rope and, throwing it over my head, jerked me along to her wickiup. She held me there while her girl tied my feet and hands, and then she got a butcher knife and was going to cut my head off.

A sick Indian who happened to be lying nearby, jumped up and held the squaw while a little boy ran and told mother. Mother came in double quick time and took the knife away from the squaw. She cut the strap they had me tied with, took me by the arm, and and made me hike for my wickiup. When she saw my leg where the dog had bitten me, oh! how mad she got. She went back to the squaw and said, "If you do not kill that dog before sundown I will kill you." I had followed mother. "Look here," she said, "and see this poor boy with his leg nearly bitten off." The old Indians that had gathered around stopped the fracas, or I guess there would have been another camp fight.

Mother went for the medicine man. When he came he said it was a very bad bite, and that we would have to be careful or blood poison would set in. He said the dog would have to be killed. I said I thought the dog would die if they would let him alone; but he said, "The dog must be killed before he dies." That almost made me laugh. The cut in my leg was "V" shaped, and the piece of flesh hung only by the skin. When he went to put it back in place I said, "Ouch!" He asked, "What did you say?" I said, "Ouch!"

"What is that?" I said I did not know. He said, "Oh!" He put the piece back in place and stuck it there with something, then he got some weeds, mashed them up and made a poultice and put it on the wound. He said he would go and have the dog killed. I told him he would have to hurry up or the dog would be dead. "When I have had the dog killed I will come back and put another poultice on your leg," he said. I asked, "What are you going to put two poultices on for?" He replied that he intended to take that one off and put a fresh one on. I said, "Oh!"

Now, when the medicine man told anyone to do anything he had to do it. He sent a big boy to kill the dog, and when the boy got to the wickiup the old squaw and her girl pitched onto him and beat the poor fellow nearly to death. Then the medicine man sent two big Indians to see what they could do. When they reached the place, I could hear very loud talking, so I got up and went to the door to see the fun. One Indian had hold of the old squaw and the other had the girl, and they were shaking them for all that was out. I said, "Go after them, old boys." Mother said, "Shut your mouth and come in here and lie down." I told her I wanted to see the squaw and her girl get a good shaking. Well, they killed the dog before he died, anyway.

When everything was again quiet in camp, the medicine man came and changed the poultice on my leg. It had swollen very badly by this time. He told mother to boil sage leaves, and with the tea to bathe my leg very often. I could hear mother crying while she was gathering the sage, and when she came in I asked her what she was crying about. She said she was afraid I would be lame all my life from the hurt. I told her I would be well in a week; that a little thing like that would not make me lame very long. My leg pained me so that I did not get much sleep that night.

The next morning the squaw and her girl and their wickiup were gone, but the sick Indian was left lying there alone in his bed. I told mother to let him come into our wickiup and stay until his squaw got back. She had gone with Washakie to sell her robes and skins and had left her wounded husband with her sister-in-law to take care of until she got back. Mother did not like to take him in until I told her that he had saved my life by keeping the old squaw from cutting my head off, then she went out and told him to come into our wickiup and stay until his wife got back.

The poor fellow was very sick, and so weak that he could hardly walk. He had been shot three times with arrows—in the arm, in the leg, and in his side. His side was the worst. The medicine man had to take out a part of two ribs, and the hole left was big enough for me to stick my fist in. It kept the medicine man busy to tend to me and all of the wounded Indians. Mother bathed my sore leg three times a day with the sage tea, and the swelling all went away, and I was getting along fine. In about a week I had mother get me some sticks and I made some crutches, then I could get around out of doors. When the others that were lame saw how well I could move about they had me make them some crutches so they could get out, too.

After staying here about two weeks we had to move, for the wood was getting scarce near camp. I hobbled around and helped mother pack up, and we went over through the sand hills and came to a good sized stream, which they called Tonobipa. This stream ran south through the sand hills and lava beds, and the Indians told me that down farther it sank out of sight into the ground.

The sick Indians had a very hard time of it while we were on the move, but I stood it very well. We could not stop at this place very long, for we had to go to the place where we were to meet Washakie. That was five days' travel away, so we only stopped here four days, then we started on again. One day we had to make a twenty-mile drive to reach water. We could not travel very fast because of the sick Indians, and we could not get started very early in the morning on account of having so many horses to pack, and I was not much help to mother. It seemed an awful long ways until we got to Piupa.

That day was too hard on our sick Indians, and we had to leave two of them in the sand hills and go on until we came to water, and oh! how tired I got, and how my leg did hurt me. When we left the two Indians, one old Indian started ahead to get them some water and bring back to them. Well, it was away after dark when we got to the river, and you bet I was glad to get a good drink of water, and lie down to rest awhile. My leg hurt me so much that mother would not let me help her do a thing. She unpacked all of the horses and put up the wickiup alone.

The medicine man came to fix my leg, and when he unwrapped it to put on a poultice he found it had turned black. He said that it had begun to mortify and would have to be cut off. Then mother began to cry so that the whole camp heard her, and a lot of the Indians came up to see what was the matter. She told them that her poor boy had to have his leg cut off. I said, "Not by a d—n sight." I told the old medicine man to pike away to his wickiup and not to come back any more. Mother cried and begged the medicine man not to go. She said I was out of my head, and did not know what I was saying. "Yes, he does," said the old rascal, "and I do not care if the little, white devil does die." I said, "I know you don't or you would not want to cut my leg off." I said that I knew very well what I was saying, and I wanted him to get, and get quick, too, and that when Washakie came I would see that all of his legs were cut off. Away he went, as mad as fire.

After he had gone, mother said, "Now you have run the medicine man off, you will die." I said, "Not half as quick as I will if he keeps putting his poisoned poultices on my leg." I said that I would have been well long ago if it had not been for him, and that the old fool did not know as much as a last year's bird's nest with the bottom out; that I knew he had been trying to kill me ever since he began to doctor me, and I was not going to let him do anything for me any more.

Mother gathered more sage and bathed my leg. The poor old woman worked with me nearly all night, and the next morning my leg was better, but I could not move it without a great deal of pain. Mother said she would not leave that place until I got well, even if we had to stay there all winter. A couple of squaws brought in the two Indians we had left in the sand hills the night before. The next morning, when mother got up, she said she dreamed that Washakie came and killed a sage-hen and put the entrails on my leg and it cured it right away. I told her to keep on with the sage tea, and I thought it would be all right in a few days.

After we had been here two or three days, some of the Indians wanted to go to the place where we were to meet Washakie and the crowd that was with him, but mother said she would move not one peg until I got better, so five wickiups stayed with us and the rest went on. When they reached the place they found Washakie and his party there waiting for us. When they told him how I was, he started out that night, and in two days he got to us. When he saw my leg and was told about it, he was very angry and said it was bad enough to be bitten by the dog without having the squaw threaten to cut my head off. He said she would have to leave the tribe.

When I told him that every time the wound started to heal the old medicine man would squeeze it and break it open again, and that he nearly killed me every time he put the poultice on, he was very mad and said he would fix him when we got down to where we were going to winter. He said he had left his things in a bad shape, and would like to get back as soon as I could be moved. I said I thought I could travel, so the next morning we all packed up for the start. When I went to get on my horse, it hurt my leg so that I began to cry. Washakie said, "Hold on, I will fix you so you can ride better than that way." Then he and some more Indians went to work and tied some wickiup poles on each side of two horses, and then wove some rope between the poles. A lot of buffalo robes were thrown on, and this made a fine bed. Mother led the front horse, and away we went in first-class style.

After we got started, Washakie came up and asked me if they were traveling too fast for me. I said, "No, you can run if you want to." He laughed and said I was all right. As we went along that day mother got some boys to shoot some sage-chickens for her. The boys killed three and brought them to her, and when we camped that night she put the entrails on my sore leg. Oh, how well I slept that night!—the first good sleep I had had for more than a week. As we traveled along, mother took good care of my leg in this way, and by the time we got to the main camp, I could walk again with my crutches.

The next morning after we arrived here Washakie told the War Chief to send down the river for the best medicine man in the tribe. I told Washakie I would not let any more of his medicine men fool with my leg. He said he only wanted him to see it. That day the good doctor came, and when he looked at it he shook his head and said it was a wonder I was alive, for the old medicine man had been putting poison weeds on it, and if he had kept it up two days longer I would have been dead now. Washakie sent for the old medicine man, and when he came, said to him, "What have you been doing to this boy?" He said he had been doing all he could for me. Washakie said: "I don't want any more of your lies. Let me tell you that you have been making poultices out of poison weeds and putting them on his leg, and you have squeezed it until you can see the prints of your fingers yet. If this boy had died I would have had you tied to the tail of a wild horse and let him kick you to death and drag you until not one bit of meat was left on your bones. Now go, and don't let me see you any more, for you are hated by every Indian, squaw, and papoose in this camp." We stopped here about two weeks, and my leg got so much better that we moved down the river to where we were going to stop for the winter. Here fishing was good, and white tail deer, sage-hens, ducks, and rabbits were very plentiful.

CHAPTER 11 — **Old Morogonai**

During the time that I was disabled and had to stay in the wicki-up, my old friend, Morogonai, would come and talk to me for hours. He told me all about the first white men that he ever saw. Lewis and Clark, he said, were the two chiefs, and they had about thirty-five white men with them. He said he sold them some horses and they were good, honest, white men. He said he traveled with them for ten days, and would catch fish and swap them for shirts.

He said he had nothing against the white men only that they had spoiled his country, and he believed that in a few years there would be no buffaloes, and the elk would all be gone, so that the Indians would have a hard time to get something to eat. He said before any white men came to this country they had plenty of game of all kinds. "We hear," he said, "that away east of us the white men are killing the buffaloes by the thousands, and only taking the best of the skins and leaving all the meat to the wolves and the buzzards." He said that some of the white men that traveled through the country used their squaws very badly and had also brought diseases among the Indians that had killed many of them.

He told about an emigrant train that was on its way to Oregon, and while they were camped at the Humboldt Springs some of Pocatello's Indians went to their camp to swap buckskins for flour. The white men took three of their squaws and drove the rest of of the Indians off. That made the Indians mad, so they gathered a lot more Indians and followed the white men and killed every one of them and took everything they had and burned their wagons. There were eighteen men and women in the train.

He said that the men who carried the mail from Salt Lake to California would steal horses from the emigrants and take them to the Indians to herd, and when the emigrants were gone they would come and get the horses. He said: "I know this to be too true, for at one time these same men stole some very fine, big horses from a large train that was going through to Oregon, and brought them to my camp to keep for two moons, and then they were coming to get them and give us fifteen new red blankets for keeping them.

"In a few days, the emigrants found the tracks of their horses and following them up found the horses around our camp, and thinking we had stolen them, they let in to shooting without giving us a chance to explain. Well, they killed seven of my men before we knew what was up, and took their horses and some of ours. I was away at the time with most of our men. When I got back to camp, I found my oldest boy and five more Indians dead. One more died that night. Well, we got what was left of our band together and followed the white men for eight days before we could get a chance to do anything, for there was a good many of them and they kept a strong guard around their camp at night. But on the eighth day it was very stormy, and we stampeded their horses and got away with twenty-two head of them. The whites followed us and would have overtaken us had it not been that we happened to run into a large camp of Pocatello's Indians. We did not stop, but kept right on, and when the emigrants saw this camp, they thought these were the Indians that had stolen their horses. They had a big fight and men were killed on both sides, but the Indians finally got the worst of it. The best of it was, that we got away with the horses.

"After we got back to the main tribe, Washakie came to hear of it, and he sent for me and made me tell him all about it. When he heard the story, he said he did not blame me, but it was a bad scrape and he did not want any of his tribe to get into trouble with the whites. He said I had better keep away from the road where the white men travel, and not have anything to do with them, for they have crooked tongues, and no one can believe what they say.

"We did not know what the whooping cough, measles, and smallpox were until the whites brought these diseases among us. A train of emigrants once camped near my band and some of their children had the whooping cough and gave it to our children. Our Medicine Men tried to cure it like they would a bad cold, and over half of our children died with it. Hundreds of our people have died with the smallpox, and we lay it all to the white man.

"The white men keep crowding the Indians that are east of here west, and they keep crowding us west, and they will soon have us away out in Nevada where there is nothing but lizards, snakes, and horned toads; and if they crowd us any further, we will have to jump off into the great water."

He told me of so many low-down dishonest things that the white men had done to the Indians that I am ashamed to write it all in this book. Now, I believe that every word he told me is true. Now, my dear friends, I am glad to have you know that there is an Indian side to the tales of the early days in the "Great West."

When poor, old Morogonai was telling me his pitiful tales, I did not know how to sympathize with him then as I do now. Since I have seen so many bloody fights between the white men and the Indians, and being pretty well acquainted with both sides, I find that I cannot blame the Indians as some folks do. I know that they are a treacherous people, and revengeful, and if a white man kills an Indian, the Indians want to kill a white man to pay for it, and more than one if they can.

Nearing the Hunting Grounds

CHAPTER 12 — **The Big Council**

Our winter camp was in a very beautiful place with plenty of game and lots of good, dry wood and nearly everything that was needed to make one happy. My leg and all the sick Indians got well, and we were having a fine time.

One day some of Pocatello's Indians came to our camp, and that night Washakie called a council of the tribe to meet at the war chief's wickiup. I thought this strange, for he always held his councils in our wickiup. The next morning they held another council, so I thought I would go and see what was going on. When I got to the door of the council wickiup, I met an Indian who told me to run back, that they did not want me there. I thought that funny, for I had never before been sent away from their councils. When I got back to our wickiup I found mother and Hanabi both crying. I knew then that something was up, but I did not know what, and they would not tell me a word about it. I thought Pocatello's Indians wanted Washakie to help them out in some bloody affair with the whites. This ran along for four days, and I could not find out anything. I saw other squaws come to our wickiup and talk to mother, but when I came up they would stop talking, so I began to think it must be something about me, and it bothered me quite a little.

On the fifth morning Washakie sent for me and when I got there, I found about fifteen Indians gathered for the council. The war chief asked me how old I was. I told him I was nearly fourteen years old. He asked how old I was when I ran away from home. I told him I was nearly twelve years old then. He asked me if I was stolen away from home, or if I came of my own accord. I told him that I ran away from home; that nobody forced me to come, but two Indians coaxed me and gave me my pinto pony. Then he told me I could go. When I got back to the wickiup, mother and Hanabi wanted to know what they said to me and I told them all about it.

That night they held their council in Washakie's wickiup and the war chief asked me how long I had been with the Indians, how they had treated me, and why I ran away from home. I told him I had been with them two years, that I had been treated as well by the Indians as I ever had been at home, and that I ran away because I did not want to herd sheep all alone. I said the only way I could get the little pinto pony was to come with the Indians; and besides, they told me if I would come I would be treated well and would have plenty to eat and wear, so I came. The war chief asked if they had done as they said they would. I told him they had done everything they said they would do, and that I was not finding any fault. Washakie spoke up and said: "I told the Indians to offer the horse to the boy if he would come of his own accord. So when he came, we gave the squaw who owned the pinto, four colts for him. I gave her one yearling, mother gave her two, and Morogonai gave one. We never told the boy he could have the horse, but we knew the horse belonged to him all the same. I gave him another pony more to get him used to riding wild horses. He broke several colts for me and some for mother, and now he can ride anything in the shape of horseflesh."

The war chief asked me if I would rather live with the white people or with the Indians. I told him I would sooner live with the Indians. Then the council broke up and all the Indians went to their wickiups. I told Washakie I would like to know what it all meant. He said I would know in the morning. I told him if I thought they were going to take my pinto away from me, I would skip out that night with him. "They are not going to take your horse away from you. Wherever you go, that horse goes, too," said my mother. We all went to bed that night wondering what was going to happen in the morning. It was a very long night for me, for I did not sleep much.

Morning came at last, and after breakfast the war-chief and a lot more Indians came to our wickiup and with them were those Pocatello Indians. When they all got into the wickiup, Washakie told me that these Indians had been down to where my people lived; that my father said I had been stolen by the Indians; that he was raising a big army to come and get me; and that he was going to kill every Indian he could find. Washakie asked me what I thought of that. I told him it was not so. "In the first place, my people do not want to fight the Indians; and another thing, if my father had been coming after me, he would have come long before this. I don't believe one word of it," I said. Washakie said he looked at it just as I did.

Then one of Pocatello's Indians said he had just come from Salt Lake City and lots of folks asked him if he knew anything of the boy that had been stolen from the white folks. He said that all through the white people's towns they were fixing to fight, and he knew very well they were coming after me. I said I knew they were not, for I heard my father say many times that if ever one of his boys ran away he could never come back again. "Besides, my father has an old Gosiute Indian living with him that knows all about my running away." Washakie said that he could hardly believe they were coming after me. "It doesn't look reasonable to me," he said, "that they would let this run so long, and then come to hunt the boy at this time of the year, and I don't think they will do it."

This made the Pocatello Indians mad and they said, "If you believe that white boy before you believe us, you can do it; and if you get into a fight with the white men, you need not ask us to help you." Washakie said he was not going to get into any trouble with the white people if he could help it. They said, "No, you are too big a coward to fight anything." Then they got up and strutted off. As they went out they said to one of our Indians that they would like to get that little white devil out in the brush and they would have another white, curly-headed scalp to dance around when they got back to their camp.

When the council met that night, it was plain that they did not have very much to say. They all appeared to be in a deep study. After a little while Washakie said he had been thinking that it would be a good thing to send some of our Indians down among the white settlements to see for themselves what was going on. Old Morogonai said it was the best thing that could be done, but "Who will go?" Washakie said it would not be hard to get enough to go. The war chief said he thought it would be better for the boy to go himself, for that would end all the trouble, and if his folks were after him it would stop them and settle all disputes. Nearly the whole council thought this was the best thing that could be done. Washakie asked me how I thought that would do. I replied that I did not know the way home and I would not go. He said if the council thought it best for me to go, they would find a way for me to get home safe. He asked each member of the council to say what he thought about it, and all of them said they thought it was the best thing that could be done.

Mother talked and cried a great deal. I do not remember all she said, but I know that she begged them to send somebody else. Washakie was silent a long time, then he said I had better go; that he would send two of his best men with me to the nearest white people's town, and then I could get on to my home myself. He said: "I want you to go home, and when you get there, tell the truth. Tell your father that you came with us on your own accord; and then, if you want to come back, we will be glad to have you come and live with us forever." I said, "All right, I will go home if you want me to, but I will not stay there." How mother did take on! It did seem as though it would break her poor, old heart; and Hanabi took it very hard, too. I told them not to feel bad, for I would soon be back.

In a few days I was to start for home, so we commenced getting ready for the journey. Hanabi and some more squaws went to work to fix me up in first class style, and in two or three days they had all my clothes made. The Indians gave me so many buffalo robes and buckskins that one horse could not carry them, and Washakie said I might have one of the horses that they had captured from the Crows. When the two Indians that were going with me said they were ready, we packed up. I had in my pack seven buffalo robes, fifteen large buckskins, and ten pairs of very fine moccasins. It was quite bulky, but was not very heavy. Just as I was leaving, the little boys gave me so many arrows that I could not get them all in my quiver.

CHAPTER 13 — **Homeward Bound**

When we started to leave the village, how my mother did cry! I tried to comfort her by telling her not to cry, for I would soon be back. Little did I think it would be the last time I would ever see her, for I felt certain that I would come back that fall.

We took with us plenty of dried buffalo meat to last us through the trip, and away we went. On the fourth day, at noon, we came to a place on the Bear River about twenty miles north of Brigham City, Utah. We stayed there the rest of that day to give our horses a little rest. The two Indians said they would go no farther, for I could find the way from there very well. As I left them, I said, "You may look for me back in a few days." "Don't try to come back this fall," they said, "for it is getting too late to cross the mountains, and we are apt to have a big snow storm at any time now. It will take you six days to get home from here, and that will make it too late for you to return. You stay at your home this winter and there will be Indians there next summer and you can come back with them."

They helped me pack my horses the next morning, put me on the right trail, and told me not to ride too fast, for I could get to the white settlement long before night. About noon, I came to some warm springs, and I thought it would be a good idea to wash my face and hands, as I had not done it very often during the last two years. I saw that I would have plenty of time for the sun was high, so I unpacked my horses and staked them nearby, undressed and went to work to give myself a good scrubbing. I ran my fingers through my hair and tried to get the snarls out, but after I was dressed again, I could not see that I looked any better. My hands were like an Indian's and my costume was in the latest Indian fashion. My leggings were made of new red flannel, my shirt of antelope skins, and my frock was heavy buckskin, smoked to a nice red color, and with beads of all colors in wide stripes down the breast and on the shoulders, and fringes all around the bottom that reached nearly to my knees. My cap was made of rawhide, with notches all around the top, and looked like a cross-cut saw

Chief Washakie, his wife Hanabi holding their baby papoose, and Nick Wilson's dear old Indian mother. Note the sadness in their eyes. Picture probably taken in 1858, shortly after Yagaiki (Nick Wilson) left to return to his home in Grantsville, Utah, when Washakie took his family to the trading post at Salt Lake City, Utah.

turned upside down. It came to a peak in front, and mother put a crown in it with a muskrat skin.

After I had scrubbed off all the dirt I could, I packed up and started again. I could see the little town long before I came to it, and at the first house I came to, a man had just driven up with a load of hay. I asked him if he could tell me where I could find a place to camp. He said I could stop there if I wanted to; that he had plenty of hay, and I was perfectly welcome, so I thought I would take him at his word. I unpacked my horses and tied them under a shed and gave them some hay. By that time, the man came out and said supper was ready. I told him I had plenty to eat with me and would rather not go in. "Come and eat with me," he said, and he took me by the hand and led me into the house. The women and children stared at me so that I did not know what to do. The children would look at me, then they would turn to one another and laugh. The lady said, "I guess you would like to wash before you eat," and she gave me some water and soap. It was the first soap I had seen for two years. After I had washed, she told me to sit down at the table; then the man asked me, "Don't you take your hat off when you eat?" I said, "No." He said, "Will you please take it off here?" I pulled it off. They had bread and butter and potatoes and gravy and milk—the first I had seen since I left home, You bet, I was glad when I got away from the table.

I went out and watered my horses and gave them some hay. By this time it was dark, so I made my bed and turned in. Just as I was getting into bed, I saw this man go down town and pretty soon he came back with three more men. I saw them go into the house and soon he came out to where I was and said the bishop was in the house and would like to have a talk with me. I said I did not want to talk, but he kept at me until I got up and went in.

The bishop said his name was Nichols, or something like that. He said, "I see by your dress that you have been with the Indians, have you not?" I told him that I had been with the Indians for a year or two. He said he had read in the papers a year or so ago about a little boy running off with the Indians, "And I should judge," said he, "that perhaps you are the boy." I said, "Maybe I am." He asked me what tribe I belonged to. I told him that I belonged to Washakie's tribe. He said, "I have heard that Washakie is a chief among the Shoshones, and that his tribe is friendly to the white people. But you can tell us more about them than anybody else can." I said that Washakie's Indians were good Indians, and that I heard Washakie say many times that he was a friend to the white people who lived in Utah, and that he had seen the big chief who was a very good tibo. "What is that?" he asked me. I said, "I forgot I was talking to a white man; 'tibo' means white man."

I told him he had no need to fear Washakie's tribe, but that old Pocatello had drawn away some of Washakie's Indians, that they were bad Indians, and were doing everything against the white people they could. I said they would steal cattle and horses, and would kill white people if they were found away from the settlements. Washakie says they are bad, and that they kill a great many emigrants and steal their horses and burn their wagons.

Well, this bishop talked and talked and asked me ten thousand questions. After a while the woman said, "Do let the poor boy rest." I told them I had always been in bed by dark and that I felt pretty tired. "Well," he said, "you can go to bed now, and I will see you in the morning. You had better come down to my house and stay all day. I would like very much for Brother Snow to have a talk with you." I thought that neither Snow nor rain would catch me in that place another day, so I was up by the peep of day, and away I went.

I traveled seven or eight miles and stopped at some more hot springs, unpacked my horses, and got me something to eat. I thought I would not stop any more in towns where bishops could get hold of me and talk my lungs out. I thought I would camp out by the side of the road after that.

Well, after my horses got filled up—I was already filled up from that bishop the night before—I started on my way again and traveled eight or ten miles and came to a place they called Ogden. As I was going down the main street a man standing by a store stopped me and began talking Indian to me. He asked where I had been. I told him. While we were talking a lot more men came up to us and one of them asked me where I was going to stop that night. I said I did not know, but that I would go down the road a piece until I found grass and water and then I would camp. He asked me to put my horses in a corral there and give them all they could eat. "No," said I, "I would rather go on." "No, you must stop here tonight," and he took the rope out of my hand and led my horses into the corral. I followed him, and when I unpacked, I asked if he was the bishop. He said he was. I told him I thought he was. He asked me why I thought he was the bishop. I said, "Because you talk so much." He laughed and said I must not notice anything like that for they seldom saw a person like me, and they wanted to find out all they could about the Indians. After a while he said, "Come into the house and we will have supper." I did not want to go, but he would have it that way, so I went in with him. I think he said his name was West.

This Bishop West, if that was his name, asked me quite a few questions, but he said he would not weary me by talking too long. I went to bed soon after dark that night, and I thought I would get off early the next morning and give them the slip again; but just as I was packing up, the bishop came out and said, "Hold on, there, you are not going before breakfast?" I told him I had plenty to eat along with me. "Well," he continued, "you will surely eat with me this morning." So I had to stop until after breakfast. He asked me a great many more questions, but he was very nice about it. I felt glad to talk with him, he was so kind and good to me.

He said I would be a very useful man if I was treated right. He asked me if I had been to school much, and was much surprised when I told him that I had never gone to school one day in my life. He said I must go to school, and if I lived near him he would see that I did go. When I started he asked me to go and see Brother Young when I got to Salt Lake City. I thought I did not want any Brother Young in mind, but I was a young boy then, and did not know what I was talking about.

That day I got to a place they called Farmington. Just as I was nearing the town, I saw some boys driving cows. I asked them where I could camp. "Up on that mountain if you want to," said one. I said to him, "You think you are pretty smart, don't you?" He said, "I am smart enough for you, Mr. Injun. If you don't believe it, just get off the buzzard head and I will show you." I jumped off my horse and he ran. I got on again and started after them, but they got through a fence and ran away across the fields. I went on through the town and camped in a field, after getting permission from a man who lived near by, and I was not bothered with questions that night.

The next morning I was off pretty early and reached Salt Lake City, went through the city, and stopped at the Jordan bridge for noon. I knew where I was then, for I had been in the city a few times before. That afternoon I went on to what we called Black Rock, those days, and camped that night near the great Salt Lake. I was now within a short day's ride of home. Oh, home! sweet, sweet, home! I could hardly stay there 'till morning, I wanted to get home so badly.

Just as I was making camp, a team drove up with three people in the wagon. I knew them. They were John Zundel, his sister

Julia, and Jane Branden, my nearest neighbors when I was at home, but they did not know me at first. I had a fire, and was broiling a rabbit I had killed, when Julia came up to where I was and tried to get a good look at me, but I kept my face turned from her as much as I could. Finally she got a glimpse of my face and went to the wagon and I heard her say to Jane, "That is the whitest Indian I ever saw, and he has blue eyes." Jane said, "I'll bet a dollar it's Nick Wilson." Then they came to where I was and Jane said, "Look up here, young man, and let us see you." I looked at her. "I knew it was you, you little scamp!" and she took hold of me, shook me, patted me on my back, and said she had a notion to flog me. She said, "Your poor mother has nearly worried herself to death about you." I cannot begin to tell all that was said that night, but they told me that the soldiers were coming to kill the Mormons, and all of the men that had horses were out to stop them. They said that the whole country was in an uproar.

Well, morning came at last, and I packed up in a hurry and started for home, and I did not stop until I got there. I was mighty glad to see my dear old home again. As I rode up, two of my little sisters, who were playing by the side of the house, ran in and told mother that an Indian was out there. She came to the door and knew me as soon as she saw me. And, oh! my dear friends, I cannot tell you just what passed during the next hour, but they were all glad to have me back safe at home again. I forgot all about my horses, and when, finally, I thought of them and went out to unpack them, all the folks followed me and mother said, "Where did you get all those horses? Did you take them from the Indians and run away?" I told her they were mine, and that I had not run away from the Indians as I had done from her.

After I had put my horses in the field, I told them all about what I had seen and passed through while I was away, and answered everybody's questions the best I could.

CHAPTER 14 — **Year Of The Move**

Soon after reaching home, another call was made for men to go out and stop the soldiers at Echo Canyon. I wanted to go, but my father would not let me. I said I could kill soldiers with my bow and arrows as well as the others could with their old flint-lock guns, but they said I was too young, so my older brother went, and I let him have one of my buffalo robes and my roan pony.

All of the grain was not out of the field yet, and all of the men had gone off to the Echo Canyon war, except a few very old men who could not do much work. You could see the women and little boys out in the fields with oxen hauling grain and stacking it. There would be about half a dozen women to a team, with a little boy driving the oxen. I have seen as many as fifteen or twenty teams at a time out in the big public field hauling grain, and just as many women and children as could get around the wagons. They seemed to be as happy as larks, and you might hear the children singing in every part of the field.

"Old squaw-killer Harney is on the way, doo da;
He swears the Mormons he will slay, doo da, doo da, day."

Another song we used to sing ran something like this:

"I looked to the west, and I looked to the east,
And I saw General Johnston coming
With four white mules and a pack of d——n fools,
And he landed on the other side of Jordan, O!"

Well, after the grain was all hauled, it had to be threshed. An old man by the name of Baker, who could just get around by the aid of two walking sticks, took charge of the threshing machine. It was not much like the steam threshers we have these days. This one had a cylinder fixed in a big box and it was made to turn by what we called horse power, but we had to turn it with ox power. Old Daddy Baker, and as many women as could get around the machine, started in to do the threshing. We put on four yoke of oxen to run this old chaff piler, as we called it.

Women and kids were left to harvest the crops while the men were off fighting Government soldiers and Indians near Salt Lake

Brother Baker put us oldest boys to pitch the grain and feed it into the old machine. One of the biggest boys started up the cattle and away she went. I was to do the feeding. At first, the boys pitched the grain so fast that I would let three or four bundles in at a time and choke the old thing up and cause the belt to break, then it would take half an hour to get started again.

The straw and chaff and grain all came out together. About fifteen women with rakes would string out and rake the straw along until they left the grain behind, then about forty kids would stack the straw. After we threshed an hour or two we would stop and cave up, as we called it; that was pushing the grain and chaff into a pile to one side, then we would go on again. We would keep this up until we got through with Brother Martendial's job, then we would move the old rattle-trap over to Brother Pumpswoggle's place.

We had an old home-made fanning mill that would follow up the threshing machine and clean the chaff from the grain. Some of the women would take turns turning the old thing, while others would take milk pans and buckets and put the grain into the hopper, then the chaff would go one way and the grain the other. We would thresh only a hundred and fifty bushels a day, and we had over twenty thousand bushels to thresh, so you can see that it looked very discouraging, with winter so near.

As luck would have it, some of our men came in with a large band of mules and horses they had taken from the soldiers, and four of the men stopped at home to help with the threshing. 'Lonzo Mecham took charge of the threshing from that time on. We used some of our Uncle Sam's mules to do the rest of the threshing and got along first rate. They were good mules.

During the fall you could see the women hauling wood from the mountains, digging potatoes in the fields, and gathering in their garden and farm products. Women that were hardly able to be out had to work like this while their husbands and fathers and brothers were away in the mountains defending their homes and families. They were poorly dressed, too, for cold weather.

Most of the people were very poor. The Indians and grasshoppers and crickets had kept them down so that it was hard for them to make a living at the best, and now there was a United States army coming to make a finish of us, and to hang every man, it was said, that had two wives, for they had ropes quite handy, and I believe they would have done it, too, if Lot Smith had not burned their wagon trains on the Sandy. After the Mormons got away with

Mormons in Utah threshing oats between times of fighting Indians and U.S. Government troops sent to quell polygamy.

all the army's mules and cattle, and the snow became very deep in the mountains, the soldiers made winter camp on Ham's Fork, and most of our men came home, so we got our threshing done by the middle of the winter.

As poor as the people were, they were as happy as could be. We would have dances two or three times a week, and to pay the fiddler, we would take a peck of wheat or a peck of potatoes or carrots, or sometimes, a squash. My folks had raised some very fine squash that summer, and when I went to a dance, I would take a very large squash and get a few carrots back as change, and at recess my partner and I would eat the carrots for lunch. It may seem funny now to think of doing these things, but many people are yet living who remember them well, and they know we had very pleasant, happy times, too.

I said that the people were very poor. They were poor in house furniture, bedding, clothing, and such things, but we had plenty to eat and most of the people had cattle, sheep, hogs, and chickens. The people had been driven out of Missouri and Illinois and had traveled over thousands of miles to the Rocky Mountains to find a home where they could live in peace. In this long, rough journey, they had worn out their clothes and broken so much of their furniture and dishes that they had hardly any of these things left. Sometimes a coat or dress would be patched so many times and with so many different kinds of cloth that you could hardly tell which kind of cloth it had been made of in the first place.

The people came that long, dreary journey across the plains to find a place where they could dwell in peace, but it seems that they were not to be allowed to do this, for they were followed by bad men who did all they could to cause these innocent people more trouble. They wrote many lies about the Mormons to the President of the United States, until the government thought it had to do something, so it sent out a governor and a set of officers with an army to investigate matters. After this army had been driven into winter quarters in the mountains, Brigham Young sent out and asked the governor to come and find out for himself how things were.

When spring came, things had not been fixed up to suit all the officers, so the people of Utah were ordered to leave their homes and move south. Everybody had their crops in when the order came to move. A guard was to remain to look after what was left behind, and if it came to the worst, to burn everything that might be useful to the army that was expected. My father and his family

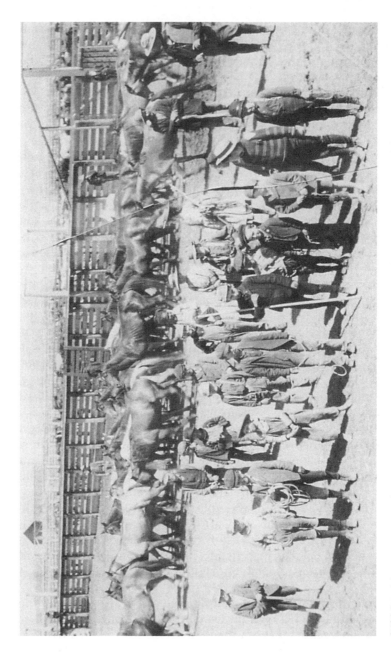

Wild Spanish mustangs were brought in to sell to the settlers and Army at Fort Lloyd, Utah. Nick Wilson leaped from the fence and rode one of these wild horses, and it was given to him. 1856.

and most of neighbors moved down to Spanish Fork, Utah, where we stopped for further orders. I wanted to go back to live with Washakie and my dear, old, Indian mother, but I hated to leave until I found out what the army was going to do. By this time, I had traded my Crow pony for a white man's saddle and a two-year-old heifer.

While this move was going on, you could sit by the road-side for half a day and see any kind of outfit you might desire, from a wheel-barrow up to a fine, eight-mule team. An old wagon, with a cow and a horse hitched up together, was a common sight. You could see the finest buggies, drawn by big teams, or you could see one old ox hitched between the shafts of a rickety, old, two-wheeled cart. You could see women leading the family cow with their bedding and a little food packed on her back. So, some of these people were rich and many were poor, but they were all traveling the same road, and all appeared to be happy and none of them very badly scared.

We had not been in Spanish Fork long, when one day some Spaniards brought in a lot of wild horses to trade for cattle, and a good many folks had gathered around the corral to see the mustangs. While sitting on the corral fence, I saw a little black, three-year-old mare that took my fancy. I asked the man what he would take for her. He said, "I will sell her for sixty dollars, but if you will jump from that fence onto her back and ride her, you can have her for nothing." I said, "That is a whack, I'll do it." He told me to wait until they were ready to turn the horses out. It was not long before he said, "Now we are ready to see the fun." He had no idea whom he was talking to. He thought the colt would throw me off the first jump, and they would all have a good laugh on my account.

They let down the bars and drove the horses around so that the black colt came near enough for me to jump off the fence to her back. As she came around, I gave a jump and landed fairly on her back, and away she went out through the bars and down the street. It seemed as if every dog in town was after us. We passed through the town in no time, crossed the bridge, went up over the hill, and away off towards Pond Town. Then we circled around towards Goshen. We soon left behind the band of horses we started with, and ran away from all the dogs.

A man went over and told my folks that I was on a wild horse, that the horse was running away with me, and that I would be killed. Mother was not much worried, for she knew I had been on a wild horse before. My brother mounted my pinto pony as soon as he could and followed me, but when he got to me, the colt I was riding had run itself down and had stopped. He rode up and handed me a rope which I put around the colt's neck, and then got off to let her rest. After a while I mounted her again and my brother drove her back to town.

When we got back, all of the men that had seen us start off came up to see the colt. Among them was one, Mr. Faust, Doc. Faust, they called him. He said I beat all the boys riding he ever saw; that he had a great many horses he wanted broke, and if I would go with him he would give me fifty dollars a month. When I told mother about it she said I could not go, for my father was very sick, and she was afraid he was not going to live much longer.

We stayed in the neighborhood of Spanish Fork until about the first of August, when word came that we could go back home, that everything was fixed up with the officers all right, and that the soldiers were going to pass through Salt Lake City and on to Cedar Valley, where they intended to build a fort.

We all started for home with a "hurrah!" and when we got back, we all went to work with a will, and I never saw such crops as we raised that year. We raised from fifty to seventy-five bushels of wheat to the acre. All through Utah it was the same. That fall, wheat sold for five dollars and eight dollars a bushel, and the best of it was, everybody had plenty of it to sell. Wheat straw that winter sold at from forty to sixty dollars a ton, and hay brought from seventy-five to one hundred dollars a ton.

The harvesting all had to be done by hand, for there were no reaping machines in those days. We hired Owen Baston to cradle our grain, and my brother and I bound it. That fall, after we got the wheat all cut, my father died.

After the death of my father, my brother and I could not get along very well together. He was a very hard worker, and I had never done much work, and it went pretty hard with me. I would rather ride horses than work, so I thought I would go over to Mr. Faust and help him break horses for a while, and then I would go back to Washakie.

Mr. Faust lived in the south end of Rush Valley, Utah. When I got to his ranch, Mr. Faust was very glad to see me. He said to his other riders: "We will have that old outlaw of a horse broken now, for here is a boy that will ride him as long as he has hair in his tail." I told him that I did not know about that, for I had not ridden a bad horse for more than a year. He said, "What do you call that jumping off the fence onto a wild mustang?" I said that she was not a bad animal to ride, for she did nothing but run. He said his horses were not bad to break, only this one had thrown two or three of the boys and that made him mean; "but," he said, "I want him broke, for he is about as good a horse as I have, and I know you can break him."

The next morning one of Mr. Faust's best riders and I went out to bring in the band that the outlaw was with. This man told me if I was not a very good rider that I had better keep off of that horse or he would kill me. I said I was not a very good rider, but I was not afraid to try him anyhow. So we brought in the band and roped the outlaw. Mr. Faust came out and said, "Well, what do you think about old Outlaw? Do you think you can ride him?" I said I would try. Mr. Faust said, "That's the stuff! I bet you can ride him." Then the man that had been talking to me telling me to stay off the horse, told Mr. Faust not to let me ride him for he was sure to kill me.

I began to think that this man did not want me to ride the horse because he had been thrown by him two or three times. He was afraid I might prove to be the better rider. So I piled on Mister Outlaw and he started off all right. I rode him around a little and began to think they were making a fool of me, when pretty soon the old boy turned loose and fairly made my neck pop. He did the hardest bucking I ever saw, but he did it straight ahead. He didn't whirl like some horses do, so I stayed with him all right. When he stopped bucking, I sent him through for ten miles about as fast as he ever went, and when I got back to the ranch, I rode up to the corral where the man was saddling another horse, and, standing up in my saddle, I said, "Do you call this a bad horse? If you do, you don't know what a bad horse is." That man didn't like me very much after that. I got along with old Outlaw first rate after that, but I had to give him some very hard rides before he finally gave up and acknowledged me the master.

CHAPTER 15 — **The Pony Express**

About the time I was thinking of starting to rejoin my Indian friends, the word came that the pony express was going to start, and Mr. Faust induced me to stay and be one of the pony riders. I sold my roan pony to a sergeant in Camp Floyd for seventy-five dollars, and I sold the little black mare for one hundred dollars. I took part of the money to mother and bought some clothes with the rest.

A great pow wow was going on about the pony express coming through the country. They had started to build roads and stations. These stations had to be built every ten miles apart and as near to water as possible. Well, the time came for the express horses to be strung along the line, and the riders were sent to their stations. Mr. Faust and Mr. Howard Egan went my bonds, and I was sent out west into Nevada to a station called Ruby Valley. This station was a home station and was kept by a man named William Smith, and Smith had a hostler whose name was Samuel Lee.

When we were hired to ride the express we had to go before a Justice of the Peace and swear that we would at all times be at our post, and not at any time be over one hundred yards from the station, except when we were carrying the mail. When we started out we were never to turn back. no matter what happened, until the mail was delivered at the next home station. We had to be ready to start back at a half-minute's notice, let it be day or night, rain or shine, Indians or no Indians.

Our saddles, which were all furnished by the company, had nothing to them but the bare tree, stirrups, and cinch. Two large pieces of sole leather about sixteen inches wide by twenty-four inches long were laced together with a strong leather string and thrown over the saddle. Fastened to these were four pockets, two in front and two behind on either side of the saddle. The two hind ones were the largest. The one in front on the left side was called the "way pocket." All of these pockets were locked with small padlocks and each home station keeper had a key to the way pocket. When the express arrived at the home station, the keeper would unlock the way pocket, and if there were any letters for the boys between the home stations, the rider would distribute them as he went along, and there was, also, a card in the way pocket that the station keeper would take out and put down on it the time the express got to this station and when it went out. He would tell the rider what time he would have to make up on his run if the express was behind time.

Well, the time came that we had to start. The express would leave St. Joseph, Missouri, and Sacramento, California, at the same time every day. The home stations were from forty to sixty miles apart, and one man's ride was from one home station to another. Between the home stations were other stations, ten miles apart, where horses could be changed. Not many riders could stand the long, fast riding at first, but after they had ridden for about two weeks they would be all right. At first the rider would be charged up with the saddle he was riding, and the first wages were kept back for it, and if we had no revolver and had to get one from the company, that would be forty dollars more to come out of our wages. Many a poor boy was killed by the Indians before he got the company paid for these things. Our wages were too small for the hard work we did, and the dangers we went through.

Everything went along first rate for a while, but after six or eight months of that kind of work the big, fine horses began to play out, then the company sent to California and bought up all of the wild horses they could get, brought them in, strung them along the road, and put the best riders to breaking them. Peter Neece, our home station keeper, was a big, strong man, and a good rider. He was put to breaking some of these wild mustangs for the boys on his beat. After these wild horses had been ridden two or three times, they would be put on the regular line for the express boys to ride. Generally just as soon as the hostler could lead them in and out of the stable without getting his head kicked off, they were considered broke, and very likely they had just been handled enough to make them mean. I found it to be so with most of the horses they gave me to ride.

I was not a bit afraid of the Indians, but for some reason or other, the way they had told these big yarns about the Indians killing the riders rather worked me up, so that while I could not say I was afraid of them, I was pretty badly scared, just the same.

Well, my home station was at Shell Creek. I rode from Shell Creek to Deep Creek, and one day the Indians killed the rider out on the desert, and when I was to meet him at Deep Creek, why,

The Scout

he was not there. I had to keep right on until I met him. I went to the next station, Willow Creek, the first station over the mountain, and there I found out that he had been killed. My horse was about jaded by this time, so I had to stay here to let him rest. I would have had to start back in the night as soon as the horse got so he could travel, if those Indians had not come upon us.

About four o'clock in the afternoon, seven Indians rode up to the station and asked for something to eat. Peter Neece, the station keeper, picked up a sack with about twenty pounds of flour in it and offered it to them, but they would not have that little bit, they wanted a sack of flour apiece Then he threw it back into the house and told them to get out, and that he wouldn't give them a thing.

This made them pretty mad, and as they passed a shed about four or five rods from the house, they each shot an arrow into a poor, old, lame cow, that happened to be standing there under the shed. When Neece saw them do that, it made him mad, too, and he jerked out a couple of pistols and commenced shooting at them. He killed two of the Indians and they fell off their horses right there. The others ran. He said, "Now, boys, we will have a time of it, tonight. There are about thirty of those Indians camped up in the canyon there, and they will be upon us as soon as it gets dark, and we shall have to fight."

A man by the name of Lynch happened to be there at the time. He had bragged a good deal about what he would do and we looked upon him as a sort of desperado and a very brave man. I felt pretty safe until he weakened and commenced to cry, then I wanted all of us to get on our horses and skip for the next station; but Pete said, "No. We will load up all the old guns that are around here and be ready for them when they come. There are four of us, and we can stand off the whole bunch of them." Well, just a little before dark, we could see a big dust over towards the mouth of the canyon, and we knew they were coming. It was about six miles from the canyon to the station.

Pete thought it would be a good thing to go out a hundred yards or so, and lie down in the brush and surprise them as they came up. When we got out there he had us lie down about four or five feet apart. "Now," he said, "when you fire, jump out to one side, so if they shoot at the blaze of your gun, you will not be there." We all took our places, and, you bet, I lay close to the ground. Pretty soon we could hear their horses' feet striking the ground, and it seemed to me as if there were thousands of them; and such yells as they let out, I never heard before. The sounds were coming straight towards us, and I thought they were going to run right over us.

It was sandy where we lay, with little humps here and there, and scrubby grease-wood were growing on the humps. Finally the Indians got close enough for us to shoot. Pete shot and jumped away to one side. I had two pistols, one in each hand, cocked all ready to pull the trigger, and was crawling on my elbows and knees. Each time he would shoot, I saw him jump. Soon they were all shooting, and each time they shot, I would jump. I never shot at all.

After I had jumped a good many times, I happened to land in a little wash, or ravine, that the water had made. I guess my back came pretty nearly level with the top of it. Anyway, I pressed myself down so I could get right in. I don't know how I felt, I was so scared. I lay there and listened until I could hear no more shooting, but I thought I could hear the horses' hoofs beating on the hard ground near me, until I found out it was only my heart beating. After a while, I raised my head a little and looked off towards the desert, and I could see those humps of sand covered with grease-wood. They looked exactly like Indians on horses, and I could see several of them near the wash.

I crouched down again and lay there for a long time, maybe two hours. Finally everything was very still, so I thought I would go around and see if my horse was where I had staked him, and if he was, I would go back to my station over in Deep Creek and tell them that the boys were all killed and I was the only one that had got away all right. Well, as I went crawling around the house on my elbows and knees, just as easy as I could, with both pistols ready, I saw a light shining betwen the logs in the back part of the house. I thought the house must be full of the Indians, so I decided to lie there awhile and see what they were doing, anyhow. I lay there for some time, listening and watching, and then I heard one of the men speak right out a little distance from the house, and say, "Did you find anything of him?" Another man answered, "No, I guess he is gone." Then I knew it was the boys, but I lay there until I heard the door shut, then I slipped up and peeped through the crack and saw that all three of them were there all right. I was most too much ashamed to go in, but finally I went around and opened the door. When I stepped in Pete called out, "Hello! Here he is. How far did you chase them? I knew you would stay with them. I told the fellows here that you would bring back at least half a dozen of them." I think they killed five Indians that night. The next morning I went back to Deep Creek.

I was sent further west, about three hundred miles, to ride from the Carson Sink to Fort Churchill. The distance was about seventy-five miles and was a very hard ride for the horses as well as for me, because much of the distance was through deep sand. Some things were not so bad, however, for I had no mountains to cross, the winter was mild, and the Indians were a little more friendly here. East of my beat, along Egan Canyon, Shell Creek, and Deep Creek, the Indians had begun to be very saucy, and they had threatened to burn the stations and kill the people, and in the following spring they did break out in good earnest, burned some of the stations and killed one of the riders. That same spring I was changed back into Major Egan's division, and rode from Shell Creek to Ruby Valley.

That summer the Indians got very bad. They burned several stations, killed the hostlers, and also a few riders. I got very badly wounded that summer. I had been taking some horses to Antelope station, and on my way back I made a stop at Spring Valley station. When I got there the two boys that looked after the horses at the station were out on the woodpile playing cards, and they wanted me to stay with them and have dinner. I got off my horse and started him towards the stable, but instead of going to the stable he went behind it, where some other horses were grazing.

Pretty soon we saw the horses going across the meadow towards the cedars with two Indians on foot behind them. We started after them full tilt, and gained on them a little, and as we ran I fired three shots at them from my revolver, but they were too far off for me to hit them. They reached the cedars a little before we did. I was ahead of the other two boys, and as I ran around a large cedar, one of the Indians, who had hidden behind a tree, shot me in the head with a flint-spiked arrow. The arrow struck my head about two inches above the left eye. The other two boys were on the other side of the tree, and seeing the Indian run, came around to find out where I was and found me lying on the ground with the arrow sticking in my head.

They tried to pull the arrow out, but the shaft came away and left the flint spike in my head. Thinking that I would surely die, they rolled me under a tree and started for the next station as fast as they could go. There they got a few men and came back the next morning to bury me, but when they got to me and found I was still alive they thought they would not bury me just then. They decided to wait awhile. They carried me to a station that was called Cedar Well, and from there sent to Ruby station for a doctor. When he came, he took the spike out of my head and told the boys to keep a wet rag on the wound and that was all they could do for me. I lay there for six days, when Major Egan happened to come along, and seeing that I was still allive, sent for the doctor again, and when the doctor came and saw that I was no worse he started to do something for me. I lay for eighteen days and did not know anything, then I began to get better fast, and it was but a little while until I was riding again. I think if Mr. Egan had not come along when he did I would not be here now telling about it. But, Oh! how I have suffered with my head at times since then.

The Indians kept getting worse. They had attacked emigrant trains, and had done a lot of damage to the express line by burning stations, killing the riders, and running off with the horses. The Indians got so bad that it was hard to keep riders enough to carry the express, for every one that could leave would do so, and it was hard for the agents to hire men to take their places. The company had to raise the wages from forty dollars a month to sixty, and it was hard to get men even at that price.

Between Deep Creek and Shell Creek was a station we called Eight-Mile station, kept by an old man, and he had two young emigrant boys to help him.

Their mother had died east of Salt Lake City with the cholera, and when they got out here, their father was shot by the Indians, and he died when they reached Deep Creek, and left these two boys with the station keeper. The father gave him five hundred dollars in money, a big pair of mules, and a new wagon, if he would send the boys back to their relatives in Missouri, where the family came from.

It was too late to send them back that fall, so the boys had to pass the winter there with him. The old man that kept Eight-Mile station couldn't do the work very well, so the older of the two boys was allowed to go there and help him. Well, along came an emigrant train, and the old man slipped away with the emigrants and left the boy to take care of the station alone.

It was hard to get men to come out here when the Indian troubles began, and the boy wanted to keep the station and have his brother come up from Deep Creek and help him.

One day, while the two boys were tending the station, I rode up there to meet the other rider, and as I reached the station I could see him coming five or six miles out. While we were watching him, a lot of Indians broke out of the brush and took in after him. He made a great race for it, but just before he reached the station they shot and killed him. We knew the Indians would attack the station, so we hurried to the barn and brought three horses to the house.

The station house was a rock building, twelve by twenty feet, with a shed roof covered with earth so that no timbers were sticking out that the Indians could set fire to. There were portholes in each end of the building, and one on each side of the door in front.

We succeeded in getting the three horses into this house by the time the Indians surrounded the station. They kept shooting at the back of the house, for they soon learned not to come up in front of those portholes.

We killed one or two of them that were foolish enough to get in front of them. I know that one of them made a mistake by darkening my porthole. When I saw the shadow, I pulled the trigger. Three days after, when I went out, I found an Indian lying there, and I am pretty certain that he must have gotten in the way of my bullet.

We were penned up three days in this house, and it was lucky for us that the station was built on low ground, where the water had raised in the cellar under the house. We had only one pan, that the boys used to mix their dough in for making bread, so we had to feed the horses and mix our bread in the same pan. The water in the cellar was not a bit good, but we had to use it, for it was all we had during the three days and nights we were kept there by the Indians.

The younger boy was not a bit over eleven years old, and the other one was about fourteen. I was the oldest. We put the little boy to tending the horses and looking after things, while we guarded the house.

The youngest would sometimes get to crying and talking about his mother dying and his father getting killed by the Indians. The older boy was very gritty, and would try to comfort his little brother.

The first night none of us slept at all, but the next day and the following night I let them sleep a little by having one of them watch while the other slept. The third night I went to sleep and left the boys on guard.

Along towards morning, just as it was getting daylight, they came and woke me up and said there was a lot of shooting going on outside, and they wanted to know what it meant. I listened, and the first thing I heard was somebody saying, "Go to the house and see if the boy is all right." I looked through a hole and saw a lot of soldiers. Well, that is the way we got out of it that time.

Mr. Kennedy, a horse trader, was bringing a large band of mustang horses from California to Salt Lake to sell, and got belated out on the desert and found it necessary to stop at Deep Creek. He could winter his horses here without feed. The Indians were so bad that we had to send out guards with the horses in the day time, and at night corral them and place a strong guard around them.

The corral was made by digging a trench and setting in large cedar posts on end. There was a straw stack in the middle of the corral, where the boys used to sleep, but the Indians got so mean that they would shoot arrows into their bed, and this got so dangerous that they couldn't sleep there. Sometimes we would spread blankets on the straw as if we were in bed, and in the morning find several arrows sticking in the blankets.

A favorite way of guarding the corral was to remove a big picket or post on either side of the bars and have a man stand in the places.

The Indians' scheme was to get the bars down in some way, then stampede the horses and run them off. One night Peter Neece and I were standing guard in this way. He was on one side of the bars and I was on the other, each standing in the place of a big post that we had taken out. We knew there were Indians around by the way the horses in the corral behaved. I was standing on the south side of the bars, looking off into the sage brush, for I thought the Indians would be coming from that direction because the horses were looking that way.

But one Indian, instead of coming straight up from the front, as he should have done, got close up to the fence at the back and came creeping around close to the corral to get to the bars. It happened that he was coming up on my side, but I didn't see him, for I was looking off into the sage brush. Pete saw him, though, but he couldn't warn me without giving himself away.

He watched him crawl towards the bars to let them down, and just as he got about at my feet, Pete fired. The Indian gave one unearthly yell that could have been heard three miles, sprang six feet into the air, and settled down dead right where I had been standing, but I wasn't there then. When that yell was being let out I turned a back somerset and landed about a rod or more inside the corral.

Sometimes at night, when the horses were brought in, we would saddle a horse apiece and keep him saddled ready for use all night, and in the morning we would saddle fresh horses, so as to be ready at any minute to go out after Indians if it became necessary.

In the spring, when Mr. Kennedy was thinking of starting for Salt Lake with his horses, the herder was fired upon one morning as he was taking them out to graze.

The Indians closed in behind the horses and headed them towards the hills. Seven of us started immediately in pursuit. I was on a lazy, old, blue horse, and couldn't keep up with the other boys, but Mr. Kennedy rode a very good horse. He was away ahead of the rest of us and was crowding the Indians pretty close and would have overhauled them in a few minutes more. Just before he got to them, an Indian's horse fell, carrying his rider down with him, and as Kennedy charged on the Indian to run over him he received an arrow in the arm, but the Indian got a bullet through his head in return. Kennedy had to wait until we came up to pull the arrow out of his arm.

By that time the Indians had the horses in a box canyon, where the rocks were very steep on both sides. A few Indians hid among the rocks and held us back while the rest of the band rushed the horses on up the canyon. The entrance to the canyon led south for a few hundred yards, and then turned sharply around a large, steep mountain, and ran almost directly north. A short distance after it turned, the canyon opened out into a large meadow about a mile long.

When we saw that we could not pass the Indians to get to the horses, Kennedy thought it would be best to go back two or three miles and cross a low divide, and so get into the canyon at the head of the meadows. The canyon narrowed again here and he thought we might head the Indians off if we would get there first.

So we turned and went back about two miles and a half to go over this divide. When we got near the top of the divide there was a cliff of rock too steep to get the horses over, so we tied them in a clump of mountain mahogany growing nearby, and went on afoot. We could not go down the other side very fast, for the white maple brush was very thick, with a pine tree now and then.

Just before we got down to the head of the meadows, we stopped on the side of the mountain near a very large, flat-topped rock. Kennedy sat up on the rock, watching for the Indians to come out onto the meadows from the canyon below. The rest of us went down just below the rock and filled our pockets with "yarb," or Indian tobacco, that grew there. While picking the yarb, Frank Mathis laid his old, muzzle-loading, Springfield rifle down in the bushes, where he could reach it when he wanted it.

We were there about half an hour, when all at once Kennedy jumped down among us and cried, "My God! boys, we're surrounded!" In the excitement that followed. Mathis grabbed his gun by the muzzle and gave it a jerk. The hammer caught on a bush and the gun was discharged, and shot his left arm off between the shoulder and the elbow. That rattled us quite a bit, so we hardly knew what to do next.

Kennedy thought it was best for us to fight our way back to where our horses were tied. So he started Mathis up the hill ahead of the rest of us. We were to keep the Indians back if we could. We knew they were around us on every side, for we could hear the brush crack and see it shake every once in a while. When near the top we came to a bare stretch of ground about two rods across.

We stopped in the edge of the brush, for we knew that Indians could shoot us very easily as soon as we got in the open. Kennedy thought we had better make a break for it and scatter out as we ran, so the Indians could not hit us so easily. I was the shortest legged one in the lot, but I wasn't the last one over, just the same. When we were about half way across, the Indians began to shoot at us with their arrows and guns. A bullet struck a rock right beneath my feet, and it helped me over the hill just that much the quicker.

By the time we got down to our horses, Mathis was bleeding badly. He was faint and begging for water. We had to lead our horses down to the bottom of the mountain on account of the rocks. Kennedy sent me and Robert Orr down to the creek to bring water back in our hats for Mathis. When we got back with the water, Kennedy sent me on to the station, so I could be there when the express came and be ready to take it on.

That is the last time I every saw Frank Mathis. He was a brave man and a good Indian fighter. He was taken to Salt Lake, so he could be better cared for. After he got well, he and a man by the name of Eccles stole eight government mules from Camp Douglas and started with them for Montana. They were followed by the soldiers, and both of them were overhauled and killed in the Malad Valley. That was the last of poor Frank Mathis.

About the time the Indians were at their worst, a small train of emigrants came through on their way to California. They were told by all of the station agents that it was not safe for so few people to travel through the country at that time, and that they had better stop until more trains came up. They said they were well armed, and thought they could stand off the Indians all right. At that time

I was riding from Shell Creek through Egan Canyon to Ruby Valley. We all knew that this train would be attacked somewhere between Deep Creek and Ruby Valley.

We, who were acquainted with the Gosiute Indians, could tell when they were going to make a raid, for they would make signs on the mountains with smokes by day and fires by night, and so by these signs we knew that this train would be attacked as they were going through some of the bad canyons on the route. Egan Canyon was about the worst of these. It was a narrow canyon about six miles long, with cliffs on each side from three hundred to one thousand feet high, so that you could turn neither to the right nor to the left. This canyon was a dread to all that had to go through it.

The train of emigrants entered this canyon just ahead of me. I rode very fast that day to try to overtake them before they got to the worst part of it, but just before I reached them I could hear shooting, then I knew that the Indians were onto them. I stopped a moment to listen, when I saw two men coming. They were bare-headed and were running for dear life. When they got near, they said, "Go back. The whole company has been killed but us." They passed me and went on.

After a little while I could hear no more shooting, and I started and rode slowly up the canyon. At every turn around a point I would stop and listen and have a look. Soon the wagons came in sight and I stopped and looked a while, but I could not see any-thing of the Indians. Then I went up to the wagons, and such a terrible sight I never saw before. Dead men, women, and children were strewn all around the wagons. The tugs of the harness had been cut and the mules and horses were gone. I rode to the next point, and as no Indians were in sight I knew they had gone, so I went back to the wagons to see if any little children might have been overlooked by the Indians.

One woman I found lying by the side of the road who was not quite dead. She was lying on her side with her face up and her black hair spread out over a small sage brush. She gave one gasp as I rode up. I spoke to her, but she made not another move. She was dead. I cannot describe my feelings as I sat there on my horse, but I know the tears ran down my cheeks very fast as I gazed on this scene. I saw four little babes, all under one year old, lying by a wagon wheel where they had been killed, and I could see blood on the hub of the wheel where their little heads had been struck.

After I found that they were all dead, I could not stand it to look upon this dreadful scene any longer, so I started on my way. When I got out of the canyon and saw where the Indians had turned off the road, I did not spare my horse until I reached the station. The station keeper sent a messenger to Ruby Valley, where the soldiers were, and they came and buried the dead emigrants.

Pony Express saddle and mochila, described in detail on pages 84-85.

CHAPTER 16 — **Johnston Punishes The Indians**

The Indians became so troublesome that the soldiers from Camp Floyd were called out to stop their dreadful work. I got a letter from Major Egan directing me to meet him at Camp Floyd as soon as I could get there, for they wanted me for interpreter and guide for the soldiers. I started at once and made two hundred miles in three days. When I reached Camp Floyd, General Albert Sidney Johnston was all ready to start out against the Indians with four companies of soldiers. We traveled west and crossed the Great American Desert in the night, so as not to be seen by the Indians.

The soldiers stayed at Fish Springs and sent me out with three other scouts to see if we could find any signs of the Indians we were after. We took only two days' rations with us. The first day we met with no success, so the next morning we separated. I sent two of the scouts to circle around to the south, and took with me a young man by the name of Johnson, and we went northwest. That afternoon we saw two Indians crossing a valley. We kept out of sight but followed them until night, and saw them go into a small bunch of cedars. We left our horses and slipped up as close to them as we could without letting them see us.

When we got pretty near to them, I recognized in one of the Indians my old friend Yaiabi; but not feeling sure that he would be glad to see me, I told Johnson to have his shooting-irons ready and I would go up to them and see what they would do. As soon as they saw me coming they jumped up and drew their bows. I began to talk to them in their language. Yaiabi did not recognize me at first, and demanded to know what I was doing there. I told him I wanted water. He said there was no water except a very little they had brought with them. They asked me if I was alone. I told them that another young man was with me, then I called to Johnson to come up.

After Yaiabi found out who I was he felt better, for they were very uneasy at first. When I asked him how he came to be there, he said they had been out to a little lake to see some Parowan Indians that were camped there. I asked him what the Indians were doing there. He said they were waiting for some more of the

Pocatello Indians to come, and as soon as they arrived they were going to burn all the stations and kill all of the riders and station keepers. I asked him if he was going with them. He said he was not. Then I asked him why he had been over to see those Indians. He said that the Parowan Indians had stolen his sister's little boy two years before, and he went out to see if he could find the child. I asked if he had found it. He said, "No. They have sold it to the white folks." "Do you know when the Indians they are looking for would be there?" He replied that they would be there the next night.

I knew it was a big day's ride back to where the Indians were gathering and I knew it was a hard day's ride to the place where the soldiers were camped. I did not know what was best for me to do. I had these two Indians and I did not want to let them go, for I was afraid they would skip back and let the others know that the soldiers were after them. Here we were a big day's ride to water, and our horses had had none since early morning, so I decided that it would be better to take the Indians to headquarters and let General Johnston decide what to do. I told Yaiabi my plans. He said he did not want to go to the soldiers, for he was afraid of them. I told him I would see that the soldiers did him no harm. He said, "Yagaiki, you have known me ever since you were a little boy, and you never knew of my doing anything bad in your life." I told him I knew that he had always been a good Indian, "but now you know that the soldiers are after those bad Indians and intend to kill the last one of them, and if I let you go, you will go to them and tell them that the soldiers are after them. Then if General Johnston should find out what I had done he would think I stood in with the Indians and would have me shot, so, you see, you must go with us to the soldiers' camp."

The Indian that was with Yaiabi said he would not go to the soldiers' camp, and started to get his bow, but I had my pistol on him in a jiffy and told him to stand. He stopped, and I kept him there while Johnson gathered up their bows and arrows. When I told them to get ready to start, Yaiabi said they were tired and would like to stay there until morning, but I said that our horses were so thirsty, we had better travel in the cool of the night or we would not be able to get them to camp, so we set out for Fish Springs.

I told Johnson to tie the bows and arrows to his saddle and to keep a close watch over them; Yaiabi mounted my horse while I walked and led the horse. When I got tired of walking, I changed places with Yaiabi, and then young Johnson walked and let the other Indian ride his horse. In this way we traveled until morning. When daylight came, I gave the bows and arrows to young Johnson and told him to go to General Johnston's camp as soon as possible and send us fresh horses and some water. In about six hours he came back to us, accompanied by two soldiers with some water and two extra horses for the Indians to ride. By traveling pretty fast, we reached camp at one o'clock that day.

General Johnston was very much pleased with me for bringing the two Indians in. At the sight of so many soldiers the Indians were very uneasy, but after they had been given something to eat and saw that they were not going to be hurt, they felt much better.

The general was very much pleased by the way Yaiabi talked. He called him a good Indian, and said he believed he was telling the truth. I told Yaiabi what the general said. General Johnston told me to get a little rest, for he wanted me to start out again that night if I would. I lay down and had a little sleep, and when I got up he told me that I was to go to the lake and see if Yaiabi had told the truth; and if everything was all right, to send back word as soon as I could by one of the scouts that he would send with me. He said for me to do all my traveling at night and keep under cover in the day time, and to meet him as soon as I could at a spring about half way between where we were and the Indians. Then on the following night he would move his soldiers to another spring which Yaiabi had told about, and which was within six miles of the lake where the Indians were gathering.

About dark, three of us started with four days' rations. I rode the little pinto pony on this trip, the first I had ridden him for a long time. We traveled all night and reached the first spring just at daybreak. I knew it would be a hard night's ride to go from here to the lake and then reach Yaiabi's spring in the mountains before daylight.

About midnight we arrived at the north end of the lake, which was only a mile and a half long and half a mile wide. I had my two scouts stop there while I wrapped a red blanket around me and went on foot to find out what I could about the Indian camp.I had gone only a few steps when I came to a lot of horses, and as I was passing around them I heard an Indian speak to his horse. He was hobbling his horse. He had staked him but was afraid he might hurt himself in the rope, and he had ridden him pretty hard that day. I asked him if he had come with the Pocatello Indians. He said he had, and that seventeen others came with him. "We will start burning the stations, then, soon," I said. "Were you at the council tonight?" he asked. I told him I was not at the council, that I had been following a horse that had started back. He said that at the council it was decided that the Parowans were to go to Ruby Valley and burn and kill everything they came to; and that the Pocatello Indians and the Gosiutes were to start at Ibapah and burn towards the east. I asked him when we were to start from there. He said, "In four days." We were walking towards their camp as we talked, so as soon as I found out all I wanted to know I said that I had forgotten my rope and would have to go back for it. So I parted company with my Indian friend. He was a Shoshone, and he thought I was another. When I got out of his sight, I wasn't long getting back to where I had left the boys, and in a very short time one of them was carrying the news to the army.

The other scout and I went to find the spring Yaiabi had told me about. We got well into the mountains before daylight, and when it was light enough to see, we found the spring up a very rough canyon. We staked our horses so they could get plenty to eat and then crawled off into the willows for a good nap.

That afternoon I climbed a high mountain nearby to see which would be the best way to go from there to the Indians' camp in the night. After I had studied the lay of the country pretty well, I went back to the horses, ate a little cold lunch, and when it commenced to get dark, we struck out to meet General Johnston at the appointed place.

We did not travel very fast, for I knew we would reach the place before the soldiers could get there. We were at the spring about two hours before day light, and had a good nap before General Johnston came. When he got to us he wanted to know if I thought it safe to make a fire to boil some coffee. I told him I thought there was no danger, so we made a small fire and had a good cup of coffee, then we all lay down for a little sleep.

About sundown, the packers began loading the hundred pack mules we had with us, and we got started just about dark for the Yaiabi spring which was about six miles north of the Indians' camp. We reached the spring in good time, and were all unpacked before dawn.

After breakfast, General Johnston and I went up on to the mountain so that he could see the Indian camp. He had a good pair of field glasses and could see everything very plainly. He asked if I knew anything about that bunch of willows he could see a little to the west of their camp. I told him I knew it very well, for when the express first started it came this way, and we had a station right where the Indian camp is now, so I had been there many times. He said, "Then you can take me to it in the night?" I told him I could, and pointed out to him the way we would have to go. He told me he wanted to make the attack the next morning at daybreak. We went back to camp, and found all the soldiers asleep, except the guard; and in a very short time we were rolled in our blankets and dreaming of the time when all the Indians would be good Indians.

When I awoke that afternoon, I saw General Johnston and his staff going up the mountain to where we had been that morning. They got back to camp just before sundown, and held a hasty council with the remainder of the officers, then orders were given to pack up, and we got in line just at dark. I told General Johnston he would have to take his men down this canyon in single file, and in some places we would have to travel along the side of the mountain over very narrow trails; that we would have to climb above high cliffs, and pass through some very dangerous places. He said for me to go ahead, and when I came to the bad places to dismount and they would follow suit. We had about two miles to go before we would come to the bad places, and when I got off the next man would get off and so on down the line. By doing this, we got down the canyon very well, except that three of our pack mules rolled over a cliff and were killed.

The head of the company got out of the canyon about eleven o'clock that night. We were within six or seven hundred yards of the Indian camp, for the lake lay almost at the foot of the mountains. As the soldiers came down they formed into lines, and General Johnston and I started to find the bunch of willows we had seen from the top of the mountain. We soon found it, and went back to the soldiers. The general said that was all he wanted with me until after the fight, and for me to take care of the two Indians we had with us. So I got Yaiabi and his friend, and we climbed a small hill not far away, where we could see the fight when it commenced.

The soldiers didn't all get out of the canyon until about three o'clock in the morning, and the pack train was not all out when daylight came. In the meantime, General Johnston had strung the soldiers around the Indian camp.

Just as day was breaking, an old Indian chief started a fire in front of his wickiup, and was standing there calling to some of the other Indians, when a soldier shot him without orders. Then the fight commenced. Oh, my! how the guns did rattle! It was almost too dark at first for me to see much of the fight, but it was getting lighter all the time. I asked Yaiabi if he was not afraid that his people would all be killed. He said he was a Mormon, and those Indians were all bad Indians, so he did not care very much which whipped—the Indians or the soldiers. As we were coming down the canyon that night, the General gave me his field glasses to carry for him and I still had them.

Along the edge of the lake grew a lot of bulrushes. Soon after the firing began, I could see the papooses running into these rushes and hiding. From the volleys that were fired it got so smoky that I could not see very plainly, but the shooting soon stopped, and as the smoke raised, I could see everything that was going on. By this time, they were in a terrible mixup,and were fighting fiercely, the soldiers with their bayonets and sabers, and the Indians with their clubs, axes, and knives. I could see little children not over five or six years old with sticks fighting like wild cats. I saw a soldier and an Indian that had clinched in a death struggle. They had each other by the hair of the head, and I saw a squaw run up to them with an ax and strike the soldier in the back and he sank to the ground, then she split his head with the ax. While she was doing this, a soldier ran a bayonet through her, and that is the way it was going over the whole battle ground. And, what a noise they made! with the kids squalling, the squaws yelling, the bucks yelping, the dogs barking, and the officers giving their orders to the soldiers.

This was the worst battle and the last one that I ever saw. It lasted about two hours, and during that short period of time, every Indian, squaw, and papoose, and every dog was killed. After the battle, I was sent to bring up the baggage wagons to haul our wounded to Camp Floyd. General Johnston made me a present of one hundred dollars, and I was just fool enough to take it.

As we were on our way back to Camp Floyd with the wounded, and were passing through a rocky canyon, we were fired at by some straggling Indian, and I was shot through my left arm about half way between the wrist and the elbow. The same bullet that went through my arm killed a soldier at my side. The one shot was all we heard, and we did not even see the one who fired it. I have sometimes wondered if that bullet was not sent especially for me.

That spring the great war between the North and the South broke out, and General Johnston sold all of the government cattle and wagons very cheap, and went back east with his pack mules. I bought a yoke of oxen for eighteen dollars and a new wagon for ten. There must have been as many as ten thousand oxen bought at from twenty-five to fifty dollars a yoke. That summer the gold mines were opened in Montana, and everything had to be hauled with ox teams, and the same oxen we had bought for eighteen dollars, were worth from one hundred and fifty to two hundred dollars a yoke. The poor people that had been living on greens and lumpy-dick for two or three years, now began to get very wealthy, and proud. The young ladies began to wear calico dresses, and I even saw young men who could afford to wear calico shirts and soldiers' blue overcoats and smoke store tobacco. A few even got so wealthy that they apostatized.

CHAPTER 17 — **The Overland Stage**

Just before the soldiers left Camp Floyd, the daily stage started from St. Joseph, Missouri, for Sacramento, California, and a telegraph line was put through. This stopped the pony express, and I started to drive the stage-coach from Austin, Nevada, to the Carson sink. I drove there that summer and winter, and the next spring I was sent to drive from Carson City to Virginia City, Nevada.

I left Austin with two coaches and six gray horses, one coach trailed behind the other, and when I got to Carson City, oh, how green I was! It is a wonder that the crickets and grasshoppers had not eaten me up long ago, I was so green. I never had been in a city before, except three or four times in Salt Lake City. This was the first Gentile town I was ever in, and I was very much afraid of Gentiles, anyhow.

Well, I got to Carson City about ten o'clock one very fine morning in June. The mail agent met me just as I entered the town, and told me to drive to Tim Smith's big rock stable and put up my horses. He told me that the line I was driving on was in dispute, and he would have to go to Salt Lake City to see who had the right of way. He said: "You can stay over there until you hear from me, and you can board in that hotel across the street. I am going to start for Salt Lake right away." So he left me alone, seven hundred miles from home and among strangers. If he had left me in an Indian camp, I would have felt all right, but to be left away out there among a lot of hostile Gentiles, was more that I could bear.

I put my horses up, and while I was sitting out by the side of the stable, I saw a man come out of the hotel. He had on a white cap and a white apron that reached from his chin to his feet. In each hand he had a big, round, brass thing. He pounded these together and made a fearful racket. Now, I had never seen a hotel before, to say nothing of being in one, and as the men that worked in the barn came rushing past me, I asked one of them what was up. He said, "Dinner." I got up and went over to the hotel, and when I went in, I never saw such a sight before. They had tables all over the house, and people were rushing in and sitting down to them.

I slipped in and took off my hat and stood by the side of the door waiting for some one to come up and ask me to sit down at a table, but nobody came. I stood there a while longer, and saw others come in and sit down at the tables without being asked, so I went sneaking up to a table and stood there, and as nobody asked me to sit down, I pretty soon sat down anyhow. A waiter came up and began to mutter something to me. I said, "What?" He got it off again. I told him that I did not know what he said, so he went out and brought me something to eat. Just then a big, black-looking fellow came in and sat down on the opposite side of my table. A man that was sitting close by me said to him, "Well, Jack, I hear that you have enlisted." Jack said, "Yes, sir." "Where are you going?" "I am going to Salt Lake." "What are going to do there?" "I am going to cut the heart out of the first Mormon I come across." Well, sir, that finished my dinner. Just as he said that, I was taking a drink of coffee, and it all went down my Sunday throat and very nearly choked me to death before I could get away from the table. I went out and I thought, "By gum! I won't let anybody here know that I am a Mormon, for if they find out that I am a Mormon they will kill me in a minute."

I went over to the stable and sat down, and then I began thinking of home. I didn't go back to the hotel that night for any supper, and when I went to bed, the fleas turned loose on me and I thought they would eat what was left of me before morning. You may talk about the persecutions of Nauvoo, but they are not in it as compared with my misery and woe at that time. I didn't sleep a wink that night, and when morning came I was hungry, sleepy, tired, and homesick.

When the man with the white cap and apron came out that morning with his brass plates and began to make another racket with them, I went over and walked right in, and turned around and walked right out again. I met one of the stable men and he asked me if I had been to breakfast. I said I had not. He said, "Come on in," and took me by the arm and we went in and sat down at a table. The waiter came up and got off the same thing that he said the day before, and the man that was with me told him to fetch it along. I told the waiter to bring me the same. Well, I ate two or three breakfasts that morning to make up for what I had lost, and then I felt very much better.

After breakfast we went back to the stable, and pretty soon Tim Smith came in and said, "Young man, it may be three weeks before the right of way is settled, and if you want to go to work in the stable I will give you three dollars a day." I told him, "All right, I would like the job," so I went to work right then.

Tim Smith was a one-armed man, and he had fourteen hostlers and a clerk that worked in the stable. The office was in one corner of the stable and a young man by the name of Billy Green was the clerk. He had charge of the men and was very kind and good to me.

I was afraid to go out at night, so I stayed in the stable and helped Billy. The other men would quit at six o'clock and Billy had to do the rest of the work. It was a very large stable, holding over one hundred horses, and there was, therefore, quite a lot of work to do after dark. Sometimes we would have to hook up three or four teams, and quite often a lot of travelers would come in after night. All this work was left for the clerk to do, and I would stay and help him. One night Mr. Smith was in the stable talking to Billy, and I heard him say, "That Mormon is as good a hand as you have here, isn't he?" Billy said, "He is the best man we ever had here." I wondered how in thunder he knew I was a Mormon.

During the next day or two, first one and then another would ask how things were in Salt Lake. One day I asked one of them how he knew I was from Salt Lake. He said, "Everybody in town knows that you are a Mormon; I know lots of Mormons, and they are very good people, and I like them first rate." I asked him if all the Gentiles thought that way. He said most of them did. Then I told him what that black jack said in the hotel. He laughed, and said the fellow was just bragging, and if I had stepped up to him and told him I was a Mormon, it would have scared him to death.

Well, after I found out that everyone knew I was a Mormon and had not hurt me yet, I began to get brave. But it taught me a good lesson. I have not been in a place since, but that I have felt proud to defend the principles of Mormonism, and I hope that I shall always feel that way.

When Saturday came we all went to the race track and paid a dollar a piece to see the bull fight and horse races. We selected high seats overlooking the bull pen, and saw a man in the pen with a small red flag in one hand and a big knife in the other. When the bull made a dash at the man, he would step to one side, and as the bull passed, he would jab at him with the big knife. He kept this up until the poor bull got so weak from the loss of blood that he could hardly stand up. Then the great brute of a man jumped on the beast's back and cut large pieces of flesh from the poor, wounded thing's shoulders, and stuck them in his mouth, and looked up at the people and laughed, just to be funny. I felt as though I would give another dollar just to have a shot at the smart aleck. That was the last time I ever went to see a bull fight.

I spent my early life with the Indians, but I never saw them use a dumb beast as cruelly as that idiot did that bull. I wondered how people could look on that scene and laugh like they did. As I sat there looking on at that wicked business, I overheard a lady (maybe she was a lady) say that she had not missed a bull fight that summer, and she would not miss one for anything. I thought, "You poor thing, I wonder if you have any children; if you have, I feel sorry for them." Talk about the Indians! They are way ahead of lots of white people in a good many ways.

Well, the agent finally came back from Salt Lake, and I started to driving the stage from Carson to Virginia City. At that time Virginia City was booming. Two or three men were killed every day. I had not driven here very long before I saw a man hanged at what they called Golden Gate. I don't remember what he had done, but I saw him hanged, anyway. They drove a team under the gate and put a board on top of the bed of the wagon and made the man stand on the board. Then they put a rope around his neck and tied it to the cross bar of the gate, and drove the team out from under him and let the man drop. The fall did not break his neck, and he just hung there until he strangled to death. I drove the stage on this route for three months, and then got tired of staging; quit and went home.

In the meantime, my mother had moved to Cache Valley, and I went up there and stopped all winter with her; and oh my! would you believe it? I fell in love with a girl, and oh, how I did love her! I thought she was one of the sweetest creatures I ever saw. I felt just like I could eat her up, and I have been sorry ever since that I didn't do it. We spent the time delightfully for about a month, when I got hurt. I was riding a horse very fast, and ran onto some ice that I did not see. The horse slipped and fell, and my head struck the ice so hard that it nearly killed me. I was carried home, brain fever came on, and I lay in bed until spring.

The place in my head, where I was shot with the flint arrow, broke out again, and I did not know what I was doing part of the time; but this dear girl stayed by my bedside day after day, and could not be persuaded to leave me. I would try to get her to go and lie down, but she would not. One day her stepfather came and took her up in his arms and carried her home and put her to bed, but that night she was back again. One day they thought I was dying, and she took on so that two men carried her home and her folks had to hold her all night to keep her there. The next morning I was much better, and then I got well fast. She came as soon as she could get away from her friends, and stayed with me until I was nearly well.

After spring had come, I was quite well, and as my money was getting short, I thought I would go back and drive the stage a few months, save some money, and come back and marry my girl. So I kissed her goodbye and left her. I got my job back, saved my money, and when winter came, I sold all but one of my horses and bought cattle. I had gathered quite a bunch of calves and yearlings, and left them with a man by the name of Frank Weaver. Then I hastened to see my girl to tell her that I was ready now for matrimony. When I got home I found her plump and sweet, and oh! how pretty she was.

The people of Cache Valley used to take their surplus cattle on to what was known as the Promontory for the winter. I had been home only a few days, when the people got scared that the Indians were going to raid their cattle which were over there, so they made a call for one hundred men to go over and run the Indians off. My elder brother was called to go, but his wife taking sick very suddenly, he got me to go in his place. He said that I would only be gone five days. I kissed my girl goodbye again, and went off with the men to guard the cattle. I little thought it would be the last time I would ever kiss her, but it was. When we got to the Promontory we found no Indians, and I was getting ready to go right back home, when word came that we were to stay until spring. I told the captain that I came in place of my brother, that I had no interest there, that I had left my own cattle with a man for only two weeks, and that I would have to go back at once to attend to them. The captain said he was told to keep every man there, but he would write to Brother Benson and see what he would say about it. Well, Brother Benson saw the bishop from our town and the bishop told him to keep me there for I was nothing but a renegade, and if I were kept there, the people would have more peace.

I soon learned that I could not get permission to leave. I sent for my brother to come and take my place, for it was he that was called, not me; but the bishop told him if he did go to take my place, it would not release me, for they would keep me there anyway. So I was in for it, and would have to make the best of it.

In about two weeks I received a letter from my mother in which she said that I was about to lose my girl, for she was going in second wife to an old man that stood high in the church. I lost no time in writing to the young lady, and the next mail brought my letter back to me. I wrote again and sent them both to her, but they came back. I wrote again, and the letter came back. I then wrote to mother and enclosed a letter to the girl, and asked mother to give it to the girl herself. Mother gave it to her, but in a few days it came back. Then mother told me not to write to the girl any more, for this man was working very hard to injure me in her sight, and it would do no good for me to write to her any more.

After I had been on the Promontory for two months, I received a letter from Mr. Weaver stating that the Indians had run off his cattle and all of mine along with them, and that if I would hurry to him we might be able to get some of them back. I showed the letter to the captain and asked him if I could go. He said he could not say for me to go, but when I asked him if he would try to stop me if I went anyhow, he said he would not, but that I had better slip off in the night. Well, when dark came, I hit the trail and rode all that night, and a little after sunrise I got to the Bear River and stayed there until noon, then I started from there and reached my home town just before sundown.

Of course, I went that night to see the girl that used to be mine. Her folks would hardly speak to me, and she sat there with her head down and would not look up. Her mother, or rather the woman that raised her, said, "You need not come here for my daughter is going to marry Brother Frost. He is a good man, and very well off." I asked the young lady if that was so. She said it was. Well, my kind friends, I cannot begin to tell you how I felt just then. I wanted to fall through the floor and never come back. I asked the girl if I could have a talk with her, but the old woman said, "No, you can't, and I want you to get out of this house." I hesitated a minute, and then the old gal went to the door and said,"Come, get out of here, and that mighty quick, too." Well, I got out.

The next day was Sunday, and I went to meeting. The bishop called me to the stand to report how things were at the Promontory. I told them everything was all right, that the cattle looked fine, and the men were all well. Then the Bishop got up and said that he did not know whether I told the truth or not. He said he had received a letter the night before to the effect that I had run away from the cattle guards without asking permission from anybody, and had therefore, betrayed my trust, and he could not believe one word I said. He called me a stagedriver, and said I was worse than a Gentile, and that he would not trust me to carry guts to a bear across the street! And, if he had a daughter, he would rather follow her to the grave than have her marry a traitor such as I. He said, if he was in my place he would sneak off and hide where he would not be seen by anybody he knew.

After he had run out of something to say, he sat down, and then my rival got up, and said he could bear his testimony to what the Bishop had said, for he knew that he had spoken the truth. He said, "Brethern and Sisters, what do you think of a man with whom you have trusted your property for protection, to sneak off in the night and leave it to the mercy of hostile Indians? If I was a young lady, I would hate to put myself under his protection, but I do not believe that such a worthless scoundrel can ever get a wife. I certainly hope he cannot!"

I could not stand it to hear any more of this talk, so I got up and went out. I do not know what was said after I came away, nor do I care, for my heart was full of sorrow. A mist of darkness seemed to come over my eyes, and I did not know where I was until I found myself in my mother's house. I knew that I had never wronged a man in my life, and I knew that all of this talk was to get my girl from me.

My dear old mother had left the meeting house before I did, and I found her in the house crying. I said, "Mother, I am sorry that I have brought all of this trouble upon you." She said, "My son, I do not blame you. I would have done the same." My mother was a good Latter-Day Saint, and she gave me a good, long talk for she knew the danger I was in. I had been away from my people so much she was afraid that the way I had been talked to by these men, might drive me out of the church entirely, but I am thankful to say that it did not.

Well, I went to see about my little bunch of stock, but they were all gone. I never got one of them back. I did not care to stay in that town any longer, so I gave mother what little money I had left from my savings for my wedding stake, and started for the road again. I had lost my cattle, but the worst of all, I had lost my girl.

Buffaloes

CHAPTER 18 — **A Terrible Journey**

That summer I worked for John Balwinkle of Salt Lake City, as his wagon boss, and freighted from Carson City, Nevada, to Salt Lake City. The summer passed without anything happening worth speaking of. That fall a mail route was established from Salt Lake City to Bannock, Montana, and Mr. Smith, of Salt Lake City, obtained the contract to carry this mail. Knowing that I was a good hand he induced me to drive the stage from Salt Lake north, that winter for him.

We started out some time in November with a wagon load of dry goods to trade for horses along the road. We also had one light coach, two buggies, and seven passengers.

As we were traveling quietly along between Ogden and Brigham City, whom do you think we met? In a wagon were my — oh! no, not my girl—but Mr. Frost and his girl going to Salt Lake to be married, and as they drove up they both said, "How do you do, Nick?" but I was too thunder struck to speak to them. I guess they thought I was mad, but I felt—well, no matter how I felt, I just felt and that was all.

When we got to the little town where Mr. Frost lived, we stopped there to buy a few horses, and I drove over to my mother's to stay with her a few days. In the meantime, Mr. Frost and his new wife got back. In two or three days, Mrs. Frost, number two, came to my mother's house, and as I happened to be there alone, she came up to me and said that she was very sorry for what she had done, and she cried bitterly. I said, "Mrs. Frost, it is too late now for you to repent. You are a married woman, and you have a good man, and he is very well off. He is a good Church man, and a better man than I am, and now that you have married him, you must stay with him and make him a good wife. I am nothing but a stagedriver and worse than a Gentile, and not fit to carry guts to a bear! I feel sorry for you Mrs. Frost, I loved you very dearly, and would have married you, but now it is too late!"

She said her husband was not half as good as I was, and that she could never love him like she did me. She said her folks and the Bishop and all of the neighbors had turned loose on her and she saw no peace until she promised to marry him. When the Bishop and Mr. Frost were abusing me in the church that time, she said she decided then to make up with me if she could, for she knew she was the cause of it all. She said she came to my mother's house to see me, but was just too late, for I had gone, and she was ashamed to write to me. After that talk, we shook hands and parted forever. I thought to myself that if I was just half as mean a man as Mr. Frost that I could bring to him a great deal of shame and misery.

Mr. Smith had bought all the horses in that town he could get, so we went on and stopped a few days at Soda Springs to see about making a mail station there. At that time quite a large company of soldiers was wintering in the town. Mr. Smith said he would make me division agent to have charge of the line from there to Salt Lake City, but I was to go on with him to Bannock so as to become acquainted with the route. When we got to Bannock, winter had set in. It snowed very hard while we were there, and kept snowing all of the way back. By the time we got to Snake River, the snow was deep, and there was no place where we could buy feed for our horses. We had two passengers with us, and Mr. Smith had not provided us with supplies enough to last us half way back to Soda Springs.

We could not travel as fast as he had planned on account of the deep snow, and the horses were getting very weak for want of food. For these reasons, we could not come back on the road we went out on, so we kept down the Snake River to where the Black Foot empties into it. There we ate the last of our provisions and were still one hundred miles from any place where we could get more, and the snow was becoming deeper every day. When we got up the Ross Fork Canyon we had to stop for the night. Here three of the horses gave out, and we had to leave them and one of the buggies. We had left the coach at Beaver Canyon.

The next morning we started before breakfast, for we had eaten the last thing the morning before. The snow kept falling all the time, and by noon, it was at least three feet deep. All of us but the driver would walk ahead of the team to break the road. We had four horses on the buggy, and it would push up the snow ahead of it until it would run into the buggy over the dash-board and sides. Well, that day two more of the horses gave out and we had to leave them, but we reached the head of the Portneuf.

That night we all turned out and kicked the snow off of a little space so the poor horses could get some frozen grass, but it was so very cold and they were so tired that they would not eat very much.

The next morning we made another early start, and Mr. Smith said we would get to Soda Springs that day, but I knew we could not get there that day, nor the next day, either. I told the passengers that if we were to leave the buggy, we might make it in two days, but the way we were fooling along with the worn-out horses, we never would get there. They told Mr. Smith what I said and he gave me a going over for it. He said I had scared the passengers nearly to death and he wanted me to stop it.

Well, by noon that day we came to the road we had come out on, but Mr. Smith did not know the place and wanted to follow the road over which we had traveled in going to Bannock. I told him the way we wanted to go was south, but the way he wanted to go was north. He told me I was off my base, and to shut my mouth. I said, "I will go to Soda Springs and you can go to the other place," so I took what I wanted out of the buggy and started off, but I had not gone far when I heard some one calling me. It was so foggy and the frost was falling so fast that I could see only a few yards, and as I hesitated about going back, one of the passengers came up to me and asked me if I was sure I knew where I was going, and begged me to come back to the buggy.

One of the passengers was a large, strong Irishman, and appeared to be well educated; the other was a sickly looking Englishman. I don't remember their names, but they called each other Mike and Jimmy. I went back to the buggy and Mike saw that I did not want anything to say to Mr. Smith, so he did the talking. He questioned Mr. Smith and then me for quite a while, and then he said he believed that I was right. He told the driver to turn the team around and follow me, which was done, although it made Mr. Smith very angry.

After turning south we had not traveled over four miles, when one of the remaining horses gave out and we could not get the poor thing to move, so we had to leave the buggy. We went on about three or four hundred yards to a clump of quaking-asp, and built a large fire. When we all got warm, I went to bring up the horses and buggy and when I got back to the fire, Mr. Smith and Mike were quarreling. Mr. Smith said that we were going away from Soda Springs, and that he intended to turn and go the other way.

It was already quite dark, but we could travel just as well in the night as in the day, for we could not see very far anyhow on account of the fog. I said I knew I was right and for all those who wanted to go to Soda Springs, to fall in line, for I was going to start right then. I went to the buggy and got a pair of buffalo moccasins I had there, put them on, and started down the trail. Mike said, "Hold on, I will go with you." Then Jimmy said he was not going to stay there and starve to death, that he would go with us, too. So the three of us went our way and left Mr. Smith and the driver standing there in the fog and snow.

It was about eleven o'clock at night when we left the buggy, and we did not feel much like pushing our way through the snow, for we had already walked many miles that day, and had been three days without anything to eat. Mike said he would take the lead to break the path, I was to come next, and Jimmy was to follow me. There was about a foot of snow with a crust on it, not quite hard enough to hold one up, and on top of this was about two feet of frost, so you see it was very hard traveling.

We decided that we must not stop to rest more than ten minutes at any time, and that at least one of us must keep awake, for we knew that if all went to sleep at the same time we would never again wake up.

It was a bitter cold night. There was no wind blowing, and it was very still, not even a bird, rabbit, or coyote was to be seen or heard—not a sound but the ringing in our ears. By this time I had gotten over being hungry, but I was very thirsty, and I had eaten so much frost to satisfy my thirst that my mouth and tongue had become so sore and swollen that I could scarcely speak. Jimmy was so used up by this time that we could hardly get him to move after we had stopped to rest, and Mike would sometimes carry him a little ways, but Jimmy said it hurt him, so Mike would have to put him down.

Well, night was coming on again, and I do not think we had traveled over three or four miles that day, but we were doing the best we could. About four o'clock in the afternoon we stopped for a few minutes' rest, I settled back in the snow and put one foot out for Jimmy to lay his head on. Soon it was time to start again and I shook Jimmy, but he did not stir. Mike had already started, so I pulled my foot out from under Jimmy's head, and as I did so his head sank in the snow. Then I took hold of him and tried to raise him, but I could not. I called for Mike, and when he came back, we raised Jimmy up, and I saw that he was dead.

I cannot tell you what happened in the next half hour, but from what he said in his sorrow over Jimmy's death, I learned for the first time that Jimmy had married Mike's sister. After a while I scraped the snow away clear to the ground, and while doing this, I found a dry thistle stalk about fourteen inches long. I took the dead man's coat off, laid him in the hole, spread the coat over his face, and covered him with snow, making a little mound like a grave. I tore some of the lining from my coat, tied it to the thistle, and stuck it over the grave.

It was hard work to get Mike started again. He said we were all going to die anyway, and he would rather stay there with Jimmy. I told him we were nearly to Soda Springs, and if he would try, we could get there; but he said I had told him that so much that he now believed I did not know where Soda Springs was. He said I had told him when we first started from the buggy that it was only thirty miles and he knew we had traveled over seventy miles by this time. I told him I knew if we traveled as fast as we could that we would be in Soda Springs in two hours.

We talked there a long time, and I began to think that Mike had really made up his mind not to try to go on any more, when just before dark he seemed to take fresh courage. He jumped up and started out so fast that I could not keep up with him. After a little while he stopped and sat down again in the snow, and when I caught up to him I found him sound asleep. I let the poor fellow sleep a few minutes, and then I had the hardest time to get him awake again. After pulling and shaking him, I finally got him on his feet, but he would start off the wrong way. Then I would get hold of him and start him off right, but he would turn around and go the wrong way. He did not know what he was doing, so I had to take the lead. Then he would stop and I would have to go back and get him.

After a little time he seemed to come to himself, and took the lead again for about a mile, and then he sat down in the snow and said he was done for, and that he would not go another step. I did all I could to arouse him, but he would not stir. He gave me a small memorandum book and a little buckskin bag full of gold dust, and told me he had a sister living in Mississippi, and that I would find her address in the book. I talked to him a long time to try to get him to come with me, but he would not move.

I saw that it was of no use, and that I would have to leave him or lie down in the snow and die with him. This I felt like doing, but for the sake of my mother and sisters, I thought I would make one more effort to reach the town, so I left him and had gone about seventy-five yards, when I stumbled over something and fell headlong into the snow. I cleared the snow away from my face, and sat there thinking about home and how badly my mother would feel if she knew where I was, and how easy it would be to lie there in the snow and go to sleep.

Drowsiness had nearly overcome me when, suddenly, I heard the faraway tinkle of a bell. I knew then that I was not far from Soda Springs. I jumped up and ran back to Mike as fast as I could go, and when I got to him, I found him stretched out on the snow with his hands folded over his breast and sound asleep. I had the hardest work to get him awake enough to tell him about the bell; the sound had ceased. He would not believe what I told him about it, so I could not get him to come with me.

I went back to the place where I first heard the bell and sat down again. In a few minutes I heard it louder than before. Then I rushed back to Mike and found him awake and when I got him to listen, he heard the bell this time, too. He jumped up and started so fast in the direction of the sound that I could not keep up with him. When he would see me falling behind, he would come back and take hold of my hands and pull me along. I begged him to let me alone and told him it hurt me to be jerked over the snow in that way. Then he would kick the snow and say that he would make a good road for me if I would only come.

We had traveled this way for about half an hour, when the fog raised a little and we saw, a short distance ahead of us, a faint light. He then left me and started for the light as fast as he could go. I tried to follow, but slipped and fell, and found that I could not get up again. Many times I tried to rise, but fell back every time. I thought if I lay there a while and rested, then perhaps I could get up and go on. I guess I must have fallen asleep, for the first thing I knew, two men had hold of me and were carrying me to the hotel where we had seen the light. Mike had reached there and had told the men in the hotel that one of his companions was dead and another was out there just a little ways dying in the snow.

When we got to the door, Mike was standing there with a big glass of whiskey in his hand. He said, "Down this, old boy, and it will be the making of you," but I could not bear the smell of liquor, to say nothing of drinking it.

They sat me down in a chair near the stove, but the heat soon made me feel sick and I had to move as far from the fire as I could get. The cook brought something for us to eat, but my mouth and tongue hurt me so that I could hardly eat anything. Then the light began to grow dim and I could feel them shaking me and could hear them talking to me, but I could not answer for my tongue was so swollen. Then I seemed to go away off.

The next thing I remember, they were telling me that the doctors had come, and I saw that the house was full of people. They told me Mike's feet were frozen and that two men were holding them in a tub of cold water to try to draw the frost out. The doctor was pulling my moccasins off and I heard him say that my feet were all right. It seems that they were giving me hot soup or something every minute, but I was so sleepy that I hardly knew what was going on. I soon found myself in bed with two doctors standing over me. One of them was the faithful Doctor Palmer who, years afterwards, became a dear friend and neighbor of mine. He told me they had just brought in the dead man, and that they did not know what to do with him until either Mike or I was able to talk. They were going to hold an inquest over the body and wanted witnesses to tell how he died. I tried to ask if they had sent for Mr. Smith, but they could not understand what I said.

I don't know how much time had passed, when an army officer came in and began talking to Doctor Palmer. I heard Doctor Palmer say, "Is that so?" The officer said it was. Then Doctor Palmer said, "My God! I did not know he was that bad." I raised up to ask what was the matter, but Doctor Palmer pushed me back onto the bed and told me to lie still. The officer said, "Shall I tell him?" Doctor Palmer said, "Not now, let the other doctor tell him." The officer went out and soon the old doctor came in. He told me that the man who came with me had his feet so badly frozen that he could not save them and they would have to be taken off. He said he would leave Sergeant Chauncey with me while Doctor Palmer assisted him in cutting off Mike's feet. He told me to keep very quiet and in a few days I would be all right.

About two hours after Mike and I reached the hotel, a company of men started out to find Mr. Smith; and when they reached the buggy, they found Mr. Smith and the driver all right. They had the meat of two horses cut up and hanging in the trees. When they told Mr. Smith that Mike and I had reached Soda Springs but that Jimmy was dead, he said he was surprised that we were not all dead, for he was certain that I was leading them right away from the town.

The party that went out for Mr. Smith got back the day the doctors were going to cut Mike's feet off. Mr. Smith came in to see me, and he almost cried when he saw the fix I was in. He said he would take me right to Salt Lake City, where I would get better care than I could in Soda Springs.

U.S. Mail on Teton Pass, heading west to Victor, Idaho.

After a little while he went out and had a bed made in a light, spring wagon, and was putting a stove in the wagon to make it comfortable for me. When the doctors heard that he was going to take me to Salt Lake City they told him that I could not stand the trip, but he said he knew I could stand it and that he was going to take me. Then the doctors sent for the officers, and when they came they told him they would not let me go, and that if he tried to take me, they would have him arrested. He told them to arrest and be d—d, for he was going to take me anyway. Then they locked the door and told him to keep away from the house.

When Mr. Smith got everything ready to start he came for me,and found the door locked. He told Captain Black to open it or he would break it open. Captain Black told him to get out, but he stepped back and jumped against the door and broke it in. Before he got to the room where I was, Captain Black grabbed him, but he whirled around and knocked him down. Then another captain ran up and Mr. Smith knocked him down, and he kept knocking them down as fast as they came until the soldiers arrived with guns and bayonets. After they had cornered him, he threw up his hands and they took him to the guard house, where they kept him a few days, then he got bail and went to Salt Lake City.

Owing to the skill of Doctor Palmer I got along pretty well, but it was several weeks before I was able to get around very much. Poor Mike suffered terribly after his feet were taken off, but he got well and strong as ever, except for the loss of his feet.

When I got well, I drove the mail from Soda Springs to Franklin during the rest of the winter. In the spring, along in June, Jimmy's wife came out from Mississippi. She was Mike's sister, and the most beautiful woman I ever saw. She was so kind and good and lovely that I would have tried to win her if she had not been so much older than I was. I think she was about twenty-six years old, while I was only twenty.

She and Mike induced me to stop driving the mail for awhile and take them back over the road we traveled those awful days to reach Soda Springs. I secured a buggy for us to ride in, a small spring wagon to carry the camp outfit, and a good cook to go with us to do the cooking and drive the mess wagon.

We first stopped where Jimmy died. The spot was still marked by the pieces of my coat lining that were lying around. Then we went to where we had left Mr. Smith and his driver, and could easily tell the place by the great chunks of horse meat still hanging in the trees. When we reached the place where Mr. Smith wanted to turn north and follow the old trail in the wrong direction, Mike told his sister that if it had not been for me that day, they would all have gone the wrong way and there, somewhere on that lonely trail, have perished in the snow. From there we went to the Snake River, where we had eaten our last meal on that awful trip.

We found here a large band of Indians, and among them were several that I was acquainted with. We could not get away from them, they were so glad to see me, so we stayed here four days. They wanted to know why I didn't come back in those old days and live with them all the time. Then I had to tell them all about where I had been ever since I went away from them and what I had been doing all that time. They took turns asking me questions until I thought they would talk me to death.

These were the first Indians this woman had ever seen, and she was quite scared of them until she noticed how glad they were to see me and how kind they were, then she felt better towards them. She said she was delighted to hear me talk to them, that they were certainly a queer people, and that I must have been a queer boy to leave my home and go to live with them.

She declared that if I would go east and lecture on my travels and experiences among the Indians I could make a lot of money. She said if I would go home with her she would write up my life and make a book out of it, and she knew it would take well in her country for the people there had heard so much about the many outrages and bloody massacres by the Indians that hundreds of her people would want to read my book.

Well, after I had finished my visit with the Indians we started back over the same road that was the cause of her dear husband's death, and where her brother and myself came so near losing our lives by starvation and cold. We stopped again at the place where her husband had breathed his last, and she gathered up all the pieces of my coat she could find, saying that she wanted to take them to Mississippi with her.

When we got back to mother's home, Mike and his sister stayed with us three weeks and this woman kept trying all the time to induce me to go with her to her home in Mississippi, but my mother was so against it that I would not go, although I wanted to very much.

The woman said that after Jimmy and Mike came west, her father died and left them a very large plantation on which were about fifty negroes, many large buildings, and great fields of cotton and sugar cane. She said if I would go home with her and Mike they would share this great property equally with me. Mike said, "That is just what we will do." My dear, old mother would not listen to it. She said that my name and standing in the church was worth more to me than all the negroes and cotton in the United States. I thought more of my mother than I did of anybody else in the world, so I told them I would not go with them.

CHAPTER 19 — **My Old Shoshone Friends**

" Finally she came to my white mother's home."

"What became of your old Indian mother, Washakie, Hanabi, and the rest?" This question has been asked me again and again. "Did you ever see them again?" "What other experiences did you have with the Indians?" Such queries as these have been sent to me from even far-off France by people who have read the first edition of my little book.

To satisfy my readers on these points and others that may be of interest, I have added a few more chapters to my story.

When I left my dear old Indian mother up north on "Pohogoy," or Ross Fork,—a place near the Snake River,— I promised her I would come back to her. That promise I intended to keep; but I was prevented from doing so by other pressing duties, till it was too late.

She waited a year for her "Yagaiki" to return, then her sorrow became so great she couldn't bear it longer and she started out to hunt me up. The Indians told me later that after I had been gone a few months my old mother would roam off in the mountains and lonely places and stay until hunger would drive her home. Finally she came to my white mother's home in Grantsville to find her boy. My mother made her welcome, taking my Indian mother into her home, feeding her, and providing her with a room as one of the family.

Then she wrote me that my two mothers wanted me to come home. I wished with all my heart to do so, but at that time I was about five hundred miles away, out on the mail line, badly wounded in the head by an Indian arrow. When I recovered enough to travel, I had to go to work again. The Indians at this time were burning stations and killing men every chance they got. Riders became so scarce and hard to get that I could not well leave, no matter how I felt.

When I finally did get away, I found that my own mother, as I have said before, had moved into Cache Valley, and my old Indian mother had left her, brokenhearted because she had not found her papoose. She had stayed with my white mother for more than two months. When I did not return as she expected, she grew suspicious that my white mother had hidden me away; and no words could comfort her or change her mind. Finally she went off with some Indians who came there.

My mother urged me to hunt her up. She had taken quite a fancy to the Indian woman. She thought it my duty to find and care for her the rest of her life. I felt so too. She had been a dear friend to me. She cared for me and protected me from harm, even saving my life several times.

The next word I got of my Indian mother was that she was dead. This sad news came from a band of Shoshones I found in the Bear Lake Valley. Hearing they were there, I had gone to see them, thinking to meet some of my old Indian friends. But those I wished most to see were not among the band. My dear old mother, they told me, had died about three years after I left. Washakie was then out in the Wind River country. As these Indians were going there, I decided to go with them.

We found Washakie at South Pass. He was very glad to see me, and treated me like a brother. But he could not tell me just where our mother was buried, as he had happened to be away from her when she died. He only knew that her grave was somewhere on Ham's Fork (a branch of the Green River) in Wyoming. He found an Indian who said he knew where it was. I offered to give him a pony if he would guide me to it. He agreed, and we went back to the head of Ham's Fork. We found the camping place they were at when she died, but not the grave, though we hunted for three days together, and I stayed another day after he left. Since then I have passed the place many times and have searched again and again; for I did desire to carry out my old Indian mother's wish to be buried like the whites, but I have never found her grave.

It was the custom of the Indians to bury their dead in some cleft of rocks or wash. They left no mark over the grave, but they usus-

Washakie's camp at South Pass, Wyoming. 1861.

ally buried with the body articles the deceased had treasured in
life, as weapons, clothing, etc. In the grave with my dear old
mother they placed the beaded and tasseled quiver she had made
of the skin of the antelope I had killed, the auger I had sent to Salt
Lake for, and other things of mine she had kept after I went away.
There are those who think an Indian has no heart. This dear old
woman certainly had one that was tender and true. Her soul was
good and pure. Peace to her memory.

Washakie's wife Hanabi was another good woman. She, too, had
died before I returned to the Indians. Her little girl papoose, the
baby when I was with them, grew up, I have been told, and married.

Washakie married another squaw by whom he had several children. One of them, Dick Washakie, is still living in the Wind River
country. He is a wealthy Indian, and has considerable influence.

When those Shoshone Indians made their treaty with the government there were three reservations set apart for the Shoshone
tribe—Fort Hall, Lemhi, and Wind River. Washakie was given his
choice. He took the Wind River reserve because, as he told me
afterwards, it had been his boyhood home, and his father was
buried there. Here Washakie spent the rest of his life, honored by
his tribe and respected for his goodness and his wisdom by all the
whites who knew him. During the early nineties he passed to the
Happy Hunting Grounds.

I saw Washakie many times before he died. We were always
brothers. When I lived in Bloomington, Bear Lake County, Idaho,
the chief often came and stayed with me. He was always made
welcome in my home, and his lodge was always open to me. During the time of Chief Joseph's War, Washakie brought his band and
camped for some months near my ranch on Bear River; and every
day he would come to get the news of the war. My wife would
read the paper and I would interpret it for the Indians.

While this war was on, the whites would not sell ammunition
to the Indians without a letter of recommendation, or "Tabop," as
they called it. The Indians all came to me for these letters. My
home for years was their headquarters. They would have eaten me
out of house and home if the ward authorities had not come to my
rescue and helped to feed these Red Brethren.

During the time of Chief Joseph's War, Washakie brought his band and camped for months near my ranch on Bear River in Idaho, and every day he would come to get news of the war.

Indians holding Pow Wow with Government agents and Army at Fort Laramie about 1867, regarding reservations, which many Indians objected to. But Chief Washakie convinced his tribe, the Shoshones, to yield peacefully, and they were given a choice for their reservation, which Washakie chose at Fort Washakie, Wyoming, the only reservation and fort in the United States named after an Indian chief.

Chiefs with Peace Pipe after Pow Wow, about 1867-68, at Fort Laramie; still not too happy about reservations.

Chief Washakie at 100 years of age. Taken at Fort Washakie on the Wind River Indian Reservation, shortly before he died. Chief Washakie was born in 1798. On February 23, 1900, he was buried at the age of 102 years with full military honors of a Captain in the old military cemetery at Fort Washakie. It was the only military funeral known to have been given to an Indian. Reverend John Roberts gave Washakie the bathrobe he wears in this photograph. He wore it the last two years of his life, and admired himself in the mirror.

CHAPTER 20 — Trapping With An Indian

" I would . . . ride the round of the traps."

But the Indians were not always a burden. They sometimes gave me good help. At one time in particular I found an Indian who proved a friend in need. It was during the winter of 1866-7, the year after I had brought my wife from Oxford, Idaho, to Bloomington.

"Hogitsi," a Shoshone Indian, with his family, was wintering in the town at the time. The whites called him "Hog," but he hadn't a bit of the hog in his nature. I found him to be one of the best Indians I ever knew.

After I had got well acquainted with him, he proposed that we try trapping to make some money. I was hard up; my family was destitute of food and clothing, for I had hard luck that summer, so I was ready to try anything.

We set to work over in Nounan Valley on a little stream about fifteen miles from home. The results were very encouraging. At the end of the first week we came back with sixty dollars' worth of furs. It was the easiest money I ever made in my life. Such success made us ready to try again.

"Hog" proposed that we go down to the Portneuf country and spend the winter at the trapping business. He said he knew of a stream there that was full of beaver and mink and other fur animals. I was anxious to go, but my wife protested that she could not think of my going off for a whole winter with an Indian. She was sure I would be scalped. It was hard work for me to persuade

her that under our circumstances it was the right thing to do. She
finally consented, however, and we set to work to get ready.

With "Hog" to help we soon had enough winter's wood chopped
up to last my family through the winter. I did all I could otherwise
to leave them comfortable; but the best I could do was not enough
to keep them from having a hard time of it while I was away.

I had three horses. "Hog" got two more from Thomas Rich and
Joseph Rich, who kept a store in Paris, supplied us with provisions
and campoutfit upon our agreeing to sell to him what furs we
should get.

A Mink.

It was about a week after New Year's that we struck out north-
ward through the cold and snow. The snow got deeper and deeper
as we went on towards Soda Springs. It seemed impossible to
make our destination. I suggested that we turn back, but "Hog"
wouldn't listen to me. He said that we would find the snow lighter
from there on, and it would be only a day or two more before we
got to Portneuf. So I yielded and we pushed on till we reached
Dempsey Creek, a branch of the Portneuf. Here we made our
winter camp at the base of the lava cliffs that border the stream
near where it empties into the Portneuf. We chose a good place on
the sunny side of the rock, and built our quarters. A cleft up the
face of the cliff served us well. By building up a fourth side to this
cleft, we made a fine chimney and fireplace. Around this we made
our shack—of quaking aspen poles and willows, and long grass to
thatch it. For a door we used the skins of two white-tailed deer
stretched over a quaking aspen frame. Our house was a cozy shel-
ter from the storms, and roomy enough to store our bales of furs.
For wood we used cedar, which grew near by.

Within the cedars we found plenty of black-tail deer, while in
the willows the white-tail were so numerous that we had little
trouble to get all we needed. Trout we could catch at any time; so
we had food in abundance.

When it came to trapping, we found beaver and mink so thick that it was no trick at all to catch them. Otter were not so plentiful, but we did land several of these beautiful animals.

I tended the traps and did the cooking. Hogitsi skinned the animals, stretched the fur, and kept watch of the horses. He was a good worker—not a lazy thing about him. Usually he was in bed an hour before me, and up an hour earlier. By the time I was ready to tumble out, he had the fire roaring, and was at work on the skins. While I got breakfast, he would look after the horses, and bring my old buckskin mare to camp. After breakfast I would get on her and ride the rounds of the traps to see what luck the night had brought. Usually I found the traps all sprung and a beaver or mink or sometimes an otter in them, tail up, and drowned in the stream. For we weighted the traps with a rock to hold the animal, when caught, under water. If the animal is not drowned, he will often gnaw off his foot and get away. After taking out the game, I would reset the traps, and return to camp with my load.

To keep the traps going kept me busy all day. We caught animals so fast that I had sometimes to stop and help Hogitsi catch up with his skinning and stretching. We would sit up at times late at night at this work. Evidently little trapping, if any, had ever been done on this stream, for the animals seemed not to know what a trap meant.

If it hadn't been for the worry I had for my dear ones at home, the winter would have been a pleasant one in every way. It was one of the easiest I ever spent, and most profitable. I never have made money faster than I did that winter. When springtime came, we had about seven hundred pounds of fur. At that time mink and

Beaver and beaver lodge.

beaver skins sold at two dollars per pound; otter was worth one dollar a foot. A stretched otter skin would often bring nine dollars or more.

When we turned over our pack to Mr. Rich, we found we had $900.00 due us after paying all our expenses. He paid us in gold, silver, and greenbacks. Hogitsi was scared when he saw the pile; and when it came to dividing, he certainly proved that he was no hog; for he simply would not take his full share. He insisted that we should not have had any if it hadn't been for me; that it would "make him too rich."

This streak of good luck gave me a new start. My wife felt better about the trapping business; but she had no desire to repeat the experience of that winter; and, as I found other profitable work to do, I did not turn to trapping again as a business, though I have done a good deal of this work at various times since. And I have also done a good deal of trading in furs with the trappers.

This trading has brought me into acquaintanceship with a good many of the mountaineers. It was through this that I came to know Kit Carson, who came to my home hunting his trapper son-in-law, Sims, one winter. Sims was wintering near at the time. Kit stopped over night with me. I brought his son-in-law to my home and they made up their troubles. Kit wanted to stay with me for a while. I took him in, and we boarded and lodged him for several months. We had a good time together swapping yarns that winter, I can tell you.

CHAPTER 21 — Working On The Indian Reservation

" 'We intend to tie you to that tree and burn you alive.' "

When the government undertook the task of settling the Indians on the reservations, I was given the job of helping the Indian Agent of the Fort Hall reservation gather and keep the Redmen within bounds. This was no easy task. The Indians found it hard, after their many years of roving life, to be restrained. They often grew discontented, complaining at times that they were being cheated and otherwise mistreated. It is a well-known fact that they often had much cause to complain. The Indians have been abused shamefully by the whites at times, and I know it. Our dealings with the Redmen reflect no great credit on us.

If the Indians became disgruntled, as they frequently did, they would slip away to the mountains in a sulky mood. Whenever they did this, it was my business to bring them back. This task was not only disagreeable, but sometimes dangerous.

At one time a band under the lead of old Sagwich got angry over something, and struck for the hills, strongly determined that they would not come back to the reservation again.

I was sent to bring them back; they had a week the start of me. I had a good horse, however, and taking with me an Indian boy named Suarki, to lead the pack horse, I started out. The second day we struck their trail, and knowing well the signs they always leave behind them, we followed it easily; but it led us over a hundred and fifty miles through a rough country before we found the runaway band.

Trading Post at Fort Hall Indian Reservation, Idaho.

On the sixth day we came upon them camped on the Salmon River. We pitched our camp about a hundred yards away. After unsaddling our horses, I went over to have a talk with them.

Old Sagwich was very angry. He said he knew what I was after, but he wouldn't go back; and I would not go back either, for they would fix me so that I couldn't give them any more trouble. He said I ought to be their friend, but instead of that I was helping to bring more trouble to them. The whites he accused of lying to them and robbing them of their hunting ground and forcing them to work at something they knew nothing about. They would bear it no longer; they would fight first. The old chief grew angrier as he went on.

"You need not think of escaping this time," he said to me. "We intend to tie you to that tree and burn you alive." I tried to reason with them, telling them I knew I was in their power; but it wouldn't do them any good to kill me. If they did, the soldiers would soon follow and kill the last one of them.

"We are not afraid of the soldiers," he retorted. "We would rather die fighting than starve."

"Well," I replied, "if you kill me, you will kill one of the best friends the Indians ever had."

But nothing I could say seemed to make any difference with old Sagwich. He was determined to carry out his threat. If he had his way I knew he would do it. The other Indians, however, were not so devilish. One of them gave me some fresh elk meat, and I went back to my camp. Things looked rather black for me that night. My only hope was that the other Indians would not stand by old Sagwich.

If the worst came, I had determined to sell my life as dearly as possible. The Indians held a council that night. We kept close watch till morning, but as no one offered to harm us, we began to feel a

At the Indian Agency.

little easier. After saddling our horses, I told Suarki I was going over to have another talk with them, and instructed him that if they made a move to kill me, he should leap on my horse and strike for home to tell the Indian Agent.

Old Sagwich was so sulky he wouldn't even speak to me. The other Indians, however, acted better. They said nothing of what had been decided, but that day they packed up and took the trail towards home. We followed them. On our way down the river we came upon one of the Indians fishing. He told me about the council. Old Sagwich was stubborn in his determination to kill me, but the rest wouldn't consent and he had to give up his bloody plan.

This experience made me feel that my job was too risky for the pay I was getting. The Agent wouldn't raise my wages, so I quit him and went back to my home at Oxford, Idaho.

Piute Indian girl.

CHAPTER 22 — **Frontier Troubles**

"Two Indians were behind them, both on an old horse of mine."

Later, we moved back into the Bear Lake, where we made our home for twenty years. During this time I was often called on to do dangerous service in the interest of our settlements. After the Indian troubles were over, we had outlaws to deal with who were worse than Indians. For a long time the frontier communities suffered from depredations committed by cattle rustlers and horse thieves. Organized bands operated from Montana to Colorado. They had stations about a hundred miles apart in the roughest places in the mountains. They would often raid our ranges and steal all the cattle and horses they could pick up, driving them into their mountain retreat. They got so daring finally that they even came into the settlements and robbed stores and killed men. The colonists did not get together to stop these outrages till after a fatal raid was made upon Montpelier, when a store was robbed and a clerk was shot dead. This roused the people of the valley to action. Gen. Charles C. Rich called upon the leaders of the towns to send two men from each settlement—the best men to be had—to pursue and punish the outlaws. Fourteen men responded to the call, among them four of the leaders themselves. It fell to my lot to be one of this posse.

We struck across the mountains east of Bear Lake, following the trail of the robbers to their rendezvous on the Big Piney, a tributary of the Green River. We knew that they had hidden themselves in this country, for two of the men with us, whose stock had been stolen, had followed the robbers to their den to recover their property. Finding the outlaws in such force, they didn't dare to claim their stolen stock but returned to Bear Lake for help.

These men led us to the place where they had come upon the outlaws; but the outlaws had evidently feared pursuit and moved camp. To hide their tracks they had driven their wagons up the creek right in the water for over a mile. Then they had left the creek and driven up a little ravine and over a ridge. As we rode up this ravine, to the top of the ridge, the two men who were in the lead sighted the tepees of the robbers in the hollow below. They dodged back to keep out of sight, and we all rode down into the thick willows on the Big Piney, hiding our horses and ourselves among them. The two men that had sighted the outlaw camp then slipped up the hill again on foot, secreting themselves in the sagebrush at the top of the ridge, and watched the rest of the afternoon to see whether the outlaws had mistrusted anything; but they showed no sign of having seen us. At dark they came and reported.

We held council then to decide what plan to pursue to capture the outlaws. As the robbers outnumbered us, more than two to one, and were well armed, it was serious business. Our sheriff weakened when the test came; he said he couldn't do it, and turned his papers over to Joseph Rich, as brave a man as ever went on such a trip. There were others who felt pretty shaky and wanted to turn back, but Mr. Rich said we had been picked as the best men in Bear Lake and he didn't feel like going back without making an attempt to capture the thieving band. One man said he was ready to go cut the throats of the whole bunch of robbers if the captain said so, but Mr. Rich said, "No; we did not come out to shed blood. We want to take them alive and give them a fair trial."

Every man was given a chance to say how he felt. Most of us wanted to make the attempt to capture the outlaws, and the majority ruled.

How to do it was the next problem. It would have been folly for so few of us to make an open attack on so many well-armed men. The only way we could take them was by surprise, when they were asleep. This plan agreed upon, Mr. Rich proposed that we go down the hill with our horses and pack animals, get in line at the bottom, then, just at the peep of day, charge upon their camp, jump from our horses, run into their tents and grab their guns. When we had decided on this plan of action, Mr. Rich said that this probably meant a fight. If it did we should let them fire first. Should they kill one of us, we must not run; for if we did so they would kill us all. We should give them the best we had. With our double-barreled shotguns loaded with buckshot, we would make things pretty hot for them if they showed fight.

In order that we might know exactly the situation, and have our tents picked out beforehand, so as not to get in a mix-up, two volunteers were called for to go down through their camp in the night and get the lay of things. Jonathan Hoopes and I offered to go. Their tepees were pitched on both sides of a little stream, which was deep enough for us to keep out of sight by stooping a little. Down this stream we stole our way, wading with the current so as not to make any noise, till we got right among the tepees. The biggest one was pitched on the brink of the stream. We could hear some of the men inside of it snoring away lustily. Hoopes reached his hand up and found a blanket on which were some service berries spread out to dry. Being hungry, we helped ourselves, filling our pockets with them. After taking in the situation fully, we slipped back to our boys.

There were seven tents in all, and fourteen of us—two to each tent. Hoopes and I were to take the largest, the other boys were assigned theirs. We waited for day to break; just as it did, the word was given; we popped spurs to our horses and away we went. A few seconds and we had leaped from them, rushed into the tents and begun to grab the guns from the robbers, who, wakened so rudely, stared stupidly, while we gathered in their weapons. By the time Hoopes was through passing them out to me, I had my arms loaded with rifles and revolvers. Mr. Rich told me to carry them up the hill a piece and stack them. "Shoot the first man who makes a move to touch them," was the order. When I looked around, there sat three of our men on their horses; they hadn't done their duty, so some of the tents were yet untouched. I told Hoopes, and he jumped over the creek to one of them. I was just gathering up some weapons I had dropped when a big half-breed made a jump at me, grabbed my shotgun and we had a lively tussle for a few minutes. He might have got the better of me, for he was a good deal bigger than I, but Hoopes jumped to the rescue and cracked him on the head with his revolver so hard that it knocked him senseless for some time.

When the outlaws rallied themselves enough to sense what had happened, they broke out of their tents in double-quick time, swearing and cursing and demanding what we wanted.

Captain Rich told them to keep quiet, that they were all under arrest, that we had the advantage, but we would not harm them

Uncle Nick landing a big trout on Jackson Lake, Wyoming.

if they behaved themselves. Seeing that it was useless to resist, they settled down.

The captain then ordered them to kill a calf for us, as we had not had anything to eat since noon the day before. They obeyed orders and we soon had a good breakfast. Later in the day part of our men went out and searched their herds. A good many cattle and horses belonging to our men were found among them.

The leaders of the outlaws were not in this band. They were off making another raid somewhere. One of the band of outlaws was deaf and dumb. Captain Rich took this fellow aside and carried on a conversation with him by writing. From the man he learned that the rest of the band were expected in that night, but as they didn't come, we concluded that they had seen us and were lying off in the hills waiting a chance to ambush us and rescue their comrades. We were too sharp to give them the chance to do that. For three days we waited, guarding our prisoners. Then, as we thought it too risky to try to take so large a band of desperate men through the rough timbered country we must pass to get home, we took forty head of their horses as bond for their appearance at court in thirty days, and let the prisoners go.

When we were ready to set out, we carried their guns to the top of a hill, and Hoopes and I were left to guard the weapons till we were sure our men were far enough away to be safe; then we left the weapons and struck out for home after them.

As no one ever came to redeem the horses, they were sold at auction. This nest of outlaws was broken up for good the following year. Since then that part of the country has had no serious trouble with horse thieves and robbers.

One more rather exciting experience that befell me and then I shall close these stories of my life in the rugged West.

It happened in 1870. Jim Donaldson, Charley Webster, or "Webb," as we called him, and I were taking a peddling trip to Fort Stanbow, the soldier post that was temporarily established near South Pass for the protection of the miners and emigrants. We had loaded up our three wagons with butter, eggs, and chickens.

The Sioux Indians were then on the warpath. We had been warned to keep an eye on our horses, but we thought little about it till one day we were nooning on the Big Sandy—about where Lot Smith burnt the government wagon trains—when, just as we sat down to eat, "Webb" looked up to see our horses, which we had turned loose to graze, disappearing in a cloud of dust. Two Indians were behind them, both on an old horse of mine, and they were whooping the others across the hills to beat time.

Jumping to our feet we dashed after them afoot. This was useless, of course. "Webb" and Donaldson jerked out their revolvers and took several shots at the rascals, but they were out of revolver reach and getting farther away every second, while we stared and damned them.

It was a pretty pickle we were in—forty miles from nowhere, with three wagons loaded with perishable stuff, and not a horse to move them. We got madder and madder as we watched the thieving devils gradually slip out of sight beyond the sand hills.

Then we went back to our wagons—cussing and discussing the situation. For an hour or more we tried to puzzle a way out of our difficulty. It was no use. The more we worried the worse it looked. All the money I had was invested in those eggs and butter and they would soon be worse than nothing in the hot sun. The other boys were in as bad a fix as I was. We just couldn't see a way out of it; but we kept up our puzzling till suddenly we heard a rumbling noise.

A few minutes later a covered wagon drawn by a pair of mules came in sight.

An old man—"Boss Tweed" the boys nicknamed him—was the driver. In the seat with him was a boy, who had a saddle horse tied behind. They were surely a welcome sight to us.

We told them of our trouble. The old man reckoned he could help us out. He proposed that we load the supplies of two of our wagons on his larger wagon, then trailing our other wagon behind, his old mules he thought could haul us into South Pass. It looked like our only chance, but "Webb" thought he had a better plan.

The Indians, he said, must make their way out of the country through a certain pass. There was no other route they could escape by. If we three would take the mules and boy's horse and ride hard through the night, we might get ahead of the thieves and retake our horses.

"Anything for the best," said the old man; but the boy objected. We shouldn't take his horse. He started to untie his animal, but we stopped him. Our situation was a desperate one; he had to give in.

We unhitched the mules, and strapped quilts on their backs. Donaldson and I jumped on them; "Webb" took the horse. Then we struck the trail single file, my old mule on lead with Jim to whip him up and "Webb" behind him to whip Jim's mule. It was a funny sight. I never meet Jim but he calls up that circus parade loping along over the hills out on the Big Sandy.

The old mules were slow, but they were tough. They kept up their steady gait mile after mile through the night. We couldn't see any trail—just the gap in the mountains against the sky to guide us as we loped and jogged and jogged and loped through the long night.

When daylight came to light our way, we found ourselves at the place where the trail took up over the pass. Soon it forked, the two branches of the trail going up two ravines which were separated by a low, narrow ridge. We saw no fresh tracks on either trail, so we knew the Indians had not passed this point. It looked as if we had got ahead of them as "Webb" hoped.

We rode up one ravine about a mile from the forks, keeping out of the trail so as to leave no tracks to alarm the thieves if they came our way. Here we stopped and "Webb" went up on the ridge to where he could overlook the country and at the same time watch both trails. Our plan was to wait till we found out which trail the Redskins took. Then we could post ourselves on either trail and head them off as they came up the one or the other ravine, it being but a short distance between the trails.

"Webb" had not been on watch long before he sighted them coming about six miles away. He waited till they reached the forks. Luck favored us. They took our trail. Seeing this "Webb" slipped down to tell us. We hastily hid our horses in the tall brush that bordered the little creek, chose a place where the big birches hung over the trail, and got ready. "Webb" and Donaldson, having revolvers, were to take the lead Indian, while with my rifle I was to settle accounts with the other.

We hadn't long to wait till here they came crowding our horses full tilt along the trail. We held ourselves till we had the dead drop on them, then we all fired. My companions both caught their Indian in the head. I took mine right under the arm. Their horses jumped and they both tumbled off so dead they didn't know what struck them. It may seem a cruel thing to do, but we were not going to take any chances.

I never have found any joy in killing Indians. And I never have killed any except when circumstances compelled it; nor have I ever felt like boasting about such bloody work. These rascals certainly deserved what they got. They had stolen all we had and left us in a very serious difficulty. They were Sioux Indians who were escaping from a battle with the soldiers of Fort Stanbow.

You can easily believe we were mighty glad to get back those horses and strike the trail again towards our wagons. We found things all right there. The old man had taken good care of our produce while we were away. He was just as happy as we were over our success. But do you think he would take any pay for his trouble? Not a cent. It was pay enough, he said, to feel so good because he had helped us out of a bad fix. When we got to South Pass, however, we found his home and left him some supplies with our good wishes. He was away at the time, so he couldn't object.

The boy who had refused us his horse didn't object, though, to taking five dollars for his pay. I've always found a heap of difference among the human beings one meets in his travels.

The years that have followed these wild days have not been so filled with exciting adventures, yet no year has passed without its rough and trying experiences; for it has been my lot to live always on the frontier. Even now my home is in Jackson's Hole—one of the last of our mountain valleys to be settled. In 1889 I first went into this beautiful valley, and a few years later I pioneered the little town now called Wilson, in my honor.

It was here that I was brought again into close contact with my Shoshone friends—the Indians from whom for many years I had been all but lost. In 1895, when the so-called Jackson's Hole Indian war broke out and several Indians were killed and others captured and brought to trial for killing game, I was called on to act as interpreter. My sympathies went out to the Indians at this time. They were misunderstood and mistreated as they always have been. The Indian has always been pushed aside, driven, and robbed of his rights.

It is a sad thought with me to see the Redmen giving way so rapidly before our advancing civilization. Where thousands of the Indians once roamed free, only a scattered few remain. The old friends of my boyhood days with Washakie have almost entirely passed away. Only once in a great while do I find one who remembers Yagaiki, the little boy who once lived with their old chief's mother. But when I do happen to meet one—as I did last year when I found Hans, a wealthy Indian, who lives now on his ranch at the Big Bend in Portneuf Canyon—then we have a good time, I tell you, recalling the days of long ago when Uncle Nick was among the Shoshones.

Now my dear readers, I told you in the start, that I would give you only a part of my life, so I will end this book by saying that from the time this story closes until this writing, my life has been a string of sorrow. No man has passed through greater troubles than I have and still lives.

I love my country, I love my own people, and I love the Indians. I am an old man now and I realize that it will not be many winters until I too will pass on to the "Happy Hunting Grounds" where I shall find them a white and beautiful people.

Lily pond in Yellowstone Park was part of the Shoshone land.

Indians on the Wyoming Wind River Indian Reservation about 1898, trying to adapt to the white man's way of living. As Nick Wilson said, "It is a sad thought for me to see my old Indian friends giving away so rapidly before our advancing civilization!"

The Return of
the White Indian
A sequel to
The White Indian Boy
Among the Shoshones

by
Charles Alma Wilson
Son of the White Indian Boy,
Elijah Nicholas Wilson

C. A. Wilson

Contents

THE RETURN OF THE WHITE INDIAN

1. Polygamy 151
2. The Violin 162
3. Prologue to Jackson Hole 172
4. A Heritage 175
5. Were They Really Horse Thieves? 179
6. Prologue to Jackson Hole (continued) 187
7. Prologue to Jackson Hole (continued)
   Ellington (Ton) Smith 192
8. Jackson Hole Sheep War 211
9. Jackson Hole Indian War 215
10. Reminiscence 220
11. Charley Wilson 224
12. Charlotte Sarah Wilson (Tragedy) 234
13. Happy Times 248
14. A Close Call and Nick Loses His Bishopric 258
15. Virgil Ward and the Drummer 265
16. The Telephone 270
17. Brasfield and Bill Scott 279
18. Carl Van Winkle 283
19. Nick McCoy 293
20. Haley's Comet 296
21. Ogden, Utah, Not in Wyoming! 302
22. Wilderness Acres 313
23. Raum and Raum (School Days) 330
24. Jessie K. Dayton and Brady Taylor 339
25. Pioneer Teachers
   Jenny Grosh and Fostene Forrester 349
26. The Hermit 355
27. Jackson Lake Dam—Was It Worth It? 370
28. Doctor Huff and Dell Judd
   and A Great Man Dies 375

CHAPTER 1 — **Polygamy**

This old manuscript of Elijah Nicholas Wilson has never been published before in its entirety, but I thought the reader and readers who have already read some of the other books that have been revised from this old manuscript, are entitled to see the original and thereby get a more intimate look at what Nick Wilson was really like. I have also added later revisions.

I hope you have enjoyed reading this old manuscript of my father's, exactly as he wrote it, thumping away with one finger on that old French typewriter that turned with a disc like a phonograph flat record, instead of the round roller that is used on modern typewriters today.

One of the questions asked about my father was: "How was it possible for him to write this manuscript when he had never attended school a day in his life?" The answer is that his white mother taught him to read and write along with teaching her children, most of whom never had a chance to go to regular school.

Those of you, my readers, who were interested enough to read his story up to this point, will be interested in the sequel that will bring you up to date on the balance or remainder of Nick Wilson's life.

He was truly an oldtimer and pioneer in the Western United States, and traveled and played a part in its early history. He left more detail of what the Pony Express was really like than any other person ever left. His description of the old Pony Express saddles and the mail pouches, called *mochila*, is credited to Nick Wilson on a plaque in the old Pioneer Village in Nebraska, which should be visited by every American interested in Early American history.

I will now begin on the sequel to my father's life, starting about the time he finished riding in the Pony Express:

Nick got well enough to go home after being shot in the head with an Indian arrow, but he never did fully recover, because he had periods of terrible headaches all the rest of his life. In his later years, after becoming bald, he was very sensitive about the awful scar, which was about three inches above his left eye. He wore his old black hat, even at meals, unless persuaded to remove it. The wound left a hole on his left forehead that seemed to have no bone under the skin, and you could see the heart beat under the blue skin, and especially so when he suffered his severe headaches.

After his bout or experience with the Mormon Bishops over their stealing his girl from him, and making her marry a man many years her senior (who had several wives already), Nick felt very bitter toward the Mormon Church, but his mother gradually persuaded him that the Church was good and it was polygamy that was bad. But the Mormon Church gradually lost its attraction and hold on Nick, especially after his own experience with polygamy and the results which plagued him the rest of his life.

After reading the chapter, "A Terrible Journey," in which Nick tells of the awful blizzard during which one of the men lost his life, freezing to death there in the snow with his head on Nick's legs, some of you will, no doubt, like me, think that when the brother-in-law and wife of the dead man came West and had Nick take them over this terrible route in the summertime to the place where the husband died, their begging Nick to go back to their plantation in the South with them, and offering to share it with him, and the possibility of marrying this lovely widow, all have a romantic appeal that even Nick found hard to turn down, but again his mother talked him out of it and got him back into activity in the Mormon Church.

But perhaps it was for the best that he did not go, because in the Civil War that was soon to follow, lots of these fine plantations were destroyed and Nick could have been killed in the war.

When Albert Sidney Johnston was sent to Utah to squelch the Mormons and stop polygamy, he wound up fighting Indians, and Nick served him as guide and interpreter until the Civil War did start, and Johnston returned east to relinquish his commission status in the U.S. Army and fight on the side of the South. He wanted Nick to go with him and serve as his aide, an opportunity which, again, Nick's mother talked him out of. His mother seemed to have had an unusual influence on Nick's life. I know that my father would have dearly loved to have gone with General Johnston, because in his telling these stories of his serving with Johnston, it was very apparent that he loved and admired this great man with all his heart.

He often talked of visiting Shiloh, where Johnston was killed, and seeing his grave in Texas, where General Johnston's body was returned for burial.

Just a few years ago I had the opportunity to go over the great Shiloh Battle Field. I stood by the stump of the huge tree where

General Albert Sidney Johnston during the Civil War. Taken at Shiloh just before his death. Nick Wilson served as guide and interpreter for this great man, while he was subduing Indian tribes that were ravaging Mormon settlements in Utah, about 1857-58.

Johnston was shot in the leg, severing the big artery, causing him to bleed to death. Johnston's aide was not with him when he was shot, as Johnston had sent him with a message to another part of the battleground. I could just imagine that aide as being my father. I went down the little winding trail to the bottom of a ravine, where the Governor of Tennessee led Johnston's horse down out of the line of fire and helped Johnston dismount and sit against a tree, where he bled to death. I couldn't help wonder why in the world the Governor didn't attempt a tourniquet to stop the blood, for it is believed that Johnston's life could have been saved if he could have had any medical aid. I know that if my dad had been there, things would have been different.

After going over this awful battleground and seeing the simulated moving picture, and seeing the small acreage in the Big Bend of the Tennessee River where General Grant was hemmed in, I have the feeling that if Johnston hadn't been killed that day, that Grant would have been taken before sundown. The Civil War might have had a far different ending, because I believe that Shiloh was the real turning point in the Civil War. Again, this is only vain surmisal of what my father's life could have been.

Now I will get down to the business of telling what his life was really like:

I do not remember ever hearing my father say what his age was when he married his first wife, Matilda Patten. But I do know the circumstances under which their marriage came about.

The Mormon Church had just finished one of its crusades of proselytizing in Europe and a great many converts had arrived from England and Germany, of which the majority were women. It seems there are always more women conversions into any religious movement, regardless of denomination, and it was this influx of women into Salt Lake City that caused Brigham Young to emphasize the revelation that it was not only every man's duty, but "God's will," that each worthy Mormon man was to marry as many wives as was possible for him to support. Of course, the Prophet Joseph Smith was the originator of polygamy into the Mormon Church. These converts, both men and women, were all given work, and while waiting marriage, especially in the case of the women, they were boarded out among the Saints who had homes, farms, etc., as many to each home as they were able to accommodate or care for.

Nick's mother had several of these female boarders and she openly encouraged Nick and her other sons to take as many of these young women to wife as was possible.

It is a strange fact, but according to Mormon records of that time, few first wives protested very vigorously their husbands having plural marriages.

Mormons were encouraged to have large families and there was lots of hard work involved, and possibly most of these over-worked wives thought it would be great to have some younger and stronger help, because one of the first rules in plural marriage was that the first wife was boss.

Of course, my father had none of these problems yet, because this was to be his first marriage. I don't know what the courtship with the young converts was like, or what their reaction to this plural marriage idea was, but they, for the most part anyway, had no choice.

However that may be, it appears that Nick didn't have much trouble getting the one he was most attracted to, Matilda Patten, and this turned out to be a very compatible, congenial, and happy marriage, resulting in about 12 or 14 children. I do not know which number is correct, because I never heard my father mention the number. My information came mostly from the wrangling of my five elder half-sisters, who were the only ones I ever knew, except one half-brother, Bill, a product of Nick's second polygamous marriage. The girls could never agree as to the real number of kids, and so I can only let it go at that. However, these 12 or 14 were all from the first marriage. There were two children from the second or plural wife; and three from my own mother, the third wife — not a polygamous marriage, because wife number 1 was dead, and my father was legally separated from wife number 2 at the time of marriage to wife number 3.

It was in 1865 that Nick Wilson married Matilda Patten (making him about twenty-three years old). They lived a more or less nomadic life because it was hard for Nick to stay in one place very long. However, he was always a good provider as he had a knack as a trader, trapper, or whatever he turned his hand to in making money. It was said of Nick Wilson that he could start out in the morning with a three-bladed jack knife and return in the evening driving a fine, four-horse span with a new wagon, he was so good at swapping.

Nick and Matilda lived for a year or two in Oxford, Idaho, and then moved to Bloomington, Utah, where they lived the winter that Kit Carson stayed with them until warm weather in the spring, when Kit went on his way looking for his lost son-in-law and riding one of Nick's fine horses for which Kit traded his share of the furs he and Nick caught that winter. The furs were worth many times the price of the horse, but Kit didn't want to be bothered taking time to sell them, and I think Kit, being a proud man, figured the extra furs paid for his bed and board, for he was never beholden to any man.

For about fifteen years Nick and Matilda traveled around to the mining towns in Nevada, Idaho and Montana, where Nick would set up a blacksmith shop. He was a very good blacksmith, and Matilda would start a boarding and rooming house and was known as a very fine cook.

I remember my father telling a story of an event that happened when he was first learning the blacksmith trade and was still living at home. His father still had the old Goshute Indian who worked for him at the time Nick ran off with the Indians. Nick said he got a job helping the local blacksmith, a man named Judd. One day he saw this old Indian coming up the road at a gallop on one of his father's old work horses. Just as he got even with the blacksmith shop, this Judd stepped out and flapped his leather blacksmith apron and yelled,"Howdy do!" The sudden appearance and flapping apron startled the old horse, and it put on the brakes, stopping short, but the old Indian continued on over the horse's head, lighting hard on his rump in the dusty road. As Judd and Nick started laughing, the old Indian shook his fist at them and shouted, "Mr. Judd! Too much Howdy Doody!"

Nick and Matilda spent time at Virginia City, Montana, and Deer Lodge, which was the home of the Montana State Prison, and my father spent one winter as a prison guard. I can remember him telling how terribly cold it was out on those bare grey prison walls, where guards paced their lonely and weary shifts, walking the narrow cat-walk atop the old prison wall at night.

This prison is still in use at Deer Lodge, and I went through Deer Lodge in December of 1975 with my son Paul on our way to attend a meeting at Three Forks, Montana, where they were planning a state park in memory of Lewis and Clark and John Coulter, to be called "The Missouri River Headwaters Bicentennial Site." It was 28 degrees below zero at Deer Lodge as we went through that night, and looking up at those old, foreboding grey prison walls, I shuddered as I recalled the stories my father told of walking that wall nearly a hundred years ago.

Nick moved back to Bear Lake in Idaho after a year at Market Lake (Idaho Falls). He finally got a farm near Soda Springs and planned to settle down awhile because they were getting a considerable sized family by now and it was hard for so many to be on the move all the time. Here Nick's eldest daughter, Edna Jane, had married Abraham Ward and Abe helped Nick run the farm. At this time Nick had seven daughters at home and four boys, but he lost all the boys. I have an article from an old newspaper telling of the terrible epidemic of diptheria during the winter of 1890-91, when Nick and Matilda lost the four boys. It says, in part, "Nick Wilson also practiced medicine and was in great demand from his reputation in saving many diptheria victims. His treatment apparently consisted of gargle and twenty-minute throat swabbing with a concoction of herbs and golden seal and other ingredients learned from his old Indian mother, and he was doctoring people in Ashton, Idaho, when his own boys died of it." The article goes on to say, "There was no way to get word to him when he lost all four of the boys and one girl." The tragic irony of this story was that while Nick was away frantically trying to save others, he lost nearly half of his own. Nick also had a reputation as a very good doctor in smallpox cases, and in later years treated cases for Indians on both the Wind River and Blackfoot reservations. Indians were very susceptible to smallpox and nearly whole tribes were wiped out by it.

After four or five years on their farm at Soda Springs, Nick and Matilda were getting pretty well fixed with worldly goods and also family-wise, as they now had at least seven daughters and four sons, and one son-in-law, Abraham Ward, who was still living on the farm and, in fact, practically running it by himself, because Nick spent most of his time blacksmithing, trading, trapping or doctoring.

After settling down on their farm at Soda Springs, Nick and his family were once more back into the swing and influence of the Mormon Church and Nick was serving as bishop at the small church in Soda Springs. Abe was an elder. The mother church in Salt Lake kept a tight line on all these outlying churches that were now scattered through lower Wyoming, Utah, Nevada, Idaho and Montana, and by their proselytizing were still gaining many converts, especially from England, so it was that polygamy again raised its ugly head in the life of Nick Wilson.

As stated before, women were the most numerous converts, and the Church had turned back to polygamy in order to keep this trend in control.

Even though the U.S. Government had outlawed polygamy ever since the Civil War, not too much was done to stop or stifle the practice until about 1880, then the government began really cracking down on polygamy as practiced by the Mormon Church in Utah. But as the government persecution was not too strenuous at first, the practice went on all the time. About this time an unusually large influx of women converts emigrated to Salt Lake City, and the Church in Salt Lake was frantically trying to get them placed in their society. The pressure was really on every Mormon man, regardless of age or family size, to take on more wives. The delegation from Salt Lake, sponsored by Brigham Young, were really putting on this pressure, and so it was that Nick was called upon the carpet and ordered to take another wife; two more if possible. Nick was never polygamous by nature, and his first experience with it was when he lost his girl in Grantsville, Utah, so many years before. That experience still rankled in his memory, and so he protested a plural marriage very vigorously, but the bishops from Salt Lake persisted, saying, "Brother Wilson, you are a man of good standing, you are pretty well fixed, in fact, you can easily support one or even two or three more wives!" Nick protested, "But I have a wife! I don't want any more! I've got twelve kids; I've got all I can handle!!" The Bishop smiled and said, "Now, now, Brother Nick, you must calm down and be reasonable," and he went into a long-winded tirade expounding the duties and wonders of plural marriages, and wound up by stating flatly that Nick had to take at least one wife *now*, and then he could take more later when he saw his duty and obligations to the Church more fully.

Nick still protested, "But what will my wife say? How can I explain another wife to her?" The Bishop's grin was wide by now and he said softly, "That's all taken care of; we have already talked to Sister Matilda and she is for it one hundred percent." Turning to Bishop Snow, he said, "Brother Snow, please ask Sister Matilda to come out." She did, and verified what the Bishop said; she had been waiting in an adjoining room.

Nick tried to hold out, but with Matilda's urging, he finally gave in and picked a young Nordic woman named Sena Logan. It wasn't long before Matilda was sorry for persuading Nick to marry again. Sena Logan turned out to be a very hot-tempered wife, and refused to help Matilda with her big family. Nick had to build a house for her because she wouldn't live with his other family.

In about a year Sena had a son whom she called Wallace. That summer the U.S. Marshals were getting close to outlying districts like Soda Springs, and Morman men polygamists were running scared. Lots of them hid in the mountains and even left the state, but one by one they were hunted down and had to face the music.

Finally came the day when Nick was plowing in one of his fields in late autumn when Abe came riding fast, leading a pack horse. He told Nick that the U.S. Marshals were in Soda Springs making arrests and would soon be out to the farm for him, for in some way they had gotten hold of most of the plural marriage records. The only recourse was to run or be arrested. Abe urged Nick to take the saddle horse and pack horse on which was packed food, bedding, guns, ammunition, cooking utensils, etc., and go back to the Indians and live with Chief Washakie until this government harassment blew over.

Nick had always planned to someday go back to his Indian friends and live, but circumstances had always prevented it. This was really a temptation for Nick, but he finally told Abe to take the horses back to the house, that he would take his chances with the law. He said he wasn't ashamed of what he had done, that it was for the church and the church came first.

Abe said, "But what will you do? They will be coming for you soon!" Nick climbed back on the plow and said, "Let them come. I will be right here plowing." And he was!

At his trial, Nick fared much better than a lot of polygamists did who tried to skip out and hide, and some even tried to lie out of it. Nick pled guilty and said he did it by orders of his church. He was given one year in the Federal penitentiary and was ordered to keep his first wife, Matilda Patten. The other, Sena Logan, was to go, and not share his bed and board any more, by request of the U.S. Government. However, he was ordered to make a satisfactory settlement with her regarding children and property. They now had two sons, Wallace and another that had just been born, whom they named William, destined to be known as Bill Wilson.

The court gave Nick one month to make these settlements regarding Sena Logan, illegitimate wife number 2. He and Matilda were more than fair with her. They didn't consider the large family of legitimate wife Matilda Patten, wife number 1, but split everything right down the middle. They sold the farm, livestock and machinery at auction, and give Sena Logan one-half. Then it was mutually decided, in fact, insisted upon by Sena Logan, that Nick take and keep one of the sons and she the other. Because Bill was a tiny baby and needed her more, Sena gave Wallace to keep as his son with no interference from her.

Earlier in this story I stated that this polygamous marriage plagued Nick the rest of his life, and so I might as well get that part told and out of the story and over with instead of trying to drag it along through the following years. It will be getting ahead of my story, but after much thought I have decided to get Sena Logan and the polygamy story told.

Sena took her baby William and her settlement money and went up further in Idaho, first around Rexburg, then Ashton and then moved up to Alta, Wyoming, just across the Idaho border in the Teton Valley, where I believe she died and is buried.

For many years she was a real Albatross around Nick's neck, because she kept popping up in all kinds of unexpected places demanding aid and money for the support of William. It appears to me that Nick could have gotten a court order forbidding this blackmail, but Nick put up with it. Matilda felt it was a just punishment placed upon her family for her part in sponsoring this marriage in the first place, so this continued until Sena Logan finally married a man up around Ashton, named Christensen, and they wound up living on a farm near Alta, Wyoming, that I presume they owned.

Nick and Matilda really drew sighs of relief when Sena got married and off their backs, so to speak, but this didn't end it. When Bill was about sixteen years old, Sena decided it was Nick's turn to care for and support Bill. He could not get along with Sena's husband, from which there were soon other children, and Bill was wild and hard to manage, so she told Bill that old Nick Wilson owed him a living and a start in life and so sent Bill back to Nick.

Bill was about the age of Nick's youngest child, a daughter named Nellie, who was fourteen years old when I was born in Jackson Hole, Wyoming, where Nick lived at the time Sena Logan Christensen sent Bill to him.

Wallace was about two years old when his mother, Sena Logan, gave him to Nick Wilson after their marriage annulment. It wasn't considered a divorce because the government didn't recognize it as a marriage. When Wallace was about ten years old, he was splitting wood and had moved his chopping block over under Matilda's clothesline. He hooked the axe over the line and it yanked out of his hands and came down and split his head open, from which he soon died. This was but one of the many tragedies that Nick mentioned in his manuscript, that seemed to hound him so much.

Nick tried to take Bill into the family as one of them, but he was always in trouble and raising hell, stealing from everybody he could, including Nick. He was finally caught stealing horses and Nick got him out of this scrape, but it cost Nick plenty. Nick's oldest brother, Henry, lived in Oregon at this time and had quite a spread, and he offered to take Bill and let him work for him. It was either that or jail for Bill, so Bill went and Nick had no more trouble from his polygamy. The old score was settled at last.

After my father died in 1915, Bill came back to the valley and we all got very well acquainted with him and everybody really liked Bill. Uncle Henry had done a good job on Bill and he was very talented and a great talker and story teller. With some education he could have really gone places in politics or as a lawyer. But he just drifted around from one little business to another, always the confidence man but never again in serious trouble. He finally started a small factory that made horse radish, in Idaho Falls, and his horse radish got quite famous before Bill died. He raised two sons of his own, Leo and Wallace, with whom my family got quite well acquainted, and we all liked Bill's boys very much. I hadn't seen or heard from either one of the boys since about World War II in 1943, and did not know whatever became of that branch of the Wilson family until after World War II was over.

CHAPTER 2 — **The Violin**

I started writing this sequel to my father's book about 1976, when I first met John Stewart, a teacher at the Utah State University in Logan, Utah. John was then a Librarian and professor of English along with other duties at that time, among which was Master of Ceremonies at the annual Goldenspike Pageant each May 10th, held at Promontory, Utah, in memory of the completion of America's first transcontinental railroad at that point in 1869. The Civil War and the Pony Express were over by that time and the Mormon Church began having a real ceremony out there at Promontory Point, and it got to be a real ritual, acted out in great detail and with costumes depicting dress and culture of that era. The U.S. Government finally got interested and decided to do something in honor of this event, build a monument or something. They sent a representative out from Washington, DC, to attend and investigate one of these yearly pageants put on by the Mormon Church, and he was so impressed by the show and ritual as conducted by the Latter-Day Saints, that he returned to Washington and advised the powers that be, not to do anything or even interfere with the pageant as put on by the State of Utah's Mormon people, and so it has been conducted each year by the Mormons on May 10th, ever since, come rain or shine, right up to this time.

John Stewart invited my wife and me to attend the pageant in 1978, which we did, and we were both given a standing ovation when John introduced me as the son of Nick Wilson, Pony Express Rider and famous as the "White Indian Boy." Promontory consists of only a few government buildings housing Park Service Rangers who care for the two vintage locomotives that stand there on the track facing each other, as they did that day in 1869, when the line was finished and the last nail driven was a Golden Spike!

Every American who possibly can should attend one of these Golden Spike Pageants! When I was there in 1978, there were about twenty busloads of children, from all over back East who had been sent to Utah to attend this Golden Spike Pageant, and they really cheered when John Stewart introduced my wife and me and told them about the part Nick Wilson had played in the settlement of the West.

This Promontory area is where Nick went in his brother's place to help with the community cattle that were wintered out on these lonely hills, at the time the Mormon bishops stole his girlfriend, as stated earlier.

I started writing this sequel to *The White Indian Boy* about 1976, and in the previous chapter I was telling of my half-brother Bill's two boys, Leo and Wallace, and that I had lost track of them after the Second World War started. Well, In 1980, the *National Geographic Magazine* published a story regarding the Pony Express, and I had guided Greg Arness, who was photographer for *National Geographic* at that time. Greg is the oldest son of James Arness, who is Matt Dillon in the *Gunsmoke* movie drama of the Old West. Greg was snapping pictures all the time as I guided him over that part of the old Oregon Trail that lies in Wyoming, and he snapped one of me that was made into a full-blown page photograph in the July, 1980, issue of *National Geographic Magazine*.

I had lost track of Bill's boys, Leo and Wallace, and thought they were probably lost in the war. Leo saw the story in *Geographic* of my dad as a Pony Express rider and, as I had long ago left Jackson Hole where he last saw me about 1940, he also had lost track of me. These two boys often visited me and my family while I worked for the Federal Elk Refuge near Jackson, Wyoming, prior to 1943. Leo saw this Pony Express article and my picture and through them he located me in California and called me on the telephone. We were both very happy to find each other again.

Leo said both he and his brother lived in Yakima, Washington, and begged me to come see them, and I did in October of 1981. My cousin and I were on a trip and arriving at Ellensburg, Washington, only about thirty-five miles from Yakima, we decided to go and look up these boys.

I was amazed at the reception given us by this family. Leo and Wallace had both married and had sons and daughters who were also married, and even grandchildren and great-grandchildren! About thirty of this tribe met us, and what a wonderful time we had! I took movies of them that turned out very well, and plan to put pictures in this book of them, as well as other old photographs of early settlers in Jackson Hole. I think there are around seventy descendants of Bill Wilson's family living in the Yakima area. They are all fine-looking, wonderful people. They work in all kinds of jobs, and some own their own farms, and a lot of them own a fine archery factory in Yakima, and also at Walla Walla, Washington, where they employ over one hundred craftsmen, part of them family members.

The plant in Yakima has an assembly line of over eighty men and women turning out beautiful sporting equipment. When we left they presented me with a beautiful bow and arrows made from hard wood imported from South America, Africa and India.

I am astounded at this progeny of my half-brother Bill Wilson! This clan has managed to stay together. Some of them are Mormons, others are not. Leo told me that his dad, Bill, had a terrific hatred for Mormons, after his experience as a child of polygamy. But you can say or think what you will about polygamy, except for it, this wonderful people at Yakima would not exist! That is something to think about!

These two sons of Bill's, Leo and Wallace, came to see me when I was living with my family on the old Patterson Ranch near the Gros Ventre River in Jackson Hole. The ranch had been purchased by the Rockefeller Foundation, which bought up all the north end of Jackson Hole and then gave it to the U.S. Government to go into the Grand Teton National Park as it is today.

Leo and Wallace each had a big truck and were hauling supplies into Jackson Hole, and especially to the many dude ranches that had sprung up all over the valley. They would try to get something to haul back out, so as not to return to Pocatello empty. There was a great demand for calcium, so they combed the Jackson Hole Valley over for old bones, of which there were plenty, due to elk dying on the refuge each winter, as well as tons of shed antlers, which they got permission from the Department of the Interior to gather up.

The last time I saw them they stayed a couple of nights with us and got two big loads of elk antlers and elk bones, as well as skeletons of cattle and horses, to haul out to Pocatello and sell for calcium. That was the summer of 1941, and that Fall the Japs hit Pearl Harbor, and that was the last time I had seen them, and so we were very happy to get together again. Leo and I planned to meet at the Pageant of the Golden Spike on May 10th, 1982, but Leo died from a sudden heart attack before we got to meet again. Wallace was not well, as he was suffering from emphysema, but has since quit smoking and is in pretty good shape again. We were all very shocked and saddened by Leo's sudden death, and I have not seen any of the family since. I wanted to find out more of the history of this wonderful branch of my relatives and I hope to get back to Yakima yet before I die, and stay awhile with them.

Now to get back to my story:

After the settlement with Sena Logan, mother of Bill and Wallace, Matilda moved to Pocatello, Idaho, and started a boarding and rooming house, and there were twelve or fourteen children for her to support.

Nick went to jail for one year at Canyon Creek. He was a model prisoner and was trusted and treated kindly and given many privileges not enjoyed by other prisoners. Nick was a good carpenter and cabinet maker, and they let him work in the prison shops, where he made furniture and sold for a small price, and so was able to send Matilda money to help out from time to time.

One of Nick's projects turned out to affect a lot of lives and it's a story that ought to be told, and right here is a good time to tell it and get it over with, because the repercussions lasted for many years. Nick liked music and had a very good singing voice, which in later years reminded me of Burl Ives, the great radio and TV singer. While in prison, Nick decided to make a violin, a fiddle, as he called it, and the results were astonishing. He worked on this violin for over six months, between chores on his furniture and cabinet-making, and when he finished, it was a beautiful instrument with a quality tone.

After finishing it, Nick taught himself to play it very well with the help of several inmates who happened to be good old-time hoe-down fiddlers. After Nick finished his prison term, he had this old fiddle to show for it, and the rest of his life he used it for entertainment of many delighted people. He was in great demand to play for oldtime dances, which was one of the main pastimes and social events in those days. The Mormon people loved dancing, and it was allowed by the Church. Almost every Saturday night they held dances that lasted often into the daylight hours on Sunday morning. People drove for miles to these dances, and it was one of the fun events in the lives of the early settlers in the West.

I can still remember the dances held in the old meeting house in Jackson Hole, when I was a kid. Whole families came from all over the valley and they brought lots of food, of which the beautiful big cakes were my favorite, and they danced and ate all night. My dad was real popular with his old fiddle, along with John Burcher, Jake Jackson, Johnie Woodward and others who took turns playing all night long. I would eat cake and all other kinds of goodies and finally crawl under the benches that lined the dance hall walls, to keep from getting tramped to death, and listen to the lively music and watch the Virginia reels, polkas, shottishes, waltzes, two-steps and other oldtime dances, and the stamp, stamp of many feet, until I finally went to sleep. These men, along with my dad, were really among the finest of real old hoe-down fiddlers!

This old violin of my dad's was a prized possession and all my half-sisters and their families expected this violin to pass on to them someday, but it finally went to my half-sister, Etta Leek. Etta married Stephen Nelson Leek, who was later known as the "Daddy of the Elk" in Jackson Hole, for the part he played in saving this splendid animal from early extinction by his untiring efforts to get the U.S. Government interested in preserving them from starvation and wanton slaughter.

My father finished his old manuscript in 1910 and it was published by Skelton Publishing Company of Salt Lake City, who went bankrupt while publishing these books. They had about fifteen hundred copies finished, and George Skelton, publisher, put Nick to traveling with a team and wagon, peddling these books for seventy-five cents a copy to help pay his publishing bill.

I was about nine years old and for three summers I traveled with my dad selling these books, all through Wyoming, Idaho, Montana, Utah and even up into Oregon. We sold so many copies that the Skelton Publishing Company got back on its feet and finally got back full-time into the publishing business. But my dad made a deal with Professor Howard R. Driggs, who was teaching English at New York University, and the World Book Company published a later edition of *The White Indian Boy.*

About the second year that my father and I were peddling his books, one of our horses became lame, and took sick and died. We happened to be in Star Valley, Wyoming, at that time. My dad got word to Steve and Etta Leek that he needed another horse, and they sent a big, grey gelding we called Captain down to us. When we got back to Jackson Hole my sister Etta told my dad he could keep Captain if he would give her his old fiddle. She had two boys, Lester and Holly. Lester was about thirteen years old and she wanted the fiddle for him to learn to play.

My father seldom played the old violin anymore and, as Etta said, it might be lost or stolen anyway, because he left it home while we were gone, and our house was often broken into, usually by kids or bums, and we had lots of things stolen or destroyed, so father gave the violin to Etta. The other five half-sisters were pretty sore about it for awhile, but finally got over it, and Lester really became a fine violinist after being tutored by a man in Jackson named Fuller, who was a good music teacher. When Lester was about seventeen years old, Etta bought him a fine violin for three hundred dollars. Lester married a girl who was a fine pianist, and they started playing for dances and giving music lessons. Lester only played my father's old violin once in awhile.

When the First World War broke out, Lester went with the first Jackson Hole volunteers overseas to France, and he took the old violin, which he carried all over Europe and entertained the soldiers. His own company began autographing the old fiddle, and there were dozens of their names written with indelible ink all over it.

When Lester got home from the war, he and his wife resumed their music teaching and playing for dances and running a movie theatre. Along about 1927 Lester played this old fiddle at a dance in Jackson, Wyoming. He usually only played it for the last "Home Sweet Home Waltz" that ended the dance and then put it back in the old black box that my father made to keep it in while he was in prison. After the dance, Lester left both fiddles on the piano and went with his wife for refreshments, then returned and got the two violins and went home. It happened to be the last dance for the season, along in late April.

When they continued these dances the following fall, Lester opened the old violin case and the fiddle was gone! He hadn't used it all summer, and he soon remembered the last time he used it was that night seven months before. He was broken-hearted over the loss, and the concern was felt by everyone who knew the history of the old fiddle, and they were legion.

Etta died about 1931, and her son Lester died about 1935. Both were still grieving about the loss of Nick's old fiddle. The story should end here, but there is more to tell, so I might as well tell what happened to this old fiddle, which had meant so much to all the relations of Nick Wilson, both the living and the dead.

It was about 1927 that my father's old fiddle was stolen after a dance in the old Club House at Jackson, Wyoming. Now comes the hard part in telling the rest of the story regarding my dad's old violin.

I have given this much thought and have arrived at the conclusion that in writing a biography you must tell it like it was, which means the telling of the names of those individuals who are concerned. Too many biographies are spoiled because the writer tries to cover up or evade pertinent truths or embellish them with fancy exaggerations that have ruined the authenticity of much of our past history of both famous men and natural events, to the point that so very much of our history is shrouded with insinuations and half-truths, putting a shadow of doubt on the real truth pertaining to these events.

The rest of the story about my father's fiddle is mostly hear-say and would not stand up in any court of law, anyway, so the characters I name are merely incidental to the tale.

I am not accusing or charging anything to anyone mentioned, therefore it is not meant to defame or injure anyone's reputation, but only to substantiate what I and others really think happened to my dad's old fiddle.

Now, as stated above, it was about 1927 when this old violin was stolen. All the boys who had gone to war were back, either alive or in their coffins. Among the survivors was a nephew of mine, named Fay Goodrick. He served through most of World War I, being called in the draft. He left a young wife, who was pregnant with their first child. It was born soon after Fay was inducted into the U.S. Army. He never saw this child until it was about two years old, after the war. Fay and his wife became very good friends with another young couple about their age; their names were Glen and Divida Crosby. I don't think Glen married Divida until after the war, and I don't think he served with Lester Leek's company that had stuck together all through the war. Divida was a daughter of Mr. and Mrs. Dave Timmons, one of the old pioneer families in Jackson Hole. I knew them all very well.

Now the story moves ahead until about 1942, or fifteen years after the loss of my father's old fiddle. I was married in September of 1927, and with my bride I left Jackson Hole soon after Lester Leek discovered the theft of my dad's old fiddle. We returned to Jackson Hole in 1935, just before Lester died of Pernicious Anemia at the age of about 38.

Soon after returning to Jackson Hole, Fay Goodrick and I were visiting and I guess that Lester's death brought up the subject of my father's old violin, and this is Fay's story:

Although my father was Fay Goodrick's grandpa, he always referred to him as "Daddy" because that is what my little brother George and I always called him.

Fay said, "By the way, did you ever wonder what became of Daddy's old fiddle?"

"Of course I have!" I answered. "Many, many times! I can't imagine who could have ever took that old fiddle and nothing ever being heard of it again!"

Fay said, "Well, I know where it is! And I seen it not very long ago! And if you want it, I can tell you where it is!"

I couldn't believe my ears! Daddy's old fiddle! To say I was all attention now is to put it mildly!

Fay continued, "Clara and I were very good friends with Glen Crosby and of course, you have known Divida all her life. Glen and I worked together a lot on different jobs. Well, Glen and Divida moved out of Jackson Hole several years ago and went to Nampa, Idaho. We missed them a lot and kept our friendship by writing quite often."

Then I believe that Fay said that Glen had died recently and he and Clara went to Nampa to his funeral, and while there, Fay and Clara, his wife, stayed with Divida at her home.

I don't remember if Fay said how long they stayed with Divida, but Fay told me that she had a piano in the living room and he happened to be in the room alone when he noticed a violin lying on top of the piano. Upon closer inspection he said he nearly fainted when he noticed writing all over this violin, and he picked it up and it was daddy's old fiddle! Fay said there was no way that he could have been mistaken; he knew the old fiddle from the time he could walk and, also, he had seen the fiddle with all the autographs on it many, many times since Lester Leek brought it home from the war. Lester and Fay were first cousins, and his mother Kate was Etta Leek's full sister, one of my five half-sisters who had hoped to own the violin one day.

Fay said it was quite awhile before he got control of his emotions enough to ask Divida where she got the violin, and she told Fay that Glen's brother, I do not know his name, had died a few years before and had given the violin to Glen, telling him that he had carried the violin all over Europe during the war and that the autographs were the names of a lot of his old buddies! Now, here was Fay's dilemma: someone was lying! One of the brothers stole my father's old violin that night after the dance, while Lester and his wife, Helen, were down in the drug store getting refreshments. Who stole the fiddle and how could I get it back?

It was about 1972 that John Stewart, a librarian and professor at Utah State University in Logan, Utah, came into my life. He was the founder of the National Association for Outlaw and Lawman History at the University. This association was gathering material for history of the Old West.

John came to Jackson Hole to gather material on Nick Wilson, Pony Express rider, pioneer and mountain man, with fame as "The White Indian Boy"!

John had already collected quite a lot of things on Nick Wilson, and I gave him more, which made a pretty good display in a show-case at the University. I told John the story about Nick Wilson's old violin, and he really put the pressure on me to get this violin, not only for its historical value, but for the Nick Wilson collection — it would be priceless.

John couldn't understand why I had let so many years pass since Fay Goodrick told me where it was, and having not made any attempt to get it. I explained that the Timmons family were not only among the first settlers in Jackson, but they were very close and dear friends of my father. I did not want to barge in on Divida and accuse her husband or his brother of stealing my dad's old fiddle! She was a widow now, and I did not think the old violin was worth what it would take to get it back.

John countered my argument by saying that he thought the vio-lin could be recovered if Divida were approached right, and if she would let some of us see it who could identify this old fiddle as being the one made by Nick Wilson, and that she might be per-suaded to give it up without any accusations or embarrassment whatever, if she could just be convinced that the violin was really the one Nick Wilson made while serving a year in prison for polygamy. He wanted to know if I could positively identify the fiddle, if I saw it, and I said I was certain I could. So John asked permission from me to let him try to recover the old fiddle, which I gladly gave to him.

Several months later he contacted me and said he had written Mrs. Crosby for permission to see the old violin and gave her reasons to believe that the violin she had was truly the old Nick Wilson fiddle. John said he received a very nasty, hostile reply from Divida Timmons Crosby, in which she very vehemently de-nied that the fiddle ever belonged to Nick Wilson, and refused to let him or anyone else see the violin for purposes of identification. She said she was tired of having her dead husband accused of being a thief and that she really believed Glen Crosby's story that his brother gave it to him.

And so the Nick Wilson violin story ends right here. The readers can make their own conclusion, but after John told me about his effort to see and possibly get possession of this violin, I was more convinced than ever that Fay Goodrick really told me the truth about seeing Daddy's old fiddle in the Crosby home. Otherwise, why did not Divida deny possession of such a violin? She did not, and thereby acknowledged the existence of such a violin. Who could believe such a coincidence of there being two autographed violins, and two coinciding stories of it being carried all over Europe through World War I? How could this be other than my father's old violin? The names on the violin would prove whether it was Lester Leek's volunteer company or not.

The University of Wyoming at Laramie would love to have this old fiddle, and so would all the universities in the great state of Utah!

After all these surmisings, I believe that in fairness to Divida and those of us who really believe that this disputed violin is really the old Nick Wilson fiddle, and for the peace of Divida's mind, for she has no doubt pondered the truth regarding this old violin for many years, that she should come forward with this violin and let it be inspected by the few of us remaining who can identify whether or not this really is Nick Wilson's old violin.

CHAPTER 3 — **Prologue to Jackson Hole**

Nick had never forgotten his two happy years living with Chief Washakie's tribe when they were wild Indians, roving at will over this great western untamed land. He remembered the summer that Washakie had planned to go to the Jackson Hole country to hunt. He listened to the many enticing stories by the Indians regarding this fabulous hunting and fishing land where the great Yam-Pah-Pa (Snake River), mother of western waters, began her wild course along its thousand miles of rugged shore to her rendezvous with the Great Sea (Pacific Ocean).

This was nearly thirty-five years earlier, but Nick had never given up his desire and longing to visit this wonderful place, and so at this time, as Nick was back in southern Idaho and he now owned a small farm near Bear Lake, which Abe and Edna ran for him while he had a blacksmith shop in the village, and Matilda ran her famous eating and rooming house, as the family was now in quite secure circumstances again, Nick Wilson decided it was high time to go and see this fabulous Jackson Hole hunting ground which he had heard so much about. No white settlers lived there yet; only a few outlaws and horse thieves made it their hideout as law and order had not yet been established there.

However, it is well known that many outlaws and especially horse thieves, prior to, and for several years after, 1900, used Jackson Hole as a rendezvous and hiding place from the law.

Horse thieves waged a thriving business of stealing the big fine horses and mules from the farmers in Nebraska and selling them to farmers and ranchers in Oregon, from whom they stole horses and sold them to farmers in Nebraska. After settlers began homesteading Jackson Hole, this practice soon ended.

There were many white men entering Jackson Hole before Nick Wilson's families and friends came here in quest of permanent homes, but most of them came to plunder and exploit and so they could not be considered as settlers, although some of these outlaws who escaped capture did remain here after the real settlers came and they are known to have taken up land and even married some of the settlers' daughters and settled down.

U.S. Marshals were placed not only in Jackson Hole, but in many other areas of the west in order to break up the gangs of outlaws. Even some of these outlaws that married settlers' daughters had to flee when things got too hot for them, and some never dared to come back. It is believed that my half-sister Fanny married one of these horse thieves.

He left one night, never to return again, abandoning Fanny and their baby girl, Alta. His name was Clark Caswell. Anyway, that's the name he married Fanny under.

I will interrupt my story again and insert a couple of accounts of Jackson Hole and horse thieves. It is getting ahead of my story, but I think a short summary of Jackson Hole's origin and a story relating to horse thieves would be in order and interesting to the reader at this point.

Beautiful Mount Moran, so named in honor of Thomas Moran, an artist, and is a flattering monument to any man! William Henry Jackson took this picture from what is now known as Signal Mountain, near the outlet of Jackson Lake, which was named by Captain Sublette in honor of David Jackson. Signal Mountain was so named because Indians could communicate with each other all over Jackson Hole from this prominent mountain. Fire destroyed timber on the north slope about 1865.

CHAPTER 4 — **A Heritage**

Majestic Mount Moran has an altitude of 12,100 feet above sea level. It rises a mile above the waters of Jackson and Leigh Lakes, whose clear, cold waters ebb and flow at its base. This great landmark was named in honor of Thomas Moran, an artist, and is a flattering monument to any man. Moran Creek flows west past its northern extremeties and empties into Jackson Lake near its head.

Down Moran Creek Canyon, following this beautiful stream, afoot and with a pack on his back, came John Colter in 1807. Turning north at the mouth of the creek, he skirted the west shore of Jackson Lake to the inlet, which is now the Snake River, waded it here, and continued on north to Yellowstone Lake. He was probably the first white man ever to lay eyes on the Teton Range and enter Jackson Hole and what is now Yellowstone Park.

Jackson Lake and Jackson Hole were named by Captain William Sublette, as he was camping on the shores of this beautiful lake in 1832, in honor of his good friend, David Jackson, a trapper. Leigh Lake was named in memory of Richard Leigh, "Beaver Dick." Jenny Lake was named in honor of Beaver Dick's beautiful Indian wife.

In 1811 came the Hunt party, consisting of sixty-four men. Following elk trails, they passed through what is now known as the Hoback Canyon en route to the Pacific Coast. The Hunt party was the first group of white men ever to visit Jackson Hole. The canyon and river were named for John Hoback, trapper, and probably guide for this party.

For many years, before and after the Hunt party passed through, the Hoback Canyon was a favorite route for elk and antelope on their semi-annual migrations to and from Jackson's Hole and the Red Desert. On one side of the Hoback Canyon, where it narrowed down, was once a long line of piled rocks, presumably placed there long ago by Indians, either for purposes of defense or, more probably, for the concealment of Indian hunters lying in wait for the long lines of migrating animals to come in range of their bows and arrows.

The Hunt party called the Tetons "Pilot Knobs." They were named "Trois Tetons" by Vioux Pierre in 1819. The Indians called them "Tee-Win-At," which means "pinnacles." The Snake River, which flows into the north end of Jackson Lake and then on out through the southeast end, roars its way on down through its thousand miles of rugged shore to a last rendezvous with the great sea. The Indians called this wonderful stream "Yam-Pah-Pa," meaning "the stream where Yampa grows." Yampa is a plant with a bulbous root and was much used by Indians for food.

All the above-mentioned enchanting lakes were gorged out at the base of the Tetons by the terminal moraines of glaciers which, ages ago, crept down from the mountains and scoured out the great basins and pot holes that bear these testimonies to this day.

When Colter and the Hunt party came this way so many moons ago, the streams teemed with fat, native trout, but only the lakes and streams that had access to the direct waters of the great "Yam-Pah-Pa" contained any fish at all.

Then in 1892, the U.S. Fish Commission planted Mackinaw and brown trout in Shoshone and Lewis Lakes in Yellowstone Park, and they came down the waters of the Lewis and Snake Rivers to Jackson and Jenny Lakes where they are now caught in great numbers. It has been common to take Mackinaw from sixteen to twenty-five pounds in weight and one is said to have been caught by Colonel Jordon, at what is known as "Jordon Channel" in Jackson Lake, that weighed forty-two pounds. It has been claimed that before 1892, Shoshone and Lewis Lakes in Yellowstone Park contained no fish life at all.

The old trappers' trails have now given way to modern highways. Locations of the outlaws' cabins have been forgotten. But there are still signs in the dark timber of the old corrals where stolen horses were hidden during the day.

Nearly all the old landmarks have gone. Only the elk remains. But he no longer wends his carefree way over the dim and near-forgotten trails of yore. Never again will he travel back and forth on his semi-annual migration to and from the mountains.

He will never leave the valley in winter, because there is no place to go, even in summer, except to his limited summer range, where there are still sparkling streams on every hand. Conditions, in summer, are ideal for increases in the herds to many times the size which can now be cared for during the long winter months. Hence, every effort should be made to keep the size of the herds within reasonable bounds, which is the only way to prevent heavy winter loss. As time passes, we will find, more and more, that this is a job for unhampered and politics-free game management. This is a heritage.

No place to go, and nothing to eat!

CHAPTER 5 — **Were They Really Horse Thieves?**

There is so much controversy and so many different stories told about what happened at the old Cunningham Cabin site that up to now the Teton Park Commission has not used any of them. They have a historical marker on the highway south of the old cabin which does not even mention the tragedy that was enacted there so long ago when Jackson Hole was young and sparsely settled.

There were only six men in the supposed law enforcement posse that came to arrest two supposedly dangerous outlaws and horse thieves.

The lawmen were Pierce Cunningham, supposedly U.S. Marshal; Bill Manning, his deputy; and Steve Leek, Mose Giltner, Bill Crawford, and Andy Madison. The last named four were supposedly deputized to help make the arrest. To my knowledge, there is no truth whatsoever in Frank Calkins' book *Jackson Hole*, in which he describes this episode: "Officers recently fought a gun battle with suspects holed up in a Hoback River Lodge that far surpassed the shoot-out two alleged horse thieves had with a posse at the Cunningham Cabin in 1893." Calkins goes on to say that the old Cunningham Cabin there now was restored to commemorate this shooting affair, which is not true. He ascribes his authority as Ben Driggs, who claims the story begins when a few horses were stolen in Montana, and that a deputy in Teton Basin named Sam Wanner checked with Johnny Carnes, who lived in Jackson Hole, and found that these "two outlaws" he calls "George Spencer" and "Mike Burnett," were holed up in northern Jackson Hole at the old Cunningham Cabin and were holding stolen horses there. He goes on to say, "A posse led by a squawman named John Williams arrived from Montana and recruited a bunch of men in Teton Basin. The men crossed Teton Pass, wallowed through snow nearly fifty miles up to Spread Creek and in early morning hours surrounded the cabin and called for the two men to surrender. They both ran out and were shooting as they came, so they were blasted with shotguns."

I can't remember if Steve Leek mentioned the date that these men were killed at Cunningham Cabin or not, but it had to be later

Bill Manning at his ranch in south Jackson Hole about 1921, shortly before his death at 92 (?). Bill was one of the Deputy U.S. Marshals who killed the two men at the site of the Pierce Cunningham cabin on lower Spread Creek in Jackson Hole, Wyoming, about 1895.

than 1893, because the first settlers did not enter Jackson Hole until 1891. I think the date was more like 1895 or 1896 because the valley was pretty well settled when this tragedy occurred.

There have been so many lies told about this episode that it is no wonder there is no plaque at the Cunningham Cabin depicting this affair. Nobody knows who to believe, but I knew all six of the men who did go to the Cunningham Cabin, and I have heard the story from four of their own lips. I have heard Bill Manning's version so many times I know it by heart. He claimed that the two men really were outlaws and horse thieves, and he only helped kill them in self-defense. Bill Crawford was a coward and a damn liar, and I never believed a word he said. Bill Crawford was well-to-do, but when my dad, Nick Wilson, died in 1915, there was over $500 on his store, hotel and livery stable accounts owed by Crawford that he never did offer to pay. (See the account about Crawford at Battle Mountain as recorded in this book.)

The other two versions were by Steve Leek and Mose Giltner. I heard Giltner's version as told to my dad in our cabin on Fish Creek when he, Mose, came to borrow my dad's white-topped Studebaker three-seated buggy that my dad used to haul dudes from the railhead at St. Anthony, Idaho, to Jackson Hole. While Mose had the buggy, he had a run-away with a team of his spirited Morgan horses which he raised on his ranch at the mouth of Spring Gulch, which was later owned by Steve Callahan, and then by Jimmy Boyle after Giltner died. Mose never recovered from the broken bones and beating he got in his run-away, and it eventually led to his early death.

Mose Giltner told my dad that he was a damn fool to have ever gone with this posse. Mose firmly believed that the men were innocent. Mose and the other five were all concerned with being charged for murdering innocent men, and thus the many stories in order to "cover up." Mose's version coincides with that of Steve Leek, as he himself told it to me and Ray Goodrick, Jesse Wort, and a boy from Texas whose name I have forgotten. This was in early September, 1919:

The four of us were with Leek in his old Oldsmobile. He was taking us to the head of Jackson Lake to put up hay and the road passed the old Cunningham Cabin. We stopped at the spring to eat lunch and I asked Steve to tell us what really happened there and he did. He showed us where the little Trapper's Cabin stood and where the small log stable stood in which the posse made their stand. He showed us where the graves were.

Leek's version was this: It had gotten noised around that two men were holed up in the Trapper's Cabin near Spread Creek. Leek said the present buildings were built in later years by Pierce Cunningham after he homesteaded the land there and he tore the old cabin and barn down and built there because of the good spring water. Leek told us that it was thought these men were horse thieves, which Jackson Hole was trying to be rid of. These men did have about forty horses which they wintered in the slew grass meadows and along the creek and river banks. This area was always a light snowfall, as was the Buffalo River Valley up to Black Rock. Leek said he was deputized by Pierce Cunningham to join the above-named Jackson Hole posse to try and find out who these men were and what they were doing. It was nearing spring breakup in Jackson Hole, and it was feared the men would soon be moving out with their horses.

It was in late April, 1895 or 1896 when the arrest was undertaken. Leek said the posse met at a ranch near what was later Kelley, Wyoming. The next day they rode to the heavy timber known now as Cunningham Hill, about ten miles north of Kelley. It was where the first road was graded down from Antelope Flat to Spread Creek and the hill is high and steep. It was a nice, balmy spring day and the snow was going fast. Leek said as their horses traveled through the snow patches it splashed like water, it was so soft. The hill observation point is nearly a mile or more from the old cabin down under the bench in the valley, and they followed around northeast, out of sight in the timber until they could see the horses down in the partly barren meadows and could see the old cabin and barn.

He said they watched the cabin all afternoon with their binoculars as they had arrived there shortly after noon. The first movement was about 4 p.m., when a man came out of the old shack and walked a few yards to the old stable and entered, reappearing in a few minutes leading a saddle horse which he led down to the cabin and the other man came to the door. They conversed a minute or two, then the first man mounted the horse and rode at a walk down to the horses about a quarter of a mile below the cabin. The horses appeared very gentle and looked from that distance to have wintered in good shape. The man walked up to a light sorrel horse and changed his saddle and bridle to this light colored horse and walked leisurely back to the cabin and packed a few sticks of wood from a pile stacked against the south side of the cabin, into the cabin.

Leek said some of the posse wanted to go down and confront the men (that is what they should have done), but Cunningham said they would wait, so they rode back quite a ways into the timber where a fire would not be seen and built a good fire and made coffee and ate sandwiches. Cunningham said they better observe the cabin again the next day and see if the men were alone, and so the posse slept that night in overcoats and saddle blankets, using saddles for pillows.

They had hot coffee before daylight and squelched the fire so no smoke would show and were back with field glasses that morning. Just before sun up, smoke curled up from the chimney and a few minutes later a man came out and urinated near the cabin and re-entered; then another man came out with a water bucket which he slipped up on his left arm and proceeded to roll and light a cigarette. Then he, too, urinated and went on to the spring and bent down, apparently filling the pail, then went to the cabin. About an hour later one of the men walked to the barn and appeared with the light-colored horse and rode back to the horses which were nearly in the same place as the day before. The rider again caught another horse, a black one this time, and, changing saddle horses, rode back to the barn. It was evident that they always kept up one horse for during the day, and turning that one loose in the evening so it could graze, evidently having no feed in the barn. This surmisal was borne out when again in late afternoon the black horse was exchanged for a light bay. It was evident they always kept a saddled horse in the barn.

The posse took turns watching the cabin and sleeping in the warm sunlight. Cunningham decided they would again build a fire, then just before daylight all would hide in the old barn, and then arrest the men in early morning. The time arrived and they walked down in the early morning darkness. It is said the darkest hour is just before the dawn. The posse quietly took their places in the barn. They were careful not to alarm the horse, by petting and whispering to him. It was cold and cramped in the tiny stable. Leek was in the manger next to the door where Pierce Cunningham squatted, looking through the cracks. Daylight finally came and the posse grew tense. The horse could sense their tenseness and started to paw. Someone quickly quieted him and kept their hand on his warm muzzle.

Sunlight lit the Teton Range and crept down. Now smoke started to come from the old stove pipe in the cabin. The quietness was loud like thunder, hearts were pounding, eyes were squinting through the chink holes that had been made through the horse manure dobbing. Leek could see that the barn had been dobbed with horse manure and some mud to keep cold winds off the night horse. The floor was dusty and dry except where the horse stood. Then a low whisper, "They are coming out!" All eyes strained! Trigger muscles tightened! Then a man stepped from the house and shut the door. He had a water pail and a six-shooter tied to his leg. He walked straight to the spring water hole which was barely sixty feet from the barn. He bent down for the water.

Pierce Cunningham now opened the barn door part way, showing himself with six-shooter pointed straight at the man at the spring. His voice cracked like a whip. "Hold it! Hands up! You're covered!"

Like a flash, the stooping man fired. His bad squatting position was all that saved Cunningham's life. He fired twice. The first bullet cut away part of Cunningham's boot heel, the second tore through the slab door, just missing Cunningham's stomach, and splinters and dirt filled Leek's eyes.

He dropped to the ground as Cunningham barked, "Fire!" There was a volley of shots, but none of them was from Leek's gun, as he was desperately rubbing dirt and splinters from his eyes just in time to look out and see the man fall. He started to fall forward, then, with buckled knees, rolled to his side and then over on his back and lay still.

Then the cabin door flew open and out rushed a huge, hairy man with a .45 Colt in each hand. He had reached his partner before Cunningham yelled, "Halt!" At the word the man leaped past his fallen comrade and came in great strides toward the men in the barn. Cunningham yelled, "Halt!" again, but the two guns began to blaze.

"Fire! Fire!" yelled Cunningham. Again, there was a spattering of shots. The wild-eyed horse reared back, breaking the halter, and kept rearing and shrilling, and the dirt and splinters were blinding.

Then it was over. Quiet — loud quiet, reigned. Leek didn't realize until he was outside that he never fired a shot. The huge, black-bearded man lay almost against the barn door step, face down, holding two empty .45's, and both were on full cock! Leek looked at his gun, spun the cylinder and six loaded shells stared back at him. He really hadn't fired a shot! He felt stunned and dirty, sick. His first thoughts were, "Was this murder, or self-defense?"

The posse buried the two strangers, wrapped in their bedding, in a shallow grave. It was a quiet posse that returned to Jackson.

News spread; stories were told. The horses were driven to Jackson. They were all branded U.S. Uncle Sam! Messages of investigation flashed east and west. No one claimed the horses, and no one knew who the men were. A hearing was held, and finally an assignment of soldiers arrived in Jackson Hole and claimed the horses. The soldiers said these horses came from Kentucky via Missouri across Nebraska. These men were delivering them to the army at a fort near Pendleton, Oregon. The horses were gone.

More stories were told. Men were frightened. Stories were altered, retold and changed again. I never realized how complete the coverup was until I read in Frank Calkins' book the version by Ben Driggs. Even the Jackson Hole posse was never mentioned! Is it any wonder that no story appeared on the plaque at the Cunningham Cabin? Was any true story ever told? What really did happen at Cunningham Cabin will probably never be known except by a six-man posse from Jackson Hole.

Steve Leek was my brother-in-law. I knew him from the time I was a baby, up until his death in Jackson Hole in March, 1943. I never knew Steve to lie or ever even use a swear word, and thus I believe this above story as he told it to us to be true.

Ray Goodrick is dead. I don't know whatever became of the boy from Texas, but at this writing I think Jesse Wort is still alive, and Jesse is another of the same breed as Steve Leek, one of the few persons I ever knew that I never heard tell a lie. I think that Jesse would bear me out in the story as told above.

There is a lot of drama in this story, a lot of surmising and a lot of unanswered questions. Among the most pertinent was: Why did not Pierce Cunningham, a U.S. Marshal and leader of this posse, confront these men that first day after observing their actions from a hiding place? The only explanation we have is: Cunningham said, "No, we will wait and observe them again tomorrow to be sure that these are all of them!" It seems to me that after observing these two men all afternoon, it should have been enough evidence to believe there were only two of them! Anyone who knew Pierce Cunningham would not accuse him of cowardice, but we now realize that the posse should have, in broad daylight, confronted these men! In doing it the way they did shows that the two men had no way of knowing these men in the barn were lawmen. They thought they were being jumped by outlaws or horse thieves, which Jackson Hole was full of at that time, who were bent on stealing their horses! All of which turned out to be government horses! If these two men were genuine drovers who were delivering these horses to some Army fort or post near Pendleton, all they would have had to do was explain that they got caught here by winter coming on and decided this would be a good place to winter the horses. These men, no doubt, knew the country well and it was still a long way to Pendleton, Oregon. Even I, in this day and age, can't think of a better place to winter a band of horses than right here where they did.

I wouldn't accuse Cunningham of cowardice in this tragedy, but I do think he showed very poor judgment in how he handled this affair. From what I know as mentioned above, in my opinion, this was murder! But Cunningham was the U.S. Marshal, placed in Jackson Hole to handle affairs in this area, and all he had to do was cover up the posses' part in this affair. That was evidently what he did, according to the records, and the matter was dropped, but not before it caused a lot of worry to six desperate men!

Pierce Cunningham in old age. His ranch near Spread Creek was where the shoot-out occurred.

Mose Giltner in old age. He was a member of the six-man posse.

CHAPTER 6 — **Prologue to Jackson Hole** *continued*

And so it was in the year of 1889 came a lone rider, Nick Wilson, leading a pack horse. He came up and over Pine Creek Pass in Idaho and entered Pierre's Hole, now known as the Teton Basin, or Teton Valley. He rode up the heavily timbered canyon that led from the Basin's southeast corner toward the east until he climbed up into what is now the Teton Pass leading into Jackson Hole, Wyoming.

His first breath-taking view of the beautiful valley lying below brought a whistle to his lips, and with awe he sat on his fine saddle horse and gazed for a long time down into this lovely valley. He almost burst with wonder and excitement as he sized up the wide, sweeping valley floor and the big stream, which he knew was the great "Yam-Pah-Pa" — Snake River!

It was his first view of Jackson Hole, although nearly thirty-five years before, when he was a lad of fourteen years of age and living with Chief Washakie of the great Shoshone tribe, he had come near to entering this beautiful valley from the north end. The Shoshone Indians were on a hunting trip into this wonderful place that is now known as Jackson Hole, but this area was then disputed by the Crow Indian tribe of Montana. So it happened that the two tribes met at what is now known as Grassy Lake, northwest of Jackson Hole, and a great battle raged between them for two days. You have already read an account of this terrible battle from Nick Wilson's old manuscript in preceding chapters.

This battle was fought clear down to Jackson Lake, where yet to this day are found arrowheads left there from this great battle. Chief Washakie's warriors won, but so badly battered were his remaining braves that he gave up the hunt in Jackson Hole that year and returned to the beautiful Henry's Lake, now in Idaho, their campground previous to this big fight, to rest and let the wounded warriors heal.

However, the urge to see this great hunting and fishing grounds of which Nick had heard so much from the Indians had never left him since that time, and now his dream was about to come true!

If only Chief Washakie and his dear old Indian mother and his other friends could only be with him now! Nick had always planned to go back to the Indians some day, but circumstances had always prevented his return.

At this time the government was already placing the defeated Indians on reservations. The great triumph of the Indians at the Battle of the Little Big Horn sounded the doom forever for their free life that had never known harness for a million years and a day. The nomadic life of the Redman was over.

Now Nick had heard that Chief Washakie had chosen the Wind River country on the east side of the continental divide to be the home for his Shoshone tribe. As I mentioned before, the first boundaries of this great reservation extended over a great area of Wyoming and Idaho, but it was gradually whittled down until now it is confined to the Wind River proper, all east of the continental divide, on account of ingressing white settlements. However, at this time the reservation still embraced the first allotment.

What was about to happen now to Nick Wilson seems more like a dream come true, than reality, for after he gazed down into this beautiful panorama which is now Jackson Hole, his heart beat faster and his thoughts burst into sound! "This is the place!" he said. He was not thinking of Brigham Young, who first made this historical statement, when he first sighted the Great Salt Lake Valley, Nick was thinking of his family, his brothers and sisters' families, and his friends and others, who, like himself, were looking for a home, a place to settle down, for already for him the west was getting too populated! "Yes, this is it!" he said aloud. "This is the place where I want to live, and here I want to die!" Both of his ambitions were realized. This was my father, Elijah Nicholas Wilson. You will see that he did settle the Jackson Hole Valley and lived here for 26 years before he died on December 27, 1915. The story of the rest of his life will now be confined to Jackson Hole; it was his last and most beloved home.

It was getting late in the day now, so Nick decided to get off the mountain and down onto the floor of the valley before dark. The decline was very steep; the well-worn game and Indian trail dropped nearly straight down. In fact, it was so steep that Nick thought that everything or everyone who entered this way must still be down there or had left another way! It was about three miles down to the floor of the valley, which he entered through heavy timber and to his surprise, he came out on the bank of a beautiful stream teeming with huge cutthroat trout! This was later named Fish Creek, and on its banks Nick later built his homestead cabin.

But the big surprise that bordered on being a miracle was that as Nick led his pack horse through the piney grove on the west bank of Fish Creek he rode into an Indian camp! It turned out to be Shoshone hunters and Nick soon began to recognize some of his old Indian friends that were kids his age when he left their camp in about 1856, thirty-three years before! They were now adult Indians around forty-seven years old! Nick described this meeting as one of the happiest days of his life. He said they talked and feasted nearly all night, recalling the days that Nick lived among the Shoshones when they were yet truly wild Indians!

These Indians told Nick that Washakie was camped with the squaws and papooses over on Grovont (Big Belly) River, which got its name, Grovont (Gros Ventre), from the fact that it teemed with fish and there were hordes of elk, deer and antelope clear to its head up under the great continental divide. The Indians gorged themselves so heavily on this easily gotten bounty they all had great bellies and became very fat!

Nick could hardly believe his good luck and was anxious to go see his friend and brother Chief Washakie. One of the Indians who knew the country and also where Washakie's camp was located offered to guide Nick to the Indian camp. Also, the great Yam-Pah-Pa was yet flowing very high from an unusual late run-off due to cold spring weather. They told Nick that he could not just cross this mighty stream any place, but must locate fiords very carefully. Nick was told that there was a very safe crossing several miles upstream from the large prominent butte in the center of the valley, now known as Gros Ventre (Grovont) Butte.

The next morning Nick accompanied this Indian and they were in Washakie's camp by two o'clock. The camp was located about where the Gros Ventre landslide is today, that dammed off the river in 1924

Washakie was very happy to see his long lost brother, and Nick wanted to know about his old Indian mother whom he had heard was dead since many years ago when she came to Grantsville to find her curly-headed white Indian papoose.

Nick gave an account of this visit that the old Indian mother had with Nick's white mother in a previous chapter, and how she finally left after many weeks when she became convinced that Nick's white mother was hiding Yagaki (Nick's Indian name) from her. Washakie told Nick that their old Indian mother had died some-where down on the Ham's Fork of the Green River in Wyoming Territory. Washakie said he had spent many days trying to locate her grave, because he, along with Nick, had promised that they would bury her like the white folks did when she died.

Nick stayed quite awhile with Chief Washakie and returned to the Wind River Indian Agency with him and the tribe after they got through hunting in the Jackson Hole country, with which Nick fell forever, everlastingly, in love!

They arrived at the Wind River Agency headquarters, where Washakie used to like to winter when there were wild Indians because of the light snowfall and much grass for their ponies. He called it the "Valley of the Warm Winds" because of the warm chinook winds that blew and took away the snows.

Washakie had promised Nick that if he would go with him to winter quarters at Fort Washakie, after the tribe got settled down, he would go with Nick down to the Ham's Fork country and together they would try again to find their old Indian mother's grave. They went via South Pass, then west to Green River and over to Ham's Fork. It was now September, which usually brings heavy snows to Wyoming, but they usually melt and then are followed by beautiful Indian summer weather. Nick and Washakie waited at the Wind River camp until after the first heavy snow in early September before they started for Ham's Fork. They did have wonderful, warm, balmy autumn days with cold nights, until Washakie said he had to leave to get back to Fort Washakie before the passes filled with heavy winter snow. Nick and Washakie searched for many days, but both finally had to give up and, with heavy hearts, they said goodbye and headed back to their separate homes. Washakie went back the way they came, and Nick traveled via Soda Springs to Pocatello and on to Matilda and the children at Oxford, Idaho.

Washakie had told Nick that he was away on a hunting trip when their old mother died. Washakie said it was soon after she returned from Utah with some Indians who were trading there. He said that his mother was very sick when she returned to his wickiup (teepee), and he thought she had died from a broken heart, because she could not find her white Indian son.

I have heard my father tell this story of his dear old Indian mother many times, and many times I have cried when he told this sad story, because it made my heart very heavy, too.

I have heard many people ask him how, after so many years, he could hope to identify her bones if he did find them. To which he always gave the same answer. "Washakie told me that the Indians who buried my old Indian mother said she was interred in a large hole in the side of a deep ravine. They said they had killed two of her best horses, which was the Indians' custom, so she would have them to ride in the Happy Hunting Ground or Indian Heaven. They said they had buried with her these horses and all her possessions, among which was the old, battered straw hat and ragged shirt with the short tail that had been all that I had to wear when I first met my dear old Indian mother. After making me some good buckskin clothing, she had always kept these precious articles of mine. But the thing by which I knew I could identify her grave was the iron auger that Washakie had brought back to me from Salt Lake City while trading there with the whites the first fall after I had joined them. I had asked Washakie to bring me an auger, as it was the only tool I needed to build the sled I used to haul wood for my old Indian mother, the sled which me and the Indian kids wore out coasting on the hill near our winter camp."

CHAPTER 7 — **Prologue to Jackson Hole** *continued*
Ellington "Ton" Smith

Now, again, back to our story: After Nick got back to his family in Oxford, Idaho, in the fall of 1889, he spent the winter in recruiting all his close relatives and friends to migrate to Jackson Hole with him. He convinced them that it would be the answer to their dreams to own real ranches and farms of their own.

In the spring of 1890, Nick guided a lot of the men up to Jackson Hole to see it for themselves. They arrived in early June, before the Snake River started to rise to high water, which usually peaked about July 4th. The men who went consisted of his elder brother, Sylvester Wilson, who had a large family, and most of his children were grown; some already married with families.

Those of Nick's relatives who decided to join this first exodus into Jackson Hole were: his elder brother, Sylvester Wilson; Sylvester's sons, Ervin, John, Charley, George and Elias Wilson; Sylvester's sons-in-law, Sealer Cheney and Jim Robertson, and Jim's brother, Issac, all of whom left families behind while they decided on this venture after they saw the Jackson Hole Valley.

Among Nick's friends who went were several bachelors and several married men. The bachelors were: Mose Giltner, Andy Madison, Ed Robertson (no relation to Jim and Issac), Bill Blackburn, Jake Jackson, Bill Manning, Boney Bonett, Jack Smith, Johnie Counts and Brother Charley. Several more soon followed: Paul Morris, Rufus Cobern, Charlie Elsie, Judge Waterman and his son Frank, Judge Spaulding and his son Harry, and many others that I may mention later. Among the married men were: Pete Nelson, Autho Williams, the first surveyor; Pete Carns, Pierce Cunningham, Bobby Miller and Frank Peterson, and many others who soon followed and took up land.

After looking the valley over and noting all its potential, several of these men stayed and started erecting log cabins. They had been really impressed by the big swampland along what is now Flat Creek north of the present town of Jackson, Wyoming. It was decided that hundreds of tons of hay could be harvested here without any work other than cutting and stacking it. The enthusiastic men were anxious to get started making homes for themselves, and it was decided for a lot of the bachelors to start building cabins, while others returned for their livestock and families.

Pete Nelson, Bill Crawford, John Hanfinger, Willas Winagar, a man named Boucher and several others whose names I can't recall right now, decided to file squatter claims on these meadowed swamplands.

Pete Nelson, who later became known as "Slewgrass Nelson," went back to Idaho and brought his wife and ten-year-old daughter, Cora, to cook for the men. They brought in disassembled mowing machines and rakes on pack horses. They drove herds of cattle and horses from their places in Idaho over to the lush, sweet grass that covered Jackson Hole. Pete Nelson's wife and daughter Cora were the first white women to enter the Jackson Hole Valley. Cora lived to a ripe old age and played a very big part in settling this valley. Cora entered the valley riding a saddle horse behind her mother, and these two cooked and served food to the dozen or so men who put up the hay that summer and fall. I think Cora and her mother returned to Idaho that fall, leaving several men to feed and care for the large herd of community livestock that first winter in Jackson Hole.

After the men got organized and started selecting squatter claims on land, Nick staked off what is now the land immediately west of the original town of Jackson, but is now being developed into the town of Jackson as it enlarges and grows toward the west. In fact, about all of my father's first land claim is now part of the town of Jackson.

Nick returned to Idaho with some of the men who went for the haying machines, livestock and food supplies. He spent the rest of the year getting the many families ready for this migration to a new home. Farms were sold or leased out by their owners, all getting ready for the exodus to begin in the spring of 1891. However, the winter of 1891 began the terrible spread of diptheria through the west; that, along with smallpox, killed hundreds of children, and nearly wiped out whole tribes of Indians. This lasted for two years, 1891-92. As mentioned before, Nick was in great demand due to his fame in doctoring these awful diseases, and as before stated, while Nick was frantically trying to save others, he lost almost half his own.

By the summer of 1893, a lot of these families, including little children and pregnant women, were ready for the trek over the high mountains into Jackson Hole. It took twenty-eight days to cover the last eighteen miles over the Teton Pass with all these families, horses, dogs, wagons, buggies and carts that were used to haul all their belongings — stoves, furniture, clothing, etc. — over this long, wild and primitive area into Jackson Hole. They had to build every foot of roads, bridges, etc., as they inched over this steep route into Jackson Hole. They cut timber, cordorized mud holes, dug off steep hillsides, all the way up one side and down the other side of Teton Pass.

Kids had the thrill of a lifetime on this journey, and some of the babies in this caravan never left Jackson Hole again before some of them were eighteen years old! Even years later, when the railroad was built up to Victor, Idaho, which was only eighteen miles from the town of Wilson, over the Teton Pass (where, on clear days you could hear the train whistle as it pulled into Victor), lots of these kids never saw a train before they were twenty years old!

They used to tell a story, I don't know how true it is, but one of these early Jackson Hole families went "outside" for the first time since most of the kids were born. "Outside" meant going over Teton Pass to another world. Anyway, when the train pulled in, amid all its heaving and panting with blasts of steam, and squeaking of brakes, the engineer saw all these yokels standing on the platform with their mouths open, he decided to have a little fun, so he yelled, "Hey! Look out! I'm going to turn around!" And gave a blast with the whistle, and everybody nearly trampled each other to death as they scattered in every direction!

These early pioneers into Jackson Hole dribbled along from the 1890's up to 1900 and later; then they began to come and go. Nick Wilson led and aided caravan after caravan into the valley. It was in about 1893 that he took in his own immediate family. The first settlers who took their families in were Nick's brother Sylvester, who had a large family. They mostly settled in what is called South Park today, southwest of Jackson City, on the east side of the Snake River. This great river then played a big part in the life of every settler in Jackson Hole. It was like a huge wall that only lowered its gates at certain times of the year, because the Snake River ran wild, with devastatingly high waters, during two to three months every year, right at the time when the people most needed to travel back and forth, which was in June, July and August.

The only inlet and outlet in those days was over the Teton Pass, and this high water made travel into and out of the valley almost impossible to the ones on the east side. So this mighty river made a big difference as to where a lot of families finally made their

LEEK   Fourth of July Celebration at South Park, 1894

This picture shows the women dressed in the latest fashions of 1894. South Park was the most heavily settled section of Jackson Hole. This picture was taken shortly after the arrival of Sylvester Wilson's families. The first families settled in South Park Valley, south of Jackson, Wyoming.

homes. The east side of the valley was more open and less brushy or timbered than the west side.

The Snake River was like a great fence or wall partitioning off the whole valley, almost right down through the center. The west side had richer, deep, black soil, but it also was covered with thick, tall willows in the flat lands, with big brush, making it a lot harder to get started farming, as it took so much longer to clear these big thick willows and heavy brush than it did to clear flat sagebrush land on the east side of the valley. Consequently, a majority of the first settlers took up land on the east side of the Snake River, despite the transportation problem that the river posed.

In order to get "outside," these settlers had to resort to large ferry boats that could carry two or three wagons and horses at once, or especially accommodate the four- and six-horse freight outfits that had to cross on these ferries in order to get their supplies over to the Jackson side of the river.

This geographic division of the valley, due to this great river, later caused lots of rivalry between the settlers on the west side and those on the east side. One of these first rivalries was that Jackson on the east and Wilson (another town) on the west very early formed baseball teams and other divisions causing competition. The "Jacksnipes" (Jackson), or the "eastsiders," were referred to as the "African Flats," and the "Wilsonites" (Wilson), or "westsiders," were called the "Cannibal Isles."

Nick Wilson first settled on the east side, as described earlier, on the land just west of Jackson, which was really the head of South Park. Nick moved his family in about 1893, and he soon disliked this choice he had made, because the wind blew so much up through the narrow gap caused by the mountains on the southeast side and a big butte on the west side, causing a narrow gap of about one-quarter mile. This caused the prevailing southwest wind to jam in intensity and made Nick's location colder in the winter and windy. So, Nick just abandoned this location and moved back to the west side of the Snake River, and founded the little town of Wilson, named for him. Here he homesteaded 160 acres from Fish Creek one mile east toward the Snake River, making this 160 acres one mile long and one-quarter mile wide.

Nick had first been attracted to this site on Fish Creek when he first entered the valley and found the Shoshone Indian camp there by the creek. He did build his homestead cabin right on the east bank of Fish Creek, and later a hotel, store and livery stable. A post office was established in the store, which was the first store

SCHOFIELD   Both approaches to the "new" Snake River Bridge washed out in 1918. This picture shows the first really good steel bridge across the Snake River, built before the government undertook dredging and rip-rapping. This bridge was finally destroyed in the Kelly Flood in 1927. Note carriage on cables from bridge to shore. The passengers pulled the carriage across by hand. The bridge, one mile east of Wilson Village located at the foot of Teton Pass, was built about 1911. Abutments were being poured on Armistice Day (now Veterans Day) 1911. This was the first attempt at a steel bridge across Snake River between Wilson and Jackson. This bridge would no doubt have stood to this day if the Kelly Flood of 1927 had not occured. The present bridge across Snake River was built in almost the same place as the one shown here. Counting the road across Jackson Lake Dam, there are now ten steel bridges spanning this great river between Moran and Alpine, where the Snake River enters Palasade Reservoir.

Charles Alma Wilson, Author

in Jackson Hole. A village sprang up with a school house and a Mormon Church meeting house, which was a large log building near Nick's log cabin, lumber hotel and store. The big log building served as a church and dance hall, and all other civic meetings, and so was known as the Wilson Meeting House. A baseball diamond was laid out near the building, and hence began the rivalry between Jackson and Wilson. All these buildings in the little village were soon followed by saloons.

The second store built in Jackson Hole was in the town of Jackson by "Pap" DeLoney, one of the first settlers who settled and started the town of Jackson. He and his family were always merchants or politicians and lawyers. "Pap" had fought all through the Civil War on the side of the North. His was also a large family of Mormon descent, as was the majority of the first settlers. But other religious groups soon arrived in Jackson Hole, and lots of atheists, too. Religion never became an issue in Jackson Hole from the first Mormon migration clear up to now that I ever heard of.

Nick erected the old log meeting house on his farm at Wilson and was Mormon Bishop from about 1895 to about 1908, at which time he left the Mormon Church, and I will try to bring an account of that event into this story at a later date.

On the east side of the Jackson Hole Valley, Nick's elder brother Sylvester was the presiding bishop until his death on August 2, 1895. His branch of the Wilson family has held onto this position in the Church, more or less, right up to this present date.

After Nick's bishopric and records were removed from him, they were presented to Bishop May, whose large family settled the area north of Jackson and the Grovont River, known as Kelly and Mormon Row. Two brothers, Bill and John Kelly, founded the town bordering on this Mormon settlement, known as Mormon Row because Mormon settlers built their houses across the dividing road, or lane, which separated their various farms from each other for several miles along this section line — thus, "Mormon Row."

After Nick moved back to Wilson, on the west side of the valley, he sent for his son-in-law, Abe Ward, who had been associated with him in farming for a long time. Abe moved his family, wife Edna Jane and two sons, into Jackson Hole in about 1894 or 1895. The two boys were Elijah and Ercle. Their first girl, Vesta, was born after the Wards moved to Jackson Hole, and I believe Vesta was the first white child born on the west side of Jackson Hole.

Vesta still lives, at this writing on October 20, 1984, at Jackson. She was born either in 1896 or 1897 at Wilson, Wyoming. Vesta is

Nick Wilson's old cabin, left side picture. Hotel across road. Windows cut in side of cabin after Nick died. Only windows and door to cabin were on north side, facing the hotel. Picture taken about 1975.

a remarkable woman, now at the age of 87 or 88, and has a very unique story regarding her life in Jackson Hole. She is, at this time, writing her autobiography, and it will add much to this biography of her grandfather and my father, Elijah Nicholas Wilson.

Nick Wilson established the first store and post office and was the first Forest Ranger who worked under the first two Forest Supervisors, Lockwood and Miller. There are some fascinating adventures Nick had while serving on this job, that I hope to write later in this story.

When Abe Ward arrived in about 1895, he homesteaded 160 acres bordering Nick's parcel on the north. Nick's son-in-law, George Goodrick, took up the 160-acre parcel to the south of Nick's farm. My uncle Alfred Nethercott, Jr., was directly north of the Abe Wards', and my grandfather Alfred Nethercott, Sr., filed on the land bordering uncle Alfred. A man named John Beckley, who was sheriff, took the land on the east end of Nick, Abe and uncle Alfred. Its east side was the bank of the Snake River, and the river soon started movement to the west and gradually ate up Beckley's farm, until not much of it was left by the time the people elected road supervisors, who built long log jetties filled with rock, that more or less slowed this erosion by the river to the west. The town of Wilson is ten feet lower than the present Snake River and formations show that at one time the Snake River did flow along the foothills of the Teton Range through what is now Wilson, Wyoming. Due to some other catastrophe or earthquake, the course of the Snake River was changed to right down through nearly the center of Jackson Hole as it is today.

The Army Engineers in later years have finally dredged out a great channel for about ten miles down through Jackson Hole and directly east of the town of Wilson, so probably the Snake will never again leave her restless bed, and now bridges will stay in place. Many attempts in early days were made to bridge this wild river, but even the first fine steel bridge was wiped out after the Grovont River was dammed off by a giant land slide in 1924, forming a lake seven miles long. This dam was a mile wide, but in 1927 it washed out in one night, with devastating results to the town of Kelly, wiping it out and drowning at least six people. It is estimated that up to two hundred people would have drowned had the dam burst earlier in the night. However, it was discovered at daylight by an alert forest ranger, and before the one hundred-foot wall of water cascaded down, wiping out Kelly, the people were warned in time to flee. This great flood took out the steel bridges on the

On June 23, 1924, the whole side of the mountain slid out on the Grovont River above Kelly, Wyoming.

Covering most of the old Billy Beard Ranch, owned by Guil Huff, brother to Dr. Charles Huff. Guil Huff was standing on the roof of his cabin a few days after the dam, which was a mile long, went out in 1926, destroying the town of Kelly, Wyoming.

Grovont River and on the Snake River east of Wilson. Had the rip-rapping and dredging been done before this flood, it is probable that the bridges would have been washed out anyway.

Nick's brother Sylvester and his five sons homesteaded in South Park, as did two of his daughters and their husbands, and many others. Alice Wilson married Sealer Cheney, and the first white boy born in Jackson was Howard Cheney. The Cheneys had five boys and one girl. The first white girl was born about 1893. Her name was Effie Wilson, first child of Ervin and Mary Jane Wilson. Ervin was Sylvester Wilson's oldest son. Uncle Sylvester and aunt Mary had five boys and three girls.

I have an old photograph taken by Steve Leek, husband to Etta Wilson, one of my half-sisters. Steve was an Englishman and a Hudson Bay trapper. He came into the Jackson Hole Valley about the time that Nick was settling Jackson Hole. Steve took this photo about 1897. Leek homesteaded one of the finest ranches in Jackson Hole along with his half-brother Ham Wort. Leek later bought out Ham.

The ranch is about three miles south of Jackson. Leek built the first rip-saw mill and made the first lumber in Jackson Hole. His house and barns still stand on the ranch and are still some of Jackson Hole's finest workmanship, both made from rip-saw lumber from the first lumber sawed in Jackson Hole. This old photo was taken at Sylvester and aunt Mary's sod-covered cabin in South Park and it pictures nearly all the people who lived in southern Jackson Hole at that time, about 1897.

When Nick Wilson moved his family into Jackson Hole, all he had left of his fourteen children by Matilda Patten Wilson, his first wife, were six daughters. According to the Church Geneology Records, that I have seen, there were fourteen children, four boys and ten girls from Nick's first marriage; two boys from his second plural marriage; and three children from his third marriage, to my mother, two boys and one girl.

Three of Nick and Matilda's daughters were married before Nick moved into Jackson Hole: Edna Jane, the eldest, to Abraham Ward; Hanna Louise to Ellington "Ton" Smith (they settled in Idaho near Driggs); Catharene Ann "Kate" married George Goodrick. Wards and Goodricks followed Nick later. All five of his boys — four of Matilda's, and Wallace from his second plural marriage (Wallace was killed with an ax at the age of about ten), and the other four boys all died in 1891-92 during the terrible diptheria and smallpox epidemic.

This picture shows the Grovont Flood after it reached the Wilson area. Teton Pass is the low land in the mountain in upper left corner. The town of Wilson can be seen below the pass at timber edge. This natural dam caused by a mountain slide on the Grovont River, several miles above Kelly, washed out in 1927. Mr. Dibblis, a Forest Ranger, alerted the town of Kelly in time for most of the people to leave to high ground. Six people were drowned, but over 200 could have drowned had the dam washed out a few hours earlier in the morning.

Old Timers in Jackson Hole. Taken by S.N. Leek in 1897 at Nick Wilson's oldest brother's dirt-rooted and dirt-floor cabin on his homestead in South Park.

Sylvester and Nick Wilson's Families:
First Settlers in Jackson Hole's South Park

This picture was taken in 1897 at Sylvester Wilson's homestead cabin in South Park, Jackson Hole, Wyoming. Sylvester was Nick Wilson's older brother. Sylvester died about 1894. From left to right, back row, eleven men: by door, 1) John Wilson 2)Dave Cheney 3)Nick Wilson 4) Elias Wilson, with hand on 5) Ralph Cheny 6)with hat, Sylvester Cheney 7) bearded man, Selar Cheney 8) Jim Robertson 9) George Wilson 10) Abe Ward 11) George Goodrick.

Second row, all women: 1) Mary Jane Wilson, wife of Ervin Wilson (deceased), holding young son, Nate Wilson 2) Matilda Wilson, wife of Nick Wilson 3) Nellie Wilson, immediately in front of Nick Wilson, and his youngest daughter 4) Rebecca Wilson Robertson, wife of Jim Robertson, standing holding daughter Mary in front of Nick Wilson and Elias Wilson 5) Alice Wilson Cheney, wife of Selar Cheney, holding only daughter Quema Cheney 6) Mary Wilson, wife of Sylvester Wilson (deceased) 7) Fanny Wilson, daughter of Nick Wilson 8) Sarah (Etta) Welthy Wilson Leek, daughter of Nick Wilson 9) Edna Jane Wilson Ward, wife of Abe Ward, holding son Virgil Ward 10) Kate Wilson Goodrick, standing in front of her husband, George Goodrick.

Children: 1) Susana Wilson 2) Effie Wilson (first white girl born in Jackson Hole) 3) Joy Wilson 4) Jimmie Wilson 5) Joseph Robertson 6) Jimmie Robertson 7) Sylvester Robertson 8) standing back of Jimmy R. and Sylvester R. is Flemming Cheney 9) Howard Cheney (first white boy born in Jackson Hole) 10) Elijah Ward 11) Ercel Ward standing in front of Howard and Elijah Ward 12) Vesta Ward, petting dog, age two years. Vesta Ward was the first child born on the Wilson side of the Snake River at Wilson, Wyoming. The only one still living in January, 1985, of this group of oldtimers is Vesta Ward Linn, No. 12. Picture taken by Steve Leek in 1897.

I never knew Hanna Louise Smith, as she died when I was still a baby. "Ton" Smith raised his four children on their farm in Idaho. The two girls, Zora and Mabel, came often to Jackson Hole to visit their five aunts. Zora and Mabel worked one summer for my sister Etta Leek, when the Leeks ran a dude ranch and had a lot of guests that summer. I met one of Ton Smith's sons, Earl, who was five or six years older than I.

When I was nine years old and on one of the trips with my dad peddling his book. *Uncle Nick Among the Shoshones,* we stopped two or three days at the Smith farm, which was about six or seven miles southeast of Driggs, over near the foothills of the Teton mountain range on the Idaho side. The Teton peaks can be seen from Driggs, which is on the Idaho side about straight west of these beautiful peaks.

Ton's land sloped to the west and a few hundred yards east of Ton's house lived another farmer, David S. Neal. There was bad blood between Ton Smith and Neal, when Nick and I visited the Smith family in 1910.

Zora was about 20 years old that summer and was engaged to marry a man named Ed Myers, who lived in Montana, but soon after he and Zora were married they moved to Jackson Hole, and Ed started a pool hall and billiard alley with a gambling den in the rear. Zora and Ed lived out their lives in Jackson Hole. Mabel was a beautiful, dark-haired girl. She died two or three years after Nick and I visited them in 1910, very suddenly with "inflammation of the bowels," which means a ruptured appendix. She was about sixteen years old.

Earl was about 18 years old, living at home and helping Ton run their farm. There was an older boy, whose name I have forgotten, and I never knew him. He was already married and had a farm somewhere near his father, Ton Smith.

The trouble between Ton and his neighbor Neal to the east of him was over their irrigation water. They both took water from a creek or canal up near Alta, Wyoming, which was just over the state line into Wyoming. This Alta town should have been in Idaho, as it was on the west side of the Teton Range, and was a part of Teton Basin in Idaho, but the state line between Idaho and Wyoming ran north and south along the west foothills of the Teton Range, and a small spur of suitable farm land lay just inside Wyoming. This fact has been a constant headache and expense to Wyoming, as its isolation caused the State of Wyoming lots of money, far more than this little strip of farm land was worth. The Taxes from it did not begin to pay for schools, roads and other expensive maintenance and Wyoming even tried to give it to Idaho, which should have taken it, but the people in Alta liked their status as Wyoming citizens, and vigorously protested annexation by Idaho. Alta has to do all its business in Idaho and really is a liability to Wyoming to this day!

Ton Smith and his neighbor Neal lived just over the state line in Idaho. Their irrigation ditches came out of dual headgates from the creek which I think is called Darby Creek, and it heads under the Grand Teton Peak range on the west or Idaho side, but the peaks are in Wyoming. These two ditches ran parallel to each other for a distance, then Neal began use of the water in his land above Ton Smith, whose ditch ran south right near to Neal's house, and then turned abruptly on a right angle down to Smith's house. This ditch water was used for household use by the Smith family, for all their domestic use, as well as for irrigation.

Ton Smith told Nick that he thought Neal was stealing his water during the night, because in the mornings the water set for the night had spread only a few yards into Smith's meadow. Ton said that Neal took great delight in polluting Smith's drinking water, and the next morning after Nick and I got there, we were all outside when Neal came out of his house carrying an overnight urinal chamber. He called, "Hey, Smith!" We looked up, and he poured its contents into Smith's ditch! Ton was white with anger as he told my dad, "See that! I am not going to take much more of it!"

Nick asked, "Why don't you go to the law about it?"

Ton answered, "I have! But they don't do anything about it! They come up here and look at the ditch and all this waste is soon gone in the swift water. Neal always denies it! You can never get the law to do anything to stop trouble. They always wait until someone is killed or something serious happens before they will act, and then it is often too late!"

Well, that's the way we left this situation, and as Nick and I drove on peddling books, he told me he was plenty worried about Ton Smith, because he could tell that Ton was about ready to take the "law into his own hands." I didn't know what Nick meant by that, but it was only about a week later that while we were peddling around Rexburg, Idaho, where one of Nick's nieces named Sara Ann Barnes lived with her husband John Barnes and their two daughters Mary Ann and Florence, we heard that Ton Smith was in jail in Driggs waiting trial for murder!

It was only one good day's drive back to Driggs, and Nick and I returned there the next day. Nick went directly to the jail and took me with him. He told the warden that he was Ton Smith's father-in-law, and we were ushered right in to see Ton. I was plenty scared when they took us through three or four iron gates, which were all locked after us, until we reached Ton's cell. After we entered, this door was also locked, and the warden said, "Call when you are ready to go, Uncle Nick!" Everybody seemed to know my dad and they all called him "Uncle Nick."

Well, Ton was sitting on an iron cot and was unshaven and looked haggard to me. This was an awful place to be locked up in! The bed had only a thin mattress with one blanket, a tin chamber under the bed, and a tin wash basin sitting on a small stand or table with a tin water pitcher beside it. That was it except for one flimsy chair! It wasn't very light in there, and what there was came from a small skylight.

Ton stood up when we were ushered in and Nick embraced him for a few minutes. Neither man spoke a word for awhile, then Nick released his embrace and with his hands on Ton's shoulders asked, "What happened, Ton?" Ton motioned to Nick to sit in the chair and me on the iron cot beside him and he told us this story:

"Well!" began Ton. "Things got worse after you left! For two mornings straight my ditch that passes Neal's house — the one we use for drinking water — was dry! It was the first time I got up early enough to find this ditch dry, and it proved what I told you, that I thought he was stealing my water at night. He would go up to the headgates after dark when he had seen me go home. The two headgates were side by side. The water is low at this time of year, and the farmers usually took turns with the water, but Neal wouldn't share with me! The reason was because he was stealing my water at night and he didn't have to share! Well, you know I have this big, black stallion, Dick, that I keep there in the barn and corral where I have a small pasture for him. He is very gentle and I ride him bareback with my shovel over my shoulder, and after I get done changing my irrigation water I have him to ride back home on.

"A couple of mornings after you and Charley left, I got on Dick about 3 a.m. and rode up there to the headgates. It is about a mile and a half. As I suspected, my headgate was closed and all the water was in Neal's ditch! I went back home. I had been getting madder and more frustrated all the time over this water problem! And when he started pouring their piss pot into our ditch — you were there! Well! I decided it had to stop! The next morning, about 2:30 a.m., while the kids were sleeping, I got my old 45-70 rifle. It holds thirteen shells in the magazine and one in the barrel. I got old Dick and rode up to the headgates. Mine was shut and all the water in Neal's ditch, just like the morning before! I tied old Dick to some willows close by the headgates, out of sight, and waited there for Neal. He came about daylight, and he was a-foot, but he had a shovel. It wasn't very light yet, but I could see him plainly. He started to open my headgate, and I stepped out where he could see me and said, "Alright! You water-stealing sonuvabitch!" And as he stood there with his mouth open, I shot him! Gawd Damn him! And not once! I put all fourteen bullets into his cussed carcass! And here I am!"

Well, after his trial, Ton's lawyer told Nick that if Ton hadn't shot all his bullets into Neal that he might have gotten him off easier, but Ton did escape the death penalty, but got life imprisonment. This was in 1910. In 1918, during the great influenza epidemic, Ton Smith died in prison of the flu. When he was sent to prison, his son and daughter, Earl and Mabel, got the ranch, but Mabel died three or four years later, in about 1913, when she was only about sixteen years old.

Good friends — Bert Schofield and Dave Edmondson, 1913. Canada Geese! Early days at Wilson in Jackson Hole, Wyoming.

CHAPTER 8 — Jackson Hole Sheep War

When Nick and Matilda came to Jackson Hole, they brought only three girls: Sara Welthy "Etta," eighteen years old, who later married Steve Leek; Fanny Priscilla, eleven years old, who later married Clark Caswell; and Nellie Guian, six years old, who later married Enoch Ferrin. After Nick moved his family, listed above, into Jackson Hole about 1893, they lived at the location of Nick's first squatter's right near Jackson. Then they moved back to Wilson in 1895, and Abe and Edna Jane Ward homesteaded next to Nick on the north side of Nick's farm, and operated both farms.

Abe's son Ercle cleared most of the willows and heavy bushes, using a large Belgian stallion shipped from Europe, which was community-owned.

After Vesta Ward was born at Wilson in Jackson Hole about 1896, her mother, Edna Jane, lost a pair of twins. Then in 1901, she had another pair of twins, Ira and Irene, making five children who lived. Nick's three girls helped him clear the sage-covered parts of this farm at Wilson until Etta married Steve Leek about 1897, and Fanny married Clark Caswell about 1899.

From 1893 up to 1899, when Nick's wife Matilda died at Wilson, on November 11, 1899, Nick's life had settled down, and these first six years in Jackson Hole were among the happiest days of Nick's life. His first big tragedy was the death of Matilda at age 51. Looking back and studying these sheets of Geneology, it seemed that pioneer people, especially women, were very old at the age of fifty. All of my half-sisters died at what seemed to me as being old age, before age fifty, except Nell, who was fifty-two. The old west was very hard on women and horses! Now days women are just getting started at fifty years of age! Nellie was all Nick had left now, out of two families of sixteen children.

As mentioned above, Nick was acting forest ranger with the United States Forest Service. Some of the old ax blazes on the forest trees through Targhee and Bridger National Forests were made by Nick Wilson as he cut and mapped out the first trails through these forests. Many of the old blazes are there to this day, and as a boy and as a man, I have ridden many times over these old trails blazed by my dad when I have guided hunting parties on trips through these mountains.

One of the problems my dad had as a forest ranger was the large bands of sheep from Idaho that had summer ranges on the Targhee National Forest. These national forests did not recognize state lines, but lapped over from one state into another. The United States Forest Service, which controls national forests, just simply issued grazing permits to various cattle and sheep outfits on these national forests, regardless of the states in which they happened to be. Idaho sheepmen who held permits on the Targhee Forest Reserve lapped way over into Idaho and Wyoming and these sheepmen had a habit of grazing on, out of the forest, and down even to the foothills in Jackson Hole.

The first settlers agreed among themselves right at the start that they would run only cattle and outlaw sheep. When these Idaho sheep began grazing down into Jackson Hole, well past the forest boundary line, the settlers resented this intrusion into the valley and warned the Idaho sheepmen to quit allowing their herders to push sheep into the Jackson Hole valley. These warnings were ignored by Idaho sheepmen, and the so-called "Jackson Hole Sheep War" broke out.

Sheep are very noisy, and even when I was a kid, long after the war, you could and still can, hear these sheep blatting from all over south Jackson Hole. The settlers decided to stop this trespass into the valley, and the fact that they themselves ran no sheep here made them all the more furious. After a quickly-held meeting, about twenty or thirty Jackson Hole settlers rode into a sheep band and, with clubs, killed hundreds of sheep and scared hell out of the herders, who fled, abandoning their flocks.

It took only one raid from the deadly serious settlers to convince Idaho to keep their sheep within their forest leases. The results were that the U.S. Forest Service erected large red signs and nailed them to trees along the Targhee eastern border adjoining Jackson Hole to keep back of the lines or suffer the consequences, which were laid down by the Jackson Hole settlers: Any sheep caught over the line would be killed and the herders lynched!

Of course, Nick Wilson played a big part in these sheep disputes, and his duties were on the side of law and order, but his sympathies were on the side of the Jackson Hole settlers.

Among some of the equipment issued to Nick Wilson as a forest ranger was one very fine telescope in a black leather case. This telescope was so powerful that you could see the key hole in a door in a building three miles away. When Kate Carter was gathering pioneer antiques to display at the opening of the Great Library in Salt Lake City, of which she was Librarian, I loaned her this telescope, among several other items, i.e., Nick's old manuscript, a copy of the original book published by Skelton Book Company of Salt Lake City, a folding tin cup and an old celuloid hinged notebook for keeping daily itineraries which could be erased each week and was easy to carry in a pocket, a large, glass-enclosed portrait of Nick Wilson and my mother, Charlotte Nethercott, which Kate had hung over the entrance door into the display room and a few other items I can't remember. Kate Carter promised to give these loaned articles back to the owner after the opening celebration was over, but she encouraged donors to give the articles for their Library Museum. In either case, she asked permission to keep these loaned articles as long as possible as they were considered safe there.

I left all these articles with Kate Carter from about 1940 to about 1975 or 1977, when John Stewart was in Jackson Hole looking for information on Nick Wilson. I went to Salt Lake to the Library and my wife and granddaughter, Janet Wilson, went with me. I asked Kate Carter for the articles I had loaned her several — 35 — years before, and she refused to give them back. She maintained that these items had been there so long, that by law of limitations they now belonged to the Daughters of the Utah Pioneer Library in Salt Lake City. I was terribly shocked by this arrogant turn of affairs, and demanded these things of my father's to be returned to me. Kate refused! There was no one in the building, but Carter and the janitor, besides the three of us. All of these articles were on display in long, large, glass showcases, except the picture of my father and mother that hung prominently over the door entrance.

I grew very angry and threatened to kick in the glass paneling and regain my possessions, unless she unlocked them. She refused. I began to kick out the paneling, and she shouted for the janitor to stop me! The janitor refused Carter's orders, saying, "I only work here! I never hired out to fight here!" Whereupon my wife and granddaughter were both crying! Kate Carter was a tough old gal, I will say that for her, and she drove a hard bargain. My granddaughter especially wanted the fine picture of her great-grandfather and grandmother. Kate wanted to keep that, and it did have a very prominent place of honor in this beautiful library museum, and I would have let her keep that, but Janet cried all the harder and louder. So Kate had the janitor get a step-ladder and get it down for Janet.

Then came the bargaining over the stuff in the glass cases. I insisted on having the old manuscript back and the old book, *Uncle Nick Among the Shoshones*. I discovered that the pictures, including the one of Nick in the introductory pages were all cut out. Kate couldn't, or wouldn't, account for that, but very soon afterwards a very prominent publishing company came out with a new edition of exactly the old book with all the pictures. This edition is called *Among the Shoshones* by Elijah Nicholas Wilson. For years it has been a best-seller on their list.

Does this coincidence ring a bell to the reader? Kate haggled so strongly that I let her keep the old telescope and the celluloid notebook, cup and other articles, and presume they are on display at this time there in Salt Lake City at the Museum.

I guess my point in telling this story regarding Kate Carter and my father's personal belongings is that it just proves the loss of integrity in the world. I was especially surprised in this incident, because Kate Carter was born and raised during the era when a man's or woman's word was their bond. However, in this case, I still have a letter from Kate Carter written at the time I loaned her these items in which she promised to return them upon demand at any time. I just wonder, if I had not shown her this letter, would I have gotten any of my father's belongings back? She did threaten to sue me, but she never did!

However, I may add in conclusion, with all due respect to Kate Carter, that I have since learned through a reliable Daughter of the Utah Pioneer, and for the sake of integrity on both sides, that Kate's purpose was to hold these precious items in the Museum for safety and posterity, where they could always be reviewed and held in honor and esteem; and mine was to hold them for the sake of love and heritage.

CHAPTER 9 — Jackson Hole Indian War

You have already read the revised chapter called "Frontier Troubles," in which Nick Wilson mentions the so-called "Jackson Hole Indian War." I will elaborate a little more on that event which happened about 1895, four years before his wife Matilda died. The Indians that Nick Wilson mentions were Shoshones from the Fort Hall Reservation in Idaho. This reservation is also called the Blackfoot Indian Reservation, and one of my favorite towns in Idaho is the town of Blackfoot, Idaho, and I have seen some of the finest western rodeos that I have ever witnessed, second only to the great Frontier Days celebration that was held each fall in Jackson Hole in early September.

This so-called Indian War took place in Hoback Canyon where Indians were camped at the mouth of Grant Creek where it empties into the Hoback River. The high teepee-shaped butte that rises here from the north bank of the Hoback is now called Battle Mountain, where this fight is supposed to have been fought. It really didn't amount to much as a war. When the Indians were discovered hunting there, about thirty or forty men under the command of Pierce Cunningham, U.S. Marshal at Jackson, tried to apprehend them, and a small skirmish erupted in which several Indians were killed. The battle took place in thick timber, and it is believed the settlers slipped up and shot several Indians; the rest ran. They had their squaws and papooses with them. The Indians escaped through the trees, with most of their horses, leaving large piles of elk hides and their teepees behind.

The only capture made by the white settlers was that as one squaw was mounting her horse, her six-month-old papoose fell out of her back cradle, and she left without retrieving the child. The white men gathered up the squalling Indian baby, but could not catch the Indians to give it to them. When it was plain that the Indians were gone, the majority of the white men followed the Indians until it was determined that these Indians had left their reservation at Fort Hall.

A few Indian horses were captured, so the settlers loaded as much of the meat and hides as they could pack and returned to

Jackson Hole. The game hides were held for evidence, the meat divided among families to use what they could before it spoiled. The Indians had been in the process of drying and curing this meat, their way of preserving meat into what was called "Jerky."

The Indian baby was first cared for by a white woman who was nursing a baby, and later the women in South Park took turns caring for the child.

There were two rather humorous happenings from this event: First, the men taking turns carrying the Indian baby and the women who first cared for it all became very lousy! Lice and bedbugs were two of the worst problems that both Indians and whites had to contend with. And like many other things that the Indians contracted, I have a hunch they got bedbugs, diptheria, smallpox, shankers, blue-balls, clap and lice — all from their white brothers!

Second, the other funny event was that the men left a character named Bill Crawford to watch over the remaining hides and supplies of the Indians until some of them could return with more horses to pack in all this stuff abandoned by the Indians. Bill Crawford was a loud-mouthed, boisterous kind of character, who was always bragging how brave and smart he was! Bill Crawford was well-fixed when he came to Jackson Hole, and he took one of the best farms up Flat Creek in the slew grass meadows mentioned before. When my dad ran a small grocery and hardware store at the town of Wilson, he gave credit to most of his neighbors who had to charge, and others, like Crawford, who charged for convenience. When Nick Wilson died, there was over five thousand dollars on his books, owed to him by both those who couldn't pay and also by those who could have paid, but didn't! Bill Crawford was one of those who could have paid, but didn't, to the tune of over five hundred dollars on these old books!

Well. Crawford was left to guard these Indian Supplies, mostly because he was always bragging about how brave he was, and also because the men didn't think the Indians would even return to try to get their plunder back. Just below this Indian camp was a little ridge covered with timber over which the Indians had disappeared. Bill was supposed to take the teepees down and get everything ready to pack out when the white settlers returned. That very first day, after all the men had left, packing all they could on the captured Indian horses and also on Bill's saddle horse since he wouldn't need a horse until the men returned, Bill became very frightened after all the men had left. I think his imagination kind of ran away, too. Bill was sure he could hear Indians returning for their stuff. It was determined later that the wind through the trees was the noise that Bill heard and thought was Indians. Bill pulled off his shoes, so he wouldn't make any noise himself, and crept stealthily up this little timbered ridge, with his pistol all cocked and ready.

Just as Bill reached the top of this little ridge, he met an Indian — face to face! The Indian was creeping up the other side in the same manner as Bill, to see if anyone was guarding the camp! Both Bill and the Indian broke and ran for dear life. Bill dropped his shoes in his panic, and he didn't stop until he reached the first house in the white settlement in South Park in Jackson Hole! Bill had traveled all afternoon and through the night! Wearing out his stockings, he arrived at Sealer Cheney's sod-covered cabin with sore, swollen, bloody feet, and the yarn he told! He told the settlers who soon gathered, that shortly after they left, a thousand Indians bore down on him! Bill said that he had escaped by the skin of his teeth, and completely wore out his shoes climbing over the sharp shale and rocks, going up and over the pass at the head of Wilson Canyon, and arriving at Cheney's in a terrible condition.

The men who hadn't planned to go back for the Indian plunder until the next day decided that a few men should go back right then and see if anything was left at the camp. You can imagine their disgust when they arrived back at Battle Mountain and found everything exactly the way they had left it the day before — except they found Bill's shoes and pistol where he dropped them and fled in terror. They couldn't find any sign of even one Indian meeting Bill on the little ridge, let alone a thousand!

For awhile after this Indian war and scare, the white people all moved close together in South Park, by the old schoolhouse, as they feared they might be attacked by the Indians any minute. They kept close watch on their herds by day and corralled them at night, and the men took turns as night guards.

One night, just after dark, Bill Crawford, who was on night duty, came riding into camp "hell for leather," shouting that they were being attacked by Indians! Women and kids all ran into the old log schoolhouse, and the men grabbed guns, ready to defend themselves! They could hear the pounding of many hooves, and upon investigation, found it was about fifty calves running and playing like calves do after being shut up all day and then turned out after milking time. They always run and play that way. A bunch of these calves had just been turned out to pasture, after the cows were milked, and all this running and dust was what alerted Bill

Crawford to another of his false alarms — of which people were getting pretty tired!

In the meantime, as Nick Wilson tells in his story "Frontier Troubles," he was appointed interpreter for the Indians, and contacts were made to get this into court. It took over two years, but it was all finally settled. The Indian woman got back her now-two-year-old papoose, and the Indians got back their teepees and horses and other belongings. The hides were sold and the money went to the government.

The hunting by Indians stopped, and now all this once free, wild land that belonged to the Indians is now owned and over-grazed, plundered, exploited and polluted by the noble whiteman!

SHEFFIELD   A spectacular catch, not unusual at the turn of the century.

They don't catch many fish like these in the Snake River anymore. Ben Sheffield ran a terrifically successful hunting lodge at Moran on Jackson Lake in 1901. Note elk quartered in background. Plundered or exploited?

CHAPTER 10 — **Reminiscence**

There were many happy times in the life of Nick Wilson during the twenty-six years after he founded and lived in Jackson Hole. Many happy times, and times of sorrow, too, for here he buried many of his old friends, his brother, sister and many of their children, as well as two wives and one little girl of his own, and the loss of his wife and mother of fourteen children was the beginning of sorrow and tragedy for Nick before his time ran out in this beautiful little valley that he loved so much!

After Matilda took sick and died so suddenly on November 11, 1899, all he had left was his youngest daughter Nellie, who was twelve years old.

Since Abe and Edna Ward had homesteaded their farm of 160 acres adjoining Nick's land to the north, they had long since lived there the required time to prove up on their farm, and Nick and Matilda had turned the hotel, store and livery stable over to them to run. They just closed up the old two-story log cabin on their homestead and moved into the new hotel. No one lived in their old house until Elijah married Josephine Linn, about 1913, when they made the old house their home.

Nick and Matilda lived in the old sod cabin that Nick had built on the banks of his beloved Fish Creek, with daughters Etta, Fanny and Nell until Etta and Fanny both married, Etta bout 1897 and Fanny in 1899 just before her mother, Matilda, died.

Here I am showing a photograph of a painting of this first old homestead cabin of Nick Wilson's that was painted by a man traveling through the valley, an artist, and he painted this scene of the old house, hotel and store of Nick's, and Steve Leek took the photograph on an old glass lantern slide about 1898, or soon after the hotel and store were built. While rummaging through a lot of Leek's old slides and other refuse from his old photographer dark room, which had been thrown away on this junk pile, I came onto this old slide (it was about 1917, I think). Recognizing it for what it was, I took it into the dark room and proceeded to develop a picture from it. I had often helped my brother-in-law Steve Leek with his

Nick Wilson's old homestead cabin built on the east bank of Fish Creek, the start of the town of Wilson, Wyoming, 1895. First store in Jackson Hole. Caption on the false front of the store reads: General Merchandise, Wagons, Farm Implements and Hardware, E. N. Wilson. Livery stable on left center, across road from store. In 1897 a hotel was built where old cabin sets. Four more lengths were built onto the Livery Stable. Fish Creek in center, left of cabin. Barn obstructs view of the bridge.

pictures, but had not had much experience in developing them, so this picture is not very good, but it does show what Nick Wilson's old spread was like in about 1897 or 1898. Anyway, if I hadn't made this attempt, this picture would have been lost forever. I don't know of another picture showing Nick's first old sod-roofed cabin on his homestead. After the hotel and store were built, Nick decided to tear the old sod-covered cabin down, as it obstructed the view of the mountain to the west from the new hotel.

I don't know whether this was done before Matilda died or not, but I presume that it was, because Nick built another cabin just south of the original cabin and right on the creek bank, too, but about 100 yards below the old cabin and just across the road from the hotel. There was a through road with a bridge over Fish Creek that ran between this new log cabin (with a shingled roof) and the hotel and store. The long livery stable stood directly south across this road from the hotel and formed the east side of the lot for the new cabin. This old livery barn with a lean-to built on the barn's east side contained about ten double stalls for horses, with a haymow that held about four or five tons of loose hay, so I presume the old house was torn down, because the new cabin in which my mother and father and Nellie lived, was in use when I was born in 1901 — not in this house, but in my grandma and grandpa Nethercott's homestead cabin a couple of miles northeast on the bank of the old Snake River. And the first sound I ever heard, no doubt, was the singing of her waters there. When I hit that unblazed trail across the Great Divide, grant that my resting place may be by old Snake River's side!

I knew nearly all the men, women and children who lived in Jackson in 1915 when my father, Nick Wilson, died, at which time "outsiders" were starting to come into the valley and buying up lots of the old settlers land, and now, in 1984, claiming to be "oldtimers!" None of us who lived or were born in Jackson Hole prior to 1915 ever considered any of these people who came into the valley after that date of 1915 as being "oldtimers!"

Nick Wilson standing in a second cutting of alfalfa hay on his ranch at Wilson, Wyoming about 1910. Note haystacks of first cutting.

CHAPTER 11 — **Charley Wilson**

At the time Nick's wife Matilda died, he was still a forest ranger, but by November the regular work of rangers was over until spring. During the winter a ranger must do his book work from his notes and itineraries kept during the summer when his duties kept him busy, so Nick was home with Matilda and Nellie when Matilda died.

Nell was going to school. Nick was also serving as Bishop for the Latter-Day Saints Church with a small group of members there at Wilson. Abe Ward, Nick's son-in-law, was an Elder and between them they kept this little church going. I think the mother church at Salt Lake City realized what the loss of Matilda would mean to Nick, and perhaps its effect on this little church at Wilson, Wyoming, so they had him come to Salt Lake, which he did about Christmas-time in 1899. Nick sent Nell to live with her sister Etta Leek, and she continued in school. Nick left Abe in charge of the church, and he went to Salt Lake.

It so happened that Alfred Alexander Nethercott, Sr., was in Salt Lake City with his family: wife, four sons and one daughter. Before coming to America, Alfred Nethercott was an Englishman serving in the ranks of Queen Victoria of England. Alfred was one of the queen's finest swordsman, and at that time so many of the royalty were getting killed in duels, usually settled by swordsmanship, that dueling was outlawed. Everytime one of these dudes got his feelings hurt, all he had to do was slap his opponent in the mug with his gauntlet, and a date was set to try to cut off each other's head! So many of the noblemen were getting killed by each other and every other Tom, Dick and Harry, that this law was passed in England against dueling. It was a very severe law that even went as far as the death penalty in order to stop this dueling business.

Well, after this law was in effect, this Alfred Nethercott, who was in the ranks of the queen, got into a duel with some lord, or earl or count, and proceeded to run him through and through with his trusty blade. If it hadn't been that Nethercott was in the queen's guard, he would probably have been beheaded, or punished by some of the other quaint customs practiced by the English to get rid of the unruly or unwanted.

Anyway, the Mormon Church was putting on a big drive for converts in England, proselytizing for all the members they could get. Our forefathers played such cunning games with each other! And so, for Nethercott, according to records, it might have been going bad, and he just wasn't taking any chances, because he deserted the ranks of the queen and high-tailed it for America and joined the Mormon Church. Records show that his sweetheart followed him from England and they were married in the Latter-Day Saints Endowment House in Salt Lake City.

Alfred and his wife, Charlotte, moved with a Mormon colony to Sacramento, California, where they raised four boys and one girl. Alfred got into the freighting business, and finally wound up in court, involved in the famous Mountain Meadow Massacre in Utah, that was laid onto the Mormons by the U.S. Government. Many of those involved in this were jailed, and I think some even got the death penalty. I have some very old copies of the old Mormon *Deseret News*, which gives an account of the trials. Alfred Nethercott was exonerated, as they couldn't prove he was really involved. But from what I know about Alfred Nethercott, I have a hunch he was in this right up to his ears. Anyway, I am glad he escaped hanging, because my mother was not yet born, and Alfred Nethercott became my grandpa!

As stated above, Nick went to Utah and it happened that Alfred Nethercott had been pressuring the church to find him some place in the west that was still wild, as he — like my dad — figured it was getting too populated for him. He was told that an old frontiersman, mountain man, Injun fighter, and Pony Express rider, was due in Salt Lake from Jackson Hole — the wildest and last of the old west! A man named Nick Wilson!

Now, right here I am kind of playing this autobiography by ear, as I really don't know, or ever heard anyone who claims to have known what really happened either, but this is what I think happened. Nick Wilson met Alfred Nethercott, of whom he had never heard before, who was a Mormon and had a wife, four boys and a girl. One of the boys was married, and the girl was thirty years old. I am enclosing pictures of this girl, Charlotte Rebecca Nethercott, that show her as being a beautiful woman. She had a fine college education; she had never married, probably because she was a semi-cripple, having quite a pronounced hunch on her back from an injury sustained when a child, from being dropped from

Alfred Alexander Nethercott, age 24, about the time he deserted the Queen of England's Guard, came to America and joined the Mormons.

the high seat of a wagon onto the ground. How it happened I do not know. I only know that this beautiful lady became my mother!

Nick married Charlotte Rebecca on June 15, 1900, in the Great Salt Lake Temple in Salt Lake City, Utah, after several months courtship. What I think happened was that my Grandpa Nethercott was sold on going to Jackson Hole, where he could live the wild life he loved, and could homestead land. Another thing, I might add about my great swordsman grandad was, while he was a devout, tithe-paying, long-praying Mormon, he was also a good friend of John Barley Corn, to the point of being an alcoholic!

I think that after hearing Nick extol the potentials of his beloved Jackson Hole, that grandpa just said, or rather, roared, which was his custom, "Alright, Nick Wilson! I like what you said about Jackson Hole country! You have just lost a wife, and you need another one! Charlotte, it's about time you got married and you couldn't find a better husband than Nick Wilson!" And so the beautiful marriage took place as above-mentioned in the beautiful and famous Temple, in Salt Lake City, and on October 12, 1901, I was born under the Mormon Temple Covenant!

Nick took his new bride and bellicose father-in-law, my wonderful Grandma and four brothers-in-law and returned triumphantly to his home in Jackson Hole, where he was confronted by at least four of his six daughters, who were mad as hell about this marriage of their father to a woman who was younger than most of his daughters were! They say that hell hath no fury like a woman scorned! Well, I bore the brunt of, not only the fury of one woman, but five of them for many years!

Grandpa Alfred Alexander Nethercott began showing his authority and domination soon after his arrival in Jackson Hole. A few days after Nick returned home with a new wife, as was the custom in those days, all friends, neighbors and even strangers combined in planning what they called a "Shiveree!" This means they all gather at the bride and groom's house, secretly, and usually in the dead hours of night, when everyone is assumed to be sleeping; and usually after enough time since the wedding has elapsed, that the newlyweds have forgotten or quit expecting this ungodly event in their lives. The more unexpected and embarrassing time of night this invasion occurs, the better the rioters like it! It was away long into the night that all these pranksters bore down on the unsuspecting Nick and Charlotte, but they acted without taking into account the fact that Grandpa and Grandma Nethercott were there in the house, too.

When all the bedlam broke out and the unsuspecting couple were being dragged out of bed, the groom probably to be thrown into the creek and the bride half scared to death, Grandpa thought it was his first venture in an Indian uprising. He barged onto the scene with drawn sword and proceeded to scare hell out of all the would-be revelers! Several of the more stout-hearted, who protested, left with bruised heads and battered posteriors! And so my Grandpa soon became a problem to be contended with in that neck of the woods.

It wasn't very long before the drinking and gambling crowd that gathered over across the bridge in Spencers Saloon also found that their lives were soon to be interrupted, too. When Grandpa got

Charlotte Rebecca Nethercott, age 18, at high school graduation.

Charlotte Rebecca Nethercott, age 24, at her college graduation.

Elijah Nicholas Wilson, age 58, at the time of his marriage to Charlotte Rebecca.

Charlotte Rebecca Nethercott, age 30, at the time of her marriage to Nick Wilson.

about "three sheets to the wind," he often took over the saloon and usually wound up in complete and lonely possession of the premises, as he dearly loved a fight, and the greater the odds, the better he liked it. And so the ones who wanted to stay and pursue their cards and drinks soon learned to cooperate with Grandpa. Grandpa often kept control of the saloon situation for hours, or even days. When it came time for this to end, there was only one person who could break it up and get Grandpa home. He was scared of no man, but there was one little woman, only about half as tall and weighing less than a fourth his weight, that Grandpa was afraid of. And that was my beautiful, wonderful little Grandma! She would go over there to that evil place and, taking his sword away from him, would march him for home. If he didn't move fast enough, he got prodded in the rump by that trusty blade!

I can remember when I was only three or four years old, watching these fracases. I would poke my head up from behind the bed, and big-eyed, listen to Grandpa roaring like a lion as Grandma gradually quieted him down and into bed. These occurrences only happened three or four times a year, thank God!

I stated that Grandpa was a devout Mormon and a praying man. Before every meal at our house, no matter who was there or what they believed, even many atheists, got down on bended knees on the floor, before their chair with head bowed, while Grandpa poured out his thanks and ours, too, whether we were thankful or not. And we all soon learned to be very quiet during this prayer, which was long and often resulted in cold food, especially if anyone made the slightest noise. Grandpa would inteerrupt his prayer, go around, and with strong hand, bow down the restless one's head, and then start all over again!

Among my Grandpa's four sons was one who was married. He brought his entire family, five sons and four daughters. His name was Alfred Nethercott, Jr. This family was one of Jackson Hole's finest old time pioneer families. Uncle Alfred took up 160 acres of land adjoining Nick's land on the northeast side. Only two of these nine children were born in Jackson Hole, Amanda and Reigo. Two sons of Grandpa Nethercott were Charley and George. Neither of them liked Jackson Hole and soon left, making their homes back in Sacramento, California. The fourth son was named Joseph.

Nick had turned the running of his ranch over to Abe Ward and he devoted his time to the Forest Ranger job and being Bishop of the local Latter-Day Saints Church. Uncle Alfred built his homestead cabin about one-half mile northeast of Nick's cabin on Fish

Creek. Grandpa built among some very tall engleman spruce and cottonwoods, a quarter of a mile above Alfred, Jr., and only a few hundred yards from the bank of the Snake River.

My little sister Charlotte Sara was born July 8, 1903, also up at my Grandma's house on Snake River. My Grandma's name was Charlotte, too, making three Charlottes in our family. People usually think that I was named after my uncle Charley Nethercott, or my mother and Grandma Charlotte, but I wasn't. My dad named me Charles Alma after a good friend of his who lived up at Kelly at the warm springs at that time. His name was Charley Allen.

My brother George was born on George Washington's birthday, February 22, 1905, and named not after our uncle George Nethercott as presumed. It is only a coincidence that we have a Charley and George Nethercott and a Charley and George Wilson in our families.

As stated in a previous chapter, Nick Wilson built his new cabin only feet from the bank of Fish Creek. This fact changed the whole history of the lives of Nick's third and last family of two boys and one girl.

At the west end of Nick's cabin was a fine, deep fishing hole that was bordered by tall willows that hung out over this hole. Just above the fishing hole, Nick had built a short ramp about 10 feet out into the creek that was used to walk out on and dip buckets of water for household use.

Nick used to step out the door and catch a mess of trout right here anytime they wanted to eat them. My sister Nell was fourteen years old when I was born and the only one of Nick's and Matilda's family still living with them. Nell now lived with her father, Nick, and my mother. The daughters of Nick and Matilda who made life so ugly for my mother at every chance they got when Nick was away — because they would have never dared to be rude to Charlotte when he was there — were Edna Jane Ward (worst of all!), and then Fanny, Kate and Etta. Edna Jane lived right across the street from our log cabin and had more opportunity to be cruel to my mother. The others practiced their spleen on my mother whenever they could. I don't know why my mother didn't complain to Nick about this shabby treatment from Nick's daughters, but she didn't before it was too late.

Kate was the first one to drop this stupid animosity toward my mother, because of her own kids who really got to like Charlotte. The Goodricks lived only about three hundred yards south of Nick's cabin. There was a swale about half way between the two houses, with tall, thick willows growing all along it. This swale was full of water during the summer months, until after irrigation time, and then it was dry.

The reason I mention this swale that ran between the Goodrick's house and our house was that about the summer I was six years old, my half-sister Fanny and her daughter Alta lived with Nick. Alta and I used to run away and go down to play with the Goodrick kids. My dad was still Forest Ranger and was gone a lot. Fanny was in charge of things, caring for me and Alta, and doing the cooking. She didn't want me to be with the Goodricks so much, and told me boogie stories about awful monsters that lived in this swale in the thick willows, and got me so scared I hardly ever went down to Goodrick's unless someone was with me. We got milk from Goodricks, and they never milked their cows until after dark. That made it twice as scary to go through these willows as in the daytime. When it came time to go for the milk, Fanny would give me a pail with a lid on it to go for the milk. I wouldn't go because of the scary stories she told me, and then she would whip me to make me go, and even then I refused. So she either had to go herself or send Alta with me, and Alta was just as big a coward as I was, and we both really hated that swale. It seemed that people and bigger kids took great delight telling these awful Boogie stories to us little kids, and I just don't have space to dwell on this story anymore, but it accounts for why there are so many cowards in the world today. It takes more courage to be a coward than it does to be a hero!

A narrow foot-bridge spanned this twenty-foot swale. Some of the Goodrick kids were at our house nearly all the time. Charlotte baked lots of cookies for them and the bigger ones like Jay and Guy and Etta helped her with the washing and when Nick was away on the Forest job, he paid the bigger kids to carry wood and water for Charlotte. At the time I was born in 1901, there were six Goodrick kids living, about four were dead, and five more were born before 1911.

Etta Leek soon got over her hostility, too, but Edna and Fanny never did, and Nell got very fond of Charlotte also, during the three years she lived at home. Nell married Enoch Ferrin when she was seventeen.

Grandpa Alfred Nethercott Sr., took up 160 acres of farm land, as mentioned before, and also Uncle Alfred Nethercott, Jr., took land joining Nick's on the north.

In my father's manuscript where he told of "The Terrible Journey," in which one man froze to death, he also told about the

Doctor Palmer who cared for Nick and the other man whose frozen
feet had to be amputated by Doctor Palmer. Nick had persuaded
Doctor Palmer to move up to Jackson Hole shortly after Nick settled
there in 1893. Doctor Palmer was everything that Nick Wilson said
he was, except Nick didn't tell that Doctor Palmer, like my Grandpa
Nethercott, was an alcoholic. He got worse after moving to Jackson
Hole, and because of his drinking habit he became not too depend-
able, as was the case when I was born at my Grandma Nethercott's
house on the bank of the Snake River.

Nick was gone on a week's trip in the forest, and Grandma sent
Grandpa to get Dr. Palmer. Of course, they both had to stop at
Spencer's Saloon and hoist a few for the road, and by the time
these two sots arrived, Grandma wouldn't let them in the house
in their condition, but with the help of her granddaughter and my
first cousin, Edith Nethercott Cheney, who was married to Sylvester Cheney, the eldest son of Selar and Alice Cheney, they delivered
me in good shape. You can imagine Nick's joy when he returned
home to find he had another son. My half-brother Bill from the
polygamous marriage was still with his mother somewhere in
Idaho.

These were happy days for Nick. I remember my sister Nellie
telling me, that when I was about eight months old, that my dad
was fishing in the hole by the house. He had built a picket-fence
all around the house, and the blacksmith shop, and the old house,
behind our new cabin. There was a picket-gate in front of the ramp
that ran out into Fish Creek. It had a loop that slipped over the
gatepost, that small children could not reach to open the gate. This
gate was always closed before and after drawing water from the
creek. Nell said that as my dad was fishing, he called her to "Bring
Charley out!" She did, sitting me down on a little blanket quilt.
Then Nick soon caught a small trout about eight or ten inches
long, unhooked it from his fly, and tossed the flopping little fish
onto the blanket with me. Nell said that I really went after that
fish! And before they knew what had happened, baby Charley had
the wiggly little monster in both hands and its head in my mouth,
the fish slapping me on both cheeks with its tail! I guess that's how
I got initiated into being such an avid fisherman. During the next
fourteen years that I got to live with my dad, some of my happiest
and exciting memories were the many, many fishing trips we had
together. Even years later, when he began to get feeble and used
a walking cane, we would walk the one mile out to the Snake River
to fish. I would carry our lunch and fishing rod and a can of grass-

hoppers, and Nick with his cane was a common sight, slowly hiking along the narrow lane that led from the little town of Wilson out to the Snake River.

The lane was lined with thick willows where I found dozens of birds' nests all the way along. I loved the blackbirds and the bob-a-links with their beautiful red and yellow wings; killdeers and wild canaries and brown thrush; bluebirds, snipes, whippoorwills and meadowlarks! But the one I loved most of all was the robin red breast! And the thrill I always got when finding a new nest that was nearly always built at eye level, and peering down onto those four beautiful sky-blue eggs! I loved the meadowlarks, too, because they were always the first bird to return to the valley in the spring, even while there were still patches of snow. Listen to their beautiful song in the early golden morning sunlight! "Utah's a pretty-little-place!" But I was glad they came back to Wyoming anyway!

And there was the call of the great sandhill crane when they arrived in the spring, circling over the valley so high you couldn't see them. As you watched, they finally came down into sight and landed along our beloved old Snake River, where they nested along with the honking, wild Canadian geese! Ducks everywhere, the beautiful green heads and wings of teal and mallard and the red-headed Merganser, who floated proudly along down Fish Creek during high water, with her brood of ducklings, past our house! It seemed like in those days that life teemed everywhere, the willows full of partridges and the great blue grouse we called "fool hens," along the foothills and in the groves of quaking aspen and big sagegrouse out on the flats.

Fish Creek teemed with trout, but that was too close to fish! The days I spent with my dad out on Snake River were the best. Oh! How my dad could fry fish! But I am getting way ahead of my story. I guess it's because I hate so to settle down and tell of the great tragedy that was about to befall Nick Wilson — and me — and I guess about all the lives in Jackson Hole were really affected more or less by it.

CHAPTER 12 — **Charlotte Sarah Wilson (Tragedy)**

My little sister Charlotte Sarah was a beautiful, blue-eyed, curly, white-haired little girl of two years when one day in early June, my dad left on a Forest Ranger job. That day was my mother's washday, and Jay and Guy and Etta Goodrick came up to help her, as usual, and I played in the tightly-fenced yard with my little sister and a couple of younger Goodrick kids. One of the boys, Jay or Guy, was cutting wood and carrying it into the house for mother. The other was busily carrying buckets of water to fill the big copper boiler on the stove, in which was heated water for the wash. Jay was about eleven years old, Guy was about nine and Etta was seven. I was about three years old. Ray and Gail were about three and four years old, and sister Sarah was just a few days under two years old.

Now it was a strict rule that the gate to the ramp that led out into the creek was to be always kept closed, but something happened that was never really quite cleared up, but anyway this gate was momentarily left open. One story was that the boy who was carrying the water had two pails, and as he would be right back after emptying the water into the boiler, he may not have taken time to set the two pails of water down and closed the gate. But mother needed help with something and asked the two big boys to help her, which took longer than had been expected. Also, my mother didn't realize that the gate to the water ramp had been left open and, of course, the water carrier had forgotten.

During the short time the gate was left open, we four kids crowded out onto this ramp. The creek was running very high and the rapids made lots of noise. The ones in the house didn't hear us kids laughing and throwing sticks and rocks into the swollen stream. Then it happened! I will never forget that awful scene, while playing out on the narrow ramp. My little sister fell, or was crowded off, into the rushing water! In those days little children, especially girls, wore several layers of petticoats and dresses. The air bloomed up under the dresses and I can still see little Sarah as she floated, head and arms above the water, and the look of amazement on her face as she was swept out of sight, down past the flopping willows that hung out over the water from the bank!

Immediately it was discovered by those in the house that we kids were all out on the ramp! We were all yanked back through the gate by the two bigger boys, and my mother came. I have explained that she had a hunch-back, but she could move very fast, and she always did the cooking and house work and had help only on these wash days. She was very frantic when we told her that Sally — that's the name my father always called my sister — had gone down in the water! Mother did not hesitate, but ran out onto the ramp and plunged into the swift current! She was a good swimmer and soon disappeared around the willows.

I had forgotten to say that we now had a little baby brother, not yet four months old, George, who was born on February 22. Although my mother was a good swimmer, she soon weakened, but made it to the bank and crawled out. In the meantime, Edna Jane Ward, across the street at the hotel, and several other people there, were alerted by Etta Goodrick. Within minutes there were a dozen or more people running up and down the stream. My mother was soon back in the creek where the water was shallower, and she could wade downstream. It was a half-hour or more before she was pulled from the water, more dead than alive, and carried back to our cabin.

In the meantime, Jay and Guy had run down the creek and had seen Sally a couple of times, still floating, being held up by the dresses full of air. They couldn't get to her as the water was so fast, and for a half-mile the bank was thick with willows, so they couldn't get close to the bank. So they ran down through Goodrick's ranch and crossed a flume over the big spring creek. Just below the spring creek, the Fish Creek made a sharp bend to the west where Edmonstons spring entered Fish Creek, and right above the spring there was a long, shallow riffle clear across Fish Creek. The brush thinned out here and just as the running boys reached this riffle they saw Sally still floating on the water. Neither of these boys could swim, but the riffle was so shallow, although swift, that they could wade out and grab her dress and pull her to the bank, where Jay picked her up in his arms and ran for home.

The sad thing is, had the boys known a thing about life-saving and had just held her head down so the water could run out, then she could have been saved. Jay said that as he ran with the little girl that she raised her arms several times and he thought she was alright, but when he met the first adults coming down the stream, she was already dead! Although I was only three and one-half years old, I can still remember very vividly this terrible tragedy that changed the history of Nick Wilson's life and family.

Those were terrible days at our house following my sister's death from drowning. The most frightening thing was the way my Grandpa Nethercott carried on. He blamed everybody, especially my dad, for building a house on the bank of a river, which Fish Creek really is for a good part of the year. This creek was nearly a hundred feet wide by our house, and lots of streams not nearly so large are called rivers.

My mother was very sick and contracted brain fever and cried all the time. My wonderful old Grandma was the sanest one of all. She was so good to me and tried to quiet Grandpa, who raved consistently that my mother was crazy and demanded she be sent to Evanston, Wyoming, to the Insane Asylum. Doctor Palmer did all he could, but brain fever was out of his line. But he insisted that she was not crazy, nor even mentally injured, and pled with Nick to take her to Salt Lake City where he said there were doctors capable of handling her problem. Nearly fifty years later his diagnosis proved to be correct.

For a three and one-half-year-old, these things were very confusing and terrible — so many people coming and going! My father's first wife Matilda was buried in South Park over on the east side of the Snake River. As stated, Fish Creek was very high in June, and so was the Snake River. They decided to bury my little sister over in South Park by Matilda in Nick Wilson's burial plot. There must have been a lot of teams and wagons crossing Snake River for this funeral. I don't know if they took my mother, but I am sure they didn't, because she was so sick in bed.

I can remember that I rode with my dad in our light spring wagon. It had three seats and a white canvas top and was known as a Studebaker wagon. My father used it to haul passengers. For this funeral, two back seats were taken out and my sister's little coffin, inside a large, rough box, was tied in the wagon box. It was covered with a quilt that was on my bed, and we still had it when my father died ten years later, and our house was abandoned. It had three bands of cloth about two feet wide: one was black, one blue, and one yellow; all had dozens of small white stars all over them. As we crossed on a big riffle across Snake River, the water came into the wagon box, all around the quilt-covered coffin's box, and I remember how concerned I was about it, and very troubled, because I knew my little sister was in the box.

My father must have had a terrible run-in with the Nethercotts, especially over my little four-month-old brother George. My grandmother wanted him, but my grandfather forbade her. My cousin Edith Cheney, who helped Grandma deliver me, had had two children since I had been born, and was nursing one of them. As George was a breast-fed baby, Edith offered to nurse him along with hers, but my father's side of the family refused to let the Nethercotts have George. As it turned out, both George and I would have been better off if they had let the Nethercotts have us both, but my dad wouldn't give me up. So he let Vesta Ward, who was about ten years old, raise George, under the supervision of her mother, Edna Jane Ward. He gave Vesta all my mother's fine jewelry, of which she had a lot, consisting of necklaces, watches, bracelets, and other things, all made of gold, and a small diamond ring that had been handed down through generations of Nethercotts, as was most of the other jewelry.

As I said in the beginning of this story, Grandpa Nethercott dominated everything and everybody. I will never understand why, or how, my father could have ever given in to Grandfather Nethercott to put my mother in an insane asylum! But he did! And this despite Dr. Palmer's pleas to take her to Salt Lake City first.

This all happened in early June, 1905, and by late July my mother was considered well and strong enough for the ten days or two weeks it took to get her to Evanston, which was in the extreme southwest corner of Wyoming. The trip had to be made by horse-drawn wagons out over Teton Pass through Idaho and northeastern Utah, via Weber Canyon into Wyoming and to Evanston. The day they left with several wagons, men and women, one woman was Alice Cheney, because years later when I was ten or twelve years old and at her place, she told me how she hated my dad, Nick Wilson. She claimed he hired her to go on this trip with my mother. Nick was to pay Alice two dollars a day, and she said he never paid her. Alice was my father's niece, daughter of Nick's brother Sylvester Wilson. I was terribly hurt by this story that Alice rubbed into me. I told my dad about it, and he said Alice was a liar! That she had insisted on going and she went only for the trip.

When my sister drowned, my dad was out in the Targhee Forest on fire patrol and trail building. It took two days before he was found and told the awful news.

After Nick returned from taking his wife to Evanston, things were bad at home. Wards had my baby brother and me. My Grandpa and Grandma Nethercott had left the valley for good. I never saw either one of them again. I was later told that they both had perished in the Great Earthquake in California in 1906.

Nick let Wards keep and raise baby George until he was six years old, when Nick gave him to his brother Elias and his wife, of Marysville, Idaho. Uncle Elias and his wife never had any children, and she was an old maid when Elias married her. She thought she wanted a child, so prevailed on Nick to give George to them. They had George only a couple of months when Nick got word that George had been lost. Nick drove all night, and the next day arrived at Marysville, but George had been found. He had wandered off following their dog. A few miles away was an old, abandoned cellar that had caved in. George climbed down in and couldn't get back out! The dog went home alone and a search began. Nick was notified. Just before he arrived, one of the searchers found George in the old cellar. He was hungry and thirsty, but OK. Uncle Elias' wife had a nervous breakdown, and had Nick take George back, so we both lived at home with "Daddy" as we called him, until he died in 1915.

However, I am getting ahead of my story again. I started to tell the rest of the story regarding my mother, who was confined to the Insane Asylum at Evanston, Wyoming. In those days, back in 1905, most, if not all, of these public institutions were managed as what is known as a political plum. This means that all the personnel were placed there by appointment by the governor, to pay his political debts he owed to his supporters. These institutions were operated on taxpayers' money, and especially the supervisor's salary was a real bonus. Thus, the governor allotted these jobs to his best supporters, which lasted until the next election, when probably a new governor was elected and the institution's management began all over again.

Evanston, as well as many other asylums, became known as "snake pits," and these supposedly crazy people were treated shamefully, with no hope of ever returning to the outside world again. This is the kind of place my Grandpa talked, or forced, Nick into placing my beautiful mother! It was around 1945 when these institutions began to be run as they were intended, and not used as political plums anymore. I will get to this as soon as I write what happened there with my mother.

My mother wrote frequent letters to my father the first winter she was confined there, and the next summer when I was four and one-half years old, he took me to see my mother. As I have explained above, it was a long trip to Evanston from Jackson Hole with a team and wagon. I will always remember this long trip with my dad and the fun I had. We camped wherever night caught us, and we once camped near a railroad track. I had never seen nor heard a train, as this was long before the train came to Victor, Idaho, where, on a clear, quiet day you could hear the train whistle eighteen miles away! Here I saw and heard this great black monster, belching smoke and steam, go roaring by our tent which was pitched beside a beautiful trout stream. I don't know who was the most frightened, me or the horses!

I had great fun on this trip. I wanted to camp every night on a stream where we could catch fish. One night we camped early where there wan't any fish, but there were lots of ground squirrels. We called them chislers because they stood upon their hind feet and gave a loud chirring sound.

My dad showed me how to catch these squirrels by taking our fly rod and making a noose in the end of the line, instead of a fish hook, and placing the loop over the squirrel hole after chasing one in, then waiting patiently for the little cuss to stick his head back out of the hole. Then pretty quick, he poked his head up a little more until when about half out you gave a jerk, and had Mr. Squirrel around the belly! And the fight he put up was better than a good-sized trout! The first one I caught I reeled up close to the rod tip, then lay the rod down and ran and grabbed the squirrel before my dad could warn me. The squirrel socked his sharp little teeth into my thumb! I was the one doing the bawling and flopping around, instead of the squirrel! That's what they call learning from the teacher who teaches in the school called "hard knocks." If you have any sense at all, you usually remember the lessons taught in the school of "hard knocks!"

We soon arrived at Evanston to see my mother. Nick kept talking to me about her to be sure I knew what it was all about. Of course, I remembered her! Only a year had passed, but her influence had been steadily undermined in my memory, mostly because my wonderful grandma was no longer present. In fact, all the Nethercott influence was getting dimmer all the time, because my dad's side of the family had no communications with them. My life had been dominated by the Nethercotts on my mother's side of the family until she was taken away. There must have been a big falling out between the Wilson and Nethercott families, that I didn't know about, to cause this wide division between them. I never got to see any of the Nethercotts, except Aunt Ida, Uncle Alfred Nethercott's wife, who stopped in to see George and me once in awhile. Anyway, I was expecting to see my beautiful mother as I remembered her, and even my father was not prepared for what we were about to see.

We camped near Evanston, and the next morning Nick cleaned me up nice and put clean clothing on both of us and we went up to the Asylum. Nick didn't know that after he left my mother, Charlotte, there, that during the past year she had suffered with awful headaches and had begun to pull her hair out in large hanks, leaving torn, bloody scalp. To stop this self-injury, they cut her hair all off. In fact, it was clipped as close to her scalp as possible, so she could not pull it out. When we were ushered into the reception room, the matron didn't tell Nick about this hair problem. When my poor mother was led into the room she recognized us immediately, and ran across the room to us with out-stretched arms. Her words were, "Oh, Nick!" and then she grabbed me up in her arms and cried, "Oh! My baby, my baby!" I had no idea who she was! This haggard, boney-faced, bald-headed person with large sores on her head! It scared the wits out of me and Nick was also in shock, and I began screaming and hitting her in the face. She dropped me to the floor and turned in rage on my dumb-founded father and screamed, "Nick Wilson, I hate you! You let your daughters abuse me and humiliate me! And now you have let them turn my baby against me!" And she ran from the room.

The woman who had brought my mother into the room stood aghast, as she stared at my stricken father! All he could do was stammer, "I . . . I never knew she was like this! I didn't know my daughters treated her badly! I, why, they never turned Charlotte's baby against her!" The woman tried to get my mother to come back, but she wouldn't budge. They got me quieted down and gave me some good things to eat, while Nick went to my mother. I clamored quite awhile for him before he returned. I don't know whatever transpired between them, but in later years we were told that my mother never spoke another word for forty-four years, while she was there, and she never wrote another letter.

Father and I returned home to Jackson Hole, and I know there was a show-down between Nick and his daughters over how they had treated my mother. The upshot of all this was that Wards kept George, and I lived with my dad in the little log cabin by Fish Creek. I didn't see my mother again for fourteen years, when I went with my half-sister Etta Leek. Abe Ward had never made any kind of settlement regarding Nick's ranch, only claiming he was legal guardian for me and my brother George. Etta and I were on a trip to Kemmerer, Wyoming, which was our county seat to get records, etc., pertaining to Nick's ranch. While at Kemmerer, Etta decided that we should go see my mother while so close to Evanston. This was about 1918. They had added a lot onto the big, red brick building and it seemed lighter and cleaner than it did in 1906.

The receptionist seated us in a large, well-lighted room and then went and brought my mother in. They called her Lottie, and I could hear the woman tell my mother, "You have some visitors. It is a big surprise!" Mother looked different now. She seemed to stand taller, and her back was less bent, her hair was still cut short, about one inch long, and was a steel-gray color, but her scalp had no sores like before. The matron told her who we were, only she called Etta mother's sister-in-law, when in reality, Etta was Lottie's step-daughter. Mother looked us over for a moment or two, and I could see she recognized Etta, but was puzzled by me. Then she dropped her head and never uttered a word to us. This matron said she had been working for the institution for only about eight years, but had been told that my mother had never uttered a word since she came there in 1905, which, of course, was not true!

Etta tried to talk to her, and bring her up to date on the family, but Lottie appeared not to pay any attention to her. She kept staring at me, but when I looked at her she would drop her head and would not look into my eyes. I was about 17 years old then. I never saw her again for thirty-two years.

Along about 1935, things began to change at these public institutions in Wyoming, and they were no longer political plums, but began to be managed by competent and trained personnel. Good doctors were placed at Evanston, and about 1940 there was a very good doctor who also served as superintendent. He had begun to analyze each patient, and was appalled at what he found. There were many patients there who should have never been placed there in the first place. And many completely sane people were just kept there for many years because there was no family or anyone who cared to get them released. Many were just abandoned by their families, as my mother had been. I doubt if, during the forty-five years Lottie spent at Evanston, that she was ever visited — even a dozen times — by family or friends.

This fine doctor at the Evanston Asylum was Dr. Rasmussen. When he got around to checking up on Charlotte Rebecca Nethercott Wilson, he was really upset and mad. He had a terrible time finding anyone who was legally responsible for her. The only one who had tried to keep in touch with her was my Aunt Ida Nethercott, wife of Uncle Alfred, Jr. Dr.Rasmussen contacted her, and at that time she was almost dead and very senile. She and uncle Alfred had had a car accident, on August 21, 1925,with an old Model-T Ford, owned by Uncle Alfred and one of the first three cars ever owned in Jackson Hole.

Uncle Alfred ran a ferry boat on the Snake River between Jackson and Wilson. His son, Reigo, ran the farm with his mother, Aunt Ida. Uncle Alfred was, like my Grandpa Nethercott, an alcoholic. Uncle Al made good money with his ferry, and there is a real story about this ferry that should be told. I will try to tell a few important instances it played in the history of Jackson Hole.

Uncle Alfred had a habit of taking Aunt Ida one or two Sundays each month down to visit her daughter, Fanny, who was married to Ora Grisamer. They lived over across the river from lower South Park, about fifteen miles from their home on the Snake River on the Wilson side. One Sunday, Uncle Alfred was pretty well lit up, and he and Aunt Ida, all dressed up, headed for Ora's. Just in front of the Leek Ranch, which I have described in previous chapters, Uncle Alfred was really pouring it on too fast for the narrow dirt road. He ran off the road, and instead of letting up on the gas and slowing down out through the sage brush, he made the fatal mistake that is still taking lives with the automobile right up to this day: he turned the front wheels back sharply to regain the road and rolled the old Model-T. It had no top, and threw Aunt Ida clear, but broke bones and caused internal injuries that she never did recover from. Uncle Alfred was pinned down on top of a large boulder, which killed him instantly.

When Dr. Rasmussen contacted Aunt Ida, she was living with her son, Reigo, who was then married. He informed Dr. Rasmussen that Etta Leek was guardian for Lottie and the two boys, Charley and George. Etta had died in 1931 during a gallbladder operation in Salt Lake City. I was thirty years old then, and had been made guardian over my mother and what was left of her share of Nick Wilson's estate, which wasn't much, and so Dr. Rasmussen finally contacted me by telephone. I was married then, and lived on my wife's homestead on Silver Creek, near Boulder, Wyoming. Dr. Rasmussen explained that he needed to see me regarding my mother Charlotte Wilson at Evanston, so my wife Doratha and I drove down there and spent several hours in Dr. Rasmussen's office. He informed me that it had been "criminal" to have placed Charlotte in that institution, where she had now been for forty years! He said it was a simple operation to drain fluid from a sac that formed at the base of her brain, back of the neck, which was common in brain fever cases. He said that in 1905 there were lots of doctors who could have performed this operation, and that her mind and health would have been cured in a month or less! He wanted to know who was responsible for this criminal act, and I told him the story as I have told it here in previous chapters.

I could not explain why my father had ever given in to my Grandpa Nethercott's domination in this affair, and against the advice of Dr. Palmer.

Anyway, Dr. Rasmussen wanted me to give him the authority to operate on her now! My wife and I were both very concerned and shook up, and we wanted to know what the results of an operation would be now. Would it be a success after forty years? If her mind was restored, would she wake up in 1905 or 1945? And many other questions we needed answers to.

Dr. Rasmussen said he could not answer any of these questions for sure, but for the sake of science, he felt the operation should be made. He thought her memory would probably return to 1905 when it happened! My God! What were we getting into? My wife and I went outside and hashed over this new problem in our lives, pro and con, and there were so many "if's." The most terrifying one was the cruel jolt it would be to my mother to be brought back to reality after forty years, and what would it do to her? The thought was more than I could take! There was also the problem of where would she live; how could we care for her in our small home with four little kids?

In spite of his urging, we just couldn't give permission for Dr. Rasmussen to attempt this operation, with so many things that could backfire on us all. We were so upset that we didn't even try to see her, but returned home where, we promised Dr. Rasmussen, we would think it all over and let him know in two weeks. In two weeks, we were very positive, after much prayer and contemplation, that it would be morally wrong to let them operate on my mother after so long a time. This should have been done way back in 1905! God will have to be the judge as to who was the most wrong, those responsible in 1905, or me in 1945!

The next time I saw my mother she was dead. I got a call from Evanston in early May, 1950, telling me that she was sick with pneumonia, and that I should come to make arrangements as she wasn't expected to live very long. The weather was terrible, with one of those May blizzard snowstorms that could last for days. The kids were in school, so I would have to go alone. The Lord must have been with me all the way, because I was just ahead of floods, of bridges going out, of mud and snow slides!

I got to Evanston and was informed that my mother was dead. She was at Bill's Mortuary in Evanston. I went and saw her in the chapel, and was more astounded and amazed than I was that day when, at four and one-half years of age, I had been so frightened! Now I was amazed at how tiny she was! And so beautiful! Her hair was all grown out, and white as the driven snow! And the peace on her face was beyond description. You may want to take another look at the three photographs of her in this book. She was beautiful then, but magnificent now!

I had promised my father to see that my mother had the Mormon Temple garments placed on her for burial. Mr. Bill turned everything over to the local Evanston Mormon Church. It was a couple of days before the garments came from Salt Lake City. Then the Mormon people put on a beautiful funeral program for her. The choir sang so beautifully, and the Bishop gave a wonderful obituary and sermon.

A large easy-chair was placed for me in the chapel near my mother's casket, which was open, and I could see her beautiful face. I won't even try to express my feelings and memories. Right in the middle of the service, someone arrived who wanted to see me and attend the service. I said yes, show him in. It was a dear friend that I had known many years ago in Jackson Hole, when we both worked at the elk refuge. He had gone to Rock Springs and worked for many years on the Union Pacific Railroad. He and his wife Reva, and their children, now lived in Evanston, and he saw in the paper an item regarding my mother's death, and of my being there, so he came and sat with me and wept. I loved him so much for coming! His name was John Steinbrook; God sent John to be with me, and I don't know whether I could have borne up without him.

A few years later God gave me the privilege of saving John and his twelve-year-old son, Jackie, from certain death on a hunting trip. That is a story in itself!

The drama of my mother, Charlotte Rebecca, is about over now! After the funeral was over, there was a long, black funeral hearse waiting outside for her. It was sent down from Jackson to transport the body to be buried by my father and little sister and Matilda, in our family plot at South Park in Jackson Hole, Wyoming. Now I was faced with another final decision regarding my beautiful mother: Mr. Bill of Bill's Mortuary in Evanston, had made arrangements to bury my mother in the Asylum burial plot. He had taken me to see it, and it consisted of the many patients of the asylum who had died during the time my mother was there. It was on level land near the foothills, and beautifully cared for. The headstones were flat and level with the ground so the grass could be cut over them. There were rose bushes and all kinds of flowers, and flowering bushes around the cemetary. I had been very pleased with the location. I had promised my father to see to the Mormon burial clothing, but I had not promised to bury her back in Jackson Hole. Somehow, I just couldn't let that long, black hearse haul her back to the place where her life had really been snuffed out forty-five years before.

I appreciated my dear cousin, Reigo Nethercott, sending a hearse for her. If he had come to superintend the job, I might have let her go. But I didn't, and after a lot of praying with John and Reva, we decided that if Evanston was good enough for her to live in for forty-five years, and along with the fact that many of her friends were now buried here, that this was now the place for her. I knew that no one remembered her or knew her anymore in Jackson Hole, and it would only open anew the old gossips, and wounds, and I can only pray and hope that I did right in having my mother buried in Evanston, Wyoming, where she had been committed wrongfully so many years ago!

Before I leave my mother's story, I should add that only a few years after my mother died this Dr. Rasmussen committed suicide. It was said that the conditions he found at Evanston were more than he could bear.

Digging through a snowslide south of Jackson. This snow slide ran almost every winter and took out part of Steve Leek's fence. Before the slide was dug out the South Park people detoured out into Leek's hay field. This shows South Park ranchers digging the slide out. This happened so often I don't know what year is pictured, but probably it is around 1915.

The road supervisor came along while these guys were digging out this slide, and after watching them for awhile, he said, "The whole bunch ought to be fired! One little old woman with a broom could move more snow in an hour than this whole gang moved in a day!"

1910. Caught in an early September snowstorm on Teton Pass while hauling dudes from St. Anthony, Idaho to Jackson Hole.

Man-afraid-of-his-horse! Holly Leek, age 5. Picture taken about 1911, at the Leek Ranch, looking north toward Jackson, Wyoming, 3 miles.

Steve Leek's famous picture, "The Fighting Elk," taken about 1915, after the feeding program was started by the State. Photo taken at Frank Tanner Ranch, south of Leek's, Jackson Hole, Wyoming.

CHAPTER 13 — **Happy Times**

Shortly after returning home from Evanston in 1906, Nick re-signed from his forestry job and settled down to taking care of me. My brother George was living with the Wards, just across the street, and we saw him often. That fall of 1906 my brother-in-law, Steve Leek, was really getting concerned about the elk. He started taking pictures and got a moving picture machine from France. He made some marvelous films of wildlife and spent the winter of 1906-07 with Abe Ward in the east, trying to raise money for the starving elk by lecturing and showing these movies and his beauti-ful slides, which he hand-colored.

One room in Leek's large house was called the "Dark Room," where Steve spent days and nights developing his pictures. In the fall of 1906, my father and I started living at Leek's and taking care of the place while Steve was gone so much.

My half-sister, Etta Leek, had a baby on Christmas Day, 1906, and called him Holliday Leek — "Holly" for short, as he was known for the rest of his life. My dad started me and Lester Leek in the trapping business. Flat Creek flowed through the Leek Ranch for over a mile, and it teemed with native cutthroat trout and muskrats were abundant. And we often caught a beautiful mink. We learned how to catch weasels and how to skin these animals and attend to the hides, as there was a lively market in furs in those days. We received market prices from a dozen or more big fur houses, and got to selling our furs to Maas and Stevens in St. Louis, Missouri, who was our favorite.

I was only six that fall, but I was a big, strong kid. Lester was about nine years old. Early in October, Nick said it was time to set our traps on Flat Creek for "mushrats," as we called them. It was a thrill when he showed us how to make our sets and the places to look for "sign" along under the banks. Lester and I started out with one dozen traps each. Six No. 0 (ought), and six No. 1 Victor traps. These sizes were for mushrats, but we used the oughts for weasel and mushrats, too. I learned a good lesson the first day we set our traps, and that was not to question Nick's experience in where to set a trap. We had most of our traps set by noon, and I began to think I knew all about where to set my traps. The mushrat sign was so plentiful that we had most of our sets made in less than a quarter of a mile up the creek. After lunch, we had about four traps each left to set, and they were all No. 1's. Father said we should set them for mink, even though, as he said, we would probably catch a mushrat more often than a mink. He said, "Now we will look for places not usually used by rats and use fish heads for bait, or mushrat meat."

The first mink set was under the bridge across Flat Creek, where the road led out to the hay meadows, west of the house. There was a flat rock sticking out from under the abutment on the east side of the bridge, and my dad said that would be a fine place to make a set. We drew straws and Lester got this set. Nick showed Lester how to set the trap in about four or five inches of water beside the rock, too deep to catch mushrats, then hang a big fish head from a string down about a foot above the rock. He explained that mushrats seldom climbed up on the rock, except maybe a big drifter. A drifter was an old male or boar muskrat that spent his time traveling up and down the creek by himself trying to break up dens, wherever he could whip the male muskrat, then taking over the female after killing her litter. These big, old drifter muskrats were usually almost twice the size of a common male muskrat, but he met with such fierce resistance from both the pair he was attacking that his hide was so full of holes and scars from rat bites that it was hardly worth skinning.

Muskrats brought us from ten cents for kits to as high as thirty-five cents for big, prime hides. Father explained to us that mink also traveled up and down the streams in search of food and killed lots of young muskrats and birds to eat. He said, "When a mink is traveling along the stream, he is investigating everything. The rock is a natural, and when he sees or scents the fish or meat bait, he will climb upon the rock. A mink is long-bodied, and at a place like this rock, he will stand up and his hind feet will reach bottom, so it's easy to get him by a hind foot."

The next set was to be mine, and it was only a couple of hundred yards above Lester's set under the bridge. This place my dad picked for me was a big willow bunch hanging out over the water. He said, "Take your hatchet and cut some of the thick willows away right on the bank just over the water where it's four or five inches deep, then hang a fish head up over the bare spot, which you make with your hatchet."

I didn't like the looks of this place for a set, and said, "Aw! I don't want that place!"

Lester said, "I will set one of my traps there, Grandpa!" And he did!

It took us almost all afternoon to set these last eight traps, and we could hardly wait to look at our traps the next morning! We were up at daylight, one hour before the sun would peek over the big, high mountain that rose almost straight up from about 200 yards of Leek's house. There was a heavy white frost and the trail we three made out to the creek was plain as if there had been a foot of snow. Nick went with us the first three or four mornings to look at our traps, to show us how to drown the animal that might be in our trap. He had us each cut a forked willow with about a two- or three-foot handle above the fork, and when we had a muskrat we would push him into deep water until he was drowned, which took about six minutes for a muskrat and about ten minutes for a mink.

Well, there was nothing in Lester's mink set under the bridge. Then we each had three or four sets for rats between the bridge and the big clump of willows, where Lester made his second mink set, and there was a muskrat in every one of them! The excitement of hearing the rattle of the chain and then, all shaky, trying to drown the rat! We knew there was something in Lester's mink set long before we got to it, and it was a big, black mink, growling and spitting like a cat, and really making that trap chain jingle!

You can imagine my feelings when I realized that this mink could have been mine! If only I had listened to the wisdom of my dad. Lester and I got to trap Flat Creek for about sixty days before the creek finally froze over about December 15th, but we had over 400 muskrats and seven mink. But the big beauty that Lester caught that first morning was the biggest and best one we got, and he got seven dollars for that beautiful pelt!

We made over fifty dollars apiece on our first trapping venture and that's pretty good for six and ten-year-old kids! I turned six just before we started trapping. Lester caught two mink under the bridge in that set. He got seventeen dollars for his three mink and I got twenty dollars for my four! Those days were among the happiest days of my life that I spent hunting, fishing and trapping with my father.

That winter of 1906-1907 Steve Leek and Abe Ward were showing their pictures back east and while they were in New York City, the police arrested Abe and threw him in jail! This was during the time that the outlaw gangs and horse thieves were being chased out of Jackson Hole. This gang was all done in Jackson Hole, but two or three of these leaders had never yet been caught. It was believed that they had skipped to South America, but there were Wanted Posters with the outlaws' pictures in post offices all over the United States. And someone had mistakenly recognized Abe Ward as being the leader of the horse thieves! Which, of course, he was not. But he so resembled this wanted outlaw that he was picked up and held until Steve and Nick could clear him!

Abe was held in the pokey for nearly a month before Nick could gather enough Church records and photographs of Abe to clear him and prove his innocence! There was quite a stir of excitement regarding this incident in Jackson Hole. Although Abe was cleared, it caused a lot of concern in the family before it was over.

Leek continued with his efforts regarding the starving elk of Jackson Hole until the winter of 1909-10. He finally got delegation from both the state of Wyoming and the federal government that led to the saving of the elk and the establishment of the Federal Elk Reserve as it is known today in Jackson Hole.

Steve Leek finally gained recognition nationally, becoming known as the "Daddy of the Elk!" There were several other dedicated Jackson Hole conservationists who also earned recognition for this cause: men like Dan Nowlin, one of Wyoming's first state game wardens; Albert Nelson and Oalus Murie and last, but not least, Elijah Nicholas Wilson! But for his part in settling this beautiful valley, the elk may have faired very much worse!

The summer of 1906 was spent mostly at our cabin by Fish Creek and just growing up. Nick was a great joy to me, and to every kid in the country who loved to listen to his exciting "Injun stories!" I remember his playing so much on his old violin and singing me the sad, old Irish and western songs he knew. I was a very tender-hearted child, and oh, how I would cry when he played on the old fiddle and sang his homely songs, like, "I am getting old and feeble and I cannot work no more! I have laid the rusty bladed hoe away. The hinges are getting rusty and the doors are tumblin' down, an' the roof lets in the sunshine and rain! And there is no one left to love me but that little boy of mine! In the little old log cabin in the lane!" And, "Poor babes in the woods, poor babes in the woods! They wandered away one bright summer's day and were lost in the woods, so I've heard people say! And when it was night, so sad was their plight! The moon did not shine and the stars gave no light! These poor little babes! They sobbed and they sighed, and they bitterly cried until at last they lay down and died! And when it was morning the Robin so red, brought strawberry leaves and over them spread! And all the day long, they sang them this song! Oh, who'll go find the poor babes in the wood!"

And an old Irish song about his poor old mother and how he cherished the "Three leaves of shamrock! The Irishman's Shamrock! The three leaves of Shamrock from my dear old mother's grave!"

Those were happy times! And in the early morning I would be awakened by Nick playing the old fiddle and singing! By nature my father was a jolly little Scotch-Irishman! And it was a long time before I caught on that he could change his voice and imitate a child or a woman. Many times I have been awakened by his voice out in the kitchen very loudly saying, "Good mornin' young buck! What brings you out so early?" Then a kid's voice that I couldn't catch at all, but "Charley" would be mentioned several times. Then my dad's voice, "Oh! Charley is still in bed! You might as well leave without him! I don't think he is getting up today!"

Boy! Would that bring me out in a jiffy, pulling on my faded old overalls. I would rush into the kitchen, yelling, "Who was that, Daddy? What did he want? Huh? Where did he go?" For by then I was looking outside, but never could see any kid! My dad would calm me down, saying, "Aw, it was some kid wanting you to go fishin', but I didn't think you wanted to go very bad anyway!"

I would do a lot of protesting, and then it would wind up with me and my dad rolling up some hot cakes, rolled in Karo syrup, and going out to the Snake River a fishin'! My dad made hot cakes the size of a big frying pan, and that's what I took to school in a five-pound lard bucket for my lunch. I licked many a kid for poking fun at my cold hot-cake!

The next year, 1908, when I was seven years old, my dad really broke me of smoking! In fact, he did it so well that I have never smoked to this day. Now, when I see my old friends dying from emphysema, I thank God for my dear old dad. My dad never smoked a cigarette or took a drink of whiskey in his life. But he did smoke a pipe. In fact, he kept two old pipes on the window sill in our kitchen which he took turns smoking, while sitting in his old rocking chair by the window and the woodbox.

That winter of 1907-08 Nick spent a lot of time over at Billy Raum's Saloon across the bridge from our cabin. Billy had come with his family from Sand Point, Idaho, where he ran a saloon. Billy was a little man with a very black mustache and a very big woman, three boys and a girl. The boy's name was Elmer, and he was about three or four years old that winter. The three girls were Eva, about my age; Winnie, five; and Ada, four. I never did know which one of those girls I loved the most! But that's another story, which I hope to get told in this story of Nick Wilson. Billy Raum also had a grocery store in connection with the saloon, which Mrs. Raum ran. Their business was known as "Raum and Raum," which I have seen painted in yellow paint all the way along the old highway from Jackson Hole to Rawlins, Wyoming, a distance of nearly three hundred miles, on big rocks and boulders.

Billy had bought this saloon from our original saloon keeper, named Spencer, who was a big, red-headed, red-faced, burley Irishman. Billy finally sold out to a man named Nick McCoy. All three of these saloon keepers were tough characters, as only the breed of saloon keepers who ran these joints in the early days had to be!

It was very lonely for Nick after he lost my mother, and Billy gave him a job tending bar for him while Billy ran the gambling tables. It was said that all three of these saloon keepers had killed men in riots or in self-defense in their own establishments. My dad was always with me during the day. The saloon was a night-time job and brought in the only income my dad had to live on after quitting the forest job. Abe Ward was supposed to be buying Nick's ranch, but he seldom, if ever, paid Nick anything. This story I hope to tell later.

Anyway, whenever my dad was away and I got a chance, I got to smoking one of these old pipes. One day I came into the house and Nick was sitting there smoking his old pipe. When he heard me come in, he said, "Hey Charley! I see that you have taken up smoking!" I was really taken aback and expected a good whaling! But before I could say anything, he must have seen the fright on my face. He continued, "Now don't be afraid. I am not going to do anything to you about it except I think we better have a good talk." Then he added, "Pull up a chair over here by me." Which I did. He puffed away for quite awhile, then finally said, "For quite awhile I been wishing I had someone to sit here a smokin' along with me. It gets pretty lonesome sometimes when you are off with kids playing an' me just a sittin' an' a smokin' an' a thinkin'!" I didn't say anything, so he continued, "I can't say I am overly tickled about you starting to smoke so early, but I have never whipped or even scolded one of my kids for doing anything I do, or say," he added as an after thought.

"I know it's my fault that you have started smoking. I won't punish you for that, or for any language you hear me use, but there is two things I will not tolerate, and one is never let me catch you smoking cigarettes! They are not only instruments of the Devil, but they are poison and will kill you! The other thing is, I never took a drink of whiskey in my life! I know I sell it for Billy, but it's all the income we have to live on and I try my best to tell those that I serve to quit the habit, because, like cigarettes, it will kill you, too! And it is one of the dirtiest and lowest habits you can get into. I've seen too many families starve because the father drinks up every cent he can get."

And that made me remember another pitiful song my father sang to me. It was about a little boy named Benny, who is dying for lack of food and medicine. His father is away gambling and drinking at a saloon. Benny's little sister goes and begs her father to come home, because poor Benny is dying. But the father won't go home. Then it ends, "Oh father, oh father! You need not come home with me now. The clock in the tower strikes three! And poor Benny is dead!"

Well! You can imagine I was getting pretty nervous and shook up, and hoped my torture would end. But it didn't! It was just beginning! Nick reached over and got the other old pipe from the window sill and filled and tamped it down with tobacco from his old "Union Leader" sack of tobacco! He handed it to me, and said, "Come on, light up and let us enjoy a good, old-fashioned smoke and visit!" I tried to protest, but my dad insisted! And he lit the old pipe and made a few puffs and handed it to me! We sat there puffing away in silence until my pipe went dry! I was beginning to feel a little green around the gills and started to lay the pipe down, but my father took it and filled her up again!

He let me light it myself this time, but I only got about half a bowl smoked when I really felt I had enough, but my dad wouldn't hear it. "Come on, now. We are just beginning to get chummy," he urged! Well, I finished that pipe-full and he filled her up for the third time! The floor was starting to spin and it felt like I was falling off the world! I dropped the old pipe and fell down and grabbed a table leg and held on for dear life! I started puking and bawling and spent about three days in bed! I was cured of smoking for life!

Stephen Leek, Hudson Bay trapper and son-in-law of Nick Wilson, age 85, shortly before his death in March, 1943, at Jackson Hole, Wyoming.

Stephen N. Leek

Stephen N. Leek first entered Jackson Hole in 1889, the same year that Nick Wilson came there. Nick came in the spring and by mid-summer he had guided many of his family and friends into Jackson Hole to begin the valley's first permanent settlers of Whitemen.

Leek entered Jackson Hole from the north end in the fall of 1889, not knowing that permanent homesteaders were already in the south or lower end of Jackson Hole, forty miles away, putting up hay from the swamps on Flat Creek and taking "squatter-right homesteads" in the lower part of Jackson Hole.

Leek, with a partner whom he called "Uncle Ed," were trappers for the Hudson Bay Fur Company, an English Trading Firm. They were paying $25.00 per hide for each bear skin. Leek was a native of Nebraska and was about 34 years old when he teamed up with "Uncle Ed" and they hired out to the Hudson Bay Company to supply needed bear skins. Steve Leek had heard of the great number of bears that ranged from the Yellowstone Park south through the Continental Divide and Teton ranges.

They entered Jackson Hole via Miles City up the Yellowstone River to Yellowstone Lake and on down to the great meadows at the head of Jackson Lake where they decided to winter. What they had heard regarding bear in that area was true and by Christmas of 1889 they had over one hundred dried bear skins. They had eighteen head of pack horses and two saddle horses. By Christmas these horses were strong and fat from eating the lush protein laden grass that grew as high as a horses back. What they didn't know was how deep the snow fell in this area.

They had snug winter quarters for themselves and by early February the snow was ten feet on the hay-meadows. Steve and Uncle Ed began to worry about the horses, but as the snow deepened the horses pawed for feed and by April, Steve said they had pawed tunnels under the ten feet of snow that was like a labyrinth, and they could walk almost upright through these tunnels to find and check up on the horses all winter long, and they came through the winter in great shape.

In the spring of 1890 Steve packed the bear skins out to Livingston, Montana, from where they were shipped to the Hudson Bay Company station at Miles City. Steve and Uncle Ed returned to the winter-quarters on Jackson Lake for their trapping gear and things they left and proceeded on down Snake River to Jackson Hole. Steve was amazed at the activity he found in lower Jackson Hole and he liked the friendly energetic Mormon people, and he got ahold of 350 acres of the best land in Jackson Hole, and his half-brother, Hamilton Wort, got 350 acres adjoining Steve, which Steve finally bought from Ham, and the first fine whip-saw buildings, a two-story house and huge hay and horse barn, still stand, three miles south of the town of Jackson in Jackson Hole.

Leek developed his fine location into a horse and cattle ranch and went into the first Dude business. Among his guests and hunters was George Eastman of the great Eastman Kodak Company. Eastman gave Leek a fine camera, and he became such an avid environmentalist and wildlife and flora enthusiast that he soon obtained additional photographic equipment, like stereo and panoramic cameras, and finally, from France, a Pathé Moving Picture camera, the first in the Jackson Hole region. Leek's pictures and writings drew attention from the great New York Museum of Natural History, which drew such public attention that resulted in the world famous National Elk Feeding Program in Jackson Hole, and Steve Leek became known as the "Daddy of the Elk"!

Charles Alma Wilson, Author

Billy Raum's Saloon and Store at Wilson, Wyoming, about 1914. Billy is the one on the extreme right with white shirt and his long-tailed black coat. Sure signs of a real gun-fighter! Note Billy's big black mustache!

From left to right: Edna Jane Ward, Nick Wilson's second child; Irene Ward, one of Edna's twins; and Abe Ward, about 1915. Harry Nethercott and wife Chloe ran this hotel from 1910-12. Harry painted the "Hotel" sign on the building. The old log building to the right was built by Nick Wilson about 1896-97, and was the first General Store and Hardware Store in Jackson Hole.

CHAPTER 14 — A Close Call and Nick Loses His Bishopric

The year 1908 was kind of a sad year for Nick. And this was the year that he lost his bishopric in the Latter-Day Saints Church (Mormon) as I have already mentioned in a previous chapter.

Fish Creek had unusually high water in 1908. Nick and I had been eating at least one meal a day at the hotel across the street that the Wards ran, but it belonged to my dad.

One day there were quite a few tourists on the stage and a family with one little girl about my age was staying at the hotel, waiting for another family to arrive from Salt Lake City, Utah, and the two families were going to make a trip through Yellowstone Park.

In those days, when a meal was ready, they didn't turn in and feed the kids first, like they do nowadays. Now they always get the kids fed first, before the adults start to eat. In those days, the elders always ate first, and then the kids got what was left. I can remember that when a meal was served at Wards Hotel, we kids had to wait until all the big people finished, and they often took an hour or more just visiting and smoking and laughing, until us kids were nearly dead from hunger. Even then when we got our turn, most of the food was gone and what was left was cold, and often not much was left, so we had to suffice on some bread and milk.

I was used to waiting to get to eat, and occupied myself in reading or something else to pass the time away. This day I got my dad's new fly rod and was out about halfway on the bridge that spanned Fish Creek. The water was very high and flapping against the stringers that held up the bridge. This bridge was built on cribs filled with rock and the stringers were fastened down to each crib with heavy wire cables. In fact, I have seen Fish Creek so high that a foot of water ran over the bridge, and it never budged. The planking was nailed to the big log stringers with sixty penny spikes and it still stands there today.

I was out about the center of the bridge fishing, and had a royal coachman fly, and I kept getting a strike from a small trout that looked about eight inches long when he would rise at the fly. When a trout is not hungry, it will sometimes rise at a bait and

Nick Wilson's old cabin, looking west. Teton Pass in low background. Two windows and door on north side. Window in east end where Nick sat and smoked his old pipe. The willow bush just beyond the corner of the cabin hung out over the fishing hole on Fish Creek, mentioned in the death of Charlotte Sarah and the near drowning of Charley.

slap it with its tail. I have hooked lots of fish in the tail, and even a small trout can really give quite a battle!

I was concentrating on this little trout and hoped I might catch him by the tail. This little girl was about my age, and I really wanted to impress her with what a mighty angler I really was. There was no railing on this bridge, and in my concentration, I forgot to watch my feet. Before I realized it, I was right on the edge and then fell in the fast current face down. The big willows that hung out into the creek at the end of our house — that I told about when my sister was drowned there, only three years before — still hung out and were flopping up and down in the swift water.

From where I fell in I just happened to be over just right for the current to carry me under these willows, about seventy feet below the bridge. When I fell in I dropped the fly rod and went out of sight! The little girl saw me go out of sight. She ran for the hotel screaming at the top of her lungs, which brought out everyone in the hotel before she was half way, which was only about two hundred feet. Her father grabbed her. She was so hysterical she could hardly talk, but finally yelled, "Uncle Nick! Uncle Nick! Your little boy fell in the creek!" And she pointed out to the center of the stream.

Well, while this was going on I came right up among these willows, and I grabbed onto one and held on for dear life! My weight swung me under the bank among these thick willows and I very soon scrambled out. I could see the little girl running toward the hotel screaming! I was really scared, and the only thing I could think of was getting away someplace to hide, as I had been warned about getting my clothes all wet. Now, besides that, I had lost daddy's new fly rod that cost him one dollar and fifty cents at Dell Judd's store over across the creek by Raum's Saloon. It never occurred to me that everybody would think I was drowned, and turn out hunting for me! Before any of the people came out of the hotel, I was across our yard back of the livery stable and was hiding in the heavy thick willows over on one of our ranch's south forties — before they got to that bridge.

I decided to hide and dry out my clothes, then go home and face the music over losing the fly rod. With the roar of the creek, and me away out in the willows, I didn't even hear them hollering and running down the creek. It took a couple of hours for my clothing to dry out hanging on willows. Then I slipped back through the brush until I could see our cabin and the hotel. I couldn't see a person in sight, so I decided to go to our house. The window in the east end of the house was high enough that I had to reach up and get ahold of the sill, and pull myself up to look inside. Just as my eyes were even with the bottom window pane I looked my father straight in the eyes! He saw me, and I never saw such a terrible expression on his face before! He was deathly pale, and his blue eyes seemed to look right through me! I dropped back to the ground and began to run, but Nick rapped the window and shouted for me to stop. I did, and he came out to me and took me in his arms. I had never heard him sob before, but he did then, and he held me so tight it hurt. Then he let me loose, held me at arm's length and said, "Where have you been? Everybody in town is down the creek looking for you! The little girl saw you fall in the creek?" "Yes," I said, "I did fall in, but I went under the big willows and pulled myself out and ran." "Why did you run? Don't you know that we all thought you were drowned? My God! It's only three years since we lost Sally!"

Someone came from the hotel and saw me, and all kinds of excitement broke out. I gathered that the blow was almost too much for my father to stand, and some of them helped him over to our house; then, after he said he was alright, they all ran down the stream looking for me. Several people stayed at the long, shallow riffle where the Goodrick boys got my little sister out. Some fixed up a net at Schofield's bridge, and more went on down to where Fish Creek emptied into the Snake River.

Everybody was real good to me for awhile, and I had to answer a lot of questions. It was decided that it was just by the grace of God I escaped being drowned, and I always loved that big willow bush that hung out over our old fishing hole!

It seemed that everything was happening all at once, for just a few days later these people, whose name was Allen, who were coming from Salt Lake, arrived. The people waiting for them with the little girl, who was with me when I fell into the creek, whose name was Stuart, were all back together again. The Allens had brought two white-top Studebaker wagons with four horses on each wagon. Both were three-seaters like my dad's Studebaker, and one was laden with bedding, tents and food supplies. The other was for the two families to ride in. There were three Stuarts, and the Allens had three children with them, and a cook and two drivers, which made eleven of them. Two of the seats were taken out of the supply wagon, so one driver and the cook could ride in it, and the five Allens and three Stuarts and a driver in the other wagon.

The Stuarts had already taken quite a fancy to Nick Wilson and his stories, and were also concerned about his ordeal from nearly losing me. So they decided to stay a few days, but they no more than had their tents all set up and a cook shack and beds on army cots, than we had another awful accident.

One of the Allen kids, who was only about four years old, ran in among the horses that were tied in a clump at a hitching post. Mrs. Allen ran in among the horses to get the little fellow. Her screaming at the child, and her long dresses scared the horses, and they began to rear and shrill and pull back on their halters, knocking Mrs. Allen down and trampling her very badly. The child wasn't hurt somehow, but Mrs. Allen was really banged up, with broken ribs and internal injuries. They soon had her in bed in our cabin and got Dr. Palmer, who, luckily, was sober, and my dad to help. They fixed her up pretty good, but Dr. Palmer said it would be a month or even more, before she could travel. Mr. Allen wanted to take her immediately to Salt Lake, but Dr. Palmer said she couldn't stand it, and the trip would kill her. Dr. Palmer was very good at this kind of problem, which was different from that of my mother.

After about ten days they decided to move Mrs. Allen up to my Aunt Ida Nethercott's home, about half a mile, where she could get better care, and so the Stuarts and the Allens settled down to having as good a vacation as they could. They could never have been in a better place than Jackson Hole. Before they left to go back to Salt Lake, in time to get their kids in school in September, everyone got real acquainted with these two lovely families, who were all Mormons. So they were there when the delegation from the Mormon Church in Salt Lake came in early August to check upon the churches in Jackson Hole. The one at Wilson, was under Nick Wilson, who was bishop; and the other was at South Park, under Uncle Sylvester's son-in-law, Jim Robertson, who was bishop of that ward in 1908.

It so happened at the time this Mormon delegation came that the head church in Salt Lake City had decided to begin enforcing the revelation in Section 89 of the Mormon Doctrine and Covenants, given through Joseph Smith, the Prophet, at Kirkland, Ohio, February 27, 1833, known as the "Word of Wisdom," regarding the abstinence from wine, strong drinks, tobacco and hot drinks.

The day they arrived the Allens and Stuarts and a lot of the citizens of Wilson, who loved to hang around the camp where the cook became very popular, especially when it came to a fish fry, or a wild goose meal, where everyone was welcome.

We kids had more fun from games, and all kinds of new things that the Allen kids and the little Stuart girl taught us. They had all kinds of books and I think I got a bigger boost in my reading that summer than I got all through grade school.

The day the Mormon delegation arrived there were still lots of good things to eat at the camp, and they really ate hearty of the fried trout and chicken. Then they wanted to know where Bishop Nick Wilson was. He had just gone home before these people drove in. A dozen hands pointed to the little log cabin on the creek bank, and they were told that they would find him there. Their horses were being cared for at the livery stable and I went with these men to see my father. There were five of them, of which two were young missionaries who they planned to leave in the valley for a few months. I led the way and opened the door and they all followed me inside. Nick was sitting in his old rocking chair and was peacefully smoking one of his old pipes!

The leader of this party got right down to business by saying, "Why, Bishop! I never dreamed you used tobacco! Haven't you received the bulletin on the "Word of Wisdom" that the Prophet in Salt Lake had decided that a renewal of enforcement of Section 89 of Doctrine and Covenants was to be vigorously enforced this year, especially as regarding tobacco? Because too many of our young people are beginning the use of cigarettes?" Nick laid his pipe down, and answered, "Yes! I got that bulletin! and have discussed it with one of my elders and with the priesthood! We don't feel that it applies to us here in this ward, as there is no problem with our young Mormons smoking cigarettes!"

"But how about you?" said the Mormon delegate. "You are bishop here and we caught you red-handed smoking a pipe!" I could tell that my dad was beginning to lose his temper, which was a very seldom event in his life, but when he did get mad everybody stood up and paid attention, I can tell you that!

"I am an old man," said Nick very softly. "I have been a member of the Latter-Day Saints Church since I was born in Nauvoo, Illinois in 1842. My father and mother were among Joseph Smith's first converts! My Uncle James Wilson was bodyguard for the Prophet the night he was murdered at Carthradge jail! I have went through the persecution of polygamy for my church. I have lost everything now but my two little boys. I have smoked a pipe ever since I rode the Pony Express, and now it's about the only means of relaxation and peace that I have left. I never smoke my pipe in church, and I am not going to give it up now! This Revelation is nearly a hundred years old! The Church surely could find something more worthy of the "Word of Wisdom" than waste a year trying to enforce this old ordinance! Why! It's like trying to enforce the Revelation on polygamy again!" The Mormon delegation was kind of taken back, but this elder, or whoever he was, was very persistent, and told Nick flatly, he would either quit smoking or turn in his bishopric! "The books are there in the bookcase!" Nick said. "Take them and get out." The tone of Nick's voice was like ice! The Mormons lost no time in taking the records and leaving.

The Allens and Stuarts were very devout Mormons, but they really berated these men for what Mr. Allen said "was the shabbiest deal I think the Mormon Church ever pulled!"

Well, that ended Mormonism as far as I was concerned. My dad never mentioned it again, and I never went to church again, until after I was married in 1927, when I started going to a Methodist Church with my wife, and then to a Congregational Church. I could tell a good story about that snooty church, but I won't. Later I was saved through an Assembly of God Church, where I heard the gospel preached by a woman for the first time in my life. I couldn't stand a woman preacher after I read what the Bible said about them, and finally my wife and I raised our four sons in the Baptist Church, where they have all been born-again Christians. I am very proud of my four sons — Nick's grandsons — and their wonderful families.

Stephen, our eldest son, is manager of the Fish and Wildlife Service in Alaska, and lives at Anchorage. Philip, our second son, was a draftsman for over twenty-five years for Shell Oil Company, and is now a Baptist preacher. Our third son, Stark, is an electronic engineer and takes care of all the computer and electric equipment for the University of Wyoming branch at Casper, Wyoming. Paul, our youngest, was the only one to get a PhD in education, and teaches geography at the State University of Montana at Missoula.

While the Allens and Stuarts were staying at Wilson waiting for Mrs. Allen to recover so she could travel, they persuaded Nick to write these stories of his life on the wild frontier and that fall he began, as already stated, using an old French typewriter!

CHAPTER 15 — **Virgil Ward and the Drummer**

The rest of 1908 went off pretty smooth, except that fall I had a bad run-in with Virgil Ward and Nick had a fracas with a drummer.

Although Virgil was my half-nephew, he was four years older than I and he seemed to live only to torment me. Later in life, I realized that he was apeing his mother, Edna Jane Ward, because you can always tell by a child's actions how his parents are reacting to a situation. Edna Jane hated my mother with the kind of hate that only comes from the green-eyed monster called jealousy. I can't think of any other reason that could make Edna Jane and the other sisters react so violently to my mother, and Virgil was much worse than any of the other Ward children. Elijah, the eldest, was fourteen years older than I, and he never seemed to hold any animosity toward me. In fact, he was always good to me and he was my favorite nephew, and I had a lot of them!

Ercle was kind of a funny kid, twelve years my senior. He never harmed me like Virgil did, but was kind of aloof. But in later years he warmed up to me after World War I, in which his right arm was shot off at the shoulder. Ercle liked to hunt and fish and the Government fixed him up with a wonderful artificial arm. It was amazing how well he adapted to it. While he ignored me as a kid, he was very different after the war. Ercle and I had many happy hunting and fishing trips before he died with diabetes at about age fifty-five.

Vesta, the oldest girl, was six years older than I and in later life we have grown very close. I love her like a sister, although when we were young she used to wallop me good, once in awhile, but I think it was just more kid fracas than any influence her mother may have had on her. Then the twins, Ira and Irene, were three weeks younger than I, and I could lick both of them put together, and often did. However, we were more like brothers and sister, and grew up together.

But this Virgil was something else! He took great delight in doing and saying everything he could to hurt me. He was the one who started calling my mother "old hunchback," but my dad put the quietus on that mighty quick, and Virgil nor anyone else ever let me hear that again. When Virgil was twelve he was considered a man, and was allowed to eat with the big people at the first table in the hotel. That left Ira, Irene, George and me as kids, who had to wait until the rest had eaten.

The Wards took a newspaper that had about six pages of "funnies," as we called them. I remember Jiggs, Mutt and Jeff, the Katzenjammer Kids, Mike and Ike, and many other old comics. I even remember when they ran a page on Teddy Roosevelt and his big teeth and his adventures as a hunter and soldier. These comics usually came on Saturday, and Virgil was the first one to read them. He was so selfish that even when he had already read a page and laid it down, he refused to let one of us kids touch it until he had read them all.

This night Virgil was reading the comics when supper was announced. He lay the papers down and, in his surly, dominant voice, said, "Don't none of you kids touch them papers until I get back or I'll brain a few of you!" After he left for the dinner room, I got the papers and gave one to the other three kids and one for me. Ira, Irene and I were seven years old, and could read fairly well, but George was only three and we would try to read the funnies to him.

Well, Virgil gulped his supper down and was back for the comics and caught us all with them. He started cussing us, and especially me, and I can't print the language he used, but he called me a little S.O.B. and knocked me out of the chair and to the floor, by a crack to the side of my head that made my ears ring.

Before I was on my feet, he smashed his fist into my nose and blood squirted all over. I hit the floor again, but came up with my sharp, three-inch, one-bladed muskrat skinning knife, and I really went for Virgil! The first slash I split open his shirt and drew blood! He began to scream and bawl like only a bully can do when the tide turns on him! He grabbed for my knife and got one side of his hand split open!

By then everyone was pouring into the living room to see what the riot was. All the kids were crying and yelling. Abe was the first one in. He grabbed my wrist and slapped me a winding and I dropped the knife. Abe grabbed me by the shirt collar and was shaking me like a rat terrier before my dad got there. He shouted, "Stop!" And everything stopped! I was gasping for air. "What the hell's going on here?" my dad shouted, and everybody started yelling at once, but Nick said, "Quiet!" And they did! Then he let me tell what happened, and I did.

Abe was holding my knife, and he was sheriff at that time. He said, "I've been trying to tell you, Paw! That this kid is getting out of hand and something has to be done about him!"

Nick took my knife from Abe and in a quiet voice said, "Yes! Something has to be done, and that is that I want you all to let Charley alone! I've been watching lately and I have never seen him start a fight. I hear you all a bossing and ordering him around! Now, this is going to stop!" He brought Virgil a whack with his cane that knocked him down, and he said, "If I ever catch you laying a hand on Charley again, I will whale the daylights out of you! It would have served you right if he had cut your guts out!"

Then he turned to the rest and said, "I don't want to hear any more about this! Now feed these kids!" He looked at Edna Jane and Vesta, and we kids were soon at the table. My dad and I didn't eat over at Wards again for quite awhile. I think it was Thanksgiving Day when Vesta came over and said, "Grandpa! Ma wants you and Charley to come for dinner tomorrow! There will be turkey and cakes and everything!"

Boy! Did that sound good to me! It happened that the only guest at the hotel was a drummer who was selling clothing and other items, and he had been staying at the hotel while plying his trade amongst the townspeople. This drummer was a young smart-aleck, about twenty-two years old, and he had never heard any of my dad's stories until that afternoon after dinner, when Nick started telling his "Injun" stories and other tales of the wild frontier.

That evening a few of us were gathered in the hotel lobby or living room, and among us was this young drummer. Joe Linn, who later married Vesta Ward, had a barber chair in the hotel lobby and he was cutting someone's hair. My dad had a walking cane that the Allens had sent him from Salt Lake along in October. It was a heavy hardwood cane with a round, beautifully-colored onyx ball on the end that must have weighed half a pound.

Nick was sitting in one of the easy chairs and was telling one of his yarns, when this young drummer walked over to him and said, rather loudly, "Old man! Don't you ever get tired of telling these damn lying Indian stories?" Everyone was so shocked and quiet that you could have heard a pin drop! Then, like a flash, Nick walloped this drummer over the head with the heavy onyx ball on his walking cane! The drummer went down like an axed beef! He wiggled his hind-end a little and lay still! We all thought he was dead! Someone called Abe and cold water was brought. They turned the drummer over and a knot big as a baseball was raising on his punkin' haid! He soon opened his eyes and some of the men helped him to his room upstairs. Early the next morning he was gone. Later I heard Joe telling some customers about it and he ended, "Well! That drummer went down corrected! An' he come up a different man!"

One of the reasons that Abe was getting down on me so bad was that I had a BB gun or air rifle. One day I was washing our dishes and Ira came over to our house. The air rifle was laying on daddy's bed, which was in our kitchen. I told Ira to leave the gun alone and not monkey with it in the house. We had a looking- glass above the wash basin with glass about 8" x 12". Ira was pointing the gun at himself in this little mirror. He said, " I bet I could hit that guy right in the eye!" And he pulled the trigger and glass flew all over the house! I made a jump for Ira and he threw the gun on the bed and bolted for the door! I grabbed the air gun and it had a lever with 250 BB's. I throwed in a BB and got Ira in the seat of the pants before he cleared the door, and got three or four more into him before he got out of range across the street, a headin' for home and bawling bloody murder!

My dad was somewhere out back while all this was going on and he showed up about the same time that Abe and Edna Jane arrived, and it looked like I had really started a camp fight!

Nick made Edna Jane go get Ira and had him show his naked posterior. There were three or four big welts on his butt, but the skin wasn't broken.

The upshot of this fracas was my air gun was taken away from me and I never saw it again. It really ended a lot of fun, because I had got to hiding in the livery stable and some of those smart-aleck, young, would-be cowboys were always riding their prancing steeds over to Wards Hotel where there were always several young gals, like Vesta. These young dudes with their fancy shirts and boots and spurs would ride up after spurring their horses up enough to make them prance. I would be hid in the barn, and with my BB gun, I would shoot their horse in the butt! The horse would come uncorked and more than one young drug-store cowboy wound up grabbing dust in front of their lady loves!

It got so none of them could hardly get their horses up to Ward's hitching post! They never did get onto what was causing them to be bucked off, before I was grounded from my gun! It was probably a good thing, though, because if they had known I was smoking up their broncos, they would have killed me!

Left to right: George Goodrick, son-in-law of Nick Wilson; Nick Wilson, the "White Indian;" Doctor McCaslin, Judge White's physician; and Judge White of Cleveland, Ohio. Judge White was one of Steve Leek's favorite "dudes." He died on a trip to the head of the Yellowstone River of a heart attack when near 90 years of age. Leek packed the body out on a pack horse nearly 60 miles to Moran. Dr. McCaslin accompanied Judge White on this trip. "It was the only way to go, for Judge White," said Dr. McCaslin. Picture was taken at the foot of Mt. Moran on Leigh's Lake.

Also, I draw your attention to the two boats. Steve Leek took this picture about 1910. Steve rowed the one boat with Doctor McCaslin and Judge White, while they trolled for trout, and George Goodrick and Nick Wilson used the other boat. Notice the cheap bamboo fishing rod that Nick is holding, with the cheap heavy cotton line with the bend in the middle joint from fighting heavy trout, in contrast to the two straight expensive fly rods held by Doctor McCaslin and Judge White. And Nick caught more fish than any of them.

Charles Alma Wilson, Author.

CHAPTER 16 — **The Telephone**

By 1900, the turn of the century, it was evident that the hearty Jackson Hole pioneer settlers were going to make a go of it! Already many had proved up on their 160-acre claims and were beginning to take the 320-acre desert claims, which was semi-arid land, where only part of it could be irrigated. Lastly the U.S. Government approved 640-acre homesteads, which were considered usable for pasture land or dry farming. Many of the settlers had already proved they could make a good living on this rich black soil, and crops were reported of ninety bushel of oats to the acre, hand sown! Cabbages, eighty pounds or more; potatoes and all kinds of vegetables were grown. My brother-in-law, Steve Leek, planted two acres of small fruit-berry bushes of all kinds of berries, and it produced so much fruit during the summer and fall that all the families in the valley were invited to come and pick these berries. Also the valley teemed with wild berries, such as huckleberries, wild currants, both yellow and white, large goose berries, sarvis berries, chokecherries, and other wild berries like thimble berries that resembled raspberries in taste and looks, and many others. So the housewives always had ample jams, jellies and preserves in their cellars all the year around.

By the time I was born in Jackson Hole in 1901, the settlers were beginning to feel the necessity of telephones, and among the very earliest settlers were Fred Lovejoy and his wife, Maud. Fred had been a telegraph operator, but his love of hunting and adventure brought him to Jackson Hole, where he and his wife, Maud, filed a homestead upon the Grovant River near Kelly. Fred decided to form the "Jackson Hole Telephone and Telegraph Company," and soon had many stock holders, like Charley Wort, Steve Leek, John Wilson, Nephi Moulton, Mose Giltner and a host of others, and the building of the telephone line began in earnest. Fred left Maud to operate the ranch, while he built the first telephone and telegraph office in Jackson Hole at the town of Jackson.

I was about six years old when the line was being built through Wilson and Lovejoy had a lot of men working for him, as he had been elected as Manager and Operator for the Telephone Company.

While working on the line from Victor, Idaho, over Teton Pass, and then to Jackson Central, from which spread a web of lines to individual homes scattered all over Jackson Hole. Fred had crews of five or six men working all along the line, and those on the west side of the pass ate and lodged at the Burcher Road House, which was located two or three miles west of Teton Pass. The men working east of the Pass to Snake River boarded at the Wilson Hotel, which was owned by Nick Wilson and run by his son-in-law, Abe Ward and family. It was Nick's job to keep the hotel supplied with fresh trout and wild chickens. There was no limit on fish, chickens or ducks and geese in those days, but by 1910 this practice of supplying game to hotels, etc., was stopped. It was the commercial exploitation of the buffalo that almost brought that noble animal to the point of extinction.

One day in the fall after the Snake River was very low, Nick took his spring wagon with a gentle old team of horses that even I, a little six-year-old, could drive, and we drove out the mile-long lane from Wilson to the Snake River, which divided the ranches of Nick and his son-in-law, George Goodrick. Several men were setting telephone poles and stretching wire to insulators on the poles.

At the end of the line, Abe Ward and Burt Hobson were digging holes, which were four or five feet deep. They each had a saddle horse on a picket rope, grazing, while Abe and Burt were working. They were almost to the end of the lane, and then the line was to run north along the Snake River bank to a point where my Uncle Alfred Nethercott ran a ferry boat across the river. Here, log cribs filled with rock, with heavy tripods, were the anchors for the telephone wire that had to span the three or four-hundred-yard channel of the river and were already built. As my dad and I passed, Abe and Burt waved at us and Burt yelled, "Hey! Don't you guys catch them all! I want to go fishing next Sunday!" Burt Hobson was a great character; he had a ranch adjoining Fred and Maud Lovejoy's upon the Grovant River. Burt played the big drums in the Jackson Hole Band, and that band was one of the valley's pride and joy hobbies! Everybody loved that band of about twelve or fifteen players, and it was used on every occasion from rodeos to funerals.

Nick and I had to turn south at the end of the lane to where we could get the wagon down into the riverbed as the river in high water had cut a bank eight to twelve feet high from Uncle Al's ferry for a half mile or more down to just a few yards below the Wilson lane.

After we got down into the river bottom, Nick decided to fish upstream to the ferry, where we could get the wagon back up onto the riverbank. There were dozens of big blue holes for us to fish, and in those days you could fish all day and never see another fisherman. That's a far cry from today! When we were about a quarter mile above where Abe and Burt were working, there was a big hole about three hundred feet long that flowed right next to this ten-foot bank, and Nick stopped the team at the upper end of this fishing hole. We never bothered to tie the team, as the rocks hurt their feet and they were lazy and didn't like to pull the wagon, and there wasn't anything to tie them to anyway. The river bank was so high we couldn't see Abe and Burt, but they knew where we were because the wagon made so much noise on the cobblestones you could hear us for a mile. When the river was rolling high, the madly rushing, muddy water filled with trees and driftwood was high as that ten-foot cut bank! This particular hole was probably ten or twelve feet deep here in low water, and so during high water this river was twenty or more feet deep with a very swift current, as the Snake drops pretty fast all the way from Jackson Lake to where it enters the plains of Idaho down between Swan Valley and Idaho Falls.

Nick set up his fly rod that consisted of three joints and put on is favorite fly, which was a coachman, and began catching those beautiful cutthroat trout with yellow bellies and red stripes under their gills. They were fat and beautiful, and oh, how Nick loved to catch them! The first trout he ever caught was on the Snake River while living with the Shoshone Indians. He used a bait hook with grasshoppers, and a line made from horse tail hair! As Nick caught and kept the ones he wanted to keep, the ones that weighed about two to six pounds, I was kept busy packing these beautiful fish over and putting them up in the wagon box. We kept water-soaked gunny sacks over and under the fish to keep them fresh, and my job was wetting the sacks in the river and throwing them up in the wagon, then climbing in and placing the trout side-by-side on the wet sacks and covering them with other wet sacks.

Nick was down along this big blue hole about one hundred and fifty feet, and I was in the wagon, which had only the one front seat in it. Nick had set the big iron handbrake and wrapped the lines around it. All the time this was going on, the old team just stood there. Although the fly season was over, there were always a few pesky gnats flying around, and the horses would throw their heads up and down to keep these gnats off their ears and noses. This continual flopping up and down of the horses' heads had gradually loosened the brake, and it finally worked out past the brake notch that held the brake in place. It flew ahead, loosening the lines and at the same time making a sharp, metallic ring, as steel hit steel.

The old horses jumped and started to run, and went straight into the upper end of this big hole, and were immediately in swimming water! They both went under before the wagon submerged, then they came up and started swimming toward the cut bank across the big hole, which was about fifty or sixty feet across.

When the team jumped from this unexpected noise, I was thrown down in the box. Before the wagon entered the water, I got to the wagon seat and stood up and grabbed the back of the seat! Then the wagon went under, the hind wheels sank, and the box filled with water. I saw all those beautiful trout float over the side of the box and they were gone! As the team swam, the wagon bobbed up and down; the hind wheels must have gone to the bottom, and then it would rise. Each time it went down I would go under with just my head above water, as the swimming team kept the front end high enough that I didn't go completely under. Then the team reached the cut bank and it rose many feet straight up! They got their front feet up on the side of the bank and scrambled with all their might, but could go no further, but would drop back into the deep water. Each time this happened, my head would go down under, but I held on to that seat for dear life, squalling to the top of my lungs!

My dad was yelling as loud as he could for me to hold onto the seat! In the meantime, he was trying to get his rubber boots and pants off, and was going to try to swim out and get me! Nick was getting about sixty-five years old and was rheumatic and overweight. He could have never made it, but thank God, he didn't have to, because Abe and Burt heard all the crying and yelling and knew something was awful wrong. They both arrived just in the nick of time on their saddle horses, right over me and the team, and they could see the fix we were in. Nick was just entering the big hole when the two men arrived and Abe was yelling for Nick to get back — not to try it!

Burt didn't hesitate a second, but jumped from his horse and then dove straight into the hole! Burt came up in back of the wagon — I saw him just as I went under again. I was getting awful tired, holding onto the seat, and was gulping water everytime I went under. When I came up, Burt grabbed me and yelled, "Let go!" I loosed my grip on the seat, and Burt began to swim with me over to where my dad stood in his long underwear.

In the meantime, Abe dropped down onto the horses and gathered up the lines and was in the seat pulling the frantic and tiring team off the bank. He soon had them swimming back across the hole, and they pulled the wagon out just below Nick and Burt and me.

The fish were all gone, and I felt terrible about that, but Nick had heard the brake when it slipped out and he knew that was what scared the horses and made them run, so it wasn't my fault after all!

This is just one of the many escapades I had while living with my dad; it was just incidental to the job of growing up!

I think the first close call I had while living with my father, Nick Wilson, was the winter after Nick and I returned from Evanston, Wyoming, where we went to see my mother. Things had finally settled down for Nick and me after that hectic summer of 1906. That was also the year of the great earthquake in California, where, I was told later, that my Grandpa and Grandma Nethercott were killed in San Francisco.

Nick and I had been living alone in our little old log cabin on the bank of Fish Creek ever since he got back home in the fall of 1905 after taking my beautiful mother to the insane asylum in Evanston. That winter of 1905-06 must have been very lonely and trying for Nick Wilson. Ever since he was married to Matilda Patten in Salt Lake City, when he was about twenty-three years old, he had been surrounded by family, children, friends and lots of exciting work. Now he was around 65 years of age and had lost his wives and most of his children and was now alone with just one little boy four years old!

It had gotten so that Nick spent a lot of his time over at Spencer's Saloon. It seems to me now, as I write these memories, that a lot of my early life was influenced by the saloon in our little town of Wilson, Wyoming. Although Nick never drank liquor or gambled, he got a lot of companionship at the saloon, where he liked to play a card game called sluff or solo. It was an old western card game played by three players, and Nick got to going over to Spencer's Saloon at night after he got me fed and to sleep in bed. He would turn the old coal-oil lamp down low and bank the old ZCMI cooking stove, or range, as they were called then, with only the slow, tick-tock-tick-tock of our old grandfather clock that sat on a shelf on the wall between the stove and Nick's old feather bed. I was left alone to sleep until Nick returned home, usually by 1:00 a.m.

But sometimes I awakened to find him gone, and I remember lying there in bed, listening to the old clock. The dim light cast weird shadows that looked like little men with long whiskers and long, flowing beards, and they would look at me and talk, and gesticulate, until finally, in fright, I would cover my head and crawl down deep into the old feather mattress and go to sleep! Even to this day when I think of these little people, I really believe I saw them and they were alive!

One night in early winter there was a bad snow storm and the wind was roaring outside. We could hardly see the bridge and creek only sixty feet away, through the blowing and drifting snow. I had a hunch that my dad was going to go over to Spencer's Saloon to play cards with old man Grant and Judge Spaulding. I begged my dad not to go! He assured me that everything was all right by lying on the bed with me after our supper was over and it was dark outside. We could hear the roar of the wind and hear the drifting snow against the door and windows. As we lay there, I wondered why Nick didn't take off his clothes and come to bed, but lay there with his pants on. He wore suspenders and I took a mighty grip on them with both hands, determined that he would not get away from me tonight!

It must have been about midnight when I awakened to the shudder of the old house in the howling wind. I found myself alone, and holding my dad's suspenders still clasped hard in my hands! He had unfastened his suspenders and left me quietly sleeping and warm in his old feather bed! The lamp was turned very low. I peeked out at the stove and cupboards and table where the little people usually sat and watched me, but they were gone. There was no sound but the howling blizzard and the tick-tock of the old clock!

Just in front of our house and the old hotel, the road forked. One fork went right past the livery stable and down to Goodricks, where it turned left to the east and out the old lane. The other branch of the road turned left and ran up across the hay meadow and entered thick willows, a quarter mile below my Uncle Alfred Nethercott's house.

I slept in a suit of underwear with a flap that buttoned up behind and had solid feet to keep my feet warm, both in bed and while I was running around the house on the cold floor. In what followed, the fact that this heavy underwear was fleece-lined and had heavy, fleece-lined feet or shoes in them was all that saved me from losing my feet.

I usually could see the light in the saloon from our front window, but the blizzard of flying snow obscured any light. I got out the door and began crying, "Daddy! Daddy!" and started for where I thought the saloon was, but instead of facing into the storm and crossing the bridge, I went with the wind out the snow road to the left, up through the field toward Nethercott's and Cheney's.

God only knows how I stayed on this snow road, but the wind blew me right up the road to where it entered the willows, which was about a quarter mile from our house! When the road entered the willows it turned sharp to the north, but the wind blew me on about thirty feet, and I fell into a big willow bush. I couldn't climb out as I sank down into the willows, but I was crying to the top of my lungs!

The days of miracles are never over! It happened that very night that my cousin, Edith Cheney, whom I have mentioned earlier in this story, was about to have a baby and was in labor and great pain. Her husband, Sylvester Cheney, had taken my Aunt Ida Nethercott up to help Edith, who was Aunt Ida's daughter, but she couldn't handle the problem and sent Sylvester to get help in Wilson, where she knew she could get either Doc Palmer or my dad. So it happened that Sylvester came along just in the nick of time and heard a child crying near the road! He couldn't believe his ears, but the actions of his team told him that something was really crying in that willow bush. He stopped the team and wallowed through the snow over to the bushes and pulled me out! Sylvester had no idea whose child he had found, but wrapped my freezing body in a quilt in the sled and galloped his team into town. The only light was Spencer's Saloon and Sylvester carried me in. The saloon was full of tobacco smoke and, what seemed to me, hordes of men!

Everybody was excited and hollering and cussing and crowding around Sylvester where he laid me on the bar, and then I was recognized and my dad really took over. Sylvester told them where and under what circumstances he had found me. Doc Palmer happened to be in the saloon — and sober — and two or three men went with Doc and Sylvester. The rest started in on me. They pulled off my frozen underwear and began rubbing me with whiskey and warm towels.

I guess I was about a goner. Just a few minutes more . . . if Sylvester hadn't come along when he did, it would have been all over for me. I had some badly frosted toes, hands, ears and cheeks, but by spring they were all healed up. The nice thing about it all for me was that a little bed was fixed for me under the bar at the saloon and whenever my dad decided to go card-playing, I always went along, too, and slept, many a night, under Spencer's Saloon bar with the mingled smell of whiskey and tobacco smoke in my nose.

Nick Wilson and State Game Warden, Dan Nowlin. Steve Leek's house and barn shown in background. Currant and raspberry bushes back of potato patch. About 1910.

Nick Wilson and Steve Leek on Leek's Ranch in Jackson Hole. Ranch buildings in background. These oats went 90 bushels to the acre and were hand-sown. 1910.

The way it was done in the early days. Putting up hay in Jackson Hole, 1912.

CHAPTER 17 — **Brasfield and Bill Scott**

About 1913 Billy Raum sold his saloon to a real colorful character named Nick McCoy, who owned a saloon up at Sand Point, Idaho. Billy took this Idaho saloon as part payment on the deal, but it turned out McCoy didn't own the saloon, and a shoot-out between Billy and Nick was narrowly averted by timely intervention of Nick Wilson. Before Billy could get to Nick McCoy, my dad convinced McCoy to divey up and pay Billy Raum off.

A lane ran north from Wilson to the ranches up along Fish Creek, among which were the Gene Foster family, then the Van Winkles, the John Cherry ranch and the Brasfields. Old man Brasfield had a wife and four very beautiful daughters. The eldest, Effie, was married to Gene Foster. His was the first ranch up this lane, about a half mile above the town of Wilson. Fosters had two children at the time I write about. Maude was about my age and Clyde was the age of my brother George. I think this was the year of 1906, and after Nick and I had returned from the trip to Evanston to see my mother. The other Brasfield girls, all very beautiful, were Anna with long, beautiful, black hair; then Evelyn, a blonde, and the most gorgeous one of all — but they were all pretty — and Afton, the youngest, who was a brunette.

There was another old timer I haven't mentioned, named Rube Scott. I don't think he ever settled in Jackson Hole, but had a ranch over Teton Pass in Idaho at Victor, only 18 miles west of Wilson, but over the high pass, which really made him seem a long way off. Rube Scott spent a lot of his time in Jackson Hole at Spencer's Saloon, and was a loud-mouthed sort of an extrovert like Bill Crawford, whom I have mentioned in this story. Rube had two boys, Bill and Gib. All three of the Scotts, father and sons, were very picturesque characters. It was Rube who, as a deputy sheriff in Idaho, had collaborated with law officers in Wyoming who were trying to apprehend an outlaw named Eli Whitney, who was a real badman and a celebrated gunslinger (meaning he was very fast with a six-shooter!). This outlaw, Whitney, was surrounded in some area between Wyoming and Idaho, and his only hope of escape was during a certain night he had to make a break for it, or be caught the next day. There were only two ways of escape, one into and through Wyoming; the other into and through Idaho. It was known that Whitney would make a break for it one way or the other. The Jackson Hole posse was guarding that exit, and Rube Scott, deputy sheriff, Idaho, and his posse, were guarding the Idaho exit.

Both of these posses were placed at likely spots of escape, and Rube stationed himself at a narrow bridge spanning a very swift, swollen stream that he figured was the most likely spot to apprehend Whitney. There was no moon that night, and each posse man had to depend on his hearing and instinct, for it was not known in what area or at what hour or minute to expect Whitney. But he was sure to appear some place, and so all the guards were very tense and alert.

Whitney was boxed off in a canyon with steep cliffs on both sides, with openings only on either end. It was a situation similar to the famous Hole-in-the-Wall in Wyoming, where outlaws hid from the law.

Nick Wilson was with the posse from Wyoming, and he had been sent to be with some of the Idaho posse; one member of the Idaho posse was with the Wyoming posse, so that whichever way Whitney decided to go, the posse man from either posse would ride fast and notify the other posse.

Nick was stationed only a few hundred yards from where Rube Scott took his stand at the bridge. At some unexpected moment during the small hours of the night, a horseman appeared from no where, right in front of Rube Scott! Rube swung up his sawed-off shotgun and yelled, "Halt!" The rider didn't even hesitate, but opened fire on Rube and at the same time spurred his horse right over Rube, before he could get off a shot.

The reason Rube couldn't get off a shot was because when he yelled, "Halt!", and started to pull the trigger, Whitney's bullet arrived first and shot off Rube's trigger finger! This would be one for Ripley's "Believe It or Not!" stories, but Rube lived out his life minus a trigger finger, and Eli Whitney escaped to South America or some place else where he was never heard of again!

Bill Scott, Rube's oldest son, was very sweet on Anna Brasfield and soon after this above incident, old man Brasfield, who was an alcoholic, was returning to his home up along Fish Creek, when his team ran away with him, and his body was found somewhere along the road the next day, all battered and bruised.

Bill Scott was no drinker like his dad, but he often frequented the saloon, and he happened to be at the saloon the day old man Brasfield was killed. There was also another character in the saloon that day whose name was Nick McCoy. McCoy owned a saloon up in Sand Point, Idaho, and, like Bill Raum, McCoy had a reputation of killing a man in his saloon. Both Raum and McCoy were tough characters, no doubt, the only difference was that Billy Raum was straight forward in his dealing and as honest as a man in the saloon business could be. On the other hand, Nick McCoy was really a coward at heart and dealt underhandedly, and was a very dangerous and deceptive, evil man — also an alcoholic. McCoy had been dickering with our first saloon keeper, Spencer, for his saloon, but Billy Raum beat McCoy to it, and bought Spencer's saloon business. But about 1913, McCoy finally made a deal with Raum and got the saloon at Wilson, Wyoming, in Jackson Hole.

There had been no inquest into Brasfield's death, and about one week after he was buried, this Nick McCoy started a story that he had heard Bill Scott and Brasfield having words over Brasfield's daughter, Anna, in which McCoy claimed he heard Bill Scott threaten to kill Brasfield if he didn't quit interferring in Bill and Anna's plans to get married. McCoy further claimed he saw Bill Scott get on his saddle horse and follow Brasfield out of town when Brasfield went home. He charged that Bill had murdered old man Brasfield on the way home, and then had made everybody think the old man had been killed in a runaway.

Nick Wilson was constable, mayor, doctor, bishop and about everything else in the town of Wilson, and so he was pressured to have Brasfield's body exhumed and have an autopsy done. Everybody liked Bill Scott, who was a big, burly, dark-complexioned character, with a big, black furious-looking mustache like Billy Raum's, and Bill Scott was about twice the size of Raum. In spite of his furious, mean looks, Bill Scott was really a very mild and gentle person, who wouldn't harm anyone, and everyone who knew him also knew this to be true. So Nick Wilson had Abe Ward, who was then sheriff, arrest Bill and he was taken to Jackson and put in jail, pending the outcome of the autopsy on Brasfield. Nick Wilson was very disturbed regarding this turn of events, and he told me he had Nick McCoy pegged as a liar and a trouble-maker.

They put up a tent in our front yard, and when Brasfield's body was dug up, it was held in this tent in care of Nick Wilson. The only one in the valley who could perform an autopsy was Doc Palmer, who was also coroner, but it was two days before they got Doc Palmer sobered up enough to perform the autopsy.

The fact that Brasfield's body was being held in a tent in our front yard was a matter of excitement, not only among us kids, but Nick Wilson was kept busy running off all the would-be observers of Brasfield's body, which they all wanted to see. There were no embalming methods in those days in Jackson Hole, and the body was already beginning to smell very badly after only a week in the grave, so a sagebrush fire with green willows was kept burning in the tent so the smoke could keep the odor down.

While this was all going on, it became known that Anna Brasfield was pregnant! There is always a faction in cases like this who always believe the worst about everything, and so a gang decided that a low-down scalawag who would kill a man and ruin his daughter ought to be hanged! So Abe had to keep a posse posted at the jail to protect Bill Scott from being mobbed and hanged!

My dad was furious about all this goings-on, and he maintained to the end that Bill Scott was innocent. He was borne out when Doc Palmer finally finished the autopsy and, with witnesses, declared that old man Brasfield had been killed by the runaway! There was not a shred of evidence that Bill Scott had anything to do with Brasfield's death. The body was reburied and remains, to this day, lying at peace in the Wilson Cemetery waiting Resurrection, that great day when the dead shall rise and the blue ribbons will be placed on the ones to whom they belong. There will be a lot of red faces all over the world on that day, me thinks!

Bill was released from jail and denied being the one who had caused Anna Brasfield's pregnancy. To this Anna agreed, but she would not divulge the culprit's name. Bill loved Anna very much, and tried to get her to marry him anyway, but she would not. Not long after this, she left the valley for good. No one ever heard from her again. Bill took this all very hard, and never married nor had a sweetheart again, to our knowledge.

CHAPTER 18 — **Carl Van Winkle**

One beautiful warm sunny morning I had finished my house-work, washing the breakfast dishes and sweeping the floor dirt out through the door and off the step onto the ground.

Nick had begun writing on his life story the fall of 1908, and that winter the Leeks left the ranch for Nick to attend. They left a hired man and his wife to do the chores and cooking. Their names were Ed and Lena Woodward. Ed was a wiry little Scotchman and his wife was about as big as all outdoors.

Nick spent the whole winter tapping away on Leek's old French typewriter with one finger. I rode Lester's little baldfaced sorrel pony "Jumping Jack" three miles to school at Jackson. "Jack" was a mean little cuss and I really learned to become a good rider from him that winter. He would try to buck me off and if that didn't work he tried to run away! He bucked me off plenty of times then took off for home and left me to walk! I got tired of some of these long walks and got so he just couldn't throw me anymore!

My worst problem after I got control of my horse, was with our cook, Lena. She was a good cook and a pretty fair housekeeper. While living alone with my dad, I seldom, if ever washed, except my hands, and sometimes my face, a little, let alone take a bath! Lena tried to keep me clean and she kept all our clothes washed and clean.

But I was a different matter. I was seven years old and a big strong kid for my age. Lena would order me to take a bath once a week and wash my face and hands before and after every meal. One day when Nick was pounding away in the living room on the old typewriter, and Ed was out feeding the stock, Lena was on one of her grouches and I guess she needed someone or something to take it out on, and as I was the fall-guy, she didn't like the looks of my face and long hair and claimed my neck was dirty as a pig pen! She ordered me to wash it good with lots of soap. I hated soap because it was always getting in my eyes! But I started half-heartedly on my neck, and Lena grabbed me by the hair, and ram-med my face down in the wash basin, and grabbed a stiff haired hand brush and started scraping on me. It felt like a horse rasp! I yanked my head up out of the basin, blowing soap suds and gasping for air! Lena tried to yank my head back into the wash basin again and I couldn't see for soap in my eyes and her yanking on my long hair. I started fighting and kicking and biting! I bit her on the arm and hit her with my fist in one of her large breasts! And she let a yowl out of her that brought my dad from the library and Ed from the barn! Nick arrived first, Lena was yowling so loud that Nick couldn't get head nor tail of the situation! As Ed rushed in the door, Lena fell into his arms and the great weight knocked Ed to the floor. Nick helped Lena up and Ed scrambled up red-faced to his feet, and he was in a fighting mood, because he would fight a buzz saw for his "little Lena!"

Well, Nick finally got things quieted down, and between Lena shrieking and puffing her fat cheeks out and in, and rolling her eyes until all you could see was their whites, they began to get the story of what had happened. When she got to the part where I hit her in the ti--er, in the bosom, Ed came uncorked and started to knock hell out of me. My dad grabbed Ed by the collar and shook him so hard he lost his false teeth! He sat Ed down hard in a chair, Lena was draped over another, and I got my chance to tell my version. Well, it ended by Nick telling Lena to let me alone and quit trying to wash and bathe me, and he told Ed to get out and finish his chores, or they would both go down the road talking to themselves! We all got along pretty well after that, and the Woodwards were still there working for Leeks the next winter of 1910, the year so many elk starved to death and the State of Wyoming sent State Game Warden Nowlin to investigate and he stayed all winter at the Leek ranch with Nick and I and Ed and Lena. Steve Leek finally got federal aid for the elk and a program was set up to feed and care for the elk during winter in Jackson Hole, and it is still being done to this day on the Federal Elk Reserve at Jackson. Well, to get back to my story of that beautiful July morning.

Nick was typing away at the kitchen table on his story, and I had been reading a book about *A Soldier of Fortune*, it was about a young Englishman and his adventures in the "Foreign Legion." It was real exciting and I remember it had a red back. I had taken the book into my bedroom and was lying on the bed reading this book, when suddenly, I came to my senses and realized that all the yelling and bawling I had been hearing wasn't coming from the riot I was reading about somewhere in Algeria or France or someplace! The yelling and bawling and screeching was coming from across the street at the old hotel. Nick was already up from the table and

Myrtle Schofield, Bob Nethercott and Carl Van Winkle, only a few days before Carl was drowned in Snake River.

standing in the door to see what was going on! I slipped past my dad standing in the door, and here came my nephew, Ira Ward, running as fast as he could and he was so winded, he could hardly talk. Then he began yelling! "Carl Van Winkle just drowned in Snake River! It just came over the phone from Ely's!" I never heard such a commotion in my life, most of the hysterics was coming from a bunch of females gathered over at Wards. The day before had been the 4th of July and there was always a big celebration on the 4th of July in both Jackson and Wilson. The Wilson-Jackson baseball teams had played what always turned out to be a wild baseball game, whenever they played either at Jackson or Wilson. This year it had been at Wilson and it wound up in a big gang fight!

Mike Yokel was a tough little Dutchman with a big family. Mike was also the World's Champion light-weight wrestler and had just gotten back from a big win down in Australia. Mike wrestled all over the world and was known world-wide. He first came to Jackson Hole to fish, about 1907 I think. He was an avid fisherman and Jackson Hole was the answer to a fisherman's dream! Mike loved this area so much he filed a homestead in the foot hills just west of Nick Wilson's ranch. Anyone familiar with Jackson Hole, and there are millions, know where the present "Stage Coach Saloon" stands today at Wilson, Wyoming, and it is built on the spot where Mike Yokel's house stood.

Mike only got home about once a year and only stayed long enough to get acquainted with his kids and have time to sire another, and he was on his way again to defend his title as the "World's Champion Light-Weight Wrestler!" It usually didn't take Mike long with the help of a few of his admirers, to squelch the fights, which were followed by a big all-night dance at both Wilson and Jackson. There had been a big whang-bang dance at Wilson, and in the early morning hours a dozen or more of the towns "belles" gathered at the Ward Hotel. They were there when Lewy Flemming had called the hotel from a phone at the Mart Ely ranch, just east of where Uncle Alfred's ferryboat landed on the east bank of Snake River.

There was a trio of young bucks who lived on the Wilson side of Snake River, known as "The Three Musketeers!" They were all about the same age and were nearly always together. Their names were Elijah Ward, Nick Wilson's oldest grandson, Lewy Flemming, who came into Jackson Hole in 1901 with his Uncle Jim Flemming, with whom Lewy lived, and was raised. I have a cassette tape of an interview I had with Lewy Flemming when I started gathering material to write this sequel of Nick Wilson's life. Lewy was ten years old when he came into the valley with his Uncle Jim and from the time Lewy was ten years old, up to the night that Nick Wilson died on December 27, 1915, Lewy Flemming knew and was intimately acquainted with Nick Wilson and all his family. Lewy was sitting up with Nick the night he died, just two nights after Christmas! And so Lewy has been a great help to me in getting some of these stories together that happened between 1901 and 1915, when I was too young to remember some of them. Even with Lewy's help I have probably gotten some of the dates mixed up, but the happenings were just like I am telling them just the same!

The other one in this trio was Carl Van Winkle, oldest son of John Van Winkle, one of the early settlers in Jackson Hole. These three young men were like stair steps going down the street! Elijah was about five-foot six, Lewy about five-foot ten, and Carl stood six-foot six! Whenever Carl and Elijah were together they were known as "Mutt and Jeff!" These three friends were closer than most brothers, and when Carl drowned. Elijah was at a dude ranch up near Cody, Wyoming, three hundred miles away!

Lewy Flemming's version of the drowning was: Carl owned a little "black top" one-seat buggy; four guys and girls could ride in the narrow seat, if they were "pretty well acquainted!" (Lewy's quote!)

After the ball game was over on the 4th of July at Wilson, Carl and Lewy ran across a couple girls from Jackson they knew, and the girls wanted Carl and Lewy to go to Jackson for the dance, instead of going to the dance in Wilson. Lewy and Carl decided to do it and so picked the girls up at Ward's Hotel about 7 p.m. and Uncle Alfred ferried them across Snake River about 7:30 p.m. From June 1, to Sept 1, Uncle Alfred ran the ferry from 8 a.m. to 8 p.m.

After the dance in Jackson broke up, about daylight, Carl and Lewy headed for home back in Wilson. They were at the ferry before sun up and had about three hours to wait before Uncle Alfred opened the ferry, which was on the Wilson, or west side of Snake River. Lewy told me that Carl had drunk a little too much at the dance and was pretty high all the way back to Snake River the morning of July 5. When Carl realized they had a three hour wait before Nethercott started the ferry up, Carl started cussing and got mad and said he wouldn't wait that long for the ferry, but would "Coon the Cable!" That meant that Carl would go hand over hand with his feet over the cable and gradually crawl over the big cable and bring the ferry back for Lewy and the team. Lewy tried to talk Carl out of it, the river was over three hundred yards wide and the water was very high. In fact Snake River usually peaked about the 4th of July, but it would be a week or two yet before the old man river would start to go down.

The cable out in the center of the stream sagged down and was only a few feet above the swift, muddy current. Carl would not listen to reason, he was a huge, strong man over six and half feet tall and weighed over two hundred pounds; Lewy couldn't stop him by force or argument, so all he could do was stand helplessly by and watch Carl start out "Cooning the Cable!" With his feet crossed above the cable, he would reach along the cable as far he could reach, then hunch his feet and legs forward, gaining about three feet every pull, which meant that Carl had to make about four hundred pulls with only his hands and feet supporting his weight! Lewy said Carl got out about two or three hundred feet, which wasn't a third way across the river, and the cable began to sag and Carl's back wasn't two feet above the water! Lewy could see a big tree drift wood coming, rolling and pitching in the heavy current, and he began to yell for Carl to stop and come back! As Lewy could already see that with Carl's weight the cable would be submerged long before Carl reached the center, one hundred fifty yards out in the river.

Carl must have seen the big tree coming and stopped, and it went under the cable only about twenty yards ahead of Carl and some of the branches hung upon the cable for an instant, pulling the cable under the water and getting Carl all wet. Lewy said Carl must have been completely crazy to keep going, and Lewy yelled until he was hoarse to get Carl to come back; but after the driftwood got by, Carl continued doggedly on! He made about another twenty-five yards and his back began to drag in the water, then another driftwood came and it hit the sagging cable head on and Carl and the cable disappeared. The cable soon flew back up out of the water, but Carl was gone! Lewy watched in horror a few minutes, but Carl never did appear again. Lewy jumped in the buggy and it was only about a quarter mile back to the Mart Ely ranch, and the Elys were eating breakfast. Lewy told them about what happened, then called the hotel at Wilson.

Pandemonium had broken out soon as the news hit Wilson. A lot of people were hanging around the hotel after the dance that had lasted until daylight. Kids were running back and forth across the Fish Creek bridge over to the post office and saloon. I could see a team hitched to a wagon and tied to Billy Raum's hitching post in front of the saloon, and also three or four saddle horses. There was a team and buggy tied to the hitching post in front of the post office, too, across the street from the saloon. The post office and store were run by a man named Del Judd, a thirty-year-old bachelor.

Also hitched to the post was Mrs. Badero's rat-tailed race horse. Mrs. Badero was a beautiful woman about thirty years old, who must have been of Mexican descent. She had a little boy named Travis Badero and he was very dark and very fine looking kid, about my age. Mrs. Badero was a strange woman and had bought the old Ray ranch down in the thick Willows, south of Wilson and joining George Goodrick's ranch. Mrs. Badero 's ranch was only about one mile south of the town of Wilson as the crow flies, but there was no road up from her place through the Goodrick place. Mrs. Badero had to go a mile west on a section line almost to Snake River, then north to end of the Wilson lane out by Snake River, then she had to go a mile west to get to town, making a three mile ride. Mrs. Badero had owned the old Ray place for about two years and Travis had been going to school at Wilson these years. No one seemed to know where she came from or what she did for a living on the old Ray of 160 acres, mostly willows,but twenty five or thirty acres were cleared and good hay land.

She evidently had money, because she and Travis were always well dressed and she bought the finest foods that Del Judd had in his store. She only seemed to have this one old yellowish-brown, long-backed, slim race horse. You could see more hot blood strain in him than in the common run of horses bred in Jackson Hole. This horse was long barreled and long-legged, but had one feature about him seldom seen in horse flesh, he had a long, bony tail with not a hair on it! This horse was very high spirited and nervous and a real goer! People wondered how Mrs. Badero and Travis ever could ride this skittish animal. You could always tell when she and Travis came to town. She only stopped at two places in town and tied her horse to the hitching post and that was at the Ward hotel, where she often ate a meal with Travis and mostly she tied to the hitching post at the post office, where she came in about three times a week to get her mail — of which she seemed to get quite a lot. You could always tell when Mrs. Badero was in town because this horse had a habit of pawing the ground and prancing all around as far as the tie rope would allow and held this funny bare tail straight up, and snorted out of both ends like a crack of a rifle shot, keeping up this staccatto until it sounded like a gun fight going on!

Well, on this day of excitement, people were doing the craziest things! It seems like in almost every tragedy there is some humor if you look for it, and this tragedy of Carl Van Winkle drowning in Snake River was beginning to border on humor from where me and my dad stood in our front yard watching all the commotion!

A whole flock of men ran out of Billy's saloon and all climbed in the wagon, as many as it would hold, and the saddle horses were mounted. The wagon full of men followed by the four horsemen thundered across the old Fish Creek Bridge and really made the old stringers jump up and down! And on past the livery barn and south to Goodricks and entered the Wilson lane and they were really pouring it on, out through the lane as fast as the horses could run.

"Now where does all them damn fools think they are going! There's nothing they can do when they get to the river, but watch the water go by!" My dad spoke more to himself than to anyone else.

Then we saw Billy Raum rush out of his saloon. He always wore a long, black fork-tailed coat. He ran and untied Mrs. Bandero's furiously snorting horse, and here was another queer trait of this strange horse: as soon as anyone was ready to mount him he became quiet and never moved a muscle until the rider was seated, ready to go! People always marveled at what they saw when Mrs. Badero and Travis went to mount this furious acting horse; to see him stand still, while she mounted and then reached down and got Travis by the hand and helped him on behind her! Well, Billy mounted this prancing, snorting, firey steed, and they pounded across the old bridge in the wake of the long-gone wagon and horsemen. It was a sight such as I will probably never see again in my life: Billy's swallow-tailed coat flapping in the breeze, and the little, heavy black-mustached rider leaning forward, as if trying to outrun the horse! My dad and I couldn't help laughing as he went by with a volley of snorts emitting from each end. He was in the lane and we could still hear the pounding of hoofs and snorting when he went out of sight down the willowy lane.

When Billy reached the end of the lane, the team and wagon were tied to the Beckley fence, and people were running up and down the river bank and pointing and shouting "there he goes!" "Aw! hell, that's just driftwood!" Then Billy arrived, and just as he reached the end of the Wilson lane, the old horse fell in his tracks, as if shot! Then he skidded along on his side and skinned Billy's face and hands and bloodied his nose and blacked both eyes! And when the people gathered, they rushed over to help Billy up, the old horse lay quite dead! There was nothing anyone could do, and in about an hour they came back on the walk to Wilson. Billy was sitting on the seat of the wagon with the driver, and both eyes were black and he was covered with blood and dirt, and as my dad always said, "he must not of been feeling too good himself!"

Before night there were a lot of small row boats on the river with good oarsmen like Steve Leek and my Uncle Alfred searching islands and eddies clear down to Munger Mountain, but by night fall they were all back empty handed and above the silence could be heard the ominous roar of the great yam pa-pa! a mile away, the mother of western waters!

Billy Raum gave the grave, quiet Mrs. Badero a fine little brown gelding that was real gentle and a lot quieter than her wild-eyed snorting old rat-tailed race horse!

As Elijah Ward was one of Carl's dearest friends, he was notified of the tragic event and knowing old Snake River, he was of the same opinion as about everybody else: Carl's body would not be found until after high water and maybe not even then, as a majority of old Snake River's drowning victims were never found. Elijah told his dad, who had called him about noon from the old hotel and gave Elijah the news, to keep him informed of further happenings and if the body was found he would like to come home for the funeral.

The very next morning, July 6, Sylvester Cheney came along down the river riding one of his work horses and leading the other; both had harnesses on. Sylvester was going down to Al Linn's, just below the end of Wilson lane to get his wagon that Al had borrowed. Sylvester got about even with the old blue fishing hole, where me and my dad had the escapade with me nearly getting drowned when our old team ran with me in the wagon while fishing on Snake River. But now the river was high and the water was flapping over the bank that had then risen ten feet or more higher than what the old blue hole was during low water time!

Sylvester was watching the fast, muddy water and the driftwood going by and thinking of Carl Van Winkle, somewhere out there, probably lodged against an old stump or pile of water-logged driftwood, then suddenly there was Carl! floating face up with his long blond hair floating like a hallow around his snow white face! Sylvester couldn't believe his eyes! but it was for real! There, only about thirty or forty feet out in the fast flowing stream, was Carl Van Winkle! It was only about a half mile up to the Ferry! Carl's body had only come half a mile in twenty four hours! Sylvester didn't hesitate a second, nor think of what the consequences might be, but he dropped the lead rope of the horse he was leading and plunged his harnessed workhorse off into the raging river! This horse was big and powerful and hit the swirling water a-swimming!

Sylvester reached down and grabbed Carl by the hair, then turned his horse toward the bank, and that big, wonderful horse made it in one lunge up onto the bank and Sylvester dropped Carl's cold, limp body in the grass! This turn of events was almost beyond belief and Sylvester was hailed as a hero, and he really was!

Well, that's about all of the story of Carl Van Winkle, except the fact that Elijah Ward made one of the fastest and longest trips on horseback ever made in Wyoming since Pony Express days, and probably not even then! Elijah was notified and told that Carl's body couldn't be held long, because it was July and hot and there was no embalming. By telephone it was arranged for Elijah to pick up a fresh horse every ten to fifteen miles from Cody down through Big Horn Basin to Lander and over Twogwotee Pass to Menor's Ferry on Snake River and on down to Wilson, Wyoming, a distance of just under three hundred miles in twenty four hours. But Elijah Ward came from good stock: his granddad Nick Wilson had been one of the best riders on the Pony Express!

CHAPTER 19 — Nick McCoy

Nick McCoy ran this saloon at Wilson from about 1913, when he bought it from Billy Raum, up to about 1920. Nick was a trouble maker and dearly loved to get some kind of fracas going. He used to stop the boys coming home from school and would get a bunch of them in the saloon and give them candy and nuts. Then he would get out a pair of old boxing gloves and pair the kids off according to size and the fights between these kids were really vicious, and it got to the point some of us were going home badly beaten up. The parents became concerned and it finally wound up in court at Jackson under a change of venue, where McCoy lied and bamboozeled the parents into dropping the charges by bargaining not to do this anymore.

Nick always had two or three shady characters hanging around the saloon under the pretense of running his livery stable, or bartending. It was believed, but never proved, that they were involved in cattle rustling, horse stealing, and plain robberies, and burglarizing all over the country.

I remember one day when I was about twelve years old, I was passing McCoy's saloon and he called me in. There was no one there but he and I. I had been borrowing a twelve-gauge double-barrel shotgun from him to get a duck with, once in awhile for my dad. When he was so sick the last two or three years of his life, he loved duck soup, also duck fried or roasted. It was one of his favorite gourmet dishes that he learned to like while living with the Indians.

This was an Ithica double-barrel light-weight gun, hammerless and so beautiful to handle. I really loved that little shotgun! I went in and Nick McCoy handed me a small box of salted peanuts, then he asked, "How are you and Virgil Ward getting along these days?"

I was surprised at the question, but answered with a shrug, "Oh, alright, I guess. I just avoid him all I can."

"Why?" asked Nick. "Are you afraid of him?"

I thought a moment then said, "No! I'm not afraid of him! At least not as much as I used to be!"

"What do you mean, used to be?" taunted Nick.

"Well, I am bigger now and he can't whip me like he did when I was a little kid," I stated.

"Uh, Uh," said Nick. "But you don't like him very much do you?"

"No," I answered, "I don't."

"Yes, I guess none of the kids like him very much, do they?"

"Oh, I don't know," I said, "He gets along with kids his age and over. He really is a coward and only bullies us little kids."

Nick gave me some more peanuts, and took a drink from a fifth of scotch, and said, "I heard that you once had a fight with him over there in the hotel and pulled a knife on him?"

"Yes, I did," I answered.

"Did you try to kill him?" asked Nick very bluntly.

I was startled, but after thinking an instant I answered, "Well, I didn't think of that at the time, he hit me and hurt me, I just got real mad and went for him with my pocket knife! He was a lot bigger than I was!" I defended myself.

Nick laughed and took another drink. "Say!" Nick said in a different tone of voice, "How do you like that little shotgun I loan you to get ducks or rabbits for your dad? He really likes duck or rabbit soup, don't he?"

I brightened up. "Yes! Yes, he sure does, and I can really knock them over with that gun!" I added proudly. Nick reached over and touched me on the arm and was very serious when he asked, "How would you like to own that gun?"

"What do you mean?" I blurted, "I don't have any money to buy it with!"

"Nobody said anything about money! I just asked how would you like to own that gun?"

"Well, I can't think of anything right now that I would sooner own than that gun!"

Nick grinned and said, "Well, you can have it!"

I was dumbfounded, and blurted, "Do you really mean it? I can have that gun? You are giving it to me?"

Nick laughed real good at my excitement and enthusiasm, and said, "Yes, in a way, I am giving you that shotgun, but you have to do a little something to earn it!"

I was really excited now, "What do I have to do to earn it?" I asked.

Nick looked at me a minute or two and took another drink, then said, "All you have to do to own that shotgun is to kill Virgil Ward with it!"

It was like a dash of cold ice water in the face! I couldn't believe what I had heard, "What did you say?" I yelled as I jumped from the bar stool!

Nick grabbed me and sat me back on the stool and I never heard his voice like that before, then he said, "Set down! Don't get so damn excited! You tried to kill Virgil Ward once with a pocket knife, didn't you?" Before I could answer, he went on, "Well, with this gun you can do a good job of it! Nobody will ever know, but you and me!"

I began to calm down and listened as Nick unfolded the plan: "All you have to do is hide out somewhere in the willows. He goes for the milk cows up there in their pasture and the brush is so thick you can wait somewhere along the cow-trail and when he comes along, just shoot his head off!"

I winced, but Nick continued, "No one will ever know who done it! All you have to do is keep your mouth shut until it blows over! And you've got a fine shotgun all your own!"

I was horror stricken at just the thought of such a thing, but I was only a twelve year-old kid and Nick was very persuasive, and sometimes I had hated Virgil enough to kill him, I thought! This was one of the greatest temptations I ever faced in my life. I really wanted that shotgun! But I guess I am just not a killer, I just couldn't do it! I told Nick I would think it over and decide later.

"Well, Don't take too long thinking, Charley!" And then he said, very menacingly, "And don't ever mention our little talk!" I will never forget the look he gave me as I left the saloon.

Well, I never again asked Nick McCoy for the use of his beautiful shotgun, but began using my dad's old 22 Winchester Special, and I got so I could hit a dime with that wonderful old gun at fifty paces. I could even kill a grouse or a duck on the wing with it!

Yes, Nick McCoy was a very evil man and God only knows how many crimes he committed before he poisoned himself to death during the prohibition years, drinking rotgut bootleg whiskey, before the Prohibition Act was repealed. I saw Nick McCoy just before he died and he had lost his voice!

CHAPTER 20 — Haley's Comet

Nick Wilson finished his manuscript the winter of 1910 and that fall I started to school at Jackson, and Steve Leek was showing his movies and slides in the east and had become very popular. He left Etta with the two boys in Kearney, Nebraska, where Steve's mother still lived. His father died when Steve was quite young, and she had then married a man named Wort. Steve had two half-brothers, Charley Wort and Hamilton Wort, and two half-sisters, Belle Wort, who married a man named Flanders and the other was Maggie Wort, and she married Chester Patterson. Chester and his brother Ted invented and patented a mechanism on the Remington Rifles that brought them a million dollars. I think Hamilton Wort was the eldest and not much younger than Steve Leek.

Ham Wort was a saddle maker and a good leather worker. He homesteaded in Jackson Hole with Leek and later Leek bought Ham out, and Ham then started a saddle shop in Cheyenne, Wyoming and later in Lander, Wyoming. Charley homesteaded west of Leek and he owned the livery stable in Jackson. All of Leek's half-brothers and sisters were well fixed through inheritance and their connection with the Remington Arms Company. Leek made his the hard way — "he earned it," and was considered among the wealthiest ranchers in the Jackson Hole Valley. He was an environmentalist at heart and spent most of his life helping and urging the conservation of wildlife.

When Steve Leek died in 1943, he left his life's collection of pictures and movies and written articles to the University of Wyoming at Laramie. This collection is priceless, and its real value has never been tabulated. I went to the University at Laramie, Wyoming in 1976 to see this collection and was appalled to find this great collection still boxed and stored in the big storeroom at the university. They had never gotten around to unpacking it for display!

I gave the University the original of my father's manuscript that is published in this book, after I had a few copies made to keep. The old manuscript was yellow with age and getting very fragile. I attempted to laminate it and no one told me to laminate on both sides of each page and when I went to give it to the university I found the paper had rolled up into a tight roll I couldn't unroll! I was very upset, but the university attendant told me that a firm in Germany could restore the manuscript to its original state, and that they would send it and have it restored and put it on display at the university.

The winter of 1909-10 was among the happiest years of my life and I got very well acquainted with Dan Nowlin who was, I believe, Wyoming's second State Game Warden, following Albert Nelson, who I believe was the first. There was great concern regarding the welfare of the elk that winter which was a very hard winter. In the spring of 1910, you could have walked on the bodies of dead elk for ten miles along Flat Creek, and never have stepped on the ground. It was estimated that ten thousand elk starved to death that winter. The willows along Flat Creek were browsed off down to stubs as large as your thumb. Every settler who could, gave hay to help pull a few elk through, and there was even a drive put on by the ranchers' wives to give the straw and hay in the bed ticks and many tons were donated that way. I remember sleeping on hard board slats part of that winter, after we gave all the straw from the mattresses in our house!

Only a few hundred elk survived that winter and Leek's pictures of dead elk were viewed that winter in schools and public places all over the Unted States, and from that time on the elk have never been in want of feed, but plenty of other problems have now risen regarding the control methods, that have become a political boomerang, and many environmentalists are again worried over the preservation of this wonderful animal!

There was another thing during 1910 that was of great significance world-wide, and that was the appearance of the great Haley's Comet! Nick and I lived on the Leek ranch that summer and Nick supervised the ranch and haying operations. Steve Leek was still in the East and he had also been elected one of Wyoming's United States Representatives and final arrangements were made regarding financing the elk problem and federal money began buying up what is now the Federal Elk Reserve at Jackson, Wyoming.

Steve paid Nick very generously and that fall he had money to start the publishing of his book by the Skelton Publishing Co. of Salt Lake City, and it was called *Uncle Nick Among the Shoshones*. I have already told how the book company went bankrupt, and I went with dad peddling these books.

The view from the Leek ranch of Haley's Comet was spectacular! Every evening this great comet flashed into sight from behind Old

Baldy or Old Glory as the High bare mountain that raises above the timber line from the north side of Teton Pass is called. Timber line in Wyoming is about eleven thousand feet. The comet came into view from near the top of this mountain and was then high-enough in the heavens to be seen for several hours as it passed on south over the Teton Range, Mosquito Creek and on until it finally vanished behind Munger Mountain straight south of us. Baldy was a little northeast of the ranch, thus we had an uninterrupted view of Haley's Comet about one-fourth of the sky expanse around the earth!

For a couple years I had been a paperboy selling the *Chicago Blade and Ledger.* The *Blade* was a very sensational newspaper like the *Denver Post,* only much bigger. It carried news items from all over the world, whether they were true or not! It showed col-ored pictures of the world and of the great comet and the belief that on a certain day this comet's long, blazing tail would strike the earth and we would all go out in flames! Many people believed this was the end of the world so strongly that they settled all their worldly affairs and committed suicide!

There were some churches that claimed only the one hundred and forty four thousand chosen believers as prophesied in the Bible would survive by being taken from the earth at the last minute before destruction! Hundreds of these strange people sold or gave away everything they owned and gathered in groups a-praying on the day that the comet was to come closest to earth in its orbit, and the tail was supposed to ignite the earth! Many of these people who didn't feel they were called among the lucky one hundred and forty four thousand also committed suicide!

I was nine years old and I read most everything in the *Chicago Blade* and I was really scared! One day, just before the fatal day of doomsday approached, I very tearfully clung onto my father's hand and begged of him what we should do! He sat me down on a chair by his, and placing his hands on my knees and looking me straight in the eye, he said very seriously, "Now! I will tell you what we will do! The big burn will be day after tomorrow!" I started to sob! Nick shook my knees and said "Hush up! This is no time to be crying! Now is the time for you and me to figure out what to do! And I know what I am going to do!"

"What are you going to do?" I cried.

"Well," he began, "Do you want to join in this plan with me?"

"Oh yes! yes! I do!" I exclaimed.

Nick hesitated a few minutes until I was on pins and needles, then he said, tomorrow we will go to town, to Pap DeLoney's store and I will buy two buckets of lard! A ten-pound pail for me, because I'm so big! and a five-pound pail for you! Then we will come back home and tomorrow night, just before the comet strikes the earth, we will grease ourselves all over good with this lard!"

"What good will that do?" I asked in amazement.

"Well!" answered Nick, "It will make us burn faster, won't it?" I nearly died! This was serious business to me and my Dad was a-poking fun at it! I have had many good laughs when I look back on that dreadful day that never happened!

How beautiful Haley's Comet was to me when it appeared again the evening after doomsday! From behind Old Baldy as usual! For those of you who never got to see this awe-inspiring sight, I will try to describe what Haley's Comet was like. When it appeared from behind Mount Baldy it was in its orbit around the earth. It didn't circle the earth like the sun does from east to west, but circled from north to south and taking about twenty four hours to complete its orbit, which was gradually changing, until after a few months, it went, to be seen again in about seventy-six years.

I was nine years old at that time, and never thought I might see it again, but in the year 1986 Haley's Comet is figured to again appear in sight of the earth. Astronomers claim that due to the electric lights beaming from all over the earth, it will dim the comet so much that few people will be able to see it, just like people living in cities never see all the brilliance and wonder of the stars at night, like we used to before all these lights were made possible. I am lucky at this time to live in a spot in Wyoming, called Story, where on most nights we can see the stars in all their glory, the Milky Way, the big and little dippers, the north star and see the other heavenly constellations almost as good as we could see them when I was a kid. I am eighty-three years old and if I live until 1986 I now hope to see Haley's Comet again!

As I have tried to describe Haley's Comet, I will finish this sight as it appeared to me. It was just after sundown that Haley's Comet appeared to us in the western sky, low in its orbit above the skyline. As it sped south, it appeared to me as a great, fiery ball, large as the full moon and trailing a great tail of fire behind it, so long that when the main body was about straight west of us the tail passed old Mount Glory. As the comet sped south, the sky grew darker and it was about six hours that we could see this beautiful phenomenon, and by the time it vanished behind Munger Mountain to the south of us, it would light up the earth brighter than a full moon. Haley's Comet gradually drew away from the earth, until after a few months we saw it no more!

I have stated above that it appeared for a few months. I was only nine years old, but I can remember it plain as yesterday. Perhaps it was only weeks instead of months that it appeared, but I am not going to make an issue of that or take time to look it up. I am only very happy that I was old enough to remember this wonderful sight and I hope I do get to see it again in 1986! I am only sad to think that people on much of this planet will never get to see this great comet again as it appeared to us in 1910.

Picture taken by Steve Leek in Snake River near Wilson, Wyoming. Leek called this picture, "Three pair, Kings up!" 1909.

Pictures like this were shown in eastern states by Steve Leek and Abe Ward, 1910-11-12. In the spring of 1910 it was estimated that 10,000 elk starved to death in Jackson Hole. Leek claimed it was possible to walk on dead elk along Flat Creek for eight miles and never step on the ground. Picture taken on Leek Ranch, 1910.

Leek's Ranch, 1910. The South Park ranchers gave all the hay they could spare to save a small elk herd on the Leek Ranch. Women made a drive for all the straw and hay used in bed mattresses. It all helped to save this small herd.

First elk feeding program started on Steve Leek's Ranch. Leek sold the state of Wyoming 1,500 tons of hay. More was bought from nearby ranchers as needed. Jay Goodrick, sitting, and state officials viewing first feeding attempt, which proved successful. 1911-12.

CHAPTER 21 — Ogden, Utah, Not in Wyoming!

After the work was all done in the fall of 1911, it was decided by Nick Wilson and the Leek and Ward families to spend the winter of 1911-12 in Salt Lake City, where Nick could watch over the publishing of his book and the kids could go to school.

Steve Leek would again take Abe Ward back east to help show his hundreds of slides and movies and Steve would lecture. They made very good money at this that winter.

The kids of school-age were: Lester, in the Leek family; (Holly was only five at Christmas time, and too young even for the "short class"); the Ward twins, Ira and Irene, were ten the fall of 1911, as was I. George would be six in February of 1911 and could go to short class a half a day. I had supposed that George and I would go on to Salt Lake City and be with our dad. The year 1911 was the summer that Nick had given George to his brother, Elias Wilson, who lived with his wife in Marysville, Idaho, which is near St. Anthony and Rexburg, and George got lost and Elias' wife gave George back to Nick and he lived with Nick and me then until Nick died in 1915.

The Government bought all of Leeks' hay that fall and it was about fifteen hundred tons. Leek had sold all their cattle, but kept about twenty head of horses. They hired Jay Goodrick to care for the ranch and with a couple of hired men to feed the elk in that end of the Jackson Hole Valley. This was one of the first programs of feeding the elk in Jackson Hole.

Elijah and Ercel Ward, with two wagons, hauled the eleven of us to the railhead at St. Anthony, Idaho, where we entrained for Salt Lake City with all our winter bags — George and mine only consisted of one suit case between us. You can imagine my disappointment when the train stopped at Ogden, Utah, and here Nick departed from the train with George and me. The rest went on to Salt Lake City. I asked Nick what was up.

He said, "You will see!" He took us to our half-sister Fanny's house on Washington Avenue in Ogden, and said we would stay with her for the winter and go to school in Ogden! I never liked Fanny when she lived with us in Jackson Hole, after her horse-thief

First feeding program started in South Park, south of Jackson, Wyoming. Leek's ranch buildings in center background. 1911-12.

This old Clubhouse still stands in Jackson, Wyoming. Note scaffolding as the building was nearing completion. Celebrants and flag pole are located in what is now the town square in Jackson, looking east up Cache Creek.

This was the town of Jackson about 1905. The large square building in background was called the Clubhouse, site of all civic activities; courthouse, dance hall, theatre, etc. on top level. Lower level contained drug store, hardware and undertaker. Building in lower right hand corner was the Mormon Church.

husband deserted her and her daughter Alta, who was a year older than me. But Nick had arranged to pay Fanny for our keep and she was to see that we attended school until the spring of 1912, when we would all go back to Jackson Hole.

Well, that was one of the worst winters I ever spent in my life, and for George too. George lives now at Federal Way, Washington, and we never meet that George doesn't bring up what we went through that winter with Fanny. She had been all over the West including California with Alta. I don't know what she did for a living, but she and Alta had driven a one-horse shay clear from California to Jackson Hole one summer, and they stayed that winter at Leeks' ranch. After they left I didn't know where they were until we stopped at Ogden. If I had known the plans for George and me for that winter, I would have protested very vigorously, even though it would probably have done me no good. I never knew how or when Nick had gotten in touch with Fanny and made these arrangements. At first I thought that Nick planned to stay that winter in Ogden with us, but he only stayed a few days and said he had to go to Salt Lake and take care of the publishing of his book, but would come and see us often! Well, he only came once all winter and I will write of that visit later.

Well, Fanny was very sweet and kind to George and me for awhile until after Nick left, and we were then read the riot act! Fanny was the one who seemed to hate my mother with a vengance, much worse than any of the other half-sisters did, and to say she took that vengance out on George and me that winter was to put it mildly. I had heard Nick tell Fanny before he left that he was giving her some extra money each month for our clothes and school supplies, and some for a show or maybe a circus, which Alta told us was coming to town soon. There was to be the great Barnum and Bailey Circus and the Ringling Brothers, and finally the great 101 Ranch Circus! All coming to Ogden during the next three months! I had never seen a circus in my life, but had seen many pictures of all the animals and had read *Barnum's Own Story*, a book of about six hundred pages with lots of pictures and it was Barnum's stories of catching the animals in Africa and all over the world! It was a great story! And now I was going to get to see a circus! I thought maybe it wouldn't be so bad here after all.

School soon started after we got to Ogden and I went to the Wasatch School with Alta and they started me in Third Grade "B". At Wilson I would have been in the Fourth Grade, but I started out in Third Grade "B" anyway. My teacher was named Miss Shaw and she was a mean little bitch, about twenty-one years-old and I found out about how mean she was the very first day! Looking back, I can't imagine a kid being as green and stupid as I was at first in my first experience in a big city and with city kids!

That first day, this Miss Shaw was interviewing each of the kids as to name, age, last grade in school, name of parents or guardian and residence, where you lived, etc. Well, when it came my turn, she asked all these questions, and I got along until she wanted to know my previous address and I said "Jackson Hole."

"Jackson Hole what? and where?" she said.

I answered "Just Jackson Hole!"

She got up from her desk and came down and stood by my desk and said, "Young man! I want you to answer my question! Where is Jackson Hole?"

I finally thought a minute and said, "Jackson Hole, Wyoming!"

She said, "Well! is Jackson Hole the name of the town where you lived in Wyoming?"

I answered "No! Wilson."

She said, "In what town did you live in Wyoming?" She was getting a red face and said "Are Wilson and Jackson one town?"

I said, "No, they are two towns!"

She said, "How could you live in two towns?"

I said, "I just did! I lived with my father in Wilson and I lived in Jackson with Leeks!, my sister."

Miss Shaw said, "Oh! I see! You lived sometime with your father in Wilson, and sometime with your sister in Jackson!"

"Yes!" I said.

"Well, where are you living now?"

I said "Ogden!"

She said, "Ogden, what?"

I said "Ogden, Wyoming!"

The kids started laughing and she said, "Give me your hand!"

I held out my hand and she grabbed ahold of three fingers and bent them back so it hurt, then she began to beat me on the open palm with a big heavy wooden ruler, like old Charley Driscoll used on us kids. The pain was terrible! I didn't know that you could smart and sting and hurt like my hand did, while she was rapping it so hard with this ruler! I jumped up out of my seat and started to cry!

"Shut up!" she barked. "And sit down!" She let go of my hand and pushed me hard back into my seat.

The kids had quit laughing and it was very still in that room! Miss Shaw grabbed me by the long hair and yanked my face up so

I had to look at her, and she said, "Now! I don't want any more funny business! I want you to answer me, Ogden, what?" She still held on to my forelock and was glaring me right in the eyes! "Ogden, what?" she almost screamed!

I was about to say, "Ogden, Wyoming" again, for I had no idea what else to say! Then I heard the kid in the seat behind me whisper, "Ogden, Utah!" I blurted out, "Ogden, Utah!"

She let go of my hair, and snapped my head back and said, "Why didn't you say that in the first place?"

Before I could answer she went on with the rest of her questions and I finished with no further trouble! I was eternally grateful to that kid who sat behind me!

I never did have any more trouble with Miss Shaw. Maybe she realized that I was just a dumb kid from Jackson Hole and really didn't know any better! She would have been right! I got along well in school and Miss Shaw promoted me to the Fourth Grade after New Years. She said I was way ahead of the kids in both Third Grade A and B! I went into the Fifth Grade at home in Wilson the next fall, of 1912, under Jesse K. Dayton!

Well, that's enough about the school and politics. My problem now was with my half-sister Fanny and her daughter Alta! Alta seemed to enjoy telling lies about George and me to her mother just to see us get whipped!

Fanny had married an old man named John Preston, who was at least twenty years older than Fanny. He was a fine machinist. He worked at the round house for the Union Pacific Railroad and made good money. Maybe that's why she married him. "Uncle John," as George and I called him, was a nice and kind old gentleman, and was very good to me and George, and I often heard him trying to admonish my sister Fanny. He would say, in his slow kind drawl, "Fanny, honey, don't be so hard on the boys! They are only boys and they are both very good boys! And they are your brothers!"

Fanny would always retort, "Well, that is easy for you to say! but you are not around here with them all the time like I am! The things they do to Alta that she tells me, you wouldn't believe!"

"I am sure I wouldn't!" Uncle John would say very dryly and drop the subject. Fanny was whipping one or the other or both of us all the time! I was a big, strong kid ten years old, and when the razor strap of Uncle John's, that she used on us, got to hurting too much, I would grab her hands and stop her beating on me. She finally got discouraged whipping me, but she really worked my little six-year-old brother over so I was very sorry for the little cuss! I would like to add right here what George thinks about the awful whippings she gave him, but will suffice in agreeing with him that among other things "she was the Devil's Grandmother! And is probably with him now, and showing him how he ought to run hell!"

I will not go into any more details about my half-sister Fanny, only a couple more instances I must tell! It wasn't long after Nick had left George and me at Fanny's until this first big circus came to town! The parade was over a mile long down Washington Avenue past Fanny's house! There was everything from big elephants to beautiful horses and all kinds of animals, tigers and bears and monkeys in cages, drawn by the most beautiful horses I ever saw! George and I couldn't wait to go to the circus, but when it started, Fanny left George and me home with Uncle John Preston, and took Alta and went to the circus! I pleaded and begged for her to take us to the circus but she said she could not afford it, and didn't have enough money.

"But, I heard Daddy say he left money for you to take us to a circus and a show."

"Well, you heard wrong! You have too big of ears anyway! But I will let you go to a show!" and they walked out and left us. I could tell that Uncle John was boiling inside, but he didn't say a word.

Two more circus' came to town. First the 101 Ranch Circus, and Fanny wouldn't take us to that either, then there was a moving picture show up town called *Jack and the Bean Stalk*. Fanny did let Alta take me and George to that! It was the first real moving picture that George and I had ever seen, except Steve Leek's movies of elk and other animals and one he took of the Jackson Hole Frontier Rodeo, which was one of the greatest shows on earth! Fanny gave Alta fifty cents to pay for the three of us for show tickets and we had twenty cents left over to buy popcorn. Oh! how I loved that picture and I can still see that big giant singing, "Ho! Ho! Ho! I can smell the blood of an Englishman!" And how we three hid behind our theatre seats when he came a tumblin' down after Jack cut the big beanstalk!

Well, Nick came to see us only once that winter, and it was just before the great Ringling Brothers Circus came to town. He stayed and took us all, including Fanny and Uncle John, to the circus and Oh! how I loved that show! Three rings going all the time! I never had so much fun in my life! Fanny warned me and George not to tell Nick that she didn't let us see Barnum and Bailey or the 101

Ranch Circus, or she would whale the daylights out of us! Our dad stayed several days and we really held on to him while he was there! Fanny was sweet as pie to us! The night before Nick left to go back to Salt Lake he took Alta, George and me to a good moving picture called "Black Beauty" about a wonderful black mare! We kids all did a lot of crying at how mean some of those wicked men treated Black Beauty, but I have often thought since that this beautiful horse had things a lot better than George and I did that winter!

When Nick went back to Salt Lake he found he had lost his wallet with several hundred dollars, every cent he owned, at the movie theatre! Fanny went down there to look for it. None of us ever expected to see that wallet again! But fortunately there were still honest people in this world. The manager said a wallet had been found when the theatre was cleaned, but the owner would have to come and positively identify it before they would give it up! Fanny called Nick, and he returned on the Bamburger trolley that ran between Ogden and Salt Lake, which was a very fast electrical train! Nick went to the Theatre Manager and returned with his wallet intact! Believe it or not! I was wrong saying Nick only came to see us once, but that was true, because he came back only to get his lost wallet!

We never saw him again until he came in the spring of 1912 to get George and me to take us home. He came up a day ahead of the Leeks and Wards. Abe and Steve had both gone back to Jackson Hole long ago. The rest of us left after our schools were out. We met the rest when the train stopped at Ogden the next day and our dear sister Fanny made a big deal out of kissing George and me good-bye!

When Abe and Steve met us at St. Anthony, it was late in May, but there was still lots of snow over Teton Pass from Victor on over to Wilson. We had to change from wagon to sleds about three miles east of Victor, and Oh, how beautiful Jackson Hole looked to me!

There is one more incident that happened in the fall of 1911 soon after we got to Ogden, that I meant to mention, and that was the visit of President William Howard Taft to Ogden! School was let out that afternoon when the presidential train stopped and President Taft stood on the platform at the end of the train and delivered his campaign speech! He was running for a second term in 1912, against Woodrow Wilson, a Democrat. Fanny got George, Alta and me up very close to the train where we could hear every word he said! I can't remember a bit of that speech now, but Taft lost the election to Wilson, who was our World War One, Great-President!

Howard Taft was the first and only United States President I ever saw in the flesh and heard his voice! Of course, we have all seen and heard many presidents since Taft on television, but I still cherish that memory of President Taft in Ogden, Utah! And not Ogden, Wyoming! I learned that lesson well!

LEEK   Peter Nelson expanded the Hotel Jackson in 1905. The timber on Snow King Mountain (background) had been consumed by fire.

The Jackson Clubhouse and this old Hotel were the center of attraction in the town of Jackson. Henry and Rose Crabtree built a frame hotel, cater-counter to the Jackson Hotel across the town square, and gave it strong competition for many years. The Jackson Hotel was one of the first real nice buildings in Jackson Hole. It was built of brick made in Jackson Hole. Building in left background was the old Jackson State Bank. Bobbie Miller was its founder. Tom and Dolly Estes ran the old brick Hotel for many years.

(Below) Jackson Hole Frontier Days Rodeo Celebration Parade, entering arena in front of Grandstand (lower left corner). These parades used to enter the rodeo grounds on a dead run, but after several horses fell and riders were run over, this custom was abolished.

(Above) Exchange of horses in a relay race at Jackson Hole Frontier Days Celebration, 1910. Charley Wort, coming in on left side of photo. Myron Seaton dismounting for change of horse. This relay race each year between Wort and Seaton was one of the most hotly contested events in the whole celebration!

A mean one at Jackson Hole Frontier Days about 1910. Broncs were saddled out in the open and then ridden to a finish in "them good ol' days!"

Jackson Hole Frontier Days, 1910. Walt Spicer on "Indian Killer." In rodeos nowdays, if a rider can stick on for 10 seconds without "pulling leather," he qualifies. In these early rodeos the rider had to stick to the finish, whether it was 10 seconds or 10 minutes!

CHAPTER 22 — **Wilderness Acres**

Some of Nick's old bachelor friends in Jackson Hole were real characters. One of the more colorful was John Locky Dodge. He was one of the original heirs of the famous Dodge Automobile Manufacturers and the old Dodge cars were among the finest in the world.

John was a graduate of Harvard University and earned a PhD. He majored in the practice of law. John was an outstanding student until he was hurt in gymnastics. He liked to box and during one of these bouts he was struck a hard blow on the head, and was unconscious for several days. The result left Dodge with some brain damage. It wasn't apparent at first that anything was wrong with him, until he hung up his shingle and started his own law practice.

Everyone, including John Dodge, was very shocked, when during one of his first cases, while presenting his argument in court, he blanked out! He couldn't remember what he had been saying. At first it was thought that John was just exhausted and tired from overwork, but after reasonable rest and he again began his practice, the same thing happened and doctors realized that John really was suffering from brain damage. John discovered that when he kept a good prompter who was alert enough to just restore the train of thought, that John could continue with his case. It was apparent that he could continue with his practice, but only with a constant and alert prompter. These blackouts were very startling, and it took a real sharp and alert prompter to restore quickly, the right word to snap John out of it. But as time went on his parents realized that John was getting worse with these lapses of memory, and finally their doctor suggested that John be given a long period of absence, clear away from his law practice, like perhaps an extended trip out west, away from it all, and see if that might help.

John Dodge had always been very interested in the west and the lure and lore of the west really appealed to him. And so it was arranged for John to receive a liberal allowance, enough that he could live well and have all the money he needed, but not enough to do anything too dramatic, and that word "dramatic" is the right word to describe John Locky Wood Tick Dodge!

I don't know how it ever happened, but John wound up in Jackson Hole along with the first settlers and he fell in love with this wonderful and beautiful valley, just like Nick Wilson did! John Dodge filed on six hundred forty acres of the most rocky, washed-out, worthless land along the bank of Snake River, about five miles northeast of the town of Wilson, and under the west shadow of Gros Ventre Butte, which I have already mentioned. It stands about the center of the valley on the east side of Snake River. In fact, Snake River flows against this Butte, which forms the east bank for about a half mile.

I believe this six hundred forty acres was the most worthless, hopeless section of land along that noble stream's thousand miles of rugged shore! But John Dodge loved it! It was his passion! It was his dream! It was his everything! And John Dodge was one of the Lord's richest blessings that he ever sent into Jackson Hole! And John was also one of its staunchest atheists. He was a devout follower and disciple of Robert Ingersoll, I guess, who was probably the world's best known atheist and left lots of literature that is known as *The Works of Robert Ingersoll*. John had reached a point in higher education that believes only fools and fanatics could believe in a living God! But even Robert Ingersoll himself, said at his brother's funeral, which Ingersoll conducted: "It is all poppy-cock to believe that there is life after death!" Then after a moment of silence he continued, "But love listening, can hear the rustle of a wing!"

The blessing that Dodge brought into Jackson Hole was the fact, that but for him, it is doubtful that many a poor family could have ever survived the rigors of frontier life, and would have faced certain starvation, but John gave work to those who needed it, or anyone who wanted to work, building the ramshackle of log buildings, and the attempt to make this land produce hay and grain, which was John's dream, a dream that never came true.

About every kid on the Wilson side of Snake River worked at one time or another for John Dodge, as did these poor people I have mentioned.

And so the summer of 1912 it became my nephew, Ira Ward, and my turn to work for John Dodge. We were eleven years old that fall. I turned eleven on the 12th of October, Columbus Day, 1912 and Ira with his twin, Irene, on election day, November 2nd, 1912.

The story that follows is a tribute to the memory of a great man, John Locky "Wood Tick" Dodge! And as our closest neighbor, Gus Nicholation, a fat Dutchman, would say, "an' dats di trute!" The story follows:

There were seven eggs left in the paper sack on the shelf. We had three cups of flour, a little baking powder, salt, a cup of sugar, and a small piece of dried bacon. There were three of us. We decided to fry two eggs apiece in the bacon grease, make water-sugar syrup, and use the seventh egg in the hotcake dough. After breakfast John L. would hitch up the mules, Hobo and Bobo, and go to town for more grub.

Monk and I knew we wouldn't eat again until John L. got back, so we were very careful in preparing this meal — to see that we didn't waste, burn or spill a thing!

Monk sliced the bacon and started it frying while I carefully browned the sugar and added just the right amount of water. John mixed the hotcakes and hummed his favorite song. It didn't have any particular tune: "She could play on the pee-an-a, my leet-tle act-ter-ass!"

Everything was going fine. The delicious vapor of the scorched sugar-syrup mingled with the tantalizing aroma of frying bacon. John finished mixing the hotcakes as he bawled the last bars of his beloved song: "She never knewww my love was trooo, my leet-tle act-ter-ass!"

He had to wait for Monk to finish frying the bacon and eggs so he could have the pan for the hotcakes. The syrup came to a boil and I pushed it back to cool. Suddenly, we were all startled by a loud squeeking in the corner of the cabin. Two mice brust into sight and came tearing along the top log of the wall. The lead mouse — guess it was a she — was being rapidly overtaken by her pursuer. To save her honor — just as she was right over our precious hotcake dough — she sailed out into space and plunked dab smack in the middle of the batter! The horrible little monster that was chasing her put on his brakes, but it was too late. He, too, skidded out into thin air and kerplunked into the soft dough and they both sank out of sight!

We were all so horrified that we just stood there with our mouths open and watched the bubbles come to the top and burst. Then up came a white lump, swimming frantically! It slid over the edge of the bowl and onto the table. It was followed by another lump of dough. They both shook, then rolled off onto the floor, kersplat!

One hunk of dough crawled through a crack in the floor and the other waddled out of sight behind the woodbox. Their ardor semed to have cooled somewhat.

The spell was broken. I looked at Monk and he looked at me and we both looked at John. The last notes of his song were still on his lips. His face lit up with a terrific smile. "Boys, did you see that? They were white when they hit the table, white when they hit the floor! I declare, I do believe they took with them all they touched!" And he began to stir the hotcake dough. I still remember those hotcakes as the best I've ever eaten.

Monk and I were about ten years old and we had been working for John L. about a week when the above episode took place. Our wages were ten cents a day and keep.

John Lockwood Dodge was one of the early settlers in Jackson's Hole and one of its most picturesque characters. He had taken up a homestead of six hundred forty acres in the river bottom area of the Snake River. This particular piece of land was, and perhaps still is, one of the rockiest, washed out, worthless 640 acres along all that noble stream's thousand miles of rugged shore. He called it "Wilderness Acres," and this was proclaimed by burned-in letters on an old, weather-beaten slab that hung from the cross-log over a big rickety pole gate near his cabin.

One of Dodge's most picturesque habits was his custom of taking an early morning cold bath. Fish Creek flowed past the hotel just across the road in front of our cabin in the town of Wilson. Even in late fall when mush-ice floated on the water, I was sometimes awakened by loud singing and, looking out the window, would see Dodge hang a towel on a willow bush and wade out to the middle of the stream. He'd have a big bar of laundry soap in one hand and a big white pottery pitcher in the other. He would fill the pitcher full of ice water and pour it on his head and, as the icy water streamed over him, rub himself down and sing at the top of his lungs: "I loved her so, and she didn't knowww, my leet-tle act-ter-ass!" It was this bathing habit that finally brought disaster down upon us.

Our next big excitement came soon after John got back from town with the load of grub. He believed in doing things in a big way and, since his allowance which he received regularly from his sister in the east was at the post office, he really went overboard. Everybody knew that Dodge had a sister named Carry who was administrator of the Dodge estate. A trust fund had been set up whereby John received an allowance about four times a year. I never knew how much he got in each payment, but it was a handsome amount for those days.

To this fact, and also because Dodge was generous to a fault, many a poor Jackson's Hole family owed their survival, because John always had some kind of work for them to do and he paid them well.

Anyway, John brought back a big load of supplies, which he bought in bulk. Eggs by the crate, one hundred pounds of cereal, five hundred pounds of flour, two hundred pounds of sugar, three or four sacks of potatoes, lard in ten pound buckets, several slabs of bacon, five gallons of honey, two casks of old-fashioned Karo syrup, a half-dozen twenty five pound bags of dried fruit and case after case of canned goods.

We were fixed for the summer, so we thought, and for several days all we did was cook, eat, and wash dishes. Monk and I would do the dishes while John played mournful and melancholy music on his old, black flute. He played nothing but long-haired classical pieces that would make a man fight the mother of his own children in the dead hours of the night!

When we first came to work for Dodge we had brought Monk's old dog, Towser, with us, but when John L. began playing his flute, old Towser howled and yelped until he got so hoarse he finally couldn't stand it any longer and went home. John was awfully disappointed. He said old Towser was the only creature west of the Mississippi that had ever seemed to really appreciate good cultured music. He said that all westerners were a bunch of damned hill-billies!

After a few days we finally got our fill of feasting and John decided it was time to get back to work. While we were hitching up old Hobo and Bobo we heard a terrifying racket down the road. It sounded worse than a four-horse team running away with a threshing machine!

Then, to our amazement, a big, long, white horseless carriage pulled up to the old wooden gate. It stopped and a blast of steam nearly tore the "Wilderness Acres" sign from its moorings. The old mules took off without waiting for a driver and we were so spellbound by the steaming monster at the gate that we didn't even notice which way they went.

It was the first automobile that Monk and I had ever seen and, as Monk said later, "We didn't know whether to run or go blind!" Only that isn't exactly what he said.

Dodge heard the commotion above the wailing of his old flute and went to the door and looked out. "My Gawd, it's Carry!" Then he added in calmer tones, "Well, it's too late to run now. I always knew she'd come some day, so it might as well be now."

We watched a man climb out who was dressed as no man we had ever seen before, or have seen since. He had on a big black cap with a heavy leather visor and his face was half covered with a huge pair of dark-colored goggles. He wore a brown and white plaid wool Jacket, and gauntlet gloves with cuffs that reached up to his elbows. The jacket was open, exposing a bright pink shirt, and he had on a pair of yellow britches with wide, puffed legs down to the knee, where they tapered down into a pair of heavy brown puttees made of bull hide and the shiniest pair of polished black shoes I ever saw.

There was a woman with him all right, but she was so wrapped up in mufflers and shawls, plus a hat bigger than an umbrella tied on her head with a bright blue scarf, that it was about five minutes before she got unwrapped enough so we could see her features. She turned out to be a big buxom blond. She crawled out and looked around at the dirt-roofed house and ramshackle out-buildings and, in a high-pitched voice, exclaimed, "Lookwood, for heaven's sake, don't tell me that this is your wonderful mansion in the wilderness!"

I can't begin to remember all that was said during the short time she stayed. Monk and I were too excited looking, from a safe distance, at the wonderful contraption that moved without horses. But I did gather that Carry was far from pleased with what she found. But John L. stood firm and finally told her, "Sister Carry, I'm sorry that you don't like this spread, but I do! I don't have any chauffeurs, maids or valets, but you're welcome to what accommodations I do have!"

Carry said, "No, Lockwood, I will stay in the village. It doesn't look much better than this, but I will have better company than mules!"

Just then old Hobo and Bobo poked their ugly heads around the barn. They had lost interest in their runaway and had slipped up behind the barn to see what was going on.

Carry calmed down then and spoke in a pleading voice. "I will stay for a few days and try to talk some sense into your stubborn head! I want you to come home with me. Can't you see that you are just throwing your life away out here? For heaven's sake, Lockwood, what do you see in the God-forsaken place?"

John took her by the arm and turned her around so she faced the Tetons and with a sweep of his arm pointed to the full view of the Teton Range. "I can see the most beautiful mountains in the world, trees, blue skies, clear water and a valley full of green grass and clean, sweet air. Ye Gods, Carry, what more does a man want when he has all that?"

It was an impressive view. I had never noticed it that way before. I guess I had just always taken this beauty for granted and hadn't realized the grandeur of it all. Even now I felt a pleasant and strange sort of thrill.

Carry didn't say anything for a long time. Then she said, "James, is the car ready?"

James had been fiddling with the monster all the time John and Carry had been talking and he had finally gotten the Old Faithful-like spouts of steam quieted down so they weren't going quite as high as the tops of the cottonwood trees and he answered, "Yes, ma'am!"

Well, Carry wound up by staying in the valley nearly all summer. Everybody in the country got real fond of her for, like John, she had a heart as big as a ham and when she wasn't out at Wilderness Acres she was helping some poor family with both money and her own two kindly hands. In fact, one of my sisters who had a baby that summer named her Carry.

John L. had about two hundred acres on an island densely covered with brush and tall cottonwood trees. The Snake River bordered on one side a slough and the spring that headed near the buildings were on the other. Because of this side channel, which overflowed into the spring and filled it with muddy water during high water time, John dug a well — with the help of about every kid in the country. This well was about twenty feet from the cabin door. It was about six feet square and about twelve feet deep and held about three-and-a-half feet of water. It was curbed by a three-foot board wall above the ground. An old oaken bucket was suspended from a pully in the center of the cross-log which was supported by two, six-foot curb posts. Just beyond the well flowed the little spring creek which was spanned by a foot bridge. The bridge led to a little rustic privy — the only thing on the place built from sawed lumber. It was Dodge's pride and joy!

John thought land that could produce as much brush as his should be top farm land, so we began clearing it with axes and grubbing hoes. When, after four or five days, we had made little impression on the jungle of brush, John decided there must be an easier and faster way. So he had us pile the brush we had cut and set it afire. Boy, what a fire! By two o'clock the whole valley was black with smoke!

Nearly everyone in the country who could travel came to see what was going on. They came by wagon, horseback and afoot. Dozens of men started back fires to keep the fire from jumping the little spring creek and burning all of Dodge's buildings and to keep it from the mainland and burning all of the rest of the country as well.

After the men got it all back-fired about half of them stayed all night and the next day when they left the grub supply that we thought would last all summer was wrecked. What they hadn't eaten they had stolen, and taken with them. About all that was left was a case of rotten eggs, five pounds of rancid butter, a little flour and a couple of teaspoons of coffee.

"My God," Dodge exclaimed, "the way these natives can eat is fantastic!" And so we were back in the same fix that we'd been in a short time before.

It was a pretty sickly breakfast we dug up the morning after the firefighters left. It consisted of a few soggy hotcakes. The butter was so strong it could have walked over and said good morning to the coffee and the coffee was so weak it couldn't have answered.

All the eggs left were rotten and John sent Monk out to get rid of them and when he didn't come back as soon as he should have John went out and found Monk throwing the rotten eggs, one at a time, at the little rustic privy.

To say that Dodge had a fit would be putting it mildly! He ranted and pulled his hair and stomped his old black hat in the ground. Finally, in a hushed voice, he told Monk to get busy and clean it up. Then he roared: "And I want it smelling like a cologne bottle when you get through!! And not like something that has been brewed in hell!" Monk was pretty scared and so was I. I offered to help but John said I could go to town with him for more grub. He said everyone had to pay for his sins sooner or later and that the sooner Monk found it out the better off he'd be.

Whenever anything went wrong, John always philosophized. "It wasn't half as bad as it might have been." But of this incident he simply said, "Ye Gods, that smell is twice as bad as anything could possibly be!"

We stopped at the Cheneys, our nearest neighbors, on our way to town and Dodge knocked at the door. Mrs. Cheney's unmarried sister, Amanda, answered it. Dodge had a habit of slipping up behind any young girl he could and giving her a big kiss, which made them furious. Amanda was no exception and when she saw who it was at the door she slammed it in his face and then peeked out a small crack to see what he wanted.

"I came to see Edith about some butter," John said, smiling from ear to ear.

"She just took all the butter to the store in town. Get some there," Amanda snapped.

"Oh, I don't want any more. What I got here the last time is so strong we can't eat it," Dodge said.

Amanda opened the door a little then and flared, "When did you get it?"

"About three weeks ago."

"Have you kept it hanging in the well?"

"No."

"Well, for Pete's sake, what do you expect in this kind of weather?"

"Well, I was just wondering what to do with it."

"Eat all of it you can and rub the rest in your hair," Amanda said, with disgust, and again slammed the door in his face!

Dodge got back in the wagon and clucked loudly at the mules. He shook his head and murmured, "Women! What's to do? Marry one and make her miserable or stay single and make 'em all miserable?" And so we drove on to town.

While John was at the store and stopping at the hotel to eat dinner and see Carry, I went home. My father and little brother were happy to see me.

"Well," my dad said, "you didn't last long on that job! But we're glad to have you home again. We've been expecting to see Dodge haul in your carcass before now!"

I told him I had only come in town to help Dodge get another load of grub and that we were going right back to his ranch.

"Gee whiz," my brother said, "you guys ain't et all that grub Dodge got the other day have you? He had so much that old Bobo balked and Sheriff Beckley had to hook his lariat rope on the tongue and drag old Hobo and Bobo across the creek before they would go!"

My dad laughed and said, "I reckon that mob they said was up there fighting fire, made short work out of the load of grub, huh?"

Dodge came for me then and Monk's mother saw him and me at our house and she came running.

"Where's my boy? Has something happened to him?"

"He's all right ma'am," Dodge said, "He stayed home to attend to a little job that was kind of pressing at the time."

She looked up at me and demanded, "Why didn't you stay and help him?"

"Aw," I defended myself, "I didn't throw any of them rotten eggs at Dodge's backhouse!"

"I do declare," she stammered, "I do declare!" And gathering up her long skirts she ran for home to tell Abram, her lesser half.

We could hear my dad and little brother laughing as we drove away. You see, Monk's mother was also one of my sisters.

Everything went pretty good for awhile. We started clearing the burned logs and stumps from the island, but old Bobo balked and refused to help in any way. So we had to do all the dragging with Hobo while Bobo just hung around and watched. Dodge would scold him, then talk baby talk to Hobo and feed him lumps of sugar.

One morning when we went to work Bobo didn't follow us as he usually did but stayed in the shade of the house and watched us tread off to work, leading Hobo who was dragging a single-tree and chain. It was an awfully hot day, even for August.

When we came in for lunch we found that Bobo had pushed the door open and was in the house. What a mess! He had torn open sacks of flour, cereal, sugar and dried apples and had gorged himself until he was swollen up so big we couldn't get him out the door!

Dodge was sure giving him a tongue-lashing when the old mule was gripped by colic. He broke out in a green sweat and started kicking his belly with both hind feet and finished wrecking everything in the room. Finally he collapsed in front of the fireplace and died.

Dodge was frantic! I never saw a man carry on like he did! All night he sobbed and coaxed and talked baby talk to his beloved Bobo. But it was no use. The old mule had crossed to the Happy Hunting Grounds.

The next morning, Monk and I were awakened by the low, mournful wailing of Dodge's flute, playing taps! Peeking in, we saw John sitting in his old, broken overstuffed chair. His long hair was disheveled and his bloodshot eyes looked like burnt holes in a saddle blanket. I slipped in and cleared my throat a couple of times but he didn't pay me the least attention. So, I got some matches, a frying pan and a couple dozen eggs and Monk and I slipped out around the house and started a sagebrush fire and scrambled eggs for breakfast.

About noon Dodge hunted us up. "Boys, I don't know how we are going to do it, but we must get Bobo out of the house!"

We went over and looked in. Bobo was already swollen up higher than the top of the fireplace opening and all four feet were sticking straight up in the air. A billion flies, more or less, had collected and above the roar of their wings Monk yelled at me, while holding his nose, "Old Bobo don't smell so good himself!"

We could see that it was hopeless to try to get Bobo out through the door. We couldn't get him out when he was alive and now he was swollen up more than twice the size he was then.

There was a double window in one end of the room opposite the fireplace and John finally decided that we could take out the windows and saw the wall down to the floor. It took us all afternoon to do this and by dark we were all so sick of the smell and flies that we moved our beds out to the barn and turned in without any supper.

The next morning we ate scrambled eggs again, cooked over a sagebrush fire, upwind from the cabin. John was gaunt and haggard, but he ate with us and quoted from Robert Ingersoll's works. He wound up by saying that it was all poppycock about men meeting again beyond the grave but, although we would never see old Bobo again, nevertheless, "Love, listening, could hear the rustle of a wing."

Monk whispered to me, "Maybe we won't see him again, but I bet we smell him for a long time!"

Well, we got busy then and Dodge thought that Hobo, with our help, could drag Bobo out of the house. But he couldn't stand the thought of dragging him by the neck, so he had us fasten the chain to Bobo's hind feet.

Dodge said for us to blindfold Hobo and bring him around the house to the opening we'd cut and hitch him on. He said he didn't want Hobo to see his old friend because it might break his heart. Although Hobo couldn't see what was going on he sure suspected something! He was trembling all over and snorting like a six-shooter.

Now that we were all ready John said he would lead Hobo and told Monk and me to pull on the chain. But Hobo wouldn't tighten a tug with the blindfold on.

Finally John said he didn't think Hobo would be able to see back around his bridle blinders anyway and he would try to keep him pulling and not let him look back. So he yanked off the blindfold and old Hobo lunged. One tug busted and the other spun Dodge around and knocked him down. Hobo turned and looked straight into the swollen hind end of his old friend. His eyes bulged! He squealed! Then he backed out of the harness and headed for the barn. And we hadn't moved old Bobo an inch!

We couldn't get Hobo near the house again, with or without a blindfold.

There was nothing left to do but to get our closest neighbor, Sylvester Cheney, to come and help us and so, riding old Hobo, I went down and got Sylvester. Cheneys had a big fine team of blazed-faced sorrel horses, the envy of every farmer in the valley.

Sylvester hooked them up and I rode back with him in the wagon and tied old Hobo on the back.

As we neared Dodge's house, Hobo began to snort and waltz from one side of the wagon to the other. Then he braced his feet, broke the halter rope, and skedaddled for the barn. The sorrels got a whiff of Bobo about then too and began to prance and rear. Sylvester pulled them over to the corral fence, tied them up and went over to the house to size things up.

When he looked in and saw Bobo I saw the crowsfeet at the corners of his eyes wrinkle up and I thought he was going to laugh, but instead, his eyes opened wide and all he said was "Gol-lee!" Only that ain't what he really said!

We hadn't seen John or Monk since we'd arrived, but then, above the drone of the flies, we heard a wailing. It was coming from the little rustic privy across the creek where John was playing his flute. Then we heard a louder wailing. It was coming from the well! We rushed over and looked in. There was Monk, standing in water up to his neck, squalling and screaming like sixty, "Get me out of here!"

Dodge had seen us. He came across the footbridge, hoisting his suspenders with one hand and waving his flute with the other.

"What's going on here?" Sylvester demanded. "What's that kid doing in the well? Why ain't you getting him out?"

"Take it easy," John said. "He got himself down there. A little while ago I came around the house and there was that little monster standing up on the well and what he was doing was worse than the time the Goodrick kid spit in my sourdough! I yelled at him and he lost his balance and fell in. When I saw he was able to stand with his head above water, I knew he was all right and decided to let him stew in his own brew!"

Monk was still yelling for someone to get him out. Sylvester told him to shut up. We ought to leave you down there," he said. We soon hauled Monk out, though, and he was a pretty well chastized boy.

Now came the smelly business of getting old Bobo's carcass out of the house. Sylvester put the chain around his neck despite John's protests. "Any damn fool knows you can't pull a mule by his feet!" he said. "His hooves are so small the chain would slip right off!" Then he got his team and double-trees from the wagon and, after about six fast laps around the house with the spooky team, he finally got them stopped close enough to the cut out window and fastened the chain to the double-tree.

It took no urging to get them to pull Bobo out. As Bobo sped through the opening one of his stiff legs caught on the wall logs and the corner of the house squeaked. The sorrels bolted! Sylvester fell over some sagebrush and rolled out of the way barely in time as Bobo whistled past!

During the next two or three minutes the old dead carcass got up more speed than it had ever known in all its long span of life! John jumped up and down and cried, "Oh, my little Bobo! My poor Bobo! Come back with my little Bobo!"

As if answering his pleas the big team circled and old Bobo's carcass mowed a big swath in the sagebrush! The big sorrels raced back around the house and came tearing straight at us! We jumped into the house just as the terrified team shot past. Old Bobo's hide was fairly smoking! The team made another circle. This time they straddled the well and the curb folded like a match box! Old Bobo slid into the well with a splash!

The impact spun the team around and Sylvester grabbed them before they could take off again. The rest of us rushed to the well. Old Bobo was deflating like a punctured balloon. As we watched the bubbles come up, the old mule sank to his last resting place.

We buried him there. There was nothing else to do. Between Monk and old Bobo the well was forever contaminated anyway. For the next two weeks all Monk and I did was haul rocks and dirt to fill the well.

To this day there are two sounds I can hear plainly when I close my eyes and listen. One is the singing of frogs, to whose music I have dropped off to sleep on many a spring night during my childhood. The other? The mournful wailing of an old black flute playing a funeral dirge for an old brown mule, as he sleeps forever, twelve feet under, along with the old oaken bucket that hung on the well.

By this time the days were getting cool, the nights real chilly. We had moved back into the house but hadn't logged the wall up and the window was still out. We started building a fire in the fireplace mornings and evenings. We would hitch up Hobo and drag a tree up to the opening in the house and then the three of us would push it, big end first, through the opening, through the house and into the fireplace. As it burned off we'd keep pushing it in until it was all burned up.

This worked fine while we were working around the house and could watch it. But the first day we left, to fix a fence in the upper pasture, we saw smoke billowing up from the house.

Dodge jumped on Hobo and took off, yelling for us to follow as fast as we could. But the single-tree hit old Hobo on the heels and he began to buck. Dodge went sailing out through the sagebrush and the fall knocked the wind out of him. Hobo stopped pitching, his big ears stood straight up, and a haughty look of disdain gleamed from his shrewd old eyes. I unhooked the single-tree and we boosted the gasping rider back on. But Hobo came uncorked again and throwed Dodge so high that, as Monk said afterwards, "the birds built a nest in his hind pocket before he hit the ground!" Only that ain't exactly where he said they built the nest.

With the single-tree no longer banging at his heels, Hobo high-tailed it for his beloved barn — his refuge in times of strife, trouble or flies! Monk and I didn't wait for John to unscramble himself from a clump of wild rose bushes; but we raced for the house.

The door between the two rooms happened to be shut, so the flames were still confined to the kitchen. Practically all the food was still in the bedroom, where we had moved it while old Bobo was dead in the other room. Luckily we hadn't moved it back yet. I climbed in the window and began to pitch stuff out to Monk — food, bedding, clothes. Dodge arrived and yelled for me to throw out his flute and music. I threw out the flute and about ten bushels of cultured music! We saved nearly everything in the room before the flames and smoke started coming in under the door and I had to get out!

Nero didn't have a thing on Dodge! John calmly set up his music rack by an old cottonwood stump, out of range of the heat and smoke, and sat down on the stump and played long-haired music while the old cabin burned to the ground.

Hobo cowered in the barn, his long, sad, yellow face and big ears protruding from the dark interior as he listened to the familiar, mournful music and fearfully watched the roaring blaze.

When it was all over Dodge got up, put his flute in the case and said, "Boys, it wasn't half as bad as it might have been. I could have lost my flute!"

Dodge examined our jumbled pile of salvage. Then he looked up and saw Hobo's inquisitive face peeking out of the barn. A big smile brightened his face and in a honeyed tone he called, "Ah, Hobo, baby, move over because you're going to have company from now on, you rascal, you!" And we moved to the barn.

But things were coming to a head. A few mornings later — just a few days before Monk and I had to quit and go back to school — the curtain fell! I was awakened by Dodge calling, "Boys, oh boys!" I got up and went outside. The sun was just hitting the tops of the Tetons, making them all pink and red. A heavy frost was on the ground. John was standing in the middle of the little creek, pouring water over his head with a frying pan. He had a big bar of white soap in the other hand. His clothes and a towel were hanging on a small bush near the little rustic privy.

"What do you want?"

"Bring me a box of matches."

I slipped on my overalls and shoes and took him the matches, wondering what kind of crazy stunt he was up to now. I soon found out.

"I might as well be doing two things at once," Dodge said, when I handed him the matches. "It just occured to me that I should burn out this dry grass and brush along the creek and, while I'm washing, I can watch it. There's such a mass of dry brush and grass around here every spring."

When we had the big fire in the summer it had burned everything but this nook of about two or three acres where the house, barn and privy stood. Only by backfiring had this area, and the buildings, been saved that time.

As I went back to bed John was tossing matches in the dry grass along the creek bank. I could hear his voice raised in happy song: "She could play on the pee-ana, my little act-ter-ass!"

I dropped off to sleep immediately as only the innocent or old can do. The next thing I knew Monk was shaking me and screaming, "Wake up! We're burning to death!"

I jumped up. The barn was full of smoke. Above the roar of flames I could hear Dodge yelling, "Boys! Boys! for God's sake, get out of there!"

Monk and I gasped for air. I was nearly blinded by smoke, but I grabbed my trousers and one shoe and staggered out to where Monk stood gasping and holding his shirt and one shoe. The shoes were old and worn out and both for the same foot.

Smoke was billowing out of the barn and the roof was all ablaze! Dodge was still yelling and, as we ran around the fire, we could see him running up and down the creek, his body black as a crow's, fighting fire with the half burned towel, trying desperately to get to the barn where he thought we were trapped.

He saw us then and ran back to where we stood on the bank and collapsed, half in the water and half on the bank, among the now dead and blackened grass. He revived immediately and sitting up gasped, "Thank heavens you're safe. I thought sure you were trapped in the barn!"

"Are you all right?" I asked.

He rolled his bloodshot eyes. His hair and eyebrows were burned off but he had kept his body wet and so outside of the fact that his hands were blistered he seemed to be okay.

Everything was gone now. The barn was still an inferno and the privy was a heap of glowing coals.

"What happened?" I asked.

John wrung out what was left of the towel and sat down on it on the bank.

"Evidently I lit too much area at once. It would have been all right only a sharp breeze came up from the east and before I realized it the privy was afire. And my clothes. I managed to reach the towel and tried to save the privy and then I saw flames climbing the barn and remembered you kids! My God, I've had enough fires to last me the rest of my life!"

The barn fell then with a crash. The land around, where the grass and brush had been, was blackened.

"Everybody in the country will be here soon," Monk said.

Dodge jumped up and looked at the pile of burned rags that had been his clothes. He tied what was left of the ragged, black towel around him. "Let them come!" he said.

Monk stood there in his short-tailed shirt with no pants, holding two shoes for the same foot. I had on a pair of ragged overalls. I looked at Monk and began to laugh. His lips were quivering, but then he started to laugh too and finally John joined in and we laughed until we cried!

"It ain't half as bad as it could have been," Dodge said. "I've lost everything, even my flute! But I could have lost you two rascals!" And he gave us a big hug.

"Nobody in Jackson's Hole gets out of bed early enough to know what goes on before sunup," Dodge said. "No one will notice this little fire, so it's up to us to save ourselves. Since Charley is the only one in the bunch who owns a pair of pants, I appoint him, without benefit of vote or ballot, or any other formality to hot foot it down to our friend and neighbor, Sylvester Cheney, for urgent help. Come spring we'll build a bigger and better Wilderness Acres!" He did, too, but that's another story.

Sylvester hitched up the big sorrel team and brought a shirt and a pair of overalls for Dodge, a pair of pants for Monk and a shirt for me.

Later, while digging around in some of the remains of the fire, we found that Dodge was right. Things weren't half as bad as they might have been. Monk found John's big billfold. It was blackened by the fire but inside it the roll of crisp new bills was virtually unharmed.

Sylvester hauled us back to his ranch where we had a good breakfast. Then we went to town and my little brother stood and watched while John outfitted Monk and me with new clothes, including shiny black shoes and warm caps.

We each had nine dollars coming at ten cents a day, but John gave each of us a crisp new ten dollar bill.

Our storekeeper's name was Roy Anderson. Just as we were leaving, his pretty daughter Trilba walked by. John grinned and rubbed his hands together. Then, in the honeyed voice he usually reserved for his mules, he said, "Aha, there goes my leet-tle act-ter-ass!" Trilba turned her pugnose to the sky and in a dry tone retorted, "Well! I'd rather be an actor-ass than a horse's ass!"

WILDERNESS ACRES, Illustration by John Coulter.

CHAPTER 23 — **Raum and Raum (School Days)**

Nick was getting along well, but very slow on his manuscript, but he kept at it and I missed our fishing trips.

One day I was out in the yard and I saw huge black clouds of smoke a couple of miles south of our house. I went in and called Nick and he came out and said, "That's about the old George Brown ranch! Warren Edmonston owns that now. It looks like their house is afire!"

We ran over to the hotel where there was a telephone and in about half an hour it rang and it was Mrs. Schofield. She said Floretta Edmonston was there with her two little girls and the baby was badly burned, she asked for urgent help. Someone soon found Dr. Palmer and Nick went with him in a buggy driven by Ercel Ward.

When my Dad got back that evening he said the baby was dead! Floretta and her oldest daughter Maud and the baby, Melvina, about four months old, were living in the old George Brown cabin, that she and Warney had bought along with the one hundred sixty acre ranch. Warney was working for Schofield cutting saw-timber and he had left early that morning, right after breakfast, to go to work. He left the milking of their three cows to Floretta. Maud was nearly six years old, I think, and her mother left her with the baby while she went to milk the cows, and told Maud she could wash the dishes. Floretta fixed the dish pan with water and left Maud standing on a chair washing the dishes. It took Floretta about forty-five minutes to feed and milk the cows and Maud had finished the dishes and got to playing with the baby, who slept in a little crib.

Warney smoked cigarettes very heavily, and he left a pack of them and a box of matches on a stand near the bed. Maud got to monkeying with these matches and got the crib clothing on fire and ran out screaming for her mother. Floretta saw the smoke and ran as fast as she could into the house and the crib was all in flames! Floretta grabbed the screaming baby up and wrapped a blanket from the bed around her and ran for the Schofield ranch about a half mile away. Maud was a big kid and ran with her mother. I think the baby was dead on their arrival from being so

Maud Edmondson and baby sister, Melvina. Picture taken a few days before their house burned down, killing the baby.

badly burned. Anyway, that's just another tragedy that was incidental to settling Jackson Hole.

Nick Wilson was also on the school board and in 1909 I was in the third grade. We were having a lot of trouble with some of the big boys who were fifteen to eighteen years old and still in the third grade, when I was in it. These big bullies disrupted the school and scared the teachers off, so that none of us were doing very good in school.

The 1909 term started about the 1st of September with a woman teacher named Jesse K. Dayton. These big kids tried to bully her and she was a very plucky young woman, but she just couldn't handle these big boys.

The Raums were living at Wilson then and Billy ran the saloon that he bought from Spencer. Billy was a little man, with one of the biggest black mustaches I ever saw, which made him look real furious and it didn't belie this little man either, because he really was a tough character. He had killed a man with a beer bottle in a saloon he owned, before he came to Jackson Hole and bought this saloon. When he and his family arrived, nobody thought Billy would last very long in the saloon business, because there were some very mean characters that frequented the saloons in Jackson Hole. It was from these saloons in Jackson and Wilson that most of our violence erupted and someone was being shot or beat to death over the drinking and gambling.

Billy had only been there a few weeks when a fight broke out in his saloon, between two bad characters, Dutch Young and John Powell. The fight started over some snide remark that Dutch made regarding John Powell's daughter, Elsie, which wasn't true, and Dutch didn't know that John Powell was her dad. John was a big red-headed Irishman, and one of the meanest fighters I ever knew, when he got to drinking, which was all too often. John floored Dutch and the fight started!

Billy had a sign hanging on the saloon wall in big letters, "No Fighting Will Be Tolerated Inside This Building!" It hung where anyone entering the door could see it the first thing! There was a lot of horse play and fun poked at Billy over this sign, and as stated before, the only thing big you could see about Billy was that big black mustache! But Billy wasn't in business long before everybody found out that Billy also had a big heart, and his size belied his fighting ability! If anyone in the community was sick or needed a helping hand, Billy was the first to their aid, and he didn't just come and ask what he could do, he did it!

In this fight between John Powell and Dutch Young, Billy also proved he meant what that sign said and he backed it up! A saloon fight can get very destructive to property and dangerous to spectators, because usually everybody gets involved.

These two big brutes Dutch and John had only just gotten started fighting and only a couple benches smashed and the leg broken off one card table, when Billy knocked John over the head with a "Black Jack" and settled his hash, the big Dutch Young nailed Billy! But Billy poked his fingers in Dutch's eyes and came up with a big beer bottle, which seemed to be one of Billy's favorite weapons, and he went to work on Dutch Young, and Doc Palmer and my dad had a lot of patching up to do on Dutch and I don't remember ever seeing him in Billy Raum's saloon again! This was the first and last fight in Billy's saloon! However, a few did start through the years, but they didn't get off the ground.

Well, our school marm boarded with Mrs. Raum, who was like I described Lena Woodward, big as all outdoors! Only there was a difference: Mrs. Raum wasn't all blubber and noise like Lena, she was almost six feet tall and dwarfed her husband Billy, and her "fat" was muscle, and she knew how to handle herself!

Miss Dayton was taking it very hard. She was one of the best qualified and best educated teachers that Wilson schools ever had, and she was badly needed. Mrs. Raum had four kids and two were in school with me. Our school house was one big room about fifty feet long and forty feet wide, with two entrance rooms at the front, and a bell house on top over these rooms and a big bell that could be heard for miles, and some of the kids did live three or four miles away. The entrance or cloak rooms were about ten by twenty foot, one for the boys and one for the girls. When it was cold or rainy, we boys used our cloak room to play marbles in. Marbles was a great game when I was a kid. Too bad kids now days can't revive marble games!

The year before Jesse K. Dayton started teaching, the big kids got so mean that the school board decided to hire a strong man teacher, more for his brawn than for his brain, and a man named Charles Driscoll applied for, and got the job.

I was in the second grade that year, 1908-9. This Driscoll was strong alright, but he didn't have much brains and scarcely any education. He soon put the quietus on the big kids and some who were 15 to 18 years old quit school. None of them could read or write and some couldn't even write their own name, but they were big enough to work and for most part their fathers needed more help developing these early homesteads, so put them to work, and for most, that ended their education. I remember one of them that when he grew up was elected Sheriff of our County, which was then Lincoln County, Wyoming, and he couldn't sign his own name, but used a mark. The County had to hire a secretary to handle the books, but he was a good Sheriff and was elected two terms.

Well, this Charles Driscoll had a family of five kids. The eldest was George, then Charles Jr., Marie, about my age which then was seven, Marguret, and a baby called Jim. I didn't like George because he was always stealing my muskrat traps! Driscoll favored his son Charley, who was a year older than I, and had red hair. To distinguish us he would call his son "Charles" and me he called "Wilson." There is nothing wrong with the name Wilson, but I did not like to be called Wilson all the time, and some of the kids started calling me "Wils" and I soon broke that habit, along with a few heads!

Well, Driscoll ran a mighty strict school. In this one room school house was one long bench about 25 feet long, called the "Recitation Bench!" It was placed up in front of all the kids' desks and just in front of an old box heater that burned about four-foot length logs. The teacher's desk was also up in front. There were about forty kids attending that school, from the "Chart Class," which we all called the "short" class, because of the sawed off little kids in it, to the eighth grade. There were a few kids over sixteen years old still in the third grade, when I was in it.

Every class in turn was called up to that long recitation bench and Driscoll would hold the reader book in one hand and a big heavy one-foot ruler in the other. He chewed tobacco and always had a big wad in his cheek. He would stand over the class and spit tobacco juice over our heads onto the hot box heater, which sat in a large box filled with dirt, and the tobacco juice would snap and pop and run down off the old heater into the box and the stink was awful! You couldn't tell whether our eyes were streaming tears from the strong fumes and odor of tobacco or from a whack on the head from this big wooden ruler! Driscoll wasn't bashful who he hit, and you better know your lesson or at least make him believe that you did, or you got the ruler on a different part of your anatomy than your head!

When spring came it was believed that the big kids who had been so unruly were either broke of it or had quit. So the fall of 1909 the school board hired Jesse K. Dayton and we began to learn something. But some of the big bullies got tired of working on their Dad's farms and claimed they would be good students. So their parents let some of them come back, and it wasn't long until Miss Dayton was at wit's end and about to quit! Mrs. Raum went to the school board and told them that these kids need to learn to respect a woman teacher, and that she wanted to take Miss Dayton's place for awhile, and promised to straighten that school out once and for all, or else! Miss Dayton agreed to tend Mrs. Raum's store and her two kids at home.

Mrs. Raum took over the school right after the Christmas and New Year holidays were over and she was a lot better teacher than Driscoll ever was. Things were going pretty good, but once in awhile she had a run-in with one of these big kids and she soon broke them of sassing and distrupting classes as they did with Miss Dayton.

She brought a big heavy black harness breast strap to school and the first day she told the big kids that if she had to punish any of them it would be with this strap and it would be applied right where their back formed sort of a mound! The kids all laughed, but only once, because a day or two later one of these bullies called her bluff and started pulling some of the things they used to on Miss Dayton, and also on other female teachers that they had run off.

Mrs. Raum nailed this kid by the back of his shirt collar and marched him up to her desk, where she pulled her chair out in plain sight, and she yanked this big kid's pants down, and with a hammer lock on his head with one arm, she put a real black leather strap polish on his sitting down place, that was red as a beet when she let him go! She only had to do that to about one other kid that had thought he could handle her, but couldn't! And the humiliation, pain and embarrassment suffered in public brought an end to any more monkeyshines.

Mrs. Raum had only one more problem to end, and that was smoking in school. Some of these big kids rolled and lit up cigarettes right in school. Mrs. Raum told them that it had to stop, and that the first kid she caught smoking in the school room would get the daylights whaled out of him.

They all took her at her word, except one big kid named Johnnie Woodward. This kid was about eighteen years old and a pretty good student. He was a wonderful oldtime fiddler and often played at the dances along with Nick Wilson, John Burcher and Jake Jackson. Johnnie Woodward was a very talented kid. He turned out to be one of the best carpenters and cabinet makers in Jackson Hole in later years.

Johnnie was a confirmed cigarette smoker. He was an addict before he was ten years old, and it was emphysema that killed him in the end. Johnnie just couldn't give up smoking and in those days we had big geography books that were about eighteen inches wide and two feet tall, and when opened up and stood on your desk, it covered the whole pupil from sight. I don't know how or when Johnnie did it, but he got into the school house and he poked a knot out of a floor board right under his desk and he had rigged up a tube which he fastened to the inkwell hole on his desk, and down through this knot hole in the floor. It was made so all he had to do was take the ink bottle out and with this big geography book standing open on his desk, it covered his body completely. While pretending to be studying, he would light up a cigarette and he inhaled every puff, and when he exhaled he would lean down behind this big book and blow the smoke down through the inkwell hole through this tube and the smoke would go under the floor.

Johnnie's desk was away back in one corner of the room and he got away with this for quite awhile. All of us kids knew that he was smoking in school, but Johnnie was a tough kid and we all knew it! He told us that the first one that told would get his head beat off! Well, one day it was study period, and no classes going on and I was busy studying my lesson and I didn't notice Mrs. Raum go down the aisle where Johnnie sat. She had gotten onto this smoking deal that Johnnie was pulling and she slipped down and jerked the geography book up from Johnnie's desk and caught him red handed, puffing away! The first thing I heard was a big whack when she popped Johnnie on the head with the big book and had him by the shirt collar and started dragging him up the aisle. Johnnie wasn't as big as some of the big kids and he wasn't a trouble maker either, but in a fight he was just as tough as, or tougher than, any kid in school. When Mrs. Raum started dragging him up the aisle, he grabbed every seat they passed and tipped them over spilling kids all over the floor. Bedlam was breaking out, but Mrs. Raum yelled, "Quiet! and we did!

Well, Mrs. Raum got Johnnie up to the open space in front of the school room and tried to take down his pants and apply the learning strap, but Johnnie fought like a tiger! He didn't take it like the other kids did, but he got in there and hit and kicked and bit with all his might. Mrs. Raum had about chewed off more than she could handle. She was hard pressed just holding her own.

All of a sudden Johnnie grabbed her dress and gave a big yank, and tore all her clothes off clear down to her waist! When those huge breasts were exposed there was a loud gasp from us kids! I had never seen a sight like that in all my life! All the female breasts I had ever seen were on the little girls when a bunch of us kids went swimming in the warm slough water out in the swales in the hay field among the willows, and we would catch pollywogs. I had never even noticed breasts on any of these little girls, but these breasts! They would have made an old brockle-faced milk cow turn green with envy! However, this exposure didn't faze Mrs. Raum and she soon had Johnnie's pants down and got the strap of knowledge applied to his posterior until it was red! red! red! We kids all ran outside and went home, and the stories that were told!

That night Nick Wilson and other members of the school board had a meeting, and it was decided that we kids weren't yet ready for sex education! So they made Mrs. Raum town constable. She told the school board she thought Miss Dayton could take over the school now, without anymore trouble, and she did! Johnnie quit school, and there was no more trouble from big kids nor any more smoking in school!

Miss Dayton taught the Wilson school for about two or three years until about the year 1912, when she fell in love with a half-breed Indian named Brady Taylor, and there was another tragedy enacted in Jackson Hole, and in the life of Jesse K. Dayton that ended her teaching for life! I will get around to that story, but as the above story about Mrs. Raum happened in the spring of 1910, there were considerable happenings yet in the life of Nick Wilson before the spring of 1912 when the career of a promising young teacher came to an end!

Snow slide at Bucket Springs, just west of Teton Pass. This was one of the worst feared snow slides on the mountain, because it got over a quarter mile swipe at you. Jackson Hole South Park Valley in upper right background.

After pulling the sled and box to a safe place beyond slide, repairs were made. Picture taken about 1912. There were four very dangerous snow slides on Teton Pass, two on east, or Wilson side, and two on west, or Victor side.

CHAPTER 24 — Jesse K. Dayton and Brady Taylor

Jesse K. Dayton taught the Wilson School the winter of 1911-12, the year my brother George and I were in Ogden, Utah.

After the wonderful summer that Ira "Monk" and I had working for John Dodge, we were ready for school, and Miss Dayton taught again that year 1912-13. I was in the fifth grade. The trouble with the big kids was over and I had wonderful teachers the next three grades, sixth, seventh and eighth, with fine accredited teachers. The year 1912-13 was the last for Miss Dayton and I am fixing to tell about that.

My sixth grade teacher was Miss Vivian Davis and we kids really learned under her. But she married Henry Dickamore, Mrs. Mike Yokel's brother, and that ended her teaching career. Too many fine teachers ended a brilliant career by marrying some cow puncher and moving into his old homestead shack and raising kids.

The only real good teacher that we ever had got away. I don't know how it ever happened, but she put her teaching above her romance. She taught my seventh and eighth grades, and to her I owe all my basic eduation. Her name was Miss Ruth Hill, a beautiful ravenhaired southern girl. I never heard what became of her after she left Jackson Hole.

As I have mentioned before, Jesse K. Dayton fell in love with a half-breed Indian named Brady Taylor. He was a handsome cuss, and I have been fascinated when watching him to see the many beautiful hues and color changes on his handsome face, on which never grew a hair. Brady had reverted back to the old original stock, or blood of the true Indian, no hair on their face, but a heavy, shiny black mane, and this type never goes bald.

As Brady talked to Miss Dayton, I have watched these color hues that were brown, red, blue, purple and pink, change in the light as he moved his head. I would think of my dad's book, *The White Indian Boy* in which he ended by saying that he realized he would soon go to the Happy Hunting Grounds, where he expected to find his old Indian friends, a white and beautiful people, I wondered what could be more beautiful than these beautiful changing colors on Brady Taylor's face!

Many a young school teacher's career ended when she married some cowboy and settled down in his homestead shack and started raising kids. Note the four kids all under four years of age. 1905.

Taylor carried the mail from Jackson to Victory, Idaho, six days a week. He hauled only the first class mail and passengers. The heavy freight was handled by men like Lue Enhon, Clary Seaton, Harry Scott and Wall Ricks, who were known as "stay chain drivers."

A stay chain driver is one that gets his heavy loads through, come snow, hell or high water! When things got tough he always carried a stay chain hung on his wrist. A stay chain is an iron extension chain to the tugs straps on a harness. When you needed longer tugs you simply snapped the stay chain into the ring or hook at the end of a tug and made whatever length was needed. A stay chain was about eighteen inches to two feet long and made a brutal but perfect club. When things got really tough every ounce of muscle was needed from every one of the six to eight horse teams used to pull these heavy rigs. It was a thrilling but terrifying sight to see these drivers climb out on the tongue between these horses or jump from back to back of the horses until he could reach the slackers or the ones needed to pull the most at that moment, and the way he laid that stay chain on was really something to see!

Teton Pass above Wilson, Wyoming, about 1915. Buildings owned and built by Harry Scott, U.S. Mail and Freight Contractor for many years between Victor, Idaho and Jackson Hole, Wyoming. Team headed west toward Victor.

For many years Teton Pass was the main artery into and out of Jackson Hole. The first record of Whitemen through the Valley was the Hunt Party consisting of 64 men. They entered via the Hoback Canyon and left over Teton Pass in 1811. The first homesteaders entered via Teton Pass. The first road into Jackson Hole Valley was made from Victor, Idaho, eighteen miles to Wilson, Wyoming, on the east side of the range. It has been the scene of many hardships and deaths due to the many vicious snowslides.

There were no automobiles in the valley prior to 1914 when Model T Fords were hauled over the rough steep mountain road with horses. The next road entrance to Jackson Hole was made via Henry Lake in Idaho via Grassy Lake to Moran, then Yellowstone Park south to Jackson. Then a road over Togwotee Pass, and a narrow road was made through the Hoback Canyon and finally through the Snake River Canyon. Jackson Hole now boasts many fine interstate highways through all its areas.

Charles Alma Wilson, Author.

Bill and Holiday Menor opened a store and built a ferry across Snake River about 12 miles north of Jackson and Wilson, Wyoming in 1892. Bill at wheel on boat in center of Snake River, transporting an old Model T Ford. Ranch building and Tetons in background.

United States Mail arriving in Wilson, Wyoming, 1913, from Victor, Idaho, over Teton Pass, heading east toward Snake River and Jackson Hole, Wyoming. Dim building in background, over horse's head, is Nick Wilson's Hotel. Picture with passengers taken while they were stopped in front of Nick McCoy's Livery Stable and Wilson Post Office.

Clay Seaton was the most aggresive and brutal of them all! And when Clay failed to get a heavy load of freight over the "Hump," as that big old mountain between Jackson Hole and Victor, Idaho, was called, then nobody that ever "pulled" leather would do it either!

Brady Taylor had three four-horse teams he used to carry this first class mail and passengers. He used light rigs: light spring wagons in summer, and a light canvas-covered sleigh with a stove inside for winter. The stove was for comfort of the pasengers as the temperature often hovered around fifty degrees below zero going over the "Hump" in winter time. A "rig" can be either a wagon or sled.

Brady kept these fine sixteen head of horses at the Jackson end of the stage or mail line. If he was on schedule or time with the mail, and did not have too many passengers, he would pull up in front of our school house door, which stood at the very bottom of the foothills below Teton Pass, just as school let out at 4 p.m. and then he would leap down from the high wagon seat and make a deep swinging bow with his big hat to the furiously blushing Miss Dayton, and then boost her gently upon the seat, and if there was room, some of us kids that lived in the village could get in behind the seat too, and we would all get a ride into town. The school house was on the outskirts of town, over by the foothills.

Brady would let us kids all out over by the hotel, then proceed the mile on to Uncle Alfred Nethercott's ferry boat, which the mail carriers used during times of high water, but they would ford the Snake River when it was low. It was only May that year, but we had an unusually early high water and Brady was crossing on the ferry in the evening with the mail from Victor, Idaho, and again of a morning on his way out.

Our school was to be let out for the summer about June 1, and a couple of weeks before school let out, a big tree came down the swollen madly rushing Snake River and took out Uncle Alfred's ferry by breaking the big two-inch cable near one of the moorings and so for two weeks, Brady had been keeping one four-horse team at Wilson where he stayed too, and another driver hauled the mail and passengers the six miles from Jackson to the Snake River, where now the mail and passengers were transported by small row boats. Steve Leek rowed the boat of a morning from the east, or Jackson side, to the west, or Wilson side, and my Uncle Alfred rowed the mail and passengers over in the evening from the Wilson side. Mail and passengers were picked up by the driver that Brady had on the Jackson side.

Brady kept this one team in my dad's livery stable in Wilson and Brady boarded and slept at the Ward Hotel. This was a beautiful arrangement for Brady and Miss Dayton, as she boarded only a few hundred feet down the road.

During this two weeks after the ferry washed out, it became common for Miss Dayton and some of us kids to ride out to the River with Brady and after he got mail and passengers all in Uncle Alfred's row boat, we would all ride back to Wilson where Brady kept his team.

When the ferry washed out it hung up about three miles down the river and it consisted of two big boats, about thirty feet long and twenty feet wide each, and the flooring and railing and butt gates that raised and lowered to let teams and wagons off and on, were all made of 2" x 10" lumber and so the ferry was too heavy to ever tow back up to the ferry site where it was moored. Uncle Alfred had given up on a ferry for that year and planned to build another which would take all winter. Travelers who had to cross the Snake River with teams and wagons had to go about twelve miles above Wilson to the Holiday and Bill Menor Ferry, which made a pretty good day's drive from Wilson to Jackson, which were only about seven miles apart!

Miss Dayton and Brady Taylor had planned a June wedding, right after our school was to let out, and they had arranged for my dad, Nick Wilson, to marry them!

Just a few days before school was to let out, it was known that Brady Taylor planned to swim his mail team of four horses across Snake River and take them to Jackson and bring back a fresh shod and rested team to use on the mail. It was a hard trip over Teton Pass and that was why Brady had bought three teams of the finest horses that money could buy. He used a span of four on this daily trip and changed teams every ten days, thus each team was used ten days then got off twenty days each month to rest. In this way, Brady always had fine-looking, fast horses, and passengers really enjoyed these trips with Brady Taylor.

Well, the evening came that Taylor was to swim his team across Snake River, then swim another team back over the next morning. That evening Miss Dayton and four or five of us kids rode to the river with him to see him cross the river with the horses. The regular way to swim horses across the river was to tie each horse to another's tail, then with a long rope on the lead horse, a man would ride in the back seat of the row boat and the oarsman would paddle across, with the horses swimming in single file behind the boat. It was a pretty risky trick, leading these horses across even with a row boat, because if the oarsman didn't keep his boat away from the horses there was always the danger that a horse might try to climb into the boat or tip it over in some other manner.

Brady was a fine swimmer himself and he hated this swimming horses behind a row boat. Brady preferred to ride the lead horse bareback, leading the other three, which he claimed was much safer. All the way out to the river, Miss Dayton had been pleading with Brady to not ride the horses across, but let Uncle Alfred take him across in his row boat. Her argument was that the water was too cold to swim in. Brady just laughed at her concern, and just then the wagon scraped against a willow bush, whose leaves were out in all their splendor. Brady stripped off a big handful of the willow leaves and laughing, gave them to Miss Dayton, and said, "Here is a big bouquet to remember me by if anything happens to me!" Miss Dayton couldn't see anything funny about it, and told him so! And she added, "I feel that something awful is going to happen!"

When we arrived at the crossing Uncle Alfred was there with his boat, but Brady Taylor told him he would rather ride a horse and swim them over that way.

Miss Dayton started to cry and plead, "But the water is too cold!"

Brady consoled her with his arm around her, and said, "It won't be too cold in the afternoon like this! But I will let Steve Leek row me back in the morning, because early in the morning the water and air are too cold!"

He kissed her good-bye, and her face was very red! Brady pulled off his boots and socks and shirt and with only his trousers he mounted his lead horse and urged them out into the muddy swirling water! He had rolled his undershirt and shirt up in a ball and shoved them down in his boots and holding the boots high above his head, plunged off into the swift water. Uncle Alfred had a long willow and he walloped the other horses and they all plunged off into the swirling water with Brady Taylor! They all went under out of sight at first, except Brady's head, neck and shoulders. Then they all came up and he headed them out into the swift water, we could see the gleam of his white teeth and the shine of water on his wet beautiful bronze skin as he waved the boots at us. We watched until we saw the horses with Brady all crawl out of the raging water on the other side, where we could see Steve Leek standing by his row boat. We kids all walked back through the mile-long lane to Wilson with Miss Dayton. She seemed rather quiet, and from time to time I noticed a queer dampness on her long beautiful eyelids.

I showed her and the other kids some of the bird nests that I had found while walking with my dad, and by the time we got home we were all laughing and having a lot of fun!

The next morning school had just taken up when there was a loud knock on the school house door. Miss Dayton opened it and Mrs. Yokel stepped in, and her face was pale as she said, "We have just got word that Brady Taylor has been drowned in Snake River."

Miss Dayton blanched, and then almost inaudibly we heard her say, "Oh, My God!" Then she fainted! We bigger kids helped Mrs. Yokel carry her over to Mrs. Yokel's house that was just across the road from the school house. We kids all walked sadly home. That ended school until the next fall.

What really happened with Brady Taylor was this, as told by Steve Leek: He said that he was waiting to row the morning mail across the river as usual, when Brady Taylor arrived with his other driver, leading four horses behind the stage. There were three passengers going "outside" and an unusually large bulk of mail. He said that Brady told him he had promised to ride in the boat and lead the horses, but on account of so many passengers and so much mail, Taylor decided he would ride and swim the horses over as he had done with the others the evening before. Steve said that Brady gave him his boots and coat and shirt to take in the boat and then Brady went first. He said Brady had quite a time getting the horses started swimming because they objected to the cold water and there was an unusual amount of driftwood for so early in the morning, but it had been a warm night and the river was rising very fast.

Brady finally got the horses swimming, then Leek followed with the passengers and mail in his row boat. He said everything seemed to be going good with Taylor and the horses, but just as they reached the channel on the Wilson side, a big bunch of driftwood came, which Taylor was unable to dodge with the swimming horses. Leek said that Brady and the horses all disappeared from sight, but the horses all came up a few yards downstream and scrambled out on the bank on the Wilson side. Brady Taylor never came up!

This tragic loss was a terrible ordeal for Jesse K. Dayton, she was sick for many weeks at the Yokel home.

Finally, the search for Brady's body was given up, until after high water was over. Miss Dayton finally left the valley to go to her home, wherever that was, and we didn't see her again until that fall.

After the water went down in late August, the search for Brady Taylor's body was resumed, but by October nothing had been found and it was decided that his body was either buried in some gravel and sand bank or had drifted on out of the valley. I remember that in later years when they were grading the road around a narrow place on the Buffalo River, over thirty miles upstream from where Taylor drowned, that a bulldozer caved off the bank and rolled with the driver into the high muddy Buffalo River about one-half mile above where it empties into the Snake River, and the body of this man was found that fall down in Swan Valley, nearly seventy-five miles from where he drowned.

After the search for Taylor's body was given up, I was fishing with my dad and Harry Nethercott, who was running the Wilson Hotel, at the time. We were right near where Brady Taylor had disappeared in the Snake River that day in late May. The river was very low and an island had formed with a huge pile of driftwood at the head of the island. There was a long blue fishing hole we could see beyond this little island, and the water was so low on our side that Nick let me go with Harry and we waded over there to try fishing the hole we could see.

Harry started fishing right where we hit the hole down near its lower end. I like to fish down stream and so I continued on up to the head of the hole that began near this huge pile of driftwood, and just as I got even with it there was the most terrible odor, I knew it was coming from the pile of driftwood, and looking inside to see what it was, I could see white bones and shreds of clothing! It was terrible. I knew at once that it was Brady Taylor! And it was! He had only gone about one hundred feet from where Steve Leek saw him disappear that morning when Brady was drowned and he lodged in this driftwood!

The remains were taken to Wilson and a smoky sage brush fire was kept going to keep down the awful odor, until after an autopsy, which identified the body as that of Brady Taylor! Brady's skull was bashed in and the authorities said it was caused by one of the horses striking him on the head with a heavy iron shoe. That was what killed Brady Taylor.

There is no odor on earth like decaying or burning human flesh. I have smelled both during the years gone by and would be able to identify the smell any place now because no animal smells that way, but man!

Well, Miss Dayton came back for the funeral when she was notified that Brady's body had been found. She was a quiet, subdued and grim woman. She stayed in the valley and married Del Judd, our postmaster, whose earlier courtship of her had been cut out by Brady Taylor. I guess Miss Dayton had really liked Del Judd, but there was soon another terrible event to happen in her life.

CHAPTER 25 — Pioneer Teachers
Jenny Grosh and Fostene Forrester

At the end of Chapter 24, I told of the finding of Brady Taylor's body and of Jesse K. Dayton returning for the funeral. Taylor and Miss Dayton had set their wedding date for June, soon after school was to be out for the summer. This was the last of Miss Dayton's teaching career.

Dell Judd had been our postmaster in the town of Wilson for many years. Dell must have come in either with the first early settlers or shortly after, because I was born in 1901 and I can't remember when I didn't know Dell Judd, he was there at my earliest recollection. Dell was a bachelor. He must have been around thirty-five years old at the time of Taylor's funeral. Jesse K. Dayton was crowding thirty.

Dell had dated Miss Dayton when she first started teaching at Wilson, which was about 1909-10 when she had so much trouble with the big kids. Mrs. Raum took over her teaching job about January 1, 1910 and turned the school back to Miss Dayton about April 1, 1910, and she continued teaching through the term of 1910-11 and 1911-12, the year I was in Ogden, Utah, then she taught the term of 1912-13, terminating only a few days before school was to end for the summer, June 1, 1912.

Dell Judd had bought the old Paul Morris ranch, about nine miles south of Wilson and started a hunting camp and dude ranch. These dude ranches were already in full swing long before Judd started his down on Taylor Creek. My father, Nick Wilson, had been hauling dudes from the railhead at St. Anthony, Idaho, to Jackson Hole for five or six years before Judd started his dude ranch. As stated before, Dell ran the Wilson Post Office and started a small general store when Nick quit the business in about 1906.

After Judd bought the Paul Morris ranch, he had his sister, Erma Judd, come up from Salt Lake City and he turned the post office and store over to Erma, who ran it until the fall of Brady Taylor's funeral in October 1912, when Erma Judd turned the business over to Jesse K. Dayton, who ran it that winter of 1912-13. Then she married Dell Judd in early 1914, probably about two years after she was to have married Taylor in June, 1912. Judd continued to run his dude ranch and Jesse K. Judd ran the store and post office.

Dell was getting a very good start in the dude business. He was a good guide and hunter and knew all the hunting area from Wilson south through the Mesquito Creek area to the Elk Creek, Fall Creek, Cobern Creek and Dog Creek areas, which covered thousands of acres of untouched wilderness area, over approximately fifty miles of the finest elk, moose, deer and bear hunting grounds in all Jackson Hole. Judd had built a nice lodge with huge fireplace and several log cabins for guests and hunters by the fall of 1914, after he and Miss Dayton were married.

The winter of 1913-14 our teacher was Miss Vivian Davis. I was in the sixth grade and through her fine teaching I really became interested in school.

I can't remember much happening in the lives of Nick Wilson and his two little boys in 1911. Nick took me and my brother George, who was now living with us, with him while peddling his books that summer, which was the last time he ever hit the road. We had lots of fun that summer. I remember an article that came out that fall, written by some outsider who had spent the summer in Jackson Hole, and in telling his or her adventures during the summer of 1911 in Jackson Hole, the article said, "One of the most touching, yet common sights I can remember, was seeing Nick Wilson with his old walking cane and his two little boys, each carrying an old willow fishing pole and a can of grasshoppers, 'agoin fishin!

"Nick Wilson, after which the little town of Wilson, Wyoming, was named, is really an outstanding person, and loved by all who know him. His stories of the early frontier days with Indians and his riding the Pony Express are spell-binding and one of my most prized memories will be my visits to his little log cabin there on the bank of Fish Creek in Wilson, Wyoming and the many happy and exciting hours I spent in listening to this fascinating old man tell his stories of long ago.

"Truly, Nick Wilson played a part in history, and the settling of the west, that cannot be surpassed or maybe even equalled by any man."

The winter of 1914-15, my teacher was Miss Ruth Hill. She was from North Carolina. She was a wonderful teacher. I was in the seventh grade that fall. There should be a tribute or story told, listing the names of the many wonderful teachers in the Jackson Hole's early history. They endured hardship, hunger and cold, and some nearly froze to death getting to and from their little one-room school building. They often had to wallow in snow early in the morning and shovel off the steps, carry wood and build fires for themselves and the school children and teach all eight grades in crowded and unsanitary conditions and mostly with shamefully low wages and sometimes no pay at all.

Two of our very early school teachers came from Nebraska riding saddle horses and leading a packhorse with all their earthly belongings to their names, and they were Miss Jenny Grosh and Fostene Forrester. They had heard of the need for good teachers in the wild Jackson Hole country that was just beginning to be settled by people from all walks of life,looking for homes, and who had courage enough to risk their all in this pursuit.

These two young women, who were in their early twenties, were excited by these stories and decided they wanted to teach on the last frontier. They started in July of about 1903, from Lincoln, Nebraska, away over on the eastern border of that huge state which was approximately seven hundred miles or more to Jackson Hole. Jenny and Fostene had written to the Wilson School Board on which Nick Wilson served and he had sent them a contract. These two brave and gallant young women set out over a long, torturous and treacherous trail of over seven hundred miles through unknown country. They left Lincoln about the middle of June and arrived at Harvey Burlingham's cow camp on Twogwotee Pass, Wyoming, about the middle of August and had been riding for nearly two months.

Harv Burlingham was a sawed-off tough little cowboy about sixty years old. He was herding the Jackson Hole cattlemen's herds of range cattle that they grazed from about July 1 to October l, each year on this high mountain range with the best and sweetest grass in all the world. The United States Government let them have it for about three cents a head and the association paid Harv forty dollars a month and keep. "Keep" means food, of which Harv got darn little, for after the scroungy food supply that the association took up to Harv's cow camp, he was forced to about live off the land, which he did. The mountains there teemed with blue grouse, partridge, deer and elk, so about all he needed and got was a little flour and baking powder, sowbelly and lard.

Harv usually returned to his camp about sundown after a hard day's ride, keeping track of over twenty five hundred beef on that great range. The association supplied him with plenty horses, a couple white wall tents eight by ten feet and someone usually came up about once a month to bring salt for the cattle and to see if Harv was still alive.

One evening Harv was surprised to look up, while unsaddling his tired horse, and the barking of his dog, to see two beautiful young ladies ride up to his camp. To say that Harv was astonished was to put it mildly, the way he told it later, "I wuz plumb flabbergasted!"

The rest of the story I got from Fostene Forrester many years later when I was working for her husband, Don Haight, on their ranch near Jackson, Wyoming. One evening after supper, Fostene got to telling us, her husband, Don, son Don Jr., and I, the story of she and Jenny Grosh's trip to Jackson Hole to teach school. They should have written a story of the seven-hundred-mile trip in 1903 through some of the wildest country that was left in the United States, and this night with Harv Burlingham was only incidental to this long, rough trip.

When they rode up to Harv's cow camp and he got his furiously barking dog quieted down, Miss Jenny Grosh asked, "Good afternoon sir! Could you tell us how far it is to some place we might camp tonight?" Harv removed his big hat and bowed his head and his long hair fell over his face and shoulders covering up his huge, unshaven black beard. Then he very politely asked, "And whare might ye ladies be from?"

They told him they had started from Lincoln, Nebraska, in June and were on their way to Jackson Hole where they had a contract to teach school at Wilson, Wyoming, and at a school they understood was six miles north of Wilson at a place called "Poverty Flats!"

Harv must have really looked flabbergasted then, with his little pig blue eyes sticking out, as Harv said, "Like a tromped on toadfrog!"

Miss Fostene Forrester added, "We stayed at a Tie Camp about twenty miles up the Wind River, above that little town, what did they call it Jenny?" and Jenny said "Dubois!"

Harv said, "Oh! That means you have come about eighteen miles today, all up hill!"

"Yes, I guess so," one of the girls answered, "And now, would you be so kind as to tell us how far to a ranch or some place we could camp tonight?"

Harv scratched his head and said, "Well, thars Beaver Tooth Neal down on Buffalo River." He hesitated a moment and shook his shaggy head: "No, you wouldn't want to stay with him, — —anyway I wouldn't reckermend Neal, he is a purty slick character, that guy is!" Harv pondered awhile and said, "Then thers old man Wolf on down on spread creek, he's a dirty old cuss, and I know a couple fine ladies like ye two be, wouldn't go fer old man Wolf!" Harv thought a minute, and finally said, "I can't think of any place else except Holiday and Bill Menor, thar brothers, old bacholoars, clean enough, but meaner than hell. They run a ferry boat across old Snake River. Yu'll hafta cross thar to get over to Nick Wilson's place at Wilson, Wyoming, an' yu'll go rite past the ole country school house on Poverty Flats. They call it that because all the ranchers are so *pore the'd starve to deth if it warn't fer ole John Dodge!*"

The girls were getting nervous and one of them asked, "Well! How far is it to this 'er, this Beaver Tooth fellah and the others?"

"Weel," answered Harv, "it's about twenty mile to Neal's place, an' another twenty to old man Wolf's about twenty more to the Menor's ferry. I wouldn't suggest stoppen there, expecially if ye get to the ferry late in the day. The ferry is on the other side of the river from where you find it, an' as I sed, them two ornery ole cusses might, or they might not, cross the ferry over to git yer until they feel ready, and so you might have to camp thar till morning, or even two or three days. Besides," added Harv, "that's sixty miles, and ye can't make that today."

Harv studied some more, then with a big smile said, "Yer welcome to stay with me. I don't have any fancy grub, but I got some grouse to fry for supper and some fresh venison!"

Jenny looked at Fostene and they both clamored, "Oh! that sounds just ducky. We'll stay!"

"You can roll yer beds over thar in that tent." He pointed to an old battered tent where he kept salt and packs, saddles, and other equipment. "No thanks," said Jenny, "we have our own tent and everything we need, but those grouse and that venison sure sound good to us!"

Harv was a great cook and he really stirred them up a tasty meal. While Harv was getting supper, the two young teachers pitched their little range tent, for which they carried folding tent poles to hold it up.

After supper, Harv stoked up the campfire and they all sat and Harv entertained them for an hour or two with his homely cowboy stories, and he played old-fashioned tunes on his harmonica, then recited for them his famous poem, which he called, "The Great Round Up!" It went something like this:

"They say there will be a big round up,
When cowboys like Dogies will stand!
They say the Great Foreman up yonder,
Will judge you in that by-and-by land!
So if you've never met up with this Foreman,
At yourself you'd better take a good look!
And for safety you'd better get branded,
And get your name in the big tally book!"

It was now time to retire. Harv said, "Good night, ladies!" and started for his tent. Miss Grosh stopped him, "Hold on young man!" she said sternly. Harv came back to her and she pulled out a small pearl-handled revolver, and said, "See this gun? Well, I am showing it to you in case you might get funny ideas! I just wanted you to know that we are armed and we both know how to use this gun!"

Harv drew a long breath and rolled his tiny blue eyes and said with unfeigned respect, "Yees Maam!"

They had only been in their sleeping bags a few minutes when Harv shook their tent and called, "Hey Maam!"

Miss Grosh poked her head out the tent flap and demanded, "Well? what do you want?"

Harv stuttered a moment or two then blurted out, "Well, Maam, I wuz thinkin' about you havin' that gun!"

"Well! what about it?" Jenny Grosh snapped.

"Weel," stammered Harv, "I got to thinkin' as how, after all, thar air two of you, and only one of me, wouldn't it be more fair fer me to have the gun tonight than fer you two in case youse guys might get some funny ideas?"

Fostene tells this story with great gusto amid a lot of laughing and I have heard Harvey Burlingham's version many times, too. That's the kind of frontier teachers that really tamed the Old West!

CHAPTER 26 — **The Hermit**

As I look back over those wonderful ten years that I spent with my father, Elijah Nicholas Wilson, or simply, Nick Wilson, but known by everyone far and wide as "Uncle Nick," I marvel at the affection felt for that name. If we were traveling even five hundred miles away from home, passersby would hail us, "Hey! Uncle Nick!" and pull their rig up close for just a greeting or a chat, and many would ask us to stay at their house overnight.

From early in the morning until late at night, people dropped in to our cabin by the creek. Sometimes just to pass the time away or to ask his advice on some problem that they could not handle alone. Many a lawsuit or even a divorce was averted by the sage counsel of "Uncle Nick." He must have been endowed with wisdom from above to handle these problems of young and old alike.

If they were getting married they came to Nick to marry them; they came to him to preach a funeral sermon. Truly, Nick Wilson had to have the wisdom of a Solomon, and it was eagerly sought. I have been awakened early in the morning by voices from the other room. Our house had two rooms. The bedroom where I slept on the west end was only ten feet from Fish Creek, whose rippling song soothed me to sleep for the fourteen years it was my home.

I remember one day a young lady came to Nick, and she was very perturbed over whether to marry or not. She was in love with a young Forest Ranger who had been sent west with the hopes the arid climate might help his tuberculosis, but he was too far gone and doctors had told him he only had a short time to live. This young girl was a neighbor's daughter. Her folks were very opposed to this marriage, but she wanted to marry the young ranger anyway. The Ranger didn't want her to marry him, knowing she would soon be a widow. So she came to Uncle Nick for advice. He talked with her for awhile and then suggested she go and bring this young man, so he could talk to him too, which she did. Nick let them talk themselves out until he understood how each felt about the situation, then he gave his advice.

"Marriage is a serious problem in our lives, there is really only three choices made during our entire life, they are: our birth, our marriage, and our death. Of these three choices we only have control over one of them, and that is our marriage. God tells us in the Bible that marriage is the most binding and sacred obligation that can be entered into on all the earth, in marriage we cleave together and become one flesh. It must be honored above mother, father, brother, sister or anything else, except the love of God, and God says, "Let no man cut asunder that which I have joined together!" Then Nick gave this advice!

"Now, after talking to you both here today, I realize that you are truly in love, I also realize the consequences of this marriage, that it may be short, that rests in the hands of God. As a man, with the authority placed upon me by the Priesthood, to unite you in Holy Matrimony, that holds only "until death do you part," it is my belief, as well as it is my advice, that you should go ahead and marry. Trust that God in His holy wisdom and mercy will give you happiness and joy all the rest of your lives, long or short as it may be!"

He married them and the young Ranger lived almost a year, and they were very happy! She followed him not long after, dying of pneumonia!

Lots of these old timers were bachelors, who took up homesteads all over Jackson Hole. They were real colorful characters and it would take a book much larger than this, which I dedicate to my wonderful father, a great man, Elijah Nicholas Wilson, better known and loved, as "Uncle Nick" by all his fellowmen and all whoever knew him!

I remember another young lady who came to Nick for advice as to whether she should marry a young man because he was kind of hard of hearing, and she worried that he might become completely deaf, and she couldn't bear thinking of spending her life with a deaf husband! Nick's advice was short and sweet: "If you really love him, you won't let a problem like that hold you back! I have known deaf people who can see more beauty, can act with more kindness and understanding to almost any situation, than all the ears in the world can or could ever hear or do!"

They were married, very happily, for more than fifty years. He never lost his hearing nor even became worse than he was at first. One night while watching TV she suffered a sudden heart attack and died in his kind and gentle arms.

As I just mentioned above, it would take a mighty large book to do credit to the lives and history of these old Frontiersmen and Mountainmen that lived in Jackson Hole, when I was a kid.

Before I close with more chapters of the story of my father's life, I would like to enter here the story of one of the oldtimers whose life may not stand out anymore than do the lives of many others, but he was unique in his story telling, probably more so than any of the others. So just for entertainment, and for fun, I now present the true? story of John Cherry, and his two beloved grizzly bears! I will call this story which follows "The Hermit":

When John Cherry first came to Wyoming he admits that Jackson Hole was a badger hole and that he packed sand from Nevada on old Buck to help Paul Bunyon build the Tetons.

According to John, Paul only spent one winter in Jackson Hole and that was the winter he nearly lost Babe, his old blue ox. After building the Tetons they cut off the wind from the Pacific Ocean and before Paul realized it, the snow had banked up so high and deep behind them in the Jackson Hole country that all vegetation, even the pine timber, was covered up and old Babe was faced with starvation! And that's the winter, as recorded in the Congressional Record in Washington, D. C., that in desperation, Paul Bunyon made a huge pair of green goggles and put them on old Babe, and Babe woke up and thought the huge snow drifts were great wind-rows of green hay and he munched away contentedly all the rest of the winter!

Paul thought he had made a wonderful discovery, because every winter it took nearly half his time providing feed for old Babe. However, when spring came, what Paul and John thought was fat on old Babe, turned out to be water belly!

In fact, the melting of the mighty snow drifts that had piled up on account of the Tetons, caused such a devastating flood that for awhile the states of California, Oregon and Washington were threatened with being washed into the Pacific Ocean! But the water finally subsided and the mighty Snake River Canyon and Gorge testify to the near disaster all the way down along its thousand miles of rugged shore to this very day!

John said that Paul got out of there as soon as he could after the water went down and old Babe was able to travel. John said that Paul was so disgusted with himself for building the Tetons that before he left he kicked a couple of holes through them, which he named Moron and Death Canyons, in order to let the wind blow in from the ocean and scatter the snow around over the rest of the west so that we would never again be faced with a flood like that! But even up to this day the Army Engineers work nearly all the time to keep the Snake River in its restless bed!

After Paul and Babe left, John got to looking around and found old Buck, his faithful old buckskin horse, dead. Old Buck had pawed great holes in search for food and these holes are known as the "potholes" below Jackson Lake to this very day. The poor old fellow had starved to death while old Babe was munching on snow drifts that looked like hay through his big green goggles.

John says he simply forgot all about poor old Buck but that it probably was a good thing that he did, because as it was we nearly lost the great states of California, Oregon and Washington.

John said he missed old Buck awful bad for awhile because he hated walking worse than a drunkard hates water. However, it wasn't long before he overcame this drawback through sheer luck and his big heart. John was tearing out a beaver dam one day on his ranch in order to lower the water so he could catch a big trout that he couldn't get to bite. It kept all the other fish scared out of that neighborhood, causing John to have to walk farther up or down the creek in order to catch a mess of fish to eat.

While John was engrossed in his labor he forgot to watch the surrounding territory for enemies, which was a dangerous and often fatal mistake to make in those days and which almost ended his colorful career right then and there! All of a sudden there was a terrifying roar and he beheld a giant grizzly bear, mouth open a yard wide, coming at him like a herd of buffalo chasing a ringtailed cat! All that saved John's life was that as he went to jump out of the way, he slipped and fell through a hole in the seat of his britches and nearly hung himself! The grizzly overshot and broke its neck slamming into a big cottonwood tree! While John was getting himself out of the mess he was in, he heard something whimpering and to his amazement there came crawling out of a big pounch on the old bear a half-grown grizzly cub! His first impulse was to batter the cub's brains out, but the little cuss crawled up and started licking John's face, and he just didn't have the heart to kill it.

So John took the cub home and raised it on milk he got from an cow moose that he kept for domestic use.

The cub grew like a weed and went every place that John did and he used to romp and play and wrestle with it by the hour. The cub would take John's head in its mouth and carry him all over the yard just like a cat playing with a mouse until it finally occurred to John that maybe that was just what the bear was doing, so he made him cut it out!

This bear got to be seventeen hands high at the shoulders and one day, on an unusually long, hard hunt, John got so fagged out he couldn't go any farther and laid down to die. The cub kept whimpering and pawing at him and finally must have realized John's predicament and so boosted him upon his own back and trotted off home! John's walking days were over. He named the cub Buck, in honor of his old buckskin horse.

One day John was riding Buck on an elk hunt when he wounded a big cow and she ran into some heavy timber. John said that Buck had one bad habit he couldn't break him of and that was this: Whenever Buck followed a blood trail he got to purring so loud it scared the wounded animal to death and sometimes the meat spoiled before he could find it. So on this particular day he made Buck stay in the open park where he had wounded the cow elk and John went on foot to look for her. The cow gave him a long hard chase before he got her and it was after dark when he got back to where he left Buck. But Buck was gone! John said the more he hollered and yelled the madder he got and just as the moon came up he saw Buck catching fish from a stream that flowed through a big meadow.

Just as John got up to him, Buck smacked the water with one of his huge paws and not only soaked John from head to heels but hit him in the face with a big sucker and knocked him down. John said he never whipped or abused Buck before but that leaving him afoot, and now this crowning indignity, was more than he could stand. So he jumped up and kicked Buck in the rump with all his might! Buck let out a roar and charged! They fought all over the meadow until it looked like a band of sheep had bedded there for a week! John said he finally got on Buck's back and with a big dry limb for a club, he beat and fought him all the way back to the ranch. It was just breaking light when the exhausted pair reached the cabin and to John's horror, there laid the real Buck sound asleep on the doorstep! John realized that he had fought and conquered a wild grizzly bear!

John said he named this new bear Babe, in honor of Paul Bunyon's old blue ox, but although he kept and rode these two bears for many years he never could trust Babe as much as Buck. He thought that taming a full grown grizzly bear might be the reason on account of the bear's different background!

John said the first man he saw after Paul Bunyon left was on one of this trips through Yellowstone Park. He said he didn't go there often because his bears were always getting their feet burned on a hot rock, for in those days not only the water was scalding but the rocks were all red hot, too. And besides, he didn't like the smell of all that sulphur water. However, he was riding Buck on one of these rare occasions up the Fire Hole River and over toward Morning Glory Spring when he smelled a stink that stunk worse than any stink ever stank there before! So he kneed Buck over that way and "Seed a feller washing his feet and throwing rocks down in the pool!" John said this "feller" introduced himself as John Colter and invited Cherry to light and rest a spell, and darned if he didn't get to visiting and washing his feet, too.

John said that Colter didn't say anything about his riding a big grizzly bear but he noticed him keep sizing Buck up out of the corner of his eye and said, if he had "airy sense at all" he would have surmised the crafty thoughts that were racing through Colter's nimble brain!

John said that after they got all cleaned up and throwed all the rocks they could find into Morning Glory Pool that he felt so good he asked Colter to go with him down to his ranch and visit him awhile. He guessed the reason he felt so good was that in washing his feet there in Morning Glory Spring he had discovered what had been hurting him for years. What he had thought was a vicious and incurable corn between his toes turned out to be just a cinder which he must have picked up while crossing the Craters of the Moon on his way to Nevada for sand with Buck, his old buckskin horse!

Colter and John Cherry camped that night at approximately what is now known as Colter Bay on Jackson Lake. Cherry said they could have made it on down to his place on Fish Creek but Buck wasn't used to packing double and Colter insisted on bringing along a couple of big buffalo robes, a sack of flint rocks and a big cross-bow gun! (I have read volumes wondering how Colter survived for years in the wilderness!) Besides, the weather was awful hot and Buck was kind of inclined to be lazy anyhow!

If Colter had stuck around awhile with John Cherry the history of Jackson Hole and perhaps the whole west might have been a different story! But, according to Cherry, Colter only spent one night in Jackson Hole, because the next morning, when Cherry woke up, Colter had stolen his bear and was gone!

History disagrees whether Colter came or left Jackson Hole by Teton Pass, Snake River Canyon, Hoback Basin, Gros Ventre River or Togwotee Pass. Cherry said he left by Togwotee Pass.

Cherry followed Buck's tracks until he started up the Buffalo River and he knew he could never catch them on foot so he swam the swollen Snake River at the mouth of the Buffalo and hot footed it the forty miles on to his ranch in less than two hours! He had to keep Babe picketed on a big chain whenever he left him alone so he wouldn't revert to the wild, and Babe was there pacing around and around in the deep trail he had worn around the pit. John grabbed some "Jerky" and mounted Babe and was soon on the trail of Buck and John Colter!

One thing in Cherry's favor was the fact that he hadn't told Colter about having another bear at home, and so, after Colter put a couple of hundred miles between them, he started taking it more easy and by the time Cherry reached the Platte River he knew Colter wasn't far ahead. Judging from the signs he was having a little trouble with Buck, who was evidently adverse to getting so far from his beloved mountains!

When Cherry caught up to Colter he was camped for noon and had Buck tied to a scrub cottonwood tree with a rawhide rope and was feeding him strips of antelope meat. Cherry said the look on Colter's face when he looked up and saw him ride up on Babe, his silver-tipped fur all white with alkali dust, was really pathetic to see! Colter just stood there with his mouth sagging open! Cherry piled off and in his own words, "Whopped the tar outen him and lambasted his ornery hide half way across the Nebrasky Territory with buffalo chips by grab!"

When John got back home both bears were gaunt and sore-footed from their long, fast journey on the hot desert, so he turned them both loose to rest and fatten up a little before the long, hard rides to his trap line during the long winter months. He said he had quite a bit of trouble over the hibernating habits of bears. He solved it by taking turns riding the bears on his trap line and thus giving each bear about two weeks uninterrupted sleep between shifts!

The day that John Cherry turned his two beloved bears loose he didn't know he might never feel the mighty muscles of their soft backs ripple beneath his legs again!

As Buck and Babe mosied off down Fish Creek to fill up on fat cutthroat trout, John decided to take a trip up into the Tetons and see what was going on in the world around him. The last time he had climbed up there he had sat two whole days on top of the Grand Teton peak and was troubled by smoke signals he coud see being sent up by Indians in Utah, Idaho, Colorado, Oregon, Montana and Nevada. He could tell by these signals that something was sure upsetting the Indians, and so he packed some jerky and dried service berries and struck out, figuring on being gone three or four days. He didn't know he wouldn't set foot on his beloved ranch again for twenty years!

It was late afternoon when John reached the top of the Grand Teton. The wind was blowing huge black clouds in from the Pacific and lightning was beating a tatoo on the rugged canyon walls way below him, and peal after peal of thunder rent the air and the big peak shook and swayed until John lost his footing and began to fall! He fell for a mile and figured his end was nigh. Suddenly his hand brushed by a small tree growing out of a crack in the canyon wall. He grasped it and held on and pulled himself up onto the ledge and discovered a large cave. He crawled back in out of the rain and went to sleep.

The next morning he ate a little jerky and dried berries and then began to size up what kind of a fix he was in! He soon found that escape was impossible and chances of survival slim! It was at least 2,000 feet straight down to the floor of the valley. Straight up and to each side was a sheer, smooth granite wall!

The jerky and service berries were soon gone and John got so hungry and heavy-hearted that he decided to not prolong his suffering any longer and decided to end it all on the jagged rocks far below! But upon looking down, his heart gave a great leap and a cry of joy escaped from his lips! For there, on the rocky canyon floor, were his faithful bears, Buck and Babe!

He yelled until he was hoarse and for hours the great canyon walls rang and echoed and the sounds came back to mock him, wave after wave! "Buck! Babe! Buck! Babe!" A dozen voices calling from all the canyon walls. The two great bears stood on their hind legs and listened and sniffed the wind, but their little eyes were too dim to see their beloved master so high and far away. But they knew he was there some place and day after day and week after week they kept their lonely vigil and paced the floor of the lonely canyon and wondered why he never came to them but always called from so many directions, "Babe! Buck! Babe! Buck!"

They couldn't see him but they knew he was there, because the shifting wind would bring them his odor and they would stand on their great hind legs and roar until the rocks trembled.

Seeing Buck and Babe gave John new hope and he started to look around for a means to live and escape! He discovered there were millions of bats living in his cave and he ate bats and bat eggs until he thought he would go batty. The sight of the faithful Buck and Babe far below always sustained him, even during the long winter months, because he could see the big cave under the ledge where the two bears always hibernated every winter. In the summers he watched them hunt and fish, while he kept on his steady diet of bat eggs!

So it went year after year. John hadn't realized it, but this steady diet of bats eggs had caused him to develop telescopic eyesight! Keen as the eagles! He could see what was going on all over Jackson Hole! He was lucky in the fact that he had fallen off the southeast side of the Grand Teton and his cave was so situated that John could see from the upper end of Jackson Lake clear around to the big bend of Snake River in the south end of the valley. It was just high enough to see the west side of the Teton Range and part of his beloved ranch at the mouth of Philips Canyon. So as the years passed John Cherry became the best authority on Jackson Hole's early history that ever lived! He saw the first horse thieves and bandits drive their stolen herds in and out of the valley and knew where all their hideouts were. He saw the first settlers enter Jackson Hole and because of his telescopic eyes, he could tell the color of a man's hair for twenty miles! He could tell a man from a woman as far as he could see them and if I told some of the things old John witnessed from his lofty perch it would make a lot of old timers turn over in their graves!

John saw the great Indian battle on the shore of Jackson Lake. He knows what happened at Dead Man's Bar and Cunningham's Hill!

Then came the day that John saw the great Babe killed by lightning while fishing at the mouth of Cottonwood Creek. He saw the flash, but before the crash of thunder reached his ears he saw the mighty bear slump and roll into the swollen waters of the Snake River, and then borne away on its bosom to eternal rest!

It nearly killed old John, but through his tears he could see his beloved Buck prowling along the west bank of Jackson Lake. He was looking over the Indian battlefield!

It was several days before Buck seemed to sense that something was wrong with his friend Babe, and John watched him begin to prowl the streams and forests and valleys in search of Babe. It made John's heart bleed to watch Buck roam day after day, farther and farther away, his great heart torn between love for his master trapped on the mountain wall and loyalty for his friend Babe. The visits back to John were becoming less frequent until finally he didn't come back anymore . . .

John could see lots of activity now in the valley as more and more settlers came and he could see more and more small log cabins dotting the valley floor.

At last John could stand it no longer. His beloved bears were gone and he could see that at last someone had moved in on his ranch. For years he had watched various bands of bandits hole up there, sometimes for months on end, but now the bandits had given way to the hardy pioneer settlers, and he could see that now a family had moved in. Of course they couldn't have known that anyone else claimed the place but it bothered John just the same.

Besides, he couldn't think of eating another bat egg! Bat eggs! Morning, noon and night! Bat's eggs! Year in and year out! Bat's eggs! Just then John's telescopic eyes spotted about a million bats winging their way high over Sheep Mountain and heading his way! And he could hear their high, supersonic cackling which meant that they were coming to lay a lot more eggs! John said the only difference between hens and bats was that hens cackled after laying an egg and bats cackled before!

Anyway, that did it! With a cry of anguish old John leaped over the ledge! As he fell his new freedom and the fact that at last he was going someplace filled him with the desire to live! Suddenly a great idea occurred to him! To save himself was so simple that even a moron would have thought of it! And, acting just in the nick of time, he reached up with both hands, and, taking himself by the hair of his head, he let himself down easy on the boulder strewn canyon floor!

John sat there and cried for hours as he thought of the wasted years in the bats' cave, of the years the faithful Buck and Babe had waited there for him! And all the time he had had the means of escape right there in his hands and on top of his head, if he had only thought of it! If he had been bald headed it would have been different! But he could never forgive himself. He cried until he washed the telescopic vision from his eyes and he could no longer hear the supersonic cackling of the bats, and so when he staggered out of the canyon and headed for home he was just a dim-eyed, gray and broken old man.

It was after dark when old John pushed open his cabin door. The cabin was dimly lighted by a tallow candle and seated at the old table was a young man and his wife. John must have presented a terrifying picture standing there in his tattered clothes and long white hair and beard, as he croaked, "Who be ye?" The woman stifled a scream as the clear-eyed young man rose and said, "Bill Redmond's the name. This is my wife, Ida, and you sir?"

"Cherry!" roared old John. "John Cherry! this hayrs my place!" "Well take it easy old timer," soothed Bill, "the people down in the settlement said someone would claim this diggings some day! We'll pull out right now if you say so!" John sank weakly to the floor. "No! Stay!" He gasped and lost consciousness.

John was a mightly sick man and lay at death's door for many months. Due only to the skillful and tender care given him by the Redmonds was old John able to pull through. In his delirium he talked and raved incessantly about Paul Bunyon, his bears, Buck and Babe, John Colter, and always, bats' eggs!

The excitement was terrific among the settlers as the news spread that Bill Redmond was nursing some old timer that had dropped in and claimed the old shack, and all winter long, after John got strong enough to have visitors, Bill let them come and see him. Some thought he was a bandit hiding out from the law, others thought he was an old Hudson Bay trapper gone balmy. There were dozens of surmises, but only one thing was for sure, and that was that no one knew him! None of the old timers had ever seen him before, none had ever heard of him and no one believed him except Bill Redmond and his beautiful wife, Ida.

Old John knew a lot of settlers had arrived in Jackson Hole during the twenty years he was stranded in the bats' cave, but even he was amazed that there were so many. That winter he met them all, men, women and children. They all came to visit him and he was always startling some unbeliever with facts regarding his supposedly private affairs, which John had seen from his lofty perch high on the wall of the Grand Teton! Or embarrasing some smart aleck with reminders of some of his more secret and intimate escapades!

When spring came Bill and Ida moved to their ranch in Spring Gulch and old John seemed strong and well as ever. John knew that the Redmonds were the only ones that believed in him. They were his best friends and so John spent a lot of time at the Redmond home. And so it was that one of Redmond's guests met old John Cherry and was so intrigued with his stories that he hung around all summer with John, gathering material for a book, and promised to send John a copy soon as he could. As it turned out this book almost broke the mighty bond of friendship between John and Bill Redmond.

That fall some visitor who happened through the valley nearly caused old John to have a stroke, when, in the course of narrating all the news he could think of to the news-hungry settlers, he happened to mention that the summer before some Indians, fishing on Snake River down around Twin Falls, had seen a great bear floating on the water and had seen it climb out on the river bank. They pursued it into the hills but upon being harassed by dogs and arrows, it had become enraged and, turning savagely upon them, slaughtered hordes of dogs, horses and Indians before the frightened Indians could escape! He said the bear ranged on west into the Owyhee mountains and was now raising havoc with cattle and sheep and there was a $1,000 bounty posted for his hide!

When John heard the story he rushed over to Redmond's and grabbing Bill said, "Good Lord Bill! That must be Babe. It don't seem possible! But it must be Babe!" John was all for starting right out to hunt for Babe but Bill pointed out to John that it was then so late in the season that all bears would now be in winter hibernation.

Long about Christmas some hardy settler decided to ski out to St. Anthony which was about 100 miles away and bring what mail he could pack for the shut in settlers. He limited himself to letters only, and only two letters to any one person. There was mail for everyone but old John Cherry! However there was a package there for John. But as there was no letter the settler decided to leave it for the regular mail carrier in the spring. And so it was that in the spring John got a copy of the book that Bill Redmond's friend had promised to send.

John was tickled nearly to death when the mail carrier handed it to him! As John could neither read nor write he hurried over to Redmond's with it. They unwrapped the book and Bill told John it was the story of his life! John couldn't wait for Bill to get started reading it to him. John wouldn't let Bill lay the book down until he finished reading it to him aloud. I never saw this book but Bill told me it was a good book, and written just like John had told his stories. But the editor made two fatal mistakes and Bill unwittingly had made a third which nearly cost him John's friendship. Bill said this author referred to old John all the way through the book as "the hermit." John listened without a word as Bill read to the end. Then John said, "Bill, what's this feller call this hayr book?" Bill said he had never lied to John and he couldn't now, so he told John right out — "Cherry's Lies and Other Lies!"

Old John's face turned purple with rage, but in a calm voice he said, "Bill, what's a hermit?" Bill answered, "Well John, all I know is what I've read. It appears that when the Lord made the world he made people, too. After he got to sizing them up he decided he had made their hind ends too big, so he sliced off pieces of hind ends until he had a big pile. He didn't know what to do with them but finally fashioned another man out of them and called him a hermit!"

The explosion was terrific! John's anger knew no bounds. He denounced Bill roundly, if for no other reason than condoning a friend that would call John a hermit! And Cherry's stories lies! He was going home to get his old .44 and "Find that varmint if it takes the rest of my life!" Bill knew that John meant it too! So he rode along home with John and tried to talk him out of it. Just as they started to ford Snake River they met "Beavertooth" Neal and he greeted them with a toothy smile and yelled in the loud and boastful manner he had, "You fellers 'pear to be headin' the wrong way!" "Depends on where you're going," Bill answered. Beavertooth grinned. "Some more o' yer business!" he said. "But it so happens I'm goin' down ter Star Valley an' collect thet five thousand smackers on them two bars!"

John Cherry had not uttered a word of greeting, but he was all attention now! "What bars?" he demanded. Beavertooth looked at him pityingly and said, "Man ain't ya heered that it got so hot fer the Owyhee grizzly thet he vamoosed outen thar an' now it 'pears he's teemed up with 'nother ornery cuss like his self an'air shore pilfering them fellers down in Star Valley! They's raised five thousand dinnero fer thar cussed hides! An thet ain't tabacey juice! Haw! Haw!" and he squirted about a quart of tobacco juice onto a flat cobble rock and rode on.

John's face was white as a sheet! He turned to Bill and said, "Bill! I kain't believe it! I kaint! But I'm gonna go 'an see!" And turning his horse he headed south. Bill caught up to him and he said, "John! You old pirate! Where are you going? What can't you believe?" John answered: "I kain't believe it's Buck and Babe, but I know they air!" And he rode on. Bill tried to argue with John but it was no use. John was determined to go to Star Valley, and so Bill went to Star Valley too! He couldn't desert his old friend now!

John was strangely silent until after they had pulled their saddles off the tired horses for the night at Cabin Creek. Using their saddles for pillows and listening to their ponies munch the sweet new grass, John finally said, "Bill I reckon as how yore the only pusson, thet is aside Idy, ter berfrend me in the hull valley. Yep! I know they's a lot of fine people livin' hayr now, also a lot o' thievin' shiffless skonks! The trouble is in tellin' who from which! They all tollerate old John an'ring and' wink, but none o' the hull passle believes airy yoarn I tole 'em yet!"

"You mean like the time you swam the Mississippi River with $30,000 in gold in your vest pocket to pay off your old Daddy's mortgage?" asked Bill. "Or the time you was frying hot cakes in one of your line cabins and the heavy snow snapped the three-foot ridge log and you stood there holding up that broken ridge log with one hand and frying hot cakes with the other until you sunk in solid rock up to your knees before you got Paul Bunyon filled up enough so he would go out and shovel off the roof?" "Why shore!" exclaimed John, "Enny fool thet ever seed old Paul eat hot cakes would believe that!" and added, "Yah do believe in Paul Bunyon don't yer Bill?" "Of course I do!" answered Bill. "Any good American does!"

"Thet's what I like about you Bill!" said old John, affectionately, and dropped off to sleep.

John and Bill arrived at the mouth of Grey's River at sun up and there was a big encampment, tents and tepees pitched all over the sagebrush flat! A big pow wow was going on around a council fire in the center of camp, and they were told that over 150 of the best wolf hunters west of the Missouri River were gathered there, not to mention dozens of ranchers and cowboys and sheep herders. All had high hopes of collecting the $5,000 bounty offered for the two grizzly bears! The story was that the Owyhee grizzly had teamed up with another giant grizzly on Caribou Mountain. They had killed several gold miners there and as the hunters moved in on them they crossed east over Salt River where they killed a sheepherder, his camp mover, and about 200 head of sheep!

They were now blocked off in a big patch of heavy timber, surrounded by rim rocks in the high mountains of Grey's River.

A dozen wolf hunters had gone in after them with their dogs the day before, but five of the hunters had been horribly mangled by the desperate bears and nearly all the dogs were killed! The hunters were now holding a pow-wow to decide what would be the best plan for attack.

John and Bill listened to the argument until it was decided to set fire to the patch of timber and either burn the bears to death or force them out in the open where the hunters could kill them with their heavy rifles.

As soon as John could make himself heard he begged the hunters to let him go into the timber and try his hand at getting the bears out, before they burned such a beautiful stand of timber or any more lives were lost! The hunters howled and hooted and laughed at the old man, but Bill Redmond was a well known and influential man and he finally persuaded them to let the old man try.

Bill doubted his wisdom in letting old John go in there after the two vicious bears, because neither he nor John knew for sure if the bears in question were Buck and Babe. Even if they were, and John was telling the truth about having tamed them, the fact remained that they were now vicious killers! They had learned to hate men and had reverted back to the wild! However, Bill knew there was nothing else he could do for his old friend.

Very sullenly, the hunters agreed to give John until noon, and if he wasn't out by then he would be considered dead and they would make no effort to retrieve his body and he could burn with the two bears!

It was with a heavy heart that Bill shook hands with his old friend and bade him good-bye. The hunters were stationed all around the big patch of timber and among the high rimrocks rifles were ready! John turned and without a word walked swiftly into the dark woods! None of the hunters ever saw him again!

Bill said it was deathly silent. But just before noon a slight breeze came up and he thought he could hear a loud steady purring sound that was probably made by the wind in the trees. But he said he couldn't help remembering what John had once told him. That Buck always purred when he was excited or happy!

Anyway, noon finally came, and no sign of poor old John! The hunters poured barrels of kerosene and turpentine along the lower edge of the timber and set it on fire!

It is a known fact that the smoke was so thick for hours that the bears could have crossed the rim rocks unseen, but as time pased, and John Cherry and the two great bears were never seen nor heard of again, it was believed that the bears perished in the fire with old John!

But Bill Redmond told me afterwards, that along in the afternoon he happened to look up just as the wind cleared the smoke away from the ridge for an instant, and he saw old John cross over the skyline, riding old Buck and leading old Babe!

THE HERMIT, Illustration by John Coulter.

CHAPTER 27 — Jackson Lake Dam — Was It Worth It?

In 1909 we had a governor who just about gave Wyoming away. Idaho wanted to develop the Twin Falls area which is located along Snake River west of Idaho Falls. But they did not have enough water, so they went to work on Wyoming's stupid governor, Cary, and he let Idaho dam off Snake River at its outlet from Jackson Lake, at a site known as Moran. It was the location of the Ben Shefield Ranch and dude operation. Not one drop of this water that was impounded in Jackson Lake came from a Idaho source.

All the tributaries below Jackson Lake clear down to the Wyoming-Idaho State line, came from the mountains of Wyoming.

This was but one of the many terrible mistakes made by Wyoming governors. Almost the entire history of Wyoming shows its governors were men of and representing the big money boys! The railroads, the gas and oil big-wigs, the Union Company Coal Mines, the cattlemen and land promotors! It is a wonder that Wyoming ever became a state, so badly was she plundered, exploited, polluted and raped by these despoilers of her resources. Even today, big and great as Wyoming is, she owns less of her own land that about any state in the union. Almost all of Wyoming's open land is Federally controlled or owned by millionaires and promoters.

Anyway, Idaho started putting a dam in Jackson Lake that created one of the worst messes in all of Wyoming's history. Thousands of acres of fine pine-timber was immersed and destroyed by the rising water behind this dam, and for years this millions of board feet of prime pine timber uprooted and drifted and filled the bays and shoreline, until it was almost impossible to reach open water on Jackson Lake, because of the mass of debris.

It is true that this project gave employment to hundreds of men for the nearly seven years it took to finish this great earthen dam. Our teacher, Charles Driscoll, worked for years on this dam following his year of teaching the school at Wilson.

Driscoll hired Nick Wilson to haul all their belongings and his family up to the dam where the workmen established a great tent city at Moran. Shefield and Festler really cashed in on this project

Here is where the trouble started about 1908, when the Cary Act allowed Idaho to start building a dam on Jackson Lake in Wyoming, to compound water that Idaho needed to develop the Twin Falls farming area. The dam was started in 1909 and the wooden structure washed out in 1910, frightening Jackson Hole settlers on the Wilson side of Snake River. A new dam was finished in 1916. Part of the tent city at Moran that housed dam workers can be seen in the background.

In 1933 the cleanup began. This ungodly blight left a scar on Wyoming's most beautiful area that will never heal. It started about 1908 and wasn't cleaned up for nearly 40 years, and is still an ugly scar around all of Jackson Lake's shoreline.

at Moran and for several years Moran was a real thriving town. Because of its location so near the south entrance to Yellowstone Park, it drew a large tourist trade in summer time as well.

Nick Wilson spent days hauling Driscolls up to Moran, which was in June. After working all summer at good wages, Driscoll had never paid Nick one penny, and so Nick had to sue to get his money out of the Charles Driscoll, by threat of garnishment of his wages. Jackson Hole had a lot of fine people among its early settlers, and it also had a lot of deadbeats, too!

It took many years and cost hundreds of thousands of dollars to clean up this worst mess in all the State of Wyoming's history. It ruined one of Wyoming's most beautiful primeval forests and was among the worst mistakes ever made by Wyoming's blundering governors! Rising waters in the reservoir killed trees on the 140 miles of shoreline on Jackson Lake, creating one of the most blighted messes in the west, bordering on a nightmare!

The results of this dam have been a headache to Wyoming and almost a permanent blight. If it hadn't been for the Government of the United States, with almost free labor of our youth, which was called the CCC (Civilian Conservation Corps) cleaning up this great mess and burning these millions of feet of one of Wyoming's most beautiful and primeval forests! However, due to the Jackson Lake Dam, the Twin Falls area in Idaho became known as the "Bread Basket of the World!"

I think it was about the second year after construction of the Jackson Lake Dam began that the impounded water washed out the dam. This was caused by a big wind storm from the west, causing ten foot waves to pound against the new structure and the dam burst.

Jackson Hole already had telephones by then and all Jackson Hole was alerted, especially that part in the Wilson area, where great flooding was expected due to the fact that the town of Wilson was ten feet lower than the Snake River one mile to the east. Great excitement was caused by the news. We received it about 11 a.m. Everyone was advised to run for the mountain and higher ground. As it would be several hours before the flood would reach Wilson, everyone began hauling perishable household goods, bedding and food. All livestock were driven up to the foothills. Goodricks had about forty pigs that ran loose around Wilson, and we kids had the time of our lives driving pigs, cows and horses up into the hills, and catching and boxing chickens! The excitement was terrific!

Some of the frightened settlers went clear up on top of Teton Pass and put up their tents. They figured to watch Jackson Hole go out through Snake River Canyon when the flood hit. When nothing had happened by dark, a lot of the watchers were very disappointed, because the flood would be at night and couldn't be seen! Morning came and still no flood. Then word was passed to the campers who had fled to the mountains that they could start hauling stuff back home. Some of them hunted livestock, pigs, and chickens for a week.

The flood had passed in the night and it wasn't enough to even bring Snake River up to high water mark!

A new and better dam was started and finished in 1916, and it stands there yet today!

During the clean up of the mess around Jackson Lake, horses were ferried across the lake at different points to islands and the west shore where there were no roads. Mt. Moran in background. Note scar on lake shoreline.

CHAPTER 28 — Doctor Huff and Dell Judd and A Great Man Dies!

The winter that Miss Ruth Hill taught at Wilson, 1913-14, was my seventh grade year. Nick had several bad spells of sickness that winter and we now had a fine young doctor whose name was Huff. He was the first fine surgeon and all around doctor that Jackson Hole ever had. Old Doctor Palmer who Nick loved so well died the summer of 1909, and I think that fall was when Doctor Huff arrived in Jackson Hole. His full name was Doctor Charles Huff.

The Jackson Hole people, through very hard work and donations, plus generous amounts of money given from many rich dudes who had visited Jackson Hole, built a hospital. St. John's Church, which I think was Episcopal, provided some fine nurses and some equipment. So the hospital became known as St. John's Hospital, although it was mostly Mormon labor that got out the logs from the best stands of timber in the valley and built this beautiful log building that served Jackson Hole for over sixty years.

There were no more deaths in the valley from the dreaded "inflamation of the bowels," now known as appendicitis. This operation was child's play for Doctor Huff who later became known as one of the finest brain surgeons in the world.

A whole book could be written about Doctor Charles Huff. He was one of the last of the breed that went to his patients' home, no matter where they lived, or what it took to get there. He even traveled by dog team to reach and operate on a man's wife snowed in on the head of the Grovant River. He traveled on horseback, by sled, wagon, automobile, airplane and even walked; he crossed the swollen Snake River in little row boats to save the lives of people in desperate need! During the influenza epidemic that was brought back to the United States by soldiers in the First World War, I can remember seeing Al Austin, one of our local forest rangers, make the rounds of the sick and dying victims of influenza all over the Jackson Hole Valley, from the Buffalo River clear down to Snake River Canyon. Dr. Huff was so sick with the flu himself that he couldn't sit up alone in his Buick car, which Al drove with one hand, and held Doc up with the other. This was in 1918-19! I do not have the language to give Doctor Charles Huff a fraction of the tribute that is his due! I will only say that he was a great doctor and a great humanitarian, a great human being, and a Great Man!

He told my father, on one of his trips to see him, that if he could have gotten hold of him, even two years sooner, that he could have added ten years to his life!

Nick was dying of asthma and bronchial pneumonia, and the night of July 17, 1915, Nick called me about 1:00 a.m. He was awful sick. I helped him sit up on the edge of his bed and he said he thought he was dying. He couldn't hardly breathe and lips were blue!

I wanted to run for help, but Nick said, "No, help me dress, and help me over to Dell Judd's. I want to make a will!"

I tried to dress him but he was just too sick and weak. So I ran over to Judds and after a lot of pounding, Dell Judd came to the door. Their bedroom was way in the back of another room beyond the store, that's why it took so long to arouse Dell. I told him that Nick was very sick and needed to see him. Dell quickly dressed and went back to our house with me.

My father was sitting in his old rocking chair and breathing better. Nick told Dell he wanted to make a will regarding me and my brother George, who had slept through all this commotion. Dell wanted to wait until morning, but Nick insisted on doing it now!

"I might not live until morning!" he said, so Dell went back to the post office and got his wife, Jesse K. Dayton Judd, and came back with her, and a typewriter. Mrs. Judd was also a notary public. They drew up a will for my dad and he signed it and both Dell and Jesse signed it and she notarized it. Dell said I was too young to sign as a witness. This was July and I wouldn't be fourteen until October 12, 1915. Herewith is the copy of my dad's will:

> State of Wyoming
> §§
> County of Lincoln:
> On the nineteenth day of July, A.D. 1915, Elijah Nicholas Wilson personally appeared before me, J.K. Judd, a Notary Public, in and for Lincoln County, State of Wyoming, and acknowledged that he executed and signed the within instrument of his own free will and accord!
>
> J.K. Judd
> My commission expires Feb. 11th, 1919

WILL AND TESTAMENT OF
ELIJAH NICHOLAS WILSON

State of Wyoming
§§
County of Lincoln

Be it hereby known, that, I, Elijah Nicholas Wilson, do now this seventeenth day of July, 1915, make my last will and testament, for my beneficiaries, who are my wife, Charlotte Rebecca Wilson; my two sons, Charles A. Wilson, age thirteen years, and George W. Wilson, age ten years, of Wilson, Wyoming, as follows:

All the real estate, being the home and situated on Lot Three (3) in Block two (2) in the town of Wilson, Wyoming, as shown by the plat and survey of same, being a part of the southwest quarter of the southeast quarter (SW1/4SE1/4) of section 22, township 41 north, range 117 west 6th principal meridian, containing thirty-one one hundredths 31/100 acres, shall accrue to my wife, Charlotte Rebecca Wilson, and upon her demise, shall revert to the joint and equal ownership of my two sons, Charles A. and George W. Wilson.

The personal property, consisting of the household effects shall remain intact in the home for the mutual use and benefit of my wife and two sons. The manuscript and copyright of my book, "Uncle Nick Among the Shoshones" shall revert to the joint and equal ownership of my two sons, Charles A. and George W. Wilson. The proceeds accruing from the publication and sale of this book, according to a written agreement with Howard R. Driggs, of Salt Lake City, Utah, shall be used for the maintainence and education of these two boys.

Be it hereby known, that, I have re-
quested, and do hereby appoint Abraham
Ward as guardian for Charles A. and George
W. Wilson until they reach the age of twenty-
one years; and as guardian he shall receive
all moneys due me and shall expend the
same to the best of his ability for the education and maintenance of these two sons.

Further, be it known, that, I, having re-
posed unbounded faith in the honesty and
integrity of Abraham Ward, do hereby request and pray that paper of administration
be duly granted to him.

Signed
E. N. Wilson

Witness:
D. B. Judd
J. K. Judd

After the Judds left about 3:00 a.m. I crossed the street to the
hotel and told Abe Ward that daddy was very sick, and he sent me
on home, and soon he and Virgil, Abe's son, came over. Edna Jane,
Abe's wife, who was Nick's daughter, had a stroke about a year
before and still could hardly walk or talk very well.

They fixed Nick up with pillows and a quilt so he was as comfortable as they could make him, because Nick choked up every time
they tried to lay him down on the bed.

Abe had Doctor Huff come over the next day and see my father.
He left some medicine and when he left, he motioned for Abe and
me to follow him out to his car, which was an old model "T" Ford.
Only a few cars were in the valley then. Charley Wort had two,
Steve Leek one, Doctor Huff one, and my Uncle Alfred Nethercott
had the one in which he killed himself over by the Leek Ranch.

Doctor Huff told us that Nick was in bad shape. He said he
didn't think Nick could ever lie down again. He could have him
taken over to the hospital in Jackson where he would have to be
kept sitting up in a chair anyway and cared for that way; so he
would probably be as well or maybe better off just to stay home
and sleep in his own comfortable rocking chair. Doc Huff said

about all we could do for him was keep him warm and give him a little warm soup or whatever Nick might be able to eat. As Doc Huff was leaving, Abe asked him how long my father would live, and Doc Huff said, "I don't know. He is a tough little man, but he could choke up and die any minute, or sitting up and cared for he might live weeks, or even months. But it won't be long!

I think Abe Ward and I were closer that day than in all my life with him.

Nick had been more like a father, a real father, to Abe than a father-in-law. I could tell that Abe was taking it very hard. As for me, I just couldn't feel anything! I couldn't even cry! I remembered all those years growing up under my father's loving care, how I used to worry about him going and leaving me alone. I would often get up in the dead hours of night and creep into his bedroom to see if he was breathing!

Responsibility had come to me at a very young age. By seven my baby childhood days were over. All the weight of the world seemed to rest on my shoulders! I used to lie in bed and wonder — what would happen to me if daddy died? I couldn't think of anyone I could turn to or who could ever take his place! I remember praying, "Oh God! Please don't take my daddy away until I am big enough to stand it. Please let me be old enough to know what to do!"

And God had answered my childhood prayer. I was nearly fourteen years old now; I was at least four inches taller than my dad! After hearing what Doctor Huff said, I just silently said: "Thank you Lord, thank you! I am big enough and old enough to take it now!"

Yet that was a terrible summer and fall for me.

It was a terrible time in Dell Judd's life, too! Everybody around Wilson helped to care for Nick all they could, but it became a twenty-four hour job. The worst of the burden fell on the Wards. Abe grew tired and haggard. Vesta, bless her heart, made soups and custards for her grandpa; Edna couldn't do anything because she was semi-invalid herself.

Dell Judd had a young hunter come the first of September 1915, to hunt for a month. He was very wealthy and about twenty-five years old. He had Wyoming non-resident hunting licenses for elk (two of them). He wanted a big bull and a big cow and he wanted them skinned in whole to be mounted and placed in a large collection of animals he had killed all over the world. He was an avid hunter. He also had a license for bear, and wanted a big grizzly, of which there were many in Wyoming in those days. He also wanted a big bull moose! So Dell had his hands full.

Dell came often to visit with Nick during those days that Nick was confined to a rocking chair. One day just before this dude arrived, Dell told Nick that this hunt would probably be all he would make that fall because the dude promised him twenty thousand dollars for this hunt and he would stay until he got all these animals. The way he wanted them skinned and cared for would take Dell a month and maybe more.

Well, this dude arrived on the stage from Driggs, Idaho; I think the railroad had been built on up to Driggs from St. Anthony at that time. Dell Judd met him when the stage arrived at the post office in Wilson. If I ever knew this young man's name, I have forgotten it now, so I will refer to him as "Judd's dude." He had enough equipment to load down at least four packhorses. He was a good-looking man, about six feet tall, medium blond hair, well-dressed, carried himself well, trim figure of the athletic type, with a healthy appearance.

Dell had a team and wagon to haul his dude and equipment to the ranch below Wilson. Mrs. Judd saw them off and was holding

This picture of the five women is not pertinent to Nick Wilson's story, except the lady in right front row is Fostene Forrester, mentioned in Chapter 25. These women represented the Town Council. Jackson was the first town in the United States to be ruled entirely by women. Sheriff Pearl Williams is not shown. Left to right, top row: Stella Van Velect, wife of Roy Van Velect, Merchant and Coroner. Mae DeLoney, wife of Bill DeLoney, Lawyer and Politician. Bottom row: Rose Crabtree, wife of Henry Crabtree, Hotel Owners. Grace Miller, wife of Bobby Miller, Banker. Fostene Forrester Haight, wife of Don Haight, Rancher.

Charles Alma Wilson, Author.

their six-month-old baby, a jolly little guy, dark complexioned like his dad. Dell Judd was of Jewish descent.

Dell had already established their base camp, which was at a beautiful little deep blue lake covering less than half an acre and containing no fish life. It bubbled up from the depths of the earth and was probably an old volcano crater; its water was sweet and cold and clear as crystal. This spot is now known as the head of Coburn Creek, which is the south fork of Fall Creek.

Dell had worked through the last half of August erecting tents and building a corral for the horses, along with a hitching post. He had carried in inch lumber and built a small privy, back out of sight, in the thick blue spruce. He had put up five white canvas wall tents, each about eight by ten feet. One for himself, one for his dude with a homemade wooden bunk, table and chair, and a small folding iron heating stove for the dude's comfort. Dell's tent was not quite so elaborate as was the dude's.

One tent was for food supplies, and one was for the saddles — so pack saddles and other equipment wouldn't get snowed or rained upon. The fifth tent was large, with four-foot walls and was twelve by fourteen feet. This tent was to hold the trophies, skins and hides and large enough to stretch out full length hides to be salted and fleshed to keep and be shipped back east after the hunt was

The logs for the St. John Hospital were picked from the finest timber in Jackson Hole and cut, hauled out by teams and sleighs in the winter time, all by donation labor, mostly by Mormon settlers. This hospital served Jackson Hole for 65 years.

over. It was truly an elaborate camp in a beautiful setting. The meadow of four or five acres had grass up to a horse's belly, and gently rising slopes all around covered with scattered blue spruce and acres of forage to last their horses all fall.

All that Dell Judd and the dude had to do the next morning was to get in the six horses that they would need, and pack four with the dude's duffle bags, guns, fishing equipment, etc. Riding two fine saddlers, they were on their way by nine o'clock on a beautiful clear-blue-sky day which Wyoming is famous for. The nearest route to Judd's hunting camp from his ranch was approximately twenty miles.

They arrived in camp early in the afternoon and Dell's dude was delighted with the camp setting. Along the way they had seen elk, deer, moose, great numbers of blue grouse and the speedy little ruffled grouse that is common all over the United State, from Maine to California, and south to the Gulf of Mexico. The dude had all sizes of shotguns and anticipated much fun. He also had numerous rifles that he considered the right size for any game.

The dude spent the rest of the day hanging and putting his things where he wanted them in the tents and Dell arranged for the six horses. He had a dozen more horses at the ranch, but six was all that was needed until after the hunt when he would be using them all to pack out the trophies and the camp.

Twenty thousand dollars was a lot of money for a fall's hunting income in those days, but Judd figured it would take the most of September and October for him to earn it, and he could pass up the bitter cold November hunting and be home with his beautiful wife and baby boy.

Dell's worst problems were these horses. A horse is a strange and powerful animal. The domestic breeds that have been raised in pastures and fenced in all their life consider that as being home. I have seen many horses that have only sparse pastures, almost to the point of starvation, be ridden a day's ride back into the mountains, and after being picketed for the night in more deep sweet forage than they ever saw in their lives, just stand there all night with their tail to the breeze and facing toward home, and if they got loose they never stopped until they got there! These kinds of horses are known as "homesickers." You can't leave them untied a minute, or lay down a bridle rein or rope attached to them, but what they are gone!

This was the kind of horses that Dell had, and he knew it. He had two old mares that he packed on this trip, and he knew that if he could keep these two anchored down, that the rest would stay with hobbles on. Dell's plan was to picket these two old mares each night in good forage, then keep them tied all day, while he was out hunting. By night these two mares would be hungry and thirsty enough that after watering them he could picket them, and in a few days they would settle down and not just stand while tied and look down the trail toward home all the time!

Well, this first night Dell picketed these mares down in the lush meadow below camp, hobbled the four geldings and belled a

"Shorty" Crail and family on Georgia Ely's homestead just below Johnny Count's hot springs, now known as Astoria Hot Springs. Shorty's wife, Georgia, was the daughter of Mart Ealy, whose ranch was just east of Wilson, Wyoming, one and one half miles on east shore of Snake River at the east end of Snake River bridge. Shorty Crail was a picturesque character and reminded me of Will Rogers. One day Shorty was carrying a pig on his saddle horse and the pig began to squeal and the horse came uncorked and threw Shorty off in a pile of cobblestones and broke four ribs. While Shorty was recuperating, I helped Georgia with the Post Office and ranch. The day that Doctor Huff took the tape off Shorty's ribs, pulling all the long black hair off was the funniest day of my life! Doctor Huff got the tape started and got Shorty rolling like a hoop on the bed and he was hollering his head off! He was stripped clean and white of all that long black hair, and he would not talk to anyone for about three days, not even his wife! What a day!

Charles Alma Wilson, Author.

couple of them. He knew the geldings would not leave without the mares, so he thought he had everything in control. It was a beautiful starlit night. The happy and excited dude kept Dell up much longer than he liked, telling stories of his prowess as a mighty hunter all over the world. He told Dell he had a feeling that this would be one of the best hunts he ever had!

As the two tired hunters went to their tents, after dousing the small campfire, they could hear the tinkling of the two horse bells as the horses grazed down in the little meadow. The two tired, sleepy men fell into a sound sleep, soothed by the whisper of the evening breeze through the tall, stately, blue spruce boughs. The gentle rippling song of the water as it bubbled up and flowed from the beautiful little lake in front of their comfortable tents and warm Eiderdown sleeping bags contributed to their sound sleep. In fact, neither heard the commotion that happened down among the horses, but long after the men were sound asleep, probably a bear, mountain lion, or some other large animal must have scared the horses and one old mare ran and her picket rope snapped. The other mare reared in panic as the five frightened horses fled down the trail toward home. Her rearing and jerking soon pulled the picket pin from its mooring and she took off on a run, following the rest.

Dell was an early riser. Right after daybreak he discovered that all the horses were gone. Upon investigation, Dell soon could see that the horses had all left on a run, and so he surmised what I have written above, a bear or something had spooked the horses. By the signs, Dell figured that they had not been gone very long. Dell ran back to camp and aroused his dude. He stoked up the campfire and had hot coffee and a little of something ready to eat by the time the dude as up and dressed.

They ate a little food together, and as Dell gulped down the hot coffee he explained to the dude what had happened regarding the horses. He told the dude that he didn't know how far the horses would go before he could catch them, but he thought that as soon as they ran a mile or two the hobbled horses would be getting tired and slow down, and that he hoped to catch them and be back at noon. Dell took a bridle and a few tie ropes, and told the dude, "Now, you stay here until I get back. You can clean up the camp dishes and keep yourself busy doing something. But under no circumstances leave this camp, nor even think about hunting until I get back!"

The dude said he would be alright, that he wasn't in any hurry to get started hunting anyway, but would go with Dell if he could be of any help.

Dell said, "No, I can travel faster alone, and I won't need any help." Then, as he hurriedly left camp, he cautioned the dude again: "Remember what I said! This is strange country to you, and anyone can get lost very quickly. Some of the ridges and streams can lead you fifty or sixty miles before coming to any ranch or settlement. Keep that in mind, and stay right here! I will be back as soon as I can!" and Dell left.

God only knows how many times during the next sixty days that Dell Judd must have cursed himself for not taking the dude with him to catch the horses!

Dell hurried along as fast as he could, but after an hour of fast trotting down the trail, it became apparent to Dell that he was going to have a long walk, because the horse tracks showed no sign of slowing down. It was afternoon before weary, sore-footed Dell Judd found his bunch of "homesickers" huddled against the big gate that led into his ranch. They were in deplorable condition, all except the two old mares, whose picket ropes were worn and frayed. The hobbled geldings were in sad shape — the hobbles had worn all the hair, skin and flesh off their ankles clear down to the bone!

All Dell could do for them was cut off the hobbles and cover the wounds with axle grease; not one of them would be fit to ride again that fall! Dell fixed a hasty lunch at the lodge, then ran in some more horses from the field and caught two more saddle horses. He decided to take the two mares back to pack, and these two pack animals would be all he would need anyway, until after the hunt was over. A saddle horse each, for him and the dude, and two pack horses to carry in the game. It was after four p.m. before Dell got started back to camp. The two old mares had led the hobbled horses out the twenty miles at a fast clip, and he took them back in at a much faster clip!

It was after sundown when Dell entered the little meadow at the lower end below the camp, but there was still plenty of light. When the camp came into sight up by the little blue lake he could see no sign of life. He began to sense that something was very wrong, and it was, for when Dell dismounted at the tents, things looked just like he had left them, except there was no dude! He called, then looked in the tents, but the dude was gone! The campfire ashes were cold and dead and the few dishes they had used for breakfast were still there — the dude hadn't touched them to wash them.

Dell tied all the horses tightly to the hitching post, went and looked again in the dude's tent. His coat and most everything was still there. All that was missing was the dude and one of his rifles, a 250-3000 Savage that he had shown Dell the evening before, because it was a new caliber just put out by the Savage Arms Company. The dude had not seen one before this one, which he bought, to try on light game like deer and coyotes or wolves.

This picture was taken about 1915, about the 4th of July, because you can tell by the netting on passengers' hats and blankets on horses that it was "mosquito time" of the year. Mosquitoes were and still are terrible along Fish Creek, from June 15th to July 15th or later. Post office and store were run by Dell Judd at this time.

This view is in the town of Wilson, Wyoming, at the foot of Teton Pass on the Wyoming side of the mountain. Nick Wilson homesteaded one hundred sixty acres of land. He built his cabin on the bank of Fish Creek; built a Hotel for his wife Matilda, a General Merchantile and Hardware Store. He built a livery stable and opened a blacksmith shop, a Post Office, and started the town of Wilson, Wyoming, named in his honor in 1878. He was ready to handle the traffic of mail carriers, tourists, passengers and freighters over Teton Pass. The village grew and soon had a schoolhouse, saloon and a Mormon Church, under the leadership of Nick Wilson, the spirited and energetic residents were ready to face any challenge.

Charles Alma Wilson, Author.

From the looks of things, Dell figured the dude must have left soon after he did. It really made him mad to think the dude would go off hunting in direct opposition to his warning him several times to not leave the camp under any circumstance! Dell sat down on one of the folding camp chairs that still sat there by the campfire ashes, and began looking the situation over and planning what to do. The country up there at the base of Wolf Mountain was scarcely timbered on the head of Coburn Creek where they had the camp. It was at least nine thousand feet elevation and already in early September it grew chilly as soon as the sun went down. Dell had noted thin ice on the pond when he made coffee that morning.

The dude could have taken off in any direction! Dell thought he had probably seen a big bull elk off on the open slopes, or maybe a bear. He knew that bear was probably what spooked his horses, and a bear likes to hang around a camp, out of sight, then at night, with his keen smell, locate goodies, like bacon, sugar or honey. There was no real heavy timber, except above camp where it spread out and was quite heavy clear up to nearly the top of Wolf Mountain, whose elevation reached about eleven thousand feet, which was near timberline in Wyoming.

Off to the west of camp was a thicket of jack pines, so called because they usually spring up around the fallen trunk of an ancient tree that was killed by fire, probably caused by lightning a hundred years ago. Out in the center of this jack pine thicket, which covered less than half an acre — about the size of blue lake by their camp — Dell could see the old rotten stump of what had once been a very big tree, about six feet through at the base. The jack pines were as thick as the hair on a dog's back, and it would even test a rabbit to crawl through this jungle. The pines averaged about eight feet tall and the old stump from which they sprang looked about four feet in diameter from where Dell sat, which was about a hundred feet.

After Dell drank some hot coffee, he took his saddle gun, an old Winchester 30.30 and climbed to the top of the ridge west of camp. The other side of the ridge was heavily timbered and sloped a half a mile down to the head of the North Fork of Fall Creek. Dell had come into camp from the northeast, and from where Dell sat on the ridge he had a great panorama view of the area for miles. He could see the Grand Tetons, poking their snowclad peaks above all the surrounding area, about sixty miles straight north. He could see snow covered Sheep Mountain to the northeast, thirty miles on beyond the town of Jackson. The Wind River Mountains, already snowclad, rose majestically to the east, with Mount Gannet, the highest peak in Wyoming. Fremont Peak to the south of Mount Gannet was climbed in error by Captain Fremont, thinking it was the highest peak in Wyoming. There he had left his old battered army hat and notebook covered with stones, to be discovered years later, and after it had been known that Gannet was about twenty-one feet higher than Fremont! But Fremont never lived to find this out! To the southeast, Dell could see part of the Grays River Range. Directly west were miles and miles of heavy timber that sloped off into Idaho and its sage brush and lava beds fifty miles away. Looking west into Idaho ones view was obstructed by the layers of lava dust that always hung over the skyline in Idaho. To the south, Dell's view was cut off by the great Wolf Mountain peak, where thick lush grass grew clear to its top.

Somewhere in all this great expanse of wilderness, was Dell Judd's dude...But where?

SCHOFIELD.　　Rich land below Wilson.
Myrtle Schofield. The oats were as high as Myrtle's eyes, about 1911, on the Schofield Ranch, quarter mile south of Wilson, Wyoming.

Dell almost panicked when these thoughts occurred to him! He knew the dude had been gone from camp for more than twelve hours now! Lost, with no coat and a cold night coming on. Dell knew this dude did not smoke, so doubted if he even had any matches!

Dell began a systematic SOS about every fifteen to twenty minutes, which was three evenly spaced rifle shots, then listened for a reply. Dell stayed upon this ridge until long after dark, continuing his three spaced SOS shots, then listened until his ears hurt. But he never received an answer! Dell finally gave up and returned to camp. He tied up the tent door flaps, and mounting his saddle horse, he led the now gaunt and hungry old mares and the dude's saddle horse back to his ranch. He turned the three horses loose inside the ranch gate and rode his tired horse on up to Wilson.

Abe Ward was the sheriff. Dell had walked more than twenty miles, plus his climb up on the ridge, and had then ridden horseback over seventy miles; all in less than twenty hours. It was now daylight by the time he got to Wilson. I heard Abe say later, "When Judd came in that morning about daylight, he looked like hell! With his bloodshot eyes and unshaven, haggard face, I knew something terrible had happened!"

They gave Dell some hot soup and Abe made him go to bed, and then he arranged a telegram to the brother of Judd's dude. By sunup he had recruited about twenty riders and they headed for Judd's camp at the head of Coburn Creek, hoping to find the dude safe and back in camp. But they didn't!

When Dell awakened he was panicky and wild-eyed. His horse had been stabled, cared for and fed and was rested. Dell wouldn't even take a cup of coffee, but mounted his horse and was back at his hunting camp in three hours! A few men were at camp, but most were out searching for the dude. They knew he was afoot and figured he couldn't be too far away, but feared he was either hopelessly lost or dead!

Well, I must cut this story as short as I can. It was terrible from there on out to the end, especially for Dell Judd and his wife, Jesse. Dell's sister, Erma Judd, came back from Salt Lake to help. Mrs. Jesse Judd became so ill with worry that she was taken to Salt Lake. Dell kept on his hopeless search day after day, along with those that could or would stay and help look for the dude. My father was getting worse and couldn't help.

The dude's brother finally arrived in Wilson. He was twenty or twenty-five years older than his brother: a man of forty or fifty years of age. He had steel grey hair and the air of a rich man who knew nothing, but had authority; a stern, grim business man.

The sheriff took him immediately to where the action was. As soon as he met Dell Judd he accused him of murdering his brother! He accused him of hiding the body, and of stealing his money and a big diamond ring which he said was worth ten thousand dollars.

Abe said, "My God man! Can't you see that Dell Judd is more than half dead himself? He keeps on this mad search day and night! I have had a hundred men down here searching for your brother!"

The dude's brother only got madder and finally in a few days, he demanded the arrest and jailing of Dell Judd. He said it was more obvious all the time that Judd had killed his bother and hidden his body!

The sheriff had to comply. He took both Judd and his dude's brother to Jackson for a hearing, and as they went through Wilson, Dell asked Abe to let him see Uncle Nick. Abe told him that Nick was too sick to see anyone, that most of the time he didn't even know anyone — yet Dell insisted, and both he and my father wept when they saw the condition of each other!

Abe's description of Judd, "He looked like hell!" was an understatement, and Nick Wilson looked even worse! He was beginning to turn yellow and was only skin and bones. To say that this "tough little man hung on to life tenaciously" was an insult!

I have seen many wicked, terrible men die in bed with a smile on their lips! My God! Why do some of the world's finest men and women have to die by inches, like a dog in a ditch!

My father could hardly talk above a whisper. After Dell and Abe left, Nick beckoned me over to him and said to bring Abe back to him. I did. While the dude's brother waited impatiently with Dell Judd while Abe went back in to talk with Nick. I could hardly hear what my father said, but I heard him say, after talking real low with Abe a minute: "You get Steve Leek and Charley Wort and anyone you can, and get bond for Dell. Don't let them keep him over there in jail!" Abe promised he would do what he could.

Dell Judd was put in prison at Jackson. The most shameful thing of all was that even Dell Judd's old friends and people who knew him for many years and could never say that Dell Judd wronged or cheated any man, some of these people sided against him, along with the dude's brother! Dell was held in jail about a week before bail was arranged for him from our county seat which was way down in Kemmerer, nearly three hundred miles away!

It was getting well up into November now, and snow and winter cold could end the search for Dell's dude any day! To the chagrin of the dude's brother, bail was set and raised for Judd's release.

Dell went straight back to the hunting camp. The dude's brother agreed to hire ten men to help Judd continue the search until he would have to give up on account of snow. Then in the spring he would come back and file charges against Dell Judd for murder! Among the ten men that were hired to search for Judd's dude was one of my cousins, Nate Wilson.

Right after Nick was told that Dell Judd was released on bond, he lapsed into sort of a coma and never spoke English again. He talked in Indian language all the time. No one could tell what he wanted and I lost so much school I almost lost hope of passing Miss Ruth Hill's eighth grade in the spring of 1916.

A few days after the men started to search for Judd's dude the weather was getting very cold and a few skiffs of snow had fallen. It was an unusually open fall, even for Jackson Hole, but skies were lowering and we all knew that winter was not far away! It

This picture was taken about 1913, after Nick McCoy had bought out Billy Raum and painted the building. Unusual high water that year, and Snake River over-flowing into Granite Creek, six miles north of Wilson, caused this flooding of the town of Wilson, Wyoming. White building and barn in upper left corner were McCoy Saloon and Livery Stable. Other buildings are Wilson Post Office and store, run by Dell Judd. Nick Wilson's cabin in right background with steep roof. Dim building beyond McCoy barn was old Wilson Mormon Church and meeting and dance hall.

was getting late in November 1915 now, and a couple of days after the men started hunting the dude with Dell Judd, my cousin Nate didn't return to camp one evening! All the other men started looking for him. Word was sent up to Wilson and Jackson. A furor began! It was demanded that Dell Judd be apprehended for his own good. It was plain that he was a demented man, crazy! and had probably killed Nate Wilson just to get more people down there on this crazy search that had gone from the dramatic to the ridiculous now! But before anything was done, Nate turned up in Idaho, he had gone off down a wrong ridge in a snow flurry. But Nate knew how to take care of himself, he had matches and he ate broiled blue grouse and pine squirrels. He finally came out at a farm near Rigby, Idaho.

Well, in December the hunt was finally called off and a few men packed Dell's camp outfit down to his ranch. They left Dell with a saddle horse, a pack horse and one tent, and he said he would hunt only one more day. It was snowing when the men left Dell there at the little lake, which was now frozen over with several inches of ice.

It was December now, and my father was in a coma more than not. Different men began sitting up with him each night, because it was felt that death was nigh.

After the men left Dell Judd alone there in the snow, he must have been a very lonely, downhearted, desperate man! It was around noon when the searchers all left, and as Dell sat there he became aware of sounds, and listening he could hear the chirping of many birds. He soon noted it was coming from the center of that jack pine thicket there by camp! After a few minutes he noticed groups of what appeared to be chickadees, small birds that winter in the pinyon groves in the high country where the blue grouse also winter and feed on pinyon needles and nuts.

As Dell listened to and watched these strange little birds he saw one fly up to the old tree stump that protruded a little above the jack pines and it looked like a piece of cloth it was carrying in its beak. Dell was alert and excited now, "There is something over in that thicket!" he thought to himself, and taking his camp axe he started cutting a path through these thick little pines. They were frozen and cut off easily with the sharp axe. It was a few minutes when Dell reached the center of the thicket and could see the bowl of a huge tree, three feet or more, all surrounded by thick jack pines, and then he saw something else, the body of a man! It was draped over this great tree, with only the rump and legs in sight on Dell's side of the tree!

In telling this story Dell said the shock nearly killed him, but on close inspection, it was his dude. It had been cold up here at nine thousand feet, and the body had begun freezing the night after he died, and so there was never any odor! Upon closer investigation, Dell saw the 250-3000 savage barrel resting against the dude's neck. He had pushed the gun over the log ahead of himself, butt first so as not to get dirt in the barrel, and the trigger guard was over a small twig or part of an old rotten limb. The dude had a shell in the chamber and the safety off on this hammerless gun, and when he put the gun over the tree stump the trigger caught on this knot and discharged, shooting the dude through the neck!

Dell left things as they were, and was soon on his horse and riding at full speed down that canyon trail, and he caught up to the men with the pack outfit and told the news. All of them were really "flabbergasted!"

The sheriff and posse got the body out! The only marks on it was the bullet hole through his neck, and the mice had eaten the lobes off both ears. The little birds were packing the loose rotting fibers off the dude's wool shirt and carrying them up into the stump of the old tree.

It was thought that shortly after Dell had left that morning back what seemed to him a hundred years ago, to catch his horses, that the dude must have seen a fox or rabbit or maybe a pine martin run into this thicket. He had been told not to leave camp, and he didn't! He followed some creature into that jack pine thicket, only a few feet away, and he had been lying there on his stomach across this old tree bowl, hardly fifty steps away, during all this heart-breaking, terrible fall of 1915, that ruined a good man's life forever. Dell Judd never did recover, nor did his wife!

The sheriff wired the dead man's brother and he returned and got his brother's body. He was now a very humbled man, for the big diamond ring was still on his brother's finger, and the one thousand dollar bills were safe in the dead man's wallet! There were many of Dell Judd's fair weather friends who were very humbled and also ashamed.

Nick Wilson was about gone now. It wasn't until many years later when I was older, that I realized that my father did his thinking in the Indian language. He had learned it first from his dear little Indian friend, Pansuk, and he talked it for two years with his old Indian mother and the Shoshone Indians. It became his native language. Truly, Nick Wilson was a "White Indian Boy!"

On the night of December 27, 1915, Elijah Nicholas Wilson passed on to the Happy Hunting Grounds.

My friend Lewy Flemming was sitting by my father's side and holding one cold boney hand as the dying old Trailmaker journeyed into the shadow land!

It was cold with a raging blizzard the day we laid "Uncle Nick" to rest, and as the howling wind blew out its woes to the homeless snows, we left him there, "Among the Shoshones," whom he loved so very much.

My stories regarding Elijah Nicholas Wilson are now over, I only hope that I have done my best.

In this biography it has not been my intent to hurt, only perhaps to humble some of us!

If anyone mentioned in this book, either the living or the dead, feel they have been unfairly presented or portrayed, I am sorry, but I can only say: That's the way it was!

As I said in the beginning, that I would not stand on the correct dates of all these happenings, but the facts are true, just the same, to the best of my knowledge, and I have presented them, I hope, to the best of my ability! I may have some dates wrong, but I don't consider that any big deal.

I do wish I could have elaborated more on some things, and less on others, and there are many incidents that are pertinent to this story that I haven't been able to present at all.

I only hope that you will bear with me. I am an old man now of eighty-three years. I have marched along through this great 20th Century, with my hand in the Palm of God. He has been my strength and my salvation, what should I fear? The Lord is the strength of my life, of whom should I be afraid?

And so I humbly finish this testimony and biography in the name of Jesus Christ. Amen.